RETHINKING DWELLING

Also Available from Bloomsbury

The Intelligence of Place: Topographies and Poetics, ed. Jeff Malpas
Political Theory and Architecture, ed. Duncan Bell and Bernardo Zacka
Is There an Object Oriented Architecture? Engaging Graham Harman,
ed. Joseph Bedford
Bare Architecture: A Schizoanalysis, Chris L. Smith

RETHINKING DWELLING

Heidegger, Place, Architecture

Jeff Malpas

BLOOMSBURY ACADEMIC
LONDON • NEW YORK • OXFORD • NEW DELHI • SYDNEY

BLOOMSBURY ACADEMIC
Bloomsbury Publishing Plc
50 Bedford Square, London, WC1B 3DP, UK
1385 Broadway, New York, NY 10018, USA
29 Earlsfort Terrace, Dublin 2, Ireland

BLOOMSBURY, BLOOMSBURY ACADEMIC and the Diana logo are
trademarks of Bloomsbury Publishing Plc

First published in Great Britain 2021
This paperback edition published 2023

Copyright © Jeff Malpas, 2021

Jeff Malpas has asserted his right under the Copyright, Designs and
Patents Act, 1988, to be identified as Author of this work.

For legal purposes the Acknowledgements on p. ix constitute an extension of this copyright page.

Cover design by Charlotte Daniels
Cover image: Colin McCahon, *On building bridges* (triptych), 1952, oil on hardboard, Auckland
Art Gallery Toi o Tāmaki, Auckland, New Zealand, purchased 1958. © Colin McCahon Research
and Publication Trust. Courtesy of the Colin McCahon Research and Publication Trust.

All rights reserved. No part of this publication may be reproduced or transmitted
in any form or by any means, electronic or mechanical, including photocopying,
recording, or any information storage or retrieval system, without
prior permission in writing from the publishers.

Bloomsbury Publishing Plc does not have any control over, or responsibility for, any
third-party websites referred to or in this book. All internet addresses given in
this book were correct at the time of going to press. The author and publisher
regret any inconvenience caused if addresses have changed or sites have
ceased to exist, but can accept no responsibility for any such changes.

A catalogue record for this book is available from the British Library.

Library of Congress Cataloging-in-Publication Data
Names: Malpas, Jeff, author.
Title: Rethinking dwelling : Heidegger, place, architecture / Jeff Malpas.
Description: London ; New York : Bloomsbury Academic, 2021. | "The volume incorporates
ideas and materials that first appeared in a range of previously published essays. None of those
essays appear here in their original form, and in many cases, only parts of those essays are
incorporated into the chapters to which they relate, with most chapters being entirely
original to this volume." | Includes bibliographical references and index. |
Identifiers: LCCN 2021004555 (print) | LCCN 2021004556 (ebook) | ISBN 9781350172913 (hardback) |
ISBN 9781350172937 (ebook) | ISBN 9781350172920 (epub)
Subjects: LCSH: Architecture, Domestic–Philosophy. | Heidegger, Martin, 1889–1976–Influence.
Classification: LCC NA7110 .M28 2021 (print) | LCC NA7110 (ebook) | DDC 728–dc23
LC record available at https://lccn.loc.gov/2021004555
LC ebook record available at https://lccn.loc.gov/2021004556

ISBN:	HB:	978-1-3501-7291-3
	PB:	978-1-3502-5314-8
	ePDF:	978-1-3501-7293-7
	eBook:	978-1-3501-7292-0

Typeset by Integra Software Services Pvt. Ltd.

To find out more about our authors and books visit www.bloomsbury.com
and sign up for our newsletters.

CONTENTS

List of Figures   vii
Acknowledgements   ix

Introduction
PLACE AND ARCHITECTURE   1

Part I
ARCHITECTURE IN TOPOLOGICAL THINKING

Chapter 1
PLACE AND DWELLING   15

Chapter 2
HOMELESSNESS AND MODERNITY   37

Chapter 3
AUTHENTICITY AND ESSENTIALISM   51

Part II
ARCHITECTURE AS TOPOLOGICAL PRACTICE

Chapter 4
DESIGN AND THE HUMAN   75

Chapter 5
ARCHITECTURE AND TRUTH   89

Chapter 6
BUILDING AND MEMORY   105

Chapter 7
THE LINE AND THE HAND   121

Chapter 8
PLACE AND PARAMETRICISM   135

Chapter 9
VERTICALITY AND THE STREET   151

Chapter 10
SPACE AND INTERIORITY 167

Epilogue
RETHINKING ARCHITECTURE 181

Notes 189
Bibliography 225
Index 238

LIST OF FIGURES

1.1 Traditional Black Forest (Schwarzwalder) farmhouse, near Triberg, Baden. Neue Photographische Gesellschaft A.-G. Steglitz-Berlin 1904. Wikimedia Commons. — 16

1.2 Heidelberg and the Old Bridge. Photo © Justin Emery. — 22

4.1 Muuratsalo Experimental House 1952–4. Patio. Photo: Eino Mäkinen, © Alvar Aalto Museum. Approximately 1953. — 81

4.2 Villa Mairea, Alva Aalto, 1938–9. Living room windows and main entrance. Photo: Martti Kapanen, © Alvar Aalto Museum. 1980 — 85

5.1 Aerial view of the Piazza del Campo, Siena. Photo: Stefano Marinari/Shutterstock. — 98

5.2 Temple of Apollo Epikourios at Bassae before restoration in the early 1970s. Photo: Tuh de/Wikimedia. — 100

6.1 Lovett Bay House, Richard Leplastrier, 1998. Photo © Leigh Woolley. — 114

7.1 Villa Sovoye, Poissy, France, Le Corbusier, 1928–31. Top, exterior view; bottom, view to the rooftop garden. Photo: Algie Said/dreamstime.com. — 125

7.2 Map of the eastern Mediterranean Sea from a Portolan atlas (c. 1544) dedicated to Hieronymus Ruffault, Abbot of St. Vaast. Agnese, Battista, 1514–64. Library of Congress Geography and Map Division – https://www.loc.gov/resource/g3200m.gct00001/?sp=11 — 127

7.3 Labyrinth, Chartres Cathedral, Chartres. Photo: © Sylvain Sonnet. — 129

8.1 Heydar Aliyev Center, Baku, Zaha Hadid Architects, 2007–12. Photo: Elnur Amikishiyev/Meashots.com, 2014. — 136

8.2 Therme Vals, Peter Zumthor, 1996. Photo: cjreddaway/Flickr, 2011. — 137

9.1 Giovanni Battista Piranesi, Le Carceri d'Invenzione, plate VII: The Drawbridge, 1761, Princeton University Art Museum, Gift of Frank Jewett Mather Jr. — 156

9.2	Pudong, Shanghai. Photo: dibrova/Shutterstock.	159
9.3	Docklands, Melbourne. Photo: Gordon Bell/Shutterstock.	159
9.4	La Défense, Paris. Photo: pisaphotography/Shutterstock.	160
10.1	The country path – *der Feldweg* – that runs from Messkirch into the surrounding countryside. Photo: © Ilona Schneider, 2017.	174
10.2	Colin McCahon, *Northland triptych*, 1959. Hocken Collections, Uare Taoka o Hakena, University of Otago, Dunedin, New Zealand. © Colin McCahon Research and Publication Trust. Courtesy of the Colin McCahon Research and Publication Trust.	178

ACKNOWLEDGEMENTS

This volume has its immediate origins in the Australian Research Council (ARC)-funded project 'Place and Parametricism: Provocations for the Rethinking of Design' undertaken during 2017–20 in collaboration with Mark Burry, Gini Lee, Stanislav Roudaski and Mark Taylor, but it also draws upon work that was part of another ARC project 'Place, Commonality, and the Human: Towards a New Philosophical Anthropology' undertaken during 2016–18 in collaboration with Andrew Benjamin. The two projects shared a focus on place, though they approached it from very different directions. The support that was made available through the respective project grants is gratefully acknowledged.

The volume also stands in relation to a much longer period of engagement with architects, artists, geographers and others from around the world over the last thirty years or so. That engagement has been significantly facilitated in Germany and Australia by the long-standing support of the Alexander von Humboldt Foundation.

The volume incorporates ideas and materials that first appeared in a range of previously published essays. None of those essays appear here in their original form, and in many cases, only parts of those essays are incorporated into the chapters to which they relate, with most chapters being entirely original to this volume. The chapters in Part I of this volume take up issues first addressed in *Rethinking Dwelling: Heidegger and the Question of Place* [essentially an edited transcript of a lecture given at the University of Auckland in 2012], with a foreword by Ross Jenner (Auckland: enigma:he aupiki – Interstices|matariki editions, 2013), reprinted in *Environmental and Architectural Phenomenology Newsletter*, 25 (2013), pp. 15–23. However, none of the text from that earlier treatment has been carried over into this volume. The original publication details of the essays from which material has been drawn in the chapters in Part II are as follows: 'Heidegger, Aalto, and the Limits of Design', in David Espinet and Toni Hildebrandt (eds.), *Suchen Entwerfen Stiften: Randgänge zu Heideggers Entwurfsdenken* (Munich: Fink-Verlag, 2014), pp. 191–214; 'Truth in Architecture', in V. Petridou, E. Constantopoulos and P. Pagalos (eds.), *The Significance of Philosophy in Architectural Education* (Athens: Michelis Foundation, 2012); 'Building Memory', *Interstices: Journal of Architecture and Related Arts* 13 (2012), pp. 11–21; 'Building on the Line: Topography in the Practice of Architecture', Scott Balmforth and Gerard Reinmuth (eds.), *Terroir: Cosmopolitan Ground* (Sydney: DAB Documents, 2007), pp. 58–85; 'Spatializing Design: Architecture in the Age of Technological Capitalism' [in Slovene], *O oblasti v arhitekturi*, edited by Mateja Kurir (Ljubljana: Maska, Društvo Igor Zabel za kulturo in teorijo, 2020); 'The Interiority of Landscape', in P. Sparke, G. Lee, P. Brown, M. Taylor and P. Lara-Betancourt (eds.), *Flow: Interior, Landscape and Architecture in the Era of Liquid Modernity* (London: Bloomsbury, 2018), pp. 149–58; 'What Is Architecture for?', *Cloud-Cuckoo-Land: International Journal of Architectural Theory,* 22 (2017), no. 36, pp. 117–26.

There are many people to whom I owe thanks for assisting in my architectural education over the years (which still continues) and for the larger engagement, as well as the specific friendships, conversations and events, out of which these essays come. In particular, I would like to acknowledge Megan Baynes, Andrew Benjamin, Richard Blythe, Mark Burry, Adrian Carter, Elias Constanopoulos, Char Davies, Jessica Dubow, Ingo Farin, Vassilis Ganiatsis, Mathew Hinds, Keith Jacobs, Ross Jenner, Paul Johnston, Leonidas Koutsoumpos, Gini Lee, Richard Leplastrier, Stephen Loo, Juhani Pallasmaa, Alberto Pérez-Gómez, Gerard Reinmuth, Mark Taylor, Edward Relph, David Seamon and Leigh Woolley. Special thanks are due to Randall Lindstrom, who has not only been an important conversational partner in relation to the topics discussed here, but who has once again provided assistance in the preparation of this material for publication. Thanks also to Justin Emery for his assistance with various technical issues, but especially in relation to the photographs and images included here.

INTRODUCTION: PLACE AND ARCHITECTURE

Architecture, whether as a practice of design or as enacted in building, has seldom been a topic that has engaged the attention of philosophers, and there are few works by philosophers that address architecture directly.[1] There have been philosophers who have engaged in architectural projects – Ludwig Wittgenstein being the most famous example,[2] also John Dewey at the University of Chicago[3] and Jacques Derrida at La Villette[4] – but often this engagement has been either apart from their philosophical work or at the periphery of it, and often, too, at the periphery of architecture. When philosophers have discussed architecture in explicit fashion – as does Arthur Schopenhauer in *The World as Will and Representation* – it is frequently within the context of aesthetic theory (although, in Schopenhauer's case, his aesthetic theory is a direct expression of his metaphysics), and its impact on architecture has seldom been great.[5] Derrida's reflections have certainly been influential, but they seem to involve less a direct engagement with architecture than a continuation of his existing philosophical thinking.[6] Moreover, inasmuch as architecture is taken up in his thinking, it is largely through being appropriated into the space of deconstructive theory,[7] with the result that, in much of the work that has followed Derrida's engagement, architecture has become another textual field across which the workings of deconstruction can be played out. In general, engagements between philosophers and architects – like that of Derrida with Peter Eisenman and Bernard Tschumi (Derrida's interlocutors at La Villette),[8] or as enacted by Jean Baudrillard and Jean Nouvel[9] – have been infrequent and have, arguably, also tended to shed little significant light on either architecture or philosophy.

Against this background, Martin Heidegger's 1951 essay, 'Bauen Wohnen Denken', translated into English as 'Building Dwelling Thinking',[10] occupies an especially interesting position. Written in a relatively non-technical style (it was not primarily intended for an audience of philosophers, but was delivered as a lecture to a group mainly consisting of architects and planners), standing completely aside from any aesthetic considerations, and eschewing the elaborations of 'theory', the essay's direct references to architecture are brief, yet it has likely had a wider impact (both positive and negative) on architects and architectural theorists than any other single work by a twentieth-century philosopher.[11] Moreover, despite the common tendency to treat him as a nostalgic anti-Modernist, when it came to architecture and design, as with painting and sculpture,[12] Heidegger seems to have had an interest in, and appreciation for, several contemporary Modernist architects and their works – most notably, perhaps, Alvar Aalto and Hans Scharoun.[13]

This volume takes Heidegger's thinking, especially as evident in 'Building Dwelling Thinking', as the starting point for a series of philosophical engagements with issues in and related to architecture that also expand out into several related fields. It does so under the banner of philosophical topology – a mode of thinking that takes place, *topos* (an idea not entirely unrelated to the *chora* of Derrida's thinking[14]), as the central notion guiding philosophical inquiry, both as a substantive focus and as a mode of investigation and analysis.[15] In aiming to bring together the philosophical with the architectural, the book inevitably faces certain difficulties, not the least of which is that of communicating with a somewhat disparate readership. For philosophers, there may be too much architecture here, and for those whose interests are primarily architectural, there will almost certainly be too much philosophy. In what may well be a vain attempt to ameliorate such difficulties, this Introduction aims to set out some of the background to the chapters that make up the book, as well as to provide clarification of key elements in the approach that is adopted. The aim is thus to orient the reader in relation to the topological inquiry that is pursued, pointing out some additional landmarks by means of which the inquiry is situated, indicating some of the directions that will be followed or looked towards, and also providing some idea of the style of travel and the nature of the pathways that are taken. Although readers may well find that their interest focuses on particular chapters more than others – and the chapters can be read more or less independently of one another – the Introduction is probably the single most important chapter of the book in providing some idea of the larger landscape into which each of those chapters is embedded, something that is likely to be important for both philosophically and architecturally inclined readers (as well as those from other disciplinary domains).

This volume *begins* with Heidegger, as does each of its chapters, and the book also *ends* with Heidegger, but it is not (despite the appearance of Heidegger's name in the subtitle) a book primarily *about* Heidegger. Different chapters engage with Heidegger's thought to a greater or lesser extent (the chapters that make up Part I are those most closely focussed on Heidegger's thinking), and the volume does not remain with Heidegger alone. Not only do the various chapters deal with issues that go well beyond Heidegger's discussions, even though they often draw on Heideggerian ideas, they also diverge from Heidegger in various ways. Moreover, whilst Part I is centred on Heidegger's 'Building Dwelling Thinking', Part II is organized around a series of issues in architectural thought and practice – the human focus of design, the question of truth in building, the significance of memory, the role of drawing and the line, the nature and limits of the parametric, the verticality of the city, the nature of interiority – explored in a way that draws on Heidegger's thinking but is not restricted to it.

Although the focus of this volume is on a set of key issues concerning the philosophical understanding of architecture rather than on the exegesis or analysis of a particular thinker, Heidegger remains a central figure throughout the volume for two reasons. The first is that he is such an important figure in the architectural engagement with philosophy. This is so notwithstanding the larger ethical and political questions that are raised, most notably, by Heidegger's involvement with Nazism and the anti-Semitic comments that appear in some of his writings. There are some who would argue – and who have argued – that these associations and comments place him beyond the pale of serious philosophical engagement. Clearly, that is not a view that is endorsed here. Instead, although the claim is not argued for in these pages (but touched upon in Chapter 3),[16] Heidegger's thinking is taken to continue to be philosophically, as well as architecturally, relevant and significant today, despite Heidegger's problematic personal and political commitments as they were evident during the 1930s and 1940s, in particular. Moreover, it remains relevant and significant precisely because of the insights it offers into those key issues that are the focus of the volume. This is, indeed, the second reason why Heidegger is so central: his work, especially as developed in the later essays, thematizes ideas that are at the heart, not only of thinking about architecture and the built environment, but also of any genuine attempt to think about the nature of the human, ideas, specifically of place and space. And in this respect, Heidegger is foundational to the topological approach that the book adopts.

The question of dwelling

If architecture is understood as having a special relation to the human – as about a certain form of articulation of human presence in the world – then the way the human is implicated here will be of special importance. As a result, this volume adopts what might be viewed as a certain sort of 'humanistic' approach to the architectural, and that would be a fair enough construal so long as the notion of the 'humanistic' is approached with some care. In a famous essay, the 'Letter on "Humanism"' from 1947, Heidegger casts doubt on 'humanism' as it has traditionally been understood.[17] He does so partly to distinguish his own position from that of the French existentialist thinker Jean-Paul Sartre, but also because of his refusal, first, to take the human (*das Menschliche* in German) as already understood (so that the human is a site for questioning in Heidegger rather than the already established basis for a philosophy), and second, because the issues at stake in any genuine questioning of the human themselves go beyond the human. These two aspects of Heidegger's approach are also important in the inquiry undertaken here. Architecture is approached as standing in an important relation to the human, but at the same time, the human alone cannot be understood as providing the sole or simple ground on which architecture stands.

The idea of the human is closely implicated in the concept that plays an important role in any discussion of Heidegger on architecture, that appears at the heart of 'Building Dwelling Thinking' (and is prominent in much of Heidegger's later thinking), and that is central to the discussion in Part I, namely, *Wohnen*, usually translated into English as 'dwelling'. Indeed, 'dwelling' has become a widely used term in English-language scholarship, not only in architecture, but also in geography, anthropology and a range of other disciplines, largely as a result of the way the term is taken to appear in Heidegger's 1951 essay. Although the issue is one also discussed in Chapter 1 (and so some of what is said here pre-empts what is to come), it is worth noting, from the very start, the strangeness that attaches to the English term. Many readers are likely, Heideggerian associations aside, to take the term as having primarily a poetic or literary usage – the sort of term that might be used, in a poem or similar work, to evoke some romantic sense of habitation or attachment. The German *Wohnen*, in contrast, is an ordinary and commonplace term in regular everyday use. Part of Heidegger's strategy, in his discussion of *Wohnen*, is indeed to complicate what might otherwise be thought to be already familiar and understood, and instead to make it strange and even perplexing. As he does so often in his later essays, his aim in 'Building Dwelling Thinking' is thus to lead his audience to question something that is usually taken for granted. The problem for most readers of Heidegger's essay, in English, is that the language of dwelling remains within the realm of the unusual, and even obscure, from the very beginning. There is thus no movement from the familiar to the strange in the English encounter with the essay – no movement from the 'homely' (as one might say) to the 'unhomely' (the *unheimlich* in German, that is, the uncanny). Even worse, if there is a sense of familiarity with 'dwelling' for many English-language readers as they come to Heidegger's essay, it is all too often a familiarity that arises as a result of the term's English deployment in discussions derived from or related to Heidegger.

In this latter sense, part of what is attempted in this volume is to move English-language readers from such an assumed familiarity with the idea of dwelling, as it has developed in the existing discussions, to a point where it is indeed rendered strange and perplexing, and where it can no longer simply be assumed. That such a rethinking of dwelling – or, better, of what is at issue in the German *Wohnen* – seems necessary is indicated by the translational matters that are evident here, but it is reinforced by the way much of the current discussion seems to diverge from Heidegger's original inquiry, and by the various difficulties to which that discussion has given rise, not only in architecture but across various fields, including philosophy. To *rethink*, according to most standard definitions, is to think again about some topic or question – to reconsider it, perhaps to reconceptualize what is at issue, even to reflect on the adequacy of the terms in which it is addressed.[18] 'Building Dwelling Thinking' is also concerned with such rethinking, although, for Heidegger, who argues that there is often a failure to think,[19] what is at issue may also be described as an attempt at *thinking* – an attempt to attend to what is really at issue in the (mostly unthinking) talk of what it is to be in the world, that is, what it is to dwell, and of what is at issue in the human activity of building.

Beginning with the obscurity that ought to be recognized as attaching to the term 'dwelling' – its appearance as a term of Heideggerian art – even as it appears in English, one ought nevertheless to be attentive to the familiarity of the phenomenon with which Heidegger begins. Rethinking dwelling ought thus to be a task for almost any reader who wants genuinely to enter into Heidegger's text and the problematic that it sets out. To read that text, one has to begin where it begins – with something apparently familiar – and follow that seeming familiarity into the region to which it beckons, a region that becomes both familiar and strange at one and the same time. Moreover, it is not only dwelling that requires rethinking – much of this volume involves both a rethinking of Heidegger's philosophy as it relates to architecture, and the terms on which it relies, as well as of key architectural notions themselves.

Place and the human

In taking as its task the rethinking of dwelling, the present volume aims to engage with a range of architectural and related issues specifically as they draw together around questions of place, hence the 'topological' framing. *Place*, it should be emphasized from the start, is not to be confused with *space*, even though the two are related, and the difference between them (as well as their relatedness) will be a recurrent theme throughout this volume. The difference, in summary terms, is that place consists in a bounded and differentiated openness (encompassing forms of both time and space), while space, taken alone, is typically associated with a mode of unbounded and largely undifferentiated extension.[20] A basic contention of this volume (as of others to which it relates) is that place is the more fundamental, with space being secondary to place (however there is also a mode of space, referred to in Chapter 10 as 'topological space', that is itself almost identical with place). Yet, although the topological is prior to the merely spatial, there is also a commonplace tendency for the reverse to be assumed – for modes of thought and action that presuppose space and the spatial to dominate over those that give primacy to place and the topological. This makes for very significant differences in the consequent modes of engagement with things and with the world. Much of Heidegger's thinking can be understood as based in an analysis and critique of purely spatialized modes of thought and action, and as an attempt to recall the way such spatialized modes remain grounded in place (and remain so despite the way this may be effaced or forgotten). In this respect, one might also say, in quite general terms, that Heidegger's thinking is a thinking and rethinking of the fundamental relation of place and being.

It is place that is essentially at issue in the reference to 'dwelling' in the title of this book, and place that is therefore the more immediate focus for the rethinking or thinking again that the book aims to undertake. The Norwegian architectural theorist Christian Norberg-Schulz writes, 'Dwelling [...] implies something more than "shelter". It implies that the spaces where life occurs are places, in the true sense of the word.'[21] Although Norberg-Schulz's account cannot be endorsed in its entirety (either in respect of its treatment of place or of dwelling), that account is certainly correct in its affirmation of the connection between place and dwelling, as well as the way both might relate to life. To speak of dwelling is thus also to speak of place, and so the title of this inquiry, 'Rethinking Dwelling', could almost be rephrased as 'Rethinking Place'. What counts against such a rephrasing, however, is that dwelling brings with it a more specific focus, and a set of issues, not immediately invoked by place alone. Dwelling brings to the fore the way in which place and the human are implicated with one another, and so the issues that surround dwelling are the issues that arise in respect of the human relation to place. Echoing the point made previously, however, this does not mean that place is only to be understood or inquired into inasmuch as it relates to the human, nor that place is to be taken as itself something human. This is so despite the ubiquitous tendency, in the architectural literature and elsewhere, to treat place as indeed a 'human' phenomenon and only such (so that place is assumed to be something constructed, often identified with a form of 'meaningful space' – an issue partly taken up in Chapter 1). Place, both in general and in its specific instantiations, stands apart from the human even as it is also related to the human.

That it stands apart in this way is so in at least two respects. First, the character of place is not exhausted by what may be evident through the engagement of any specific human individual or human community with place. There is always *more* to place, even to the very place of one's immediate situatedness. Second, even though every place involves the human, the involvement at issue always and only occurs as part of the inter-implication of place and world in which the human participates, but which the human neither determines nor founds. Place is indeed that to which the human is necessarily related – so there is no human mode of being that is not also placed being (even though such being-placed is often refused or forgotten) – and yet place is not something *merely* human, nor related exclusively to the human. Moreover, if this book aims at rethinking place as well as dwelling, then it should also be emphasized that it involves or, better perhaps, presupposes a rethinking of the human (as it does a range of other notions).

Although the point should already be clear, it is worth saying a little more about the concept of the human that is at issue here, not only as it is at work in Heidegger, but also as it is at work throughout the inquiries undertaken in the pages that follow. Perhaps most importantly, it should be clear that the human cannot be assumed, in any unqualified sense, to refer simply to a certain species of hominid – to modern *homo sapiens sapiens*.[22] This is all too often what the term 'human' is assumed to mean, even though, at the very same time, it is often also used to refer to a certain ethical category or mode – one that emphasizes a concern for the other – frequently taken to be characterized by kindness or compassion that is not restricted just to others of the same kind. To be 'inhuman' or 'inhumane' is not to fail to be a certain species of hominid, but rather to fail to exhibit a certain mode of ethical being or ethical comportment. To take the 'human' to refer just to a certain species, or species-character, would be to treat the human merely *biologically*, but Heidegger has no special interest in the human merely as a biological phenomenon, and neither is such a conception of the human of any special relevance to the discussion here. Moreover, there can be no non-arbitrary (or non-stipulative) ground on which the idea of the human could be restricted to just such a biological meaning.

If the human cannot be assumed to be a biological notion, neither can the human simply be identified with a certain mode of life as it might be defined within the frames of psychology or anthropology. Not only do such frames tend to assume some notion of the human as already given, but, like biology (including evolutionary biology), they treat human being only as it is empirically presented, and that means, once again, that the fundamental question of the human – who or what *is* the human? – can never be addressed in a fundamental manner within such frames. It is the rejection of most of these traditional ways of understanding the human that largely underpins Heidegger's refusal of most forms of so-called 'philosophical anthropology'. If there were to be such a thing – an anthropology that would indeed be philosophical – then it would have to operate with a radically different conception of the human, a more genuinely *philosophical* conception than is usually assumed. But the tendency of anthropology (and of psychology and biology) is always to rely upon already assumed and often unquestioned notions, usually empirically based, of what the human might be. Philosophical anthropology thus finds itself in a situation of tension between the philosophical demand and the anthropological one. In similar fashion, and for similar reasons, Heidegger's critique of traditional humanism is based on its assumption of the human, and so its overlooking of what is really at issue in the question of the human.

For the most part, and especially as Heidegger uses it in his later thinking, the human is, or is grounded in, that mode of individual being that is constituted in terms of a relation to its own bounds or limits (which is what is at issue in the other term Heidegger uses to refer to human beings in his later work, namely, 'mortals'). To put it in slightly different but related terms (the terms Heidegger already uses, in large part, in *Being and Time*[23]), the human is that mode of being that can ask about its own being and the limits of that being – that can address the matter of its own 'place'. Because its own being is in question for it in this way – because its own place is an issue – the human is that being which stands in an uncertain relation to itself, and so may indeed be said to stand apart from itself and its world (even though this is also that to which it is closest). The questionability that appears here is itself related to the possibility of freedom in Heidegger (which is not about escape from causality, but rather a certain relatedness to the world). It can also be argued that it is just such questionability, applied to how one acts and lives, that underpins the idea of the human as indeed an ethical notion. The questionability – or freedom – that is at issue here is also what differentiates human from other modes of being. This way of understanding the human means that the 'human' cannot be taken to be restricted in its application to the species *homo sapiens sapiens* alone, and it thereby leaves open the possibility of modes of human being that are not 'human' in the biological sense of the term (in much the same way that, for instance, functionalist accounts of the mind allow for the possibility of mind as associated with different biologies). There remains a question as to what marks out a being as human. Heidegger's short answer is that it is a certain relation to being (discussed earlier in terms of the questioning of being), and that relation to being also involves a relation to language. Once again, however, this is a much larger topic than can be properly addressed here. Indeed, it raises complex questions about, not only the idea of the human, but also the idea of language – and here, too, as is so often the case in Heidegger, the conventional understanding of what is at issue cannot be assumed.[24]

Topology and ontology

Although this book engages with architecture, it does so, as already noted, from an explicitly philosophical perspective – one that owes much to Heidegger (and in this respect, it is also quite a specific perspective philosophically). The adoption of such a perspective means, however, that the inquiry undertaken here is not one that operates primarily by looking to specific buildings or designs as the basis on which to arrive at more general conclusions. This is not, in other words, an *empirical* inquiry, even though it may draw upon and be informed by empirical (which is to say, experiential or observational) considerations and may also use specific buildings and designs as examples or illustrations. Of course, it is also not an inquiry that remains within the precincts of mere logical or analysis either, since it takes the form of reflection upon certain phenomena – one might say 'ideas' except that it should also be emphasized that the engagement is not merely ideational or conceptual either.

As with Heidegger's own work, what is attempted is a reflection, in phenomenological terms, on the things themselves. It attempts to use one of Heidegger's common locutions, to think *things* rather than merely to think *about* things (the locution is itself one also employed in the discussions that follow here). Such an approach is exemplified by Heidegger's inquiry in 'Building Dwelling Thinking', which is presented, not as an inquiry into mere concepts, but into those very 'things' named in the inquiry's title. Yet, even as Heidegger's inquiry does indeed aim to think building, to think dwelling, to think thinking, this does not mean that it functions independently *of* thinking or of that with which thinking is intimately connected, namely, *language* (as if any inquiry could function in that way). Thinking is not something that stands apart from things and somehow has to get back to them, or, at least, the thinking that is already estranged in this way is a thinking that has already lost its way *as thinking*. To think is to remain with things, even though sometimes it may also require a turning back to things and so a turning back to its own prior belonging with things. And as thinking and language also belong together, so the remaining with things is a remaining with, and an attending to, language – which is also not apart from things but already belongs with them. Language is very much at issue in Heidegger's inquiry, and the same is true of the inquiry undertaken here, but this is not, as is so often assumed, because language functions as some kind of 'prison' or constitutes a barrier that must be overcome. Instead, the genuine engagement with things, which is no mere causal or sensory activity and re-activity, is always an engagement that occurs within a space that is, itself, opened *by* and *through* language.

This is not the place to try to offer an account of how language is properly to be understood nor, indeed, of the way language and world are related. However, it is important to note that it would be a mistake to suppose that an inquiry such as this could be undertaken without attending to – without 'listening', as Heidegger would say – what can be heard in language.[25] This is not to assume any 'correlation' of language with things, nor to presuppose any form of linguistic constructionism or idealism. Language, understood in its fundamental sense (the sense at issue in Heidegger's frequent invocation of the Greek terms, from which the English 'language' comes, *logos* and *legein*), is not something that one can ever stand outside of any more than one can stand outside of the world or outside of place. Although language can certainly be *objectified*, and thereby studied *as an object*, such objectification already renders language as something less than it is – and, indeed, must do so, since any such objectification already relies on language, even in that act of objectification.[26]

At this point, it is worth going to Heidegger's characterization of the inquiry that he aims to carry out in 'Building Dwelling Thinking'. At the very start of his discussion, in a passage that could also stand as a characterization of a large part of what is attempted here, Heidegger tells us:

> In what follows we shall try to think about dwelling and building. This thinking about building does not presume to discover architectural ideas, let alone to give rules for building. This venture in thought does not view building as an art or as a technique of construction; rather it traces building back into that domain to which everything that is belongs.[27]

In trying to 'think about dwelling and thinking', Heidegger's aim is to move back to that in which building has its proper ground – to move back to building's beginning, its *arche,* in Greek, which can also mean 'first principle'. More will be said about Heidegger's comments here in the pages to come. From the start, however, there are several points that should be emphasized. First, the reference to 'the domain to which everything that is belongs' indicates that what is at issue here is already a question that has a distinctly topological character. What is at issue is a moving or tracing back, but also a moving or tracing back to a specific domain. The topological character of this language is not to be dismissed as merely metaphorical. What is at issue is indeed a certain sort of *place*. Second, the belonging to this place is a belonging that relates to everything *that is*, and, although Heidegger leaves it implicit, what this indicates is that the inquiry is an inquiry that takes up things in their *being*. In this respect, the inquiry is not only topological, but also, in an important sense, *ontological*. Third, when Heidegger says that what is to be attempted is 'to think', that has to be understood in the light of the 'tracing back' that is at issue here. Thinking, itself, is just such a turning back 'into that domain to which everything that is belongs'. In this sense, *thinking* is always a turning back to being and to place – it is both *ontological* and *topological*.

There is often, in contemporary discourse, suspicion about any talk of beginnings, or grounds, or even principles, and certainly of first principles. But even that sort of suspicion has its own beginnings, its own grounds, its own principles (even its own *first* principles) – it merely chooses, for the most part, not to talk about or acknowledge them. Sometimes, the suspicion of beginnings, grounds and principles is manifest in the suspicion of ontology or in the relativizing of the notion. Such relativizing is evident in the tendency, in some quarters, to treat 'ontology' as a specific mode of analysis, or as the outcome of such an analysis, which involves delineating the basic elements or components of a field, domain or practice – on which basis, the ontology of architecture, for instance, might be said to consist in the specification of the basic elements of design or of built form, or in the actual elements so specified. Such a relativized sense of ontology, however, is highly restricted and is always dependent on the context already having been specified, even if only implicitly. It is common to find ontology viewed, beyond such a relativized sense, as 'universalizing' and 'totalizing', and often as therefore complicit with various forms of oppression and the refusal or neglect of difference. There is no doubt that ontological claims can have such a character, but the mere fact that an ontological claim is wide in scope, or that it applies in some fundamental fashion, is not sufficient to legitimate the objection that such a claim is, by that very fact, problematic. To argue otherwise is to refuse to attend to the specificity of what is in question. The important question is not whether a claim is wide in scope or fundamental in nature, but whether and to what extent it is well-articulated, contentful and well-grounded.

The relativized sense of ontology noted above, although not illegitimate, is nevertheless *derivative*. In its more fundamental and original sense (the sense indicated by the original Greek from which the term was formed, through Latin, when it first appeared in the seventeenth century[28]), ontology concerns *being*, including specific modes of being, and it names the inquiry into being as well as the 'structure' such an inquiry lays bare – its 'logic', one might say. If architecture is understood, as it is understood in the pages that follow, to be a certain mode of responsiveness to place that is worked out through designed or built form – which is to say, through the shaping of space as that occurs within and with respect to place (place and space being distinct even if also related) – then not only will the ontology of architecture be determined by such responsiveness, but architecture will also be ontological, in its own character, through the way it contributes to the very appearing of place and space as that occurs in designed and built form.

What is outlined here under the heading of 'ontology' is very much the sort of inquiry Heidegger advances in 'Building Dwelling Thinking'. In its questioning of the nature of human being in the world, of what it is to live in the world, or to dwell, Heidegger's inquiry is both *ethical* and *ontological*, and the two are bound together in the essentially topological account that Heidegger develops (something elaborated upon, most directly, in the Epilogue). The relation between the ethical and the ontological, and their connection to the topological, is a theme that runs throughout much of this volume. In Heidegger's work, talk of ontology is not without its problems. On the one hand, Heidegger largely abandons the language of ontology and the ontological in his work after *Being and Time* (largely because of concerns about the conventional character and meaning of ontology within the philosophical tradition).[29] On the other hand, Heidegger's thinking remains fundamentally *ontological* in its concern with being and that which belongs to being. It is in this latter sense that ontology is at work here (a sense that aims to take issue with the traditional forms of ontology), and it is in this sense, too, that ontology is directly connected with the ethical. Heidegger's inquiries in 'Building Dwelling Thinking' are both ontological and ethical at one and the same time, and they are such inasmuch as they aim to address the basic condition of human being in the world and the implications for human being, which is to say, for the way human beings engage in the world that follows from this (which is essentially what is at issue in Karsten Harries's talk of the 'ethical function' of architecture). It is this question of the relation between architecture and human being that is perhaps the most important underlying question pursued through the chapters that follow, and to which the discussion will return most directly in the Epilogue.

Part I

ARCHITECTURE IN TOPOLOGICAL THINKING

Chapter 1

PLACE AND DWELLING

In a series of critically acclaimed films – *London*, *Robinson in Space* and *Robinson in Ruins* – the British film-maker Patrick Keiller provides an evocative but also critical exploration of themes of place, space, identity and politics as they appear in the post-Thatcherite landscape of England in the 1990s and 2000s.[1] The films are of interest architecturally, as well as culturally, since they are largely composed around a series of images of landscapes, both urban and rural, as well as buildings, roads, shops and factories. There are no actors, only a disembodied narrator, who speaks over a series of separate, statically shot scenes. The final film, *Robinson in Ruins*, produced in collaboration with the geographer Doreen Massey, presents itself as aiming to explore the discrepancy between 'on the one hand, the cultural and critical attention devoted to experience of mobility and displacement and, on the other, a tacit but widespread tendency to fall back on formulations of *dwelling* that drive from a more settled agricultural past'.[2]

The talk of 'dwelling' here is clearly intended as a direct reference to the discussion in 'Building Dwelling Thinking'. At one point in the film, the narrator is heard speaking of the main character, Robinson (who is never seen), having visited a local supermarket (a German-owned chain, Lidl, that is common across the UK):

> Despite his increasing insubstantiality, Robinson had returned … with two bottles of Putinov vodka, a snow shovel, and several own-brand items, in illustrated packaging, that recalled the dwelling of Black Forest farmers which, for Heidegger, let earth and heaven, divinities and mortals, enter in simple oneness into things. For which simple oneness Robinson began to search by visiting a well.[3]

What is included here is effectively a quotation from the English translation of Heidegger's essay: 'Let us think for a while', writes Heidegger, 'of a farmhouse in the Black Forest, which was built some two hundred years ago by the dwelling of peasants. Here the self-sufficiency of the power to let earth and heaven, divinities and mortals enter in simple oneness into things, ordered the house.'[4] (see Figure 1.1). In Keiller's film, Heidegger is thus invoked as exemplary of exactly the tendency to fall back on ideas and modes of thinking that derive, not

Figure 1.1 Traditional Black Forest (Schwarzwalder) farmhouse, near Triberg, Baden, 50 kms northeast of Freiburg im Breisgau. Neue Photographische Gesellschaft A.-G. Steglitz-Berlin 1904. Wikimedia Commons.

from the experience of mobility or displacement, but rather 'from a more settled agricultural past'. As such, Heidegger's work and the ideas that work expresses are presented as having little relevance to the contemporary world – even to represent an absurd response to it. It is an absurdity and irrelevance expressed in Keiller's film by the somewhat ridiculous list of supermarket purchases, and of Robinson as beginning his search for Heidegger's 'simple oneness' by visiting a well that turns out, in its contemporary form, to be little more than a barely flowing and neglected stream.

The contrast that Keiller and Massey draw, between the mobile and displaced character of contemporary experience and the settled agricultural 'dwelling' of the past, echoes the almost identical contrast that appears in Hilde Heynen's account of the situation of contemporary architecture:

> [The] modern consciousness is that of 'the homeless mind', and foreigners and migrants provide a model for the experience of every individual in a modern, mobile, and unstable society. Dwelling is in the first instance associated

with tradition, security, and harmony, with a life situation that guarantees connectedness and meaningfulness. Considerations such as these underlie the dilemmas that architecture is faced with.[5]

The contrast is repeated in Neil Leach's work, 'The Dark Side of the *Domus*', from the same year. There, Leach offers 'a critique of the concept of "dwelling"', which has, he says, 'become something of a dominant paradigm within architectural theory'. 'Dwelling', he argues, is tied to an emphasis on 'the soil, on the earth', involving 'an evocation for [sic] the *Heimat*, for the homeland',[6] and is associated with 'the rooted, the nationalistic and the static'.[7] Standing in opposition to the urban and the metropolitan,[8] 'dwelling' is said to be 'ill equipped to deal with our contemporary cultural conditions', and so Leach concludes 'that architecture must look to a more flexible theoretical model, more in tune with the fluidity, flux and complexity of our contemporary modes of existence'.[9] In *Heidegger for Architects* – a work which seems to argue that Heidegger is not really 'for' architects at all or should be administered only in very small and controlled doses – Adam Sharr repeats a similar set of conclusions, warning against the dangers of 'Heidegger's romantic provincialism'.[10]

The criticisms that appear in Leach and Heynen, in particular, pick up on lines of argument that are present in earlier architectural discussions. Anthony Vidler, for instance, deals with Heidegger as part of his own exploration of what he calls the 'architectural uncanny', and so of ideas of homelessness and the 'un-homely' (which is the literal meaning of the German term, *unheimlich*, usually translated as 'uncanny'), associating Heidegger with a 'profound nostalgia' for a 'premodern' form of belonging.[11] Mark Wigley takes the image of the 'house' in Heidegger's writings (in a way that itself prefigures aspects of Leach's account) as representative of Heidegger's complicity in political violence as well as operating to disrupt and confuse any genuine architectural sensibility – the house becomes a way of withdrawing from the spatial, the public, the modern.[12] Heynen and Leach are significant because of their focus on 'Building Dwelling Thinking', and the specific critique of dwelling that they advance. Of course, not only do their critiques not stand alone, but dwelling alone is not all that is at issue here.

As dwelling is invariably connected with place – is a mode of *being-in-place* – so the critique of dwelling is also a critique of place, or of much of the thinking that takes place as a key notion. And the sorts of claims that appear in Heynen, Leach and Sharr, as well as being implicit in Keiller, appear in a host of other works in architecture and elsewhere that take issue with a notion of place that is assumed to be no less problematic than that of dwelling. Understood as static, settled, 'rural' and *past*, and as therefore associated, too, with the 'mythic' and the 'romantic', place is itself frequently contrasted with the supposedly mobile and interconnected character of the modern world, and with a mode of thinking that, as it is tuned to such mobility and interconnectivity, is also associated with the urban and the cosmopolitan, with the real rather than the 'mythic', with the contemporary and the futural. This contrast is operative within contemporary architectural discussion – and not only in relation to Heidegger. It seems, for instance, to be at work, if not always in quite these terms, in the famous dispute between Christopher Alexander and Peter Eisenman at Harvard in 1982.[13]

The contrast at issue here might seem to be a simple and straightforward one, and certainly the terms in which it is presented appear to reinforce that impression (even if things become somewhat more complicated in Heynen's discussion).[14] Yet, as soon as one presses upon it, the contrast starts to become awkward, uncertain, problematic. Indeed, it is remarkable how many different issues and ideas are bound up together here – especially in discussions such as those of Leach and Sharr (and almost whenever Heidegger is directly at issue). They include ideas, not only of 'dwelling' as contrasted to 'modernity', or of the rural as against the urban (the 'provincial' as against the 'cosmopolitan'[15]), but also of home and 'homelessness', of settlement and exile, of the familiar and the strange, the grounded and the ungrounded, the emancipatory and the oppressive, the conservative and the progressive, the fascist and the democratic. One might wonder whether there are not too many ideas here – too many different terms and issues – than can be conjoined, as it seems they often are, into a set of simple dualities.

At this point, however, it becomes evident that what is at issue concerns not just a particular thinker, a single episode in intellectual history, or even one specific idea taken on its own. Heynen, for one, is quite clear on the way in which the questions that arise out of Heidegger's discussion of dwelling are part of a much larger constellation of issues that are central to contemporary architecture, and that she presents in terms of architecture's relation to modernity. So, although the problem of 'dwelling' may be situated in an important way in relation to Heidegger's 'Building Dwelling Thinking', the problem goes well beyond that text, encompassing place no less than it does dwelling, and raising fundamental questions about the primary orientations of architectural thought and practice.

This first part of this book takes a closer look at the cluster of issues that appear here – exploring the contrast that appears in Heynen, as well as in Leach and Keiller, according to which dwelling is opposed to the modern as well as the urban, but also, and more importantly, examining what is at stake in the idea of dwelling, and of place as connected to this, as it develops out of Heidegger's work. Chapter 1 focuses on the way 'dwelling' has entered into English-language discussion, beginning with the account Heidegger advances in 'Building Dwelling Thinking' as well as the ways dwelling has been taken up thereafter, in architecture and also geography (both areas where the notion has been especially important). Issues of translation loom large here, especially the difficulties that arise from the use of 'dwelling' to translate the original German term *Wohnen*. Although much of the focus is on dwelling, place is equally at issue in the discussion, and much of the analysis of dwelling is directly transposable into the analysis of place, although with one notable caveat. Since dwelling is always a dwelling 'in' place, so place must always retain a degree of primacy over dwelling. It may be that place is only known through dwelling, but it is place that, in one important sense, enables dwelling at the same time as it also extends beyond it. Chapter 2 continues in a similar direction but focuses more specifically on the problematic association of dwelling, and so also place, with the rural, the settled and the past. Here, one of the key questions concerns the possibility of a normative component that belongs to dwelling and so the extent to which it can be understood as a critical notion rather than simply as a 'nostalgic' reversion to some realm of comforting and unquestioning security. The last chapter in this first part, Chapter 3, takes up various questions of identity and authenticity that stand in the background of much of this discussion, considering them in relation to dwelling and place as well as to related notions of home and belonging. Although seldom interrogated directly, these notions often play a role in architectural thinking and frequently figure in the way architectural notions are articulated and critiqued – not only in connection to Heidegger but also more generally. A central issue here concerns the supposed character of dwelling and place as tied to problematic forms of essentialism or foundationalism that are necessarily exclusionary and even violent.

In exploring the way dwelling has become an issue in recent and contemporary discussions, a key aim is to enable a better understanding of what is genuinely at issue in topology (or topological thinking), especially as it is configured around the ideas of dwelling and place as they might operate in architecture and in thinking about architecture. This first part of the book thus provides a framework for the more focused discussions and explorations that occur in the parts and chapters that follow. These first chapters focus much more directly on the work of Heidegger than do those that follow (Chapter 10 and the Epilogue return the discussion to a more Heideggerian frame). But Heidegger has an important role throughout the volume, and this derives, not only from his significance as perhaps the most influential thinker of the twentieth century – whether for good or ill – but because of the way his work is indeed directly engaged, as is the work of no other twentieth-century thinker, with the very issues of space, place and the human relation to these, that are at the heart of any genuinely topological mode of thinking, and that are also fundamental to the thinking of architecture.

Heidegger on 'Man and Space'

Most discussions of 'dwelling' cite Heidegger as the source for the notion, usually by reference to the discussion in 'Building Dwelling Thinking'.[16] Heidegger's focus on 'dwelling' – *Wohnen*, as it appears in that essay – was a direct response to the theme of the 1951 conference in Darmstadt to which 'Building Dwelling Thinking' was a contribution. Titled 'Man and Space', the conference aimed to focus, according to the organizer, Otto Bartning, on 'the architectural management of our space of living [*Lebensraum*]', which means, he said 'the comprehensible and incomprehensible, the felt, willed, and creative engagement with the space of living'. And he added that the meeting would also be given over to the question concerning 'the part of architecture in overcoming homelessness [*Heimatlosigkeit*], both physical [*leiblich*] and intellectual/spiritual [*geistig*] homelessness'.[17] Heidegger addresses the questions at stake here quite directly, as well as taking up, no less directly, the larger set of issues invoked in the conference title – concerning the relation of the human ('man', *Mensch*) and the spatial – that are necessarily implicated with homelessness and dwelling, and with place.[18]

The position set out in 'Building Dwelling Thinking' includes three main interconnecting relations: between building and dwelling, between space and place, and between the human and the world. In each case, Heidegger reverses the usually assumed ordering of those relations – building is grounded in (or secondary to) dwelling, space is grounded in place, the human is grounded in the world. A fourth relation is also implicated, although it comes to the fore only towards the very end of the essay, namely, the relation between dwelling and thinking (this fourth element is one that, for the moment, will be left to one side, but will be taken up directly in Chapter 2). The entire essay is aimed at both opening up the question of 'what it is to dwell' *as a question*, but also setting out an answer to that question – or, at least, indicating the domain in which such an answer is to be found. It is in doing this that Heidegger can be seen as offering an account of the role of architecture in addressing the space and place of living – though this means recognizing that architecture belongs to a much larger task than might have hitherto been supposed.

The problem of homelessness emerges in Heidegger's discussion in such a way that, to use Bartning's terms, homelessness as 'physical' is always underlain by homelessness as 'intellectual/spiritual' – and this accords with the idea that the problem of dwelling comes before the problem of building. It is not that Heidegger considers a lack of housing to be an insignificant problem – his comments indicate quite the opposite[19] – but he claims that the mere provision of housing (of 'shelter', as one might put it) does not, in itself, address the more fundamental problem of the homelessness that pertains to our very way of being in the world. Heidegger's discussion is notable for its attempt to engage with the architectural context of the Darmstadt meeting. And, although Heidegger is often criticized for having nothing concrete to say about how one might address the real living conditions in which people find themselves, the fact that his account remains at a general and philosophical level, and does not consider detailed issues of design or take up such issues in relation to specific buildings, is neither surprising nor obviously blameworthy. Heidegger was not an architect and had no strong background in, or knowledge of, architectural practice. He thus approaches the issues, as one might expect, philosophically and from the perspective of his own thinking. The fact that he was able and willing, nonetheless, to engage with the topic at issue is an indication of the way in which questions relevant to architecture – notably questions of place and space, as well as 'dwelling' – were already centrally at work in that thinking.

Although 'Building Dwelling Thinking' is structured around the discussion of 'dwelling' and 'building', what lies at the very heart of that discussion is the question of 'world'. Heidegger rejects the idea, associated in *Being and Time* (Heidegger's master-work from 1927) with Descartes, that the world is to be understood in terms merely of an extended spatialized structure, one that is essentially homogenous and isotropic, that encompasses all that is and in which things appear as merely present (so 'to be' is 'to be present within space'). It is often assumed that, in *Being and Time*, Heidegger replaces this Cartesian view, which privileges what is often taken to be a 'theoretical' perspective, with a more engaged view, one that gives priority to the 'practical'.[20] In fact, for Heidegger, even in *Being and Time*, *both* theory *and* practice (the distinction between which is not, in any case, absolute[21]) are embedded in a structure of 'meaningfulness' that is given shape by the activities of what he calls *Dasein*, which is understood as the ground of the human. *Dasein* is 'being here/there' (*Da* in German having the sense of both 'here' and 'there'); in other words, it is that mode of being that is always given in and as a 'here/there', and so as *placed* (although, in *Being and Time*, the language of place remains implicit). *Dasein* is a term that is less common in Heidegger's later work, where he tends to refer instead to the 'human' or to 'mortals'. One of the problems in *Being and Time*, however, is that the emphasis on the activities of *Dasein*, as constituting the ordered structure of meaningfulness, can easily be read as implying that the world, or the meaningfulness of the world, is a product of *Dasein* – even that the world is a 'projection' of *Dasein*. Such 'subjectivism' (since *Dasein* can be understood as itself connected to, even if not identical with, subjectivity) was part of what *Being and Time* was intended to overcome, and this difficulty, together with other problems (including the seeming prioritization of the practical with which it is associated, and the lack of a fully developed account of space and place), meant that *Being and Time* remained an incomplete work.

In taking up the question of world, what 'Building Dwelling Thinking' attempts is essentially a re-articulation of an issue that was already central to *Being and Time* but advanced in the later work in somewhat different terms.[22] It remains the case that human being first finds itself *in* the world through its activities, but those activities are explicitly understood in very broad terms, and, most importantly, as contributing to or playing a role in the structure of the world, but not as producing it. The world is now understood as both arising from and consisting in the interplay between the multiplicity that also appears in and through the world. That multiplicity includes everything that is – persons, animals, plants, artefacts, processes, things – but at another level, it is evident in terms of an interplay across two axes involving four different but equally basic elements: earth, sky, divinities and mortals. To use Bartning's contrast once more, one might say that earth and sky are the basic components that come to the fore in physical or bodily (*leiblich*) situatedness, whilst divinities and mortals (or divinity and mortality) come to the fore in relation to spiritual/intellectual (*geistig*), and also 'historical', situatedness – the axis of earth and sky appearing as more strongly spatial, and that of divinities and mortals as more strongly temporal.[23] The two axes, and so also these four elements, are, however, necessarily interconnected, each implicating and implicated by the others, so that the above distinctions cannot be taken as absolute. The ontological structure at issue here is thus non-reductive and fundamentally *relational*, and this applies to the basic elements – earth, sky, divinities, mortals – as well as to 'things', which here does not mean only the ordinary middle-sized things, such as jug, chair or machine, but also those larger assemblages that take the form, for instance, of bridge and house. Because the world understood in this way is not merely spatialized, in the Cartesian sense, but has an ordered character to it, though one deriving from the complex structure that is the fourfold (which is not the same as any ordering that derives only from *human* activity since it incorporates the *non-human* also), the world is understood as *topological*, as constituted always in and through 'places' (and this applies, in addition, to the relationality that is at issue here – it, too, is organized around places).

In the ordering that it establishes, the farmhouse to which Heidegger refers is said to bring together the basic elements of world – the latter being what Heidegger takes to be given in the fourfold of earth and heaven, divinities and mortals. Heidegger talks of this same ordering as at work in the other example he develops of the placing and spacing that occurs through the spanning of a river by a bridge (he refers specifically to the 'Old Bridge', *Alte Brücke*, in the city of Heidelberg (see Figure 1.2). In an analysis that echoes, even though it does not acknowledge, Georg Simmel's account of the bridge in his essay 'Bridge and Door',[24] Heidegger talks of the bridge, in its character as a 'thing', but also as something 'built', establishing a place, clearing a space, and in so doing setting the elements of world into relation to one another, both unifying and differentiating them, thereby also allowing the opening of world. Significantly, here neither place nor space is 'made' by mortals. Heidegger is not describing some process of 'place-making' as it is usually understood in architectural circles. Place and space belong to the fourfold, to the world, rather than being products of human building. Building *allows* the fourfold – the unitary play of the world – to come forth (which is why Heidegger connects 'building' to 'letting-dwell', *Wohnenlassen*[25]), and so building also allows the placing and spacing that belongs to the fourfold.

Figure 1.2 Heidelberg and the Old Bridge. Photo © Justin Emery.

If the structure or 'event' at issue here is difficult to grasp, then that is because it is not something built out of already existing elements that are put together to form something else (as, indeed, one might do as part of a process of construction). Instead, Heidegger's account is one that takes the larger structure or event – the fourfold, the 'world' – to be composed out of the unifying and differentiating of the elements even as the elements are themselves composed through that same unifying and differentiating. Moreover, whilst the fourfold is always brought together in and through the thing, the thing is itself brought together in and through the fourfold. The reciprocity at work here applies at almost every level and with respect to each of the key structures and elements that Heidegger identifies – *including, it should be noted, human being, the being of 'mortals'*. Yet, inasmuch as the entire structure is compositional or 'relational', so it is also topological, and not just in the sense that it is a structure that gives rise to places. It is a compositionality that belongs to place as such (and is exemplified even in ordinary places) – a bringing together within bounds that is open as it also opens, and in which different places are established as places through their relatedness within an encompassing place or region that, in its own turn, is given in the interrelatedness of those same places.[26] Moreover, since what is opened up here always both encompasses and surpasses that which it is opened up in and through – just as the bridge is encompassed and surpassed by the world that is opened up in and through it something demonstrated by the fact that the opening of the world is not unique to, for instance, the bridge alone – so what is opened up, in an important sense, comes 'before' (is more 'originary') than that in and through which it is opened.

The way Heidegger sets out his account in 'Building Dwelling Thinking' is in relatively familiar and concrete terms (hence the examples of the bridge and farmhouse), even though the thinking that it aims to enact is intended to uncover something deeper than may at first be assumed. Yet because of its character in this regard, the account has often been read in ways that overlook or distort elements of that account, or else dismiss the account as deliberately obscure, even as indicating the collapse of Heidegger's thinking into mysticism or poetry (both of the latter terms being intended pejoratively). Yet, if there is obscurity here, it is just the obscurity that comes from a density and complexity of ideas, and from Heidegger's insistence on thinking all of the relevant elements together – refusing the usual linear mode of analysis that moves from one thing to another in a step-wise manner or that does indeed take certain primitive or assumed elements as that from which the larger structure can be constructed or to which it can be reduced. There is more to be said, as noted earlier, about the way thinking enters into the discussion of 'Building Dwelling Thinking' as itself an issue. What is important for the moment, however, is to recognize the distinctiveness of the mode of thinking that is at work in the essay as a whole, and the way it stands quite apart from the usual modes of scholarly discussion. It exemplifies what Heidegger characterizes as a mode of 'topology' (*Topologie* is the term Heidegger himself uses[27]) – and for that reason, Heidegger's way of proceeding ought to be seen as all the more significant in this context, since it does indeed seem to be so centrally oriented to place, both as it is a focus for thinking and as it also shapes the character of thinking.

'Dwelling' – from Norberg-Schulz to Ingold

Regardless of the deeper level of analysis that lies within the apparent simplicity of his account in 'Building Dwelling Thinking', Heidegger's specific focus on *Wohnen* would not itself have presented any special problems for his original audience. *Wohnen* is, as noted earlier, a common term in everyday German. The term figures in architectural discussion, in much the same way in which 'housing', for instance, figures in English-language contexts, but the term does not carry any special or technical meaning – certainly no more so than other commonplace terms to which it is related (terms like *Wohnung* meaning a 'residence' or 'apartment').

Other thinkers, including Theodore Adorno and Walter Benjamin, also discuss issues relating to *Wohnen*, most notably in Adorno's *Minima Moralia*, published the same year as the proceedings from the Darmstadt conference,[28] and in Benjamin's unfinished *Passagenwerk*, or *Arcades Project*, which he worked on from 1927 to his death in 1940.[29] The way *Wohnen* is taken up in both Benjamin and Adorno undoubtedly has relevance to Heidegger's discussion (and some of Benjamin's remarks will be returned to later), but it is important to note that both of them treat *Wohnen* as a term of everyday experience. And for the most part, their remarks, although critical, do not figure as part of a sustained argument or analysis, appearing rather in the consideration of changes in the character of contemporary living.[30] In this latter respect, however, both Adorno and Benjamin take *Wohnen* to have been made problematic by modernity. It is Adorno who asserts, and it is this that is echoed in Heynen and others, that 'dwelling, in the proper sense, is now impossible',[31] and Adorno sees this as part of a larger malaise affecting modernity, and from which there seems no escape. 'Wrong life', he writes, 'cannot be lived rightly'.[32] For Benjamin, *Wohnen* has to be seen, 'in its more extreme form', as tied to the nineteenth century, and yet also as ancient 'and perhaps eternal'.[33]

In English, 'dwelling' does appear in some architectural discussions, independent of its appearance in the English translation of Heidegger's essay, but only in the sense of a habitable structure (the most common sense in English), and so as meaning most often a house or hut (but sometimes also tent, cave and so on).[34] As used in the sense at issue in Heidegger's *Wohnen*, the term does not figure as a significant focus of discussion in English-language architectural writing or elsewhere (apart from some philosophical discussions of Heidegger's work[35]) prior to the 1970s. Heidegger's original audience in Darmstadt included some distinguished figures in German architecture, including Bartning as well as Hans Scharoun, and the architects in the audience appear to have responded well to what Heidegger had to say. There is no evidence, however, of 'Building Dwelling Thinking' having gained any significant recognition, in the period immediately after its original presentation and prior to its appearance in English translation, among architects in Britain, the Commonwealth or the United States.

Kenneth Frampton published a short essay, 'On Reading Heidegger', in 1974, twenty-three years after Heidegger spoke in Darmstadt. A line from 'Building Dwelling Thinking' is included as the epigraph to Frampton's essay,[36] and this appears to be one of the earliest references to the essay in an

English-language architectural discussion. Yet apart from the epigraph, there is nothing in Frampton's discussion that directly takes up Heidegger's account in 'Building Dwelling Thinking', nor is there any mention of 'dwelling' (and, although 'building' is one of the key terms in Frampton's essay, the term is not used in quite the sense in which it appears in Heidegger's text).[37] In fact, rather than being directly connected to Frampton, the attention given to 'dwelling' within architectural circles has been largely a result of the work of the Norwegian architect and theorist Christian Norberg-Schulz, and indeed, a great deal of the critique of Heidegger in architectural circles has been via the critique of Norberg-Schulz.[38]

Existential concerns are already evident even in Norberg-Schulz's early work, but his thinking about architecture also shifted, in the late 1960s, from a structuralist approach towards one that is more explicitly phenomenological (perhaps partly under the influence of Dalibor Vesely). This is clearly evident in Norberg-Schulz's publications from the early 1970s onwards, beginning with *Existence, Space and Architecture,* in 1971, and followed by *Genius Loci,* in 1980, and *The Concept of Dwelling,* in 1985.[39] 'Dwelling', as it refers to Heidegger's *Wohnen,* is directly taken up in the latter two volumes, and especially in *The Concept of Dwelling.* There, Norberg-Schulz distinguishes a quantitative sense of 'dwelling', in which one has a degree of shelter and space, from what he terms a '*qualitative,* existential interpretation'. The latter notion is defined in terms of a certain relation of 'belonging to' or 'being at home in' a place:

> To dwell means to belong to a given place, which might be a green field or a grey street, and furthermore to possess a house where the heart may blossom and the mind muse … To dwell in [this] qualitative sense is a basic condition of humanity. When we identify with a place, we dedicate ourselves to a way of being in the world.[40]

To belong to a place in this way involves, according to Norberg-Schulz, the experiencing of the environment to which that place itself belongs as a meaningful totality. Dwelling is thus understood as a certain relation between human being and environment, and this relation has two aspects. The first is *identification,* whereby meaning is found 'in' things ('interiorized') and so in terms of embodied qualities.[41] The second is *orientation,* whereby meaning is given through the spatial ordering of things and of the environment – an ordering that is also tied to an ordering of activity.[42] Norberg-Schulz's account implies a key role for architectural practice which he understands as essentially a bringing together of the elements of a place – the identificatory and the orientational – in built form, and so in the concrete 'figure' (hence the subtitle of the 1985 book on the concept of dwelling as 'on the way to figurative architecture').[43]

At the same time as Norberg-Schulz was developing his own phenomenological approach to architecture, a similar phenomenological shift was occurring within geography, and there, too, the idea of dwelling was explicitly drawn upon. One of the earliest instances of this is an essay by the geographer Anne Buttimer, from 1976, 'Grasping the Dynamism of Lifeworld'.[44] As with Frampton, Buttimer uses a passage from the 1971 English translation of 'Building Dwelling Thinking' as an epigraph – the same passage, in fact, that Keiller refers to in relation to *Robinson in Ruins*. Buttimer asks whether 'the notion of "dwelling," in the sense used by Heidegger, [could] offer a valuable perspective for geography today?',[45] and she goes on to offer a characterization of what it is to dwell. She writes:

> To dwell implies more than to inhabit, to cultivate, or to organize space. It means to live in a manner which is attuned to the rhythms of nature, to see one's life as anchored in human history and directed toward a future, to build a home which is the everyday symbol of a dialogue with one's eco-logical and social milieu. It has been easier to describe how people may have lived in the technologically less complex milieux of former times, or to speculate romantically on how we might live today if the wasteland had not come to be, than to wrestle with the question of whether or how 'dwelling' may be possible for contemporary man. Our heritage of intellectual constructs seems in many ways inadequate to describe contemporary styles of making a home on the earth.[46]

Buttimer moves on to a larger discussion of 'humanistic' approaches in geography, and especially the potential of phenomenology, in Gaston Bachelard and others, as well as Heidegger, for arriving at a more adequate understanding of the way human beings are situated in space and in relation to the environment. 'Dwelling' is employed as a way into the phenomenological concept of the 'lifeworld' – understood as that entire surrounding 'context' in which human life is lived, which is understood as constituted in terms of relations of meaning rather than mere connections of causality.

Although Norberg-Schulz is the key figure within architectural circles in whose work the idea of 'dwelling' takes on a significant role, Buttimer is exemplary of a much wider engagement with Heidegger and phenomenology, and so also with 'dwelling' and place, that develops among geographers in the mid-to-late 1970s and early 1980s. Moreover, since geography itself has a wide reach, encompassing urban and landscape studies, as well as the cultural, sociological, and environmental, so the geographical engagement often overlaps directly with the architectural – even, in some cases, in relation to issues of design. Edward Relph's influential work, *Place and Placelessness*, published in the same year as Buttimer's essay, also makes reference to dwelling as it appears in 'Building Dwelling Thinking'.[47] Among a wide range of source material, Relph draws explicitly on Norberg-Schulz's work,[48] and includes brief discussions of architecture and planning as part of what is undoubtedly one of the ground-breaking works in the study of place. In 1979, David Seamon published *A Geography of the Lifeworld: Movement, Rest and Encounter*, in which the idea of 'dwelling' figures explicitly.[49] In 1985, Seamon and Robert Mugerauer edited *Dwelling, Place and Environment* – a volume that was significant not only in virtue of its direct thematization of place and dwelling, as well as its explicit acknowledgement of Heidegger's influence,[50] but also because of its interdisciplinary breadth (from architecture to Goethean science) and its bringing together of many key figures, including Buttimer and Relph.[51]

The sorts of accounts to be found in Relph, Buttimer, Norberg-Schulz and others, although varying in the breadth of their source materials and the reach of their inquiries, nevertheless share a set of similar ideas and concerns. Where 'dwelling' is explicitly discussed, it is characterized in terms that draw on notions of connection, attachment, attunement (Norberg-Schulz talks of 'atmosphere'), belonging, home and in ways that emphasize holistic notions of an environmental totality or 'whole' (the 'lifeworld' in Buttimer) as well as the way that totality is manifest as a totality of meaning or meaningfulness. The body figures significantly as that around which place and world are configured – in the form of the *human body*, as given in and through action and experience, as well as in the form of the *thing*, artefactual or 'natural', towards which action is directed and that is a focus of experience and meaning. Moreover, there is a general recognition of the spatial and topological configuration of bodies and things, always within a landscape or region, as integral to the articulation of the world and of the human engagement with it.

In addition, there are two key features that mark out the type of approach that is evident here – in both its architectural and geographical instantiations (points on which, in one form of another, criticism has also frequently focused). First is its explicitly humanistic concern that, irrespective of any connection with traditional humanisms, is most immediately evident in a clear focus on issues of human life and existence (which need not, however, imply an exclusion of the non-human). In this respect the phenomenological character of work such as that of Norberg-Schulz and Buttimer can also be said to include strongly existential, and even *existentialist*, elements, even though this is manifest more in an overall attitude than in a commitment to specific existentialist theses.[52] Second is its explicit focus on providing a positive account of that in which human existence is situated or grounded. In this respect, the approach is one that comes close to engaging in the sort of ontological inquiry that is Heidegger's primary concern, and that is also central to this volume.

'Close to' is not, however, 'the same as', and neither Norberg-Schulz nor Buttimer nor Relph (nor any of the other authors mentioned) makes any explicit claim to be doing 'ontology'. Instead, they tend to present their work as drawing on ontological considerations in order to address the empirically situated problems of architecture and geography. Thus, Seamon and Mugerauer talk of Heidegger's 'ontological excavations into the nature of human existence and meaning' as providing the 'philosophical foundations' for many of the essays in *Dwelling, Place and Environment*. To some extent, the difference at issue here can be understood in terms of the focus on the existential in contrast to the ontological. The existential and the ontological are related, since the ontological determines the existential, but they are also distinct. The *ontological* concerns the determining structure of existence, that in which it is embedded and by which it is shaped,[53] whereas the *existential* concerns existence in its more concrete realization – whether understood individually or collectively. The work of those such as Norberg-Schulz, Buttimer and Relph can thus be viewed as existentially oriented, even though it typically does not engage in the same ontological analysis that is undertaken in Heidegger.

The way the notion of dwelling was taken up outside of philosophy – in architecture and geography, and from there into other disciplines – in English-language discussions during the 1970s and 1980s, was stimulated by at least two factors. The first of these was the appearance of Heidegger's later thinking in English-language translations and commentary. The second was an increasing dissatisfaction with existing approaches and paradigms in the face of contemporary problems and challenges (especially social and environmental), together with the sense that Heidegger's work, along with phenomenological, existentialist and hermeneutical approaches more generally, provided a way of more adequately thinking what was at issue – a way of thinking, moreover, that was capable of addressing the character of human being in the world in a more encompassing and integrated fashion. As is the case with almost every appropriation of philosophical thinking into other domains, however, the way Heidegger's ideas were taken up was not always entirely true to the details of that thinking. Perhaps most significantly, the tendency to assimilate the later Heidegger to phenomenological approaches that were already gaining widespread influence in social scientific circles – even though Heidegger had by that time long abandoned the terms and framework of traditional phenomenology – meant that important shifts in Heidegger's thinking were often overlooked.

This was especially true in terms of the focus on ideas of meaning and meaningfulness and, associated with this, of the notion of the 'lifeworld' (itself understood as a totality of meaning) that is evident in Buttimer. The latter notion derives from Husserl,[54] rather than Heidegger, and the term barely appears in Heidegger at all.[55] 'Meaning', *Bedeutung* or *Sinn* in German, became a common category in discussions of human society and culture, and of human life more generally, during the nineteenth century, and continues to figure as a prominent notion within hermeneutics and phenomenology. 'Meaning' is an important term in *Being and Time*, partly because of the work's phenomenological and hermeneutic character, and it figures, as noted earlier, in the account of the structure of world as developed in Heidegger's earlier work, although it disappears almost entirely, at least in terms of any significant philosophical role, from his later thinking. In a famous seminar from 1969, held at Le Thor in Provence, Heidegger comments on the way 'meaning' (*Sinn*) represents a first stage in the development of thinking, emphasizing the way it is superseded by 'truth' (*Wahrheit*) and 'place' (*Ort*).[56] The reason for the shift away from 'meaning' is the same reason Heidegger never makes significant use of the notion of 'lifeworld', namely, that both notions tend to be associated with forms of thinking that are "'anthropological,' "subjectivistic,' "individualistic," etc'.[57] Heidegger saw such forms of thinking as giving rise to troublesome issues that affect *Being and Time*, but which also surface elsewhere.[58]

Meaning is typically constituted with respect to a subject – as was briefly indicated earlier, it is seen as arising, in *Being and Time*, through the 'projective' activity of Dasein and so can easily appear as something Dasein 'brings about'. Even though Dasein is not identical with the subject as usually understood, the way meaning is indeed tied to projection suggests a continuation of something like the same subjectivist tendency as is common in more conventional positions (including idealism and in some forms of phenomenology).⁵⁹ This is a much larger topic than can adequately be dealt with here, but what is most important for the current discussion is that the thinking at work in 'Building Dwelling Thinking' is not a thinking that relies on 'meaning' as a significant or philosophically substantive notion (in 'Building Dwelling Thinking' the emphasis is on the thing rather than on the thing *as meaningful*). That may seem a small point, but it turns out to be crucial, since it means that the way dwelling is understood is not in terms of a mode of existence that is primarily shaped by the subject or, more specifically, by human beings. It is not that an otherwise objective space is given meaning through the addition of human activity, experience, thought or feeling. Instead, 'meaning', if the term is to be used here at all, is, in one sense, already 'in' the world. What comes first, then, is not the human being standing against a world of objects, but a single dynamic structure of interactivity in which the human is already involved and by which human life and existence are shaped.

During the 1970s, however, the rise of phenomenological and interpretive approaches in social science led to an emphasis on meaning in ways that also encouraged a tendency towards the sort of subjectivism, broadly understood, that is a problem for Heidegger. One of the key figures in this regard is undoubtedly Alfred Schutz, whose work had already begun to have a significant influence in areas of social scientific inquiry in the 1960s.⁶⁰ A student of Edmund Husserl, Schutz applied the basic elements of Husserlian phenomenology (including notions like that of the 'lifeworld') to the study of the social world and, in particular, focused on the way meaning was generated or constituted in and through social life. It was two of Schutz's students, Peter Berger and Thomas Luckman, who produced one of the most influential works in social science of the later twentieth century, *The Social Construction of Reality* – a book that draws heavily on Schutz, as well as Max Scheler and Karl Mannheim.⁶¹

Social constructionism is not itself a significant element in the work of Norberg-Schulz, Buttimer, Relph or any of the other writers who were drawing on and developing the notion of 'dwelling' during the 1970s and 1980s. This is partly because of the way in which the notion of 'dwelling' is indeed so closely connected with notions of place and space, and so with the idea that human existence, and indeed any sense of meaning or meaningfulness associated with it, is worked out only in terms of the structure of bodily and topological involvement in the world. That structure is not constructed or constituted by human activity (notwithstanding the enormous impact human activity has on the earth and its living environment), since human activity is itself shaped by that structure of involvement. Nevertheless, the tendency to draw on notions of meaning and meaningfulness in the work of Norberg-Schulz, Buttimer and others (and regardless of whether or not this involves any explicit connection back to Schutzian or even Husserlian phenomenology) still brings complications with it. This is perhaps most obvious in Norberg-Schulz's work, where the relatively uncritical deployment of such notions tends towards the idea of the world as made meaningful for human beings through human activity, including the activity of architectural design and construction. And this is indeed one way of reading what is at issue in Norberg-Schulz's idea of 'dwelling' as comprising not only the finding of meaning in things (identification) but also the giving of meaning to things through spatial ordering (orientation). Admittedly, there remains an ambiguity here as to the exact role of the human being, or the architect, in the ordering of space (and how fundamental it should be taken to be), but that ambiguity is not unimportant.

The issue of social constructionism is one that will recur later in this volume. Here it is the character of such constructionism as giving primacy to a certain form of subjective constitution of the world that is of immediate relevance. This, or the reaction to it, turns out to be a key element in the way dwelling is taken up in what can be thought of as the second phase in the English-language engagement with the notion – an engagement with dwelling that begins in the 1990s, and that is largely initiated by the work of anthropologist Tim Ingold. Although it has made no significant impact in architecture, Ingold's work has been extremely influential in parts of anthropology and archaeology. Moreover, in some geographical circles, it seems to have effectively erased the earlier work on dwelling by geographers such as Buttimer and Relph – thus Pau Obrador-Pons writes, in an encyclopedia entry from 2008, that 'in geography, the concept of dwelling owes its reputation to the work of Tim Ingold'.[62] In fact, the way Ingold appropriates Heidegger's treatment of dwelling has been influential not only in geography but in other disciplines also, most notably, perhaps, in archaeology and anthropology.[63]

In his 1995 essay, 'Building, Dwelling, Living: How Animals and People Make Themselves at Home in the World', Ingold distinguishes between two different perspectives, the 'building perspective' and the 'dwelling perspective'.[64] As he summarizes the distinction in a later discussion, the first of these perspectives has been 'more usual' within social and cultural anthropology, and it consists in the supposition that 'people inhabit a world – of culture or society – to which form and meaning have already been attached. It is assumed, in other words, that they must perforce "construct" the world, in consciousness, before they can act in it'. This is essentially the view that was discussed earlier – the 'constructionist' view that takes the world to be constituted as meaningful through human activity, whether understood in individual or collective (i.e. social) terms. In the 1995 essay, Ingold admits that this is the view that he once held, but now rejects. In contrast, the 'dwelling perspective' is one that 'treats the immersion of the organism-person in an environment or lifeworld as an inescapable condition of existence. From this perspective, the world continually comes into being around the inhabitant, and its manifold constituents take on significance through their incorporation into a regular pattern of life activity'.[65] It is in favour of this latter perspective that Ingold argues in 'Building, Dwelling, Living' (it is not uncommon, however, to find many who draw on Ingold's notion of 'dwelling' continuing to endorse some form of the constructionist position to which the 'dwelling' perspective is supposed to be opposed).

Although Ingold positions himself as a phenomenologist, and the terms he employs in the title of his essay deliberately invoke Heidegger's 'Building Dwelling Thinking', Ingold's development of and arguments for, the 'dwelling perspective', especially as set out in his original essay, have only a slight connection back to Heidegger's own work, owing much more to the work of the ethologist Jakob von Uexküll.[66] This reflects Ingold's interest in dismantling, not only the Cartesian idea of the subject (defined by the capacity for rational thought) as distinct from the 'objective' world, but also the separation of the human from the non-human.[67] Von Uexküll's position, which is largely a development out of a certain form of almost psychologized or perhaps 'ethologized' neo-Kantianism (the latter being itself prone to forms of psychologism and anthropologism[68]), is one that treats organisms, human and non-human alike, as inseparably bound up with their 'environing world' (*Umwelt* in German).

Heidegger also affirms the idea of the organism as intimately tied to the environmental context in which it perceives and acts, and of human being as inextricably bound up with the world in which it exists. In contrast to von Uexküll, Heidegger nevertheless sees the fundamental structure in which human being is embedded as also inevitably given over to a certain separation from the world or, as it may also be understood, to the opening up of both distance and nearness as part of the opening up of the world and the human engagement in it. The latter is an aspect of human being – and of the underlying structure of human being that Heidegger refers to, in *Being and Time*, as *Dasein* – that remains in both Heidegger's early and later thinking, despite the shifts that occur between them. In *Introduction to Metaphysics*, from 1935, it is expressed in terms of the *uncanny* character of the human (the word Heidegger uses here being the same term, *unheimlich*, 'un-homely', that is also the focus for Anthony Vidler's discussion of the 'architectural uncanny').[69] The strange character of human being as both in the world and apart from it is directly tied to Heidegger's understanding of the human, already noted in the Introduction, as not merely a psychological, sociological, biological or even 'anthropological' notion but, rather, as itself an *ontological* category. Its uncanniness is one marker of the irreducibility of the 'essence' of the human to any other category. 'Being human' is not a matter of biology, then, but is instead a certain mode of relatedness to the world – one that is, moreover, distinct from the relatedness of organism to environment that appears in Uexküll. Inasmuch as 'dwelling' is the term that is used to describe the relatedness at issue in the former sense, then von Uexküll's account, and so also Ingold's, will be inadequate as an account of 'dwelling'.

'Dwelling' and Wohnen

Ingold admits, in a 2005 essay, to some misgivings about having talked of the 'dwelling perspective', but not because such talk involves, in any sense, a misappropriation of the original Heideggerian notion. 'Looking back, I rather regret having used the phrase. The trouble with "dwelling" is that it sounds altogether too cosy and comfortable, conjuring up a haven of rest where all tensions are resolved, and where the solitary inhabitant can be at peace with the world—and with him or herself.' Ingold goes on to say that, whilst noting that this was not how he intended the phrase to be understood, 'the connotations of singular harmony, which stem from the way the term has been taken up in phenomenological literature inspired by Martin Heidegger's famous essay *Building Dwelling Thinking*, are unavoidable'.[70] The problem, it seems, is not that the use of 'dwelling' is too far removed from Heidegger, but that it remains too close. There is more to be said about the extent to which the connotations noted by Ingold are indeed present in Heidegger's original discussion of *Wohnen*. But Ingold's comments also draw attention to the issue of the meaning of the English 'dwelling', and that leads back to the question of translation, which has been noted previously but only briefly touched upon. It is time to look more closely at this matter.

The use of 'dwelling' as a translation of *Wohnen* in the standard English translation of Heidegger's essay, and in almost all subsequent English-language discussion, is almost never remarked upon, yet it is a translation ill-adapted, in several respects, to the original text. The translation can be justified by looking to many German-English dictionaries, but such sources seldom attend to the philosophical or semantic complications at issue. There are obvious differences between the terms. *Wohnen* is a common term in ordinary German usage, whereas the English 'dwelling' is not – at least, not beyond its use to denote a habitable or inhabited structure – and the same goes for the English 'dwell'. The etymology of 'dwell' is also quite different from the German, and as a result, so are some of its connotations. The English 'dwell' comes, via a Scandinavian route, from an older Germanic source, and its original meanings include 'to lead astray', 'to delay', 'to tarry', 'to linger', although it is also related to 'dull' (as in 'dullard') meaning lacking insight or intelligence. One possibility is that all these senses come from an original term that meant to run round in a circle, hence staying in one place, getting nowhere, but also being confused, muddled or plain stupid.[71] The *Oxford English Dictionary* lists several meanings for the term 'dwell', including that mentioned earlier in the Introduction, and the first of which more or less coincide with those early meanings associated with the original Germanic source:

> 1. To lead into error, mislead, delude; to stun, stupefy. *Obsolete* ... 2. To hinder, delay. (Only Old English.) ... 3. To tarry, delay; to desist from action ... 4.a. To abide or continue for a time, in a place, state, or condition. *Obsolete or archaic* ... 4.b. to let dwell: to let (things) remain as they are, let alone, let be. *Obsolete* ... c. Of a horse: *(a)* To be slow in raising the feet from the ground in stepping. *(b)* To pause before taking a fence ... d. *Mechanics*. To pause ... 5. to dwell on, upon (in): to spend time upon or linger over (a thing) in action or thought; to remain with the attention fixed on; now, esp. to treat at length or with insistence, in speech or writing; also, to sustain (a note) in music. (The most frequent current use in speech.) ... 6. To continue in existence, to last, persist; to remain after others are taken or removed. *Obsolete* ... 7. To remain (in a house, country, etc.) as in a permanent residence; to have one's abode; to reside, 'live'. (Now mostly superseded by live in spoken use; but still common in literature.) ... 8. To occupy as a place of residence; to inhabit. *Obsolete* ... 9. To cause to abide in. *Obsolete*.[72]

It is noteworthy how many of these senses of the term are specified as 'obsolete' or 'archaic' (and were so even in the first edition of the *Oxford English Dictionary* from 1933). The difference between the English 'dwell' and the contemporary German *Wohnen* is clearly evident when one considers that, whilst in ordinary German, if one wishes to know someone's place of residence, one asks *Wo wohnen Sie?*, in English, one does not say 'Where do you dwell?', but 'Where do you live?'. And to ask, in ordinary speech, 'Where do you dwell?', would already be to suggest some kind of affectation.

Because 'dwelling' is a relatively uncommon term in contemporary English (and has been so since well before the beginning of the last century), its use to translate Heidegger's *Wohnen*, although not unreasonable, nevertheless results in the transformation of a term that is ordinary in German into something out of the ordinary in English. Immediately, 'dwelling' becomes something special and even rather strange – the very word suggesting a return to something archaic. Yet much of the point of Heidegger's discussion in 'Building Dwelling Thinking', as already noted in the Introduction, is to use a term that readers think they understand – for German speakers, *Wohnen* – and then, as he does in so many of his essays, render that understanding questionable. This does not happen in the usual English translations of Heidegger's essay. There 'dwell' and 'dwelling' already appear as terms that are *unfamiliar* – and so there is no shift from the familiar and the ordinary to the unfamiliar and the questionable. 'Dwell' and 'dwelling' have thus become words of art for many readers of Heidegger – technical terms that carry a special coding with them, and that also have echoes of the poetic and even the mystical. Yet, at the same time, these terms are used, in spite of the oddity that attaches to them in English, as if their meaning were indeed already understood – such that one finds architectural theorists and commentators writing about 'the question of dwelling' as if it was clear what this might mean. Thus, in his survey of the idea of dwelling in twentieth-century architectural thinking, Pavlos Lefas writes of how, in 'Building Dwelling Thinking', Heidegger 'set the question of dwelling on a new footing', as if the question was something already familiar, and the problem it names already well-understood.[73] Certainly, the English translation of *Wohnen* as 'dwelling' does put the question onto a new footing, but in so doing, one might argue, it also puts it on the wrong footing.

Although 'dwelling' might seem an appropriate translation for *Wohnen* on the grounds that it can mean 'residing' or 'inhabiting', this merely raises the question as to why one should not use those terms instead. The idea that 'dwelling' may be thought more evocative or poetic is not, in this case, a good reason for preferring it over something more prosaic. The real problem, however, is that there is no single English term that matches the German *Wohnen* in either its noun or verb form. 'Reside', 'inhabit' and 'abide', as well as 'dwell', all overlap with the meaning of the German term, but also differ significantly from it. And although 'live' (as in 'Where do you live?') is the most obvious and direct way of translating the German *Wohnen* as it used in much ordinary English-language discourse, it also carries a different set of etymological and semantic links. An obvious way to handle the matter might be to look to some notion of 'being at home', and although such a notion is not directly connoted by the English term itself, it is notable how often the notion of 'home' figures in discussions of 'dwelling' – in Norberg-Schulz, in Buttimer, in Relph and in Ingold. A notion of 'home' certainly is at work in the German term, if only because the place of one's *Wohnen* is also typically one's home or where one is most 'at home'(*zu Hause*).

There is, however, a problem with that as well, at least in relation to Heidegger, since Heidegger explicitly contrasts being *zu Hause* with *Wohnen*. Heidegger's point, however, is to emphasize a difference between those places with which one is engaged in terms of an everyday familiarity and the places in which one actually *lives* in a sense that involves more than mere familiarity. So Heidegger writes that 'the truck driver is at home [*zu Hause*] on the highway, but he does not have his shelter [*seine Unterkunft*] there'; and similarly, 'the working woman is at home in the spinning mill, but does not have her dwelling place [*ihre Wohnung*] there; the chief engineer is at home in the power station, but he does not dwell there [*er wohnt nicht dort*]'.[74] One can certainly capture something of this in English, if in a different way: 'home' is not the same as being 'at home', and so neither the power station, the mill, nor the highway is home to those who are 'at home' within them (who know their way around there), and neither the driver, the mill worker, nor the engineer *lives* in the places in which they are nevertheless 'at home'.

The way 'home' is at issue here also connects, of course, with the way the notion of 'dwelling' is often criticized – with Leach's attack, for instance, on the supposed myth of the *domus*. There is no doubt that 'home' is tied up with what is properly at issue in 'dwelling', but it would be a mistake to assume that, alone, the connection to 'home' provides ground for treating 'dwelling' – or *Wohnen* – as an objectionable notion. Whatever the problems with which 'home' might be taken to be associated, it remains a fundamental notion, and not one that can be dispensed with lightly, if at all. If what is at issue in *Wohnen*, and so in 'dwelling' properly understood, is indeed a mode of 'being at home' in the world, then this is indeed something that deserves further exploration rather than mere dismissal. Just as Heidegger puts the question, '*Was ist, zu wohnen?*', so one can also put the question, 'What is it to be "at home"?', and, in doing so, take up an aspect of Heidegger's original question about *Wohnen*.

The question of 'home' that appears here is one that will return in subsequent discussions, but although the idea of 'home' does capture part of what is at issue in the question of *Wohnen*, or 'dwelling', it does not offer a completely adequate solution to the problem of translation. The very idea of a one-to-one match is often problematic as a translational ideal. But assuming that some such match is required, then, of the terms that are available, there are reasons for preferring to translate *Wohnen*, in the Heideggerian context, with one of those more prosaic terms considered earlier – one that is less immediately associated with an archaic or literary use. 'Living' is certainly one such alternative (though not quite as Ingold uses it) and 'inhabiting' another. Of these two, 'inhabiting' is perhaps the more suitable. *Wohnen* is sometimes translated as 'inhabiting' in other contexts, and 'Building Inhabiting Thinking' may be thought already more suggestive of what is at issue than the usual translation; and so, too, might the question, 'What is it to inhabit?', be argued to carry more of the sense that is at issue in Heidegger's original question, '*Was ist, zu wohnen?*', than does the version of that question that resorts to obscure talk of 'dwelling'.[75] The fact is, however, that 'dwelling' is now so embedded in the English-language literature that it seems unlikely that one could readily shift the usage away from it. Thus, one is indeed left with the task of 'rethinking' what 'dwelling' might be; the real point being less about what term is employed, than how that term is understood. And that means that no matter what the translational practice, it is no substitute for doing the thinking and rethinking that is required in order properly to come to terms with what is at issue.

Dwelling, place and home

To talk of dwelling inevitably involves some notion of place. Not only is that evident from the way 'dwelling' is taken up in Norberg-Schulz, as well as in Buttimer, Relph and even Ingold, but it is also clearly at issue in 'Building Dwelling Thinking'. Already, in the brief summary of Heidegger's discussion that was set out earlier, it was evident how place plays a key role in the discussion, both in terms of the way Heidegger addresses the themes that structured the Darmstadt meeting and in relation to the larger trajectory of Heidegger's own thought. The question of world that concerns him cannot adequately be addressed according to a purely 'spatial' understanding – at least not that which is commonly assumed. In English, the term 'dwelling' does itself imply such a connection to place – to dwell is indeed to be at a place – but the English 'dwelling' also seems to suggest that the way place is at issue is in some special sense, perhaps of a sort that would only ordinarily arise in 'poetic' states and situations. Crucial to the discussion in this chapter has been the uncovering of what is at issue in dwelling, despite the character of the English term, as about the most everyday and ordinary of things, namely, the fundamental character of human being in the world and the structure of possibility by which it is shaped and conditioned.

Some of the treatment of 'dwelling', even in the work of those who argue for the notion, undoubtedly sets up problems for its understanding. It is easy, for instance, for the focus on dwelling to become enmeshed in problematic forms of subjectivism or anthropologism. Nevertheless, it still remains the case that consideration of dwelling, so long as it is undertaken in a way that is responsive to the philosophical complexities of what is at issue, ought to direct attention back to a basic mode of questioning that relates to the very place in which questioning can arise. That place is tied to the human – where the human is just that which finds itself in question – and to that which goes beyond the human, which is to say, to the world. The relevance of all of this to architecture is not to be found in the direct or explicit engagement of every architect, and certainly not of every building or design, with such basic questioning. But that is not to say that such questioning falls outside of the concern of architecture; first, because no matter how it responds and whatever it claims, architecture is always itself placed, and so place is always at stake for architecture, and, second, because even when architecture is not concerned with the construction of dwellings, it always takes place in relation to 'dwelling', that is, in relation to an already given mode of worldly activity and inhabitation. And this is true of even the most modest and mundane of architectural projects. Although the answer typically remains implicit and barely even noticed, buried in the underlying structures of everyday life, and although the question itself is hardly ever spoken, let alone heard, the issue of what it is to dwell, and of what it is to dwell *here*, in this place – no matter where that might be – endures. Does it endure even today, in 'modernity'? The preliminary answer surely has to be that it does, but how and why this is so, and whether that is also Heidegger's position, are issues for the next chapter.

Chapter 2

HOMELESSNESS AND MODERNITY

The contrast that was first encountered in the discussion of Keiller at the start of Chapter 1, and that is reiterated in Leach and Heynen, is one that presents dwelling as standing in opposition to the present situation of the world – in opposition to 'modernity'. That the English 'dwelling' is indeed an archaic or obsolete term – and so a term belonging to the past – undoubtedly reinforces that contrast. One of the forms in which that basic opposition of past versus present is embodied and expressed is in the contrast between the rural and the urban – as if the city were not itself an ancient phenomenon and life 'in the country' was not also a part of modernity.[1] Yet whether expressed in terms of the urban versus the rural or the modern versus the past, the general contrast at issue is one that is invoked in architectural and geographical contexts well beyond the work just of Keiller, Leach and Heynen. It is repeated, for instance, in the encyclopedia entry by Pau Obrador-Pons referred to earlier. Obrador-Pons writes of the 'major downsides subsisting within the dwelling perspective that considerably narrow the scope of the concept, the main one being its rustic and romantic overtones'. Dwelling, he claims, 'was not originally conceived to embrace contemporary urban life. In its original usage, dwelling is almost impossible under the conditions of modernity.'[2] In this last line, of course, Obrador-Pons essentially repeats a line from Heynen, who also asserts that 'according to Heidegger – the philosopher who never faced up to "Auschwitz" – dwelling stands for a relationship with the fourfold that has become impossible under modern conditions',[3] whilst Heynen, in turn, largely repeats the same claim as it appears in Adorno: 'Dwelling, in the proper sense, is now impossible.'[4]

The issues at stake here are not restricted to the question as to whether 'dwelling' is a notion tied to some notion of the rural past. What is in question is whether the notion has any relevance to the contemporary urbanized condition, or, more generally, to the current situation, and that means that what is in question is whether the notion has any genuine *critical* import. This is all the more significant when one recalls that part of the original focus on the Darmstadt symposium was on the role of architecture in overcoming homelessness – both 'physical' and 'intellectual/spiritual' homelessness – and so there was an explicit concern with homelessness as part of the contemporary condition. To what extent, then, should one regard Heidegger's analysis of dwelling as offering a way of responding to contemporary homelessness? Or does he perhaps intend it to show that there can be no adequate response, at least not one that 'ameliorates' or 'overcomes'?

Dwelling in modernity

The idea that 'dwelling' and modernity are indeed incompatible has been associated with two different readings of Heidegger's position. One is the reading that Keiller and Leach seem to adopt according to which 'dwelling' is taken to be tied to a set of notions that, as Keiller puts it, 'derive from a more settled agricultural past', that valorize that past, and, to some extent, desire to return to it. The other attributes to Heidegger a more critical attitude towards the ideas of dwelling and place – one that does, in many ways, converge with that of Adorno. Towards the end of 'Building Dwelling Thinking', Heidegger writes: 'We are attempting to trace in thought the nature of dwelling. The next step on this path would be the question: what is the state of dwelling in our precarious age?'[5] There seems no doubt that Heidegger answers his question, even if indirectly, by asserting that the present age is one of homelessness, and so, in some sense, of a failure of 'dwelling'. What is less clear is the extent to which this is distinctive of the present age, since, although Heidegger seems, on the face of it, to affirm, with Adorno, that 'dwelling' today is impossible, he also insists, in a way that echoes Benjamin, that the 'plight of dwelling' has always been with us (Benjamin calls it 'perhaps eternal') and is perhaps eternal.[6] Looking beyond 'Building Dwelling Thinking', however, there is evidence that supports the reading that takes 'homelessness', or 'the plight of dwelling', to be characteristic of modernity, and also as unavoidable. So, for instance, in the 'Memorial Address', given in Messkirch in 1955, Heidegger talks of how homelessness (dwelling, or *Wohnen*, is not itself mentioned) is associated with a loss of 'groundedness' or 'rootedness', *Bodenständigkeit*, that 'springs from the spirit of the age into which all of us were born',[7] and thus might indeed appear to be something specifically modern and from which one cannot escape.

It is just this sort of reading that Heynen seems to endorse – despite her criticisms of Heidegger on other grounds. It is a reading perhaps best exemplified, however, in the work of Massimo Cacciari (to whom Heynen also refers).[8] Rejecting the sort of account found in Norberg-Schulz, Cacciari writes: 'No nostalgia, then, in Heidegger – but rather the contrary. [Heidegger] radicalizes the discourse supporting any possible "nostalgic" attitude, lays bare its logic, pitilessly emphasizes its insurmountable distance from the actual condition.'[9] There is something to be said for such a reading, since it is certainly closer, in several respects, to Heidegger's own position than are many of the readings, not only of those critical of Heidegger, but also those claiming to draw on his work. Moreover, what Cacciari emphasizes – namely, the radicality of Heidegger's approach and its own critical and questioning stance – is itself central to any real understanding of Heidegger's position, including his position on the nature of *Wohnen*, or 'dwelling'. Whatever the virtues of Cacciari's reading, however, and even if it does not merely repeat the seemingly simple contrast between the 'rural' and the 'urban', it maintains the contrast between 'dwelling' as something past and in contrast to the contemporary situation – 'Dwelling', for Cacciari no less than Leach, is indeed not something to be found in modernity. There is no doubt that Heidegger does talk about the 'homelessness' of modernity in various places. The question is how that talk, in the various places in which it occurs, should be understood. That it does imply the impossibility of 'dwelling' as something peculiar to modernity is not obvious, nor is it obvious either (even though this cannot be ruled out from the start) that 'dwelling' is indeed impossible in modernity.

Returning to the text of 'Building Dwelling Thinking' – the text in which Heidegger first advances a detailed discussion of 'dwelling' (and probably one of only two or three places where he does so)[10] – it is important to reiterate a point that should already be evident: there is nothing in the text of that essay that presents 'dwelling' as exclusively tied to the rural or to the past. The question of *Wohnen*, or dwelling', is one that arises, as was evident earlier, for the truck driver, for the woman at work in the spinning mill, for the engineer in the power station. And when Heidegger uses these examples, he clearly intends them both to be contemporary *and* to indicate, not that 'dwelling' is *impossible* for the truck driver, the factory worker or the engineer, but that 'dwelling' is *an issue* for them, apart from any familiarity they have in their places of work.

Just prior to these examples, which occur near the very start of the essay, Heidegger writes that 'bridges and hangers, stadiums and power stations are buildings but not dwellings; railway stations and highways, dams and market halls are built but they are not dwelling places. *Even so these buildings are in the domain of our dwelling*'.[11] The *Alte Brücke*, or 'Old Bridge', that is such a central example in 'Building Dwelling Thinking' is indeed historic – perhaps the best-known bridge in Germany, and the eighth on that particular site across the River Neckar, it dates back to the eighteenth century (although three of the central spans were destroyed by retreating German troops, against the appeals of the town, in 1945, and rebuilt in 1946–7). But it is most definitely a *city* bridge rather than belonging to the countryside alone (see Figure 1.2).[12] Moreover, in discussing the way the bridge (both specifically and in general) gathers together the elements of the world, and so the playful unity of earth, sky, divinities and mortals that is the fourfold, Heidegger also cites the example, as Hubert Dreyfus once excitedly noticed, of 'the highway bridge [*Autobahnbrücke*] ... [that is] tied into the network of long-distance traffic'.[13] And even though Heidegger is critical of the technological system of which the highway bridge is a part, there is no suggestion that the highway bridge does not also gather the elements of world just as do the other bridges to which Heidegger refers (though the highway bridge does gather, in important respects, differently[14]).

Certainly, towards the end of 'Building Dwelling Thinking', Heidegger does use as an example – the one that is most often quoted and referred to, and that is referred to by Keiller in the passage at the beginning of the previous chapter – the traditional South German (or Black Forest) farmhouse. The fact that he resorts to this as a key architectural example of how 'dwelling' might be articulated in built form is certainly significant, although how far the use of that example can be taken as indicative of a specifically 'rural' or 'provincial' mode of thinking is surely debateable. Simply to assume that it is so is already to beg the specific question at issue, as well as the larger question as to how Heidegger should be read in the first place. That Heidegger uses this example is partly an indication of his own context of 'dwelling'. Such farmhouses would have been extremely familiar to him – several such houses were located a few hundred metres down the slope from his famous hut in Todtnauberg, itself located twenty or so kilometres from Freiburg,[15] as they still are today. Farmhouses like the one Heidegger describes would also have been familiar to many in Heidegger's original audience in Darmstadt – such farmhouses remain a common sight in Southern Germany even now – and it is not at all obvious that they would have regarded the reference to the farmhouse as unusual (there is nothing in the text of the discussion suggesting that it was so regarded). Moreover, the appeal to traditional and vernacular architecture is not uncommon in architectural discussions, even in a modernist context. Alvar Aalto, for instance, looks to traditional Finnish forms in his own work (see Chapter 4). Such forms are also common in architectural discussions, of the sort noted earlier, regarding the different forms of habitable structure or dwelling.

Elsewhere, Heidegger also draws on examples or settings that evoke life outside of the city. But, again, to what extent one reads this as specifically 'provincial', whatever that really means, rather than indicative of a concern, say, with the 'natural' environment (understood in a way that need not itself imply any absolute dichotomy between the 'natural' and the 'human') or as a function of personal experience and familiarity, is by no means self-evident. The mere presence of a certain sort of example or setting shows very little in the absence of a wider body of evidence and argument. Much is often made of Heidegger's liking for the hut at Todtnauberg – a particular focus for discussion by Wigley and Sharr – and Heidegger himself talked about the importance of that place for his work.[16] Yet even this does not settle the question of Heidegger's supposed provincialism. He is certainly not alone in looking to rural solitude as a condition for philosophical reflection or for personal recreation, or even as an important background for philosophical ideas. Indeed, if Heidegger's sojourns in Todtnauberg are evidence of his provincialism, then perhaps the same should also be true of Ludwig Wittgenstein, who had a small house or hut built for himself at Skjolden, Norway, between 1914 and 1918 (demolished following Wittgenstein's death in 1951, but recently reconstructed), and which he visited regularly throughout his life.[17] Like Heidegger, Wittgenstein used his rural refuge as a place for writing and thinking, and likely, too, given Wittgenstein's own tendency towards reclusiveness, as an escape from the wider world. There are philosophical points of convergence between these thinkers, but the fact that they both made use of such huts tells us little about any 'nostalgic' or anti-modern element in their respective philosophical positions. It probably does say something about personal predilection, but the question of how much, and in what ways, the personal can indeed be related to the philosophical is a fraught one, even if, in Heidegger's case, the fact that there is such a connection (and a relatively straightforward one) is all too often taken for granted.

In 'Building Dwelling Thinking', Heidegger takes the farmhouse to provide an example of how dwelling might be articulated in built form, and, in doing so, the example he takes is a form of building that is both rural and historical. But there is nothing in the text to suggest that the structure exemplified by the farmhouse cannot be translated to more modern and contemporary buildings (even though

Heidegger does not do so himself), and he also makes very clear, as is often pointed out, that the farmhouse is an example from the past to which there can be no simple return.[18] Indeed, this insistence on the impossibility of such return and of the irretrievability of any past mode of life is a theme that recurs at various places in his work – evident, as Karsten Harries points out, in 'The Origin of the Work of Art' from 1935–6.[19] Moreover, neither in Norberg-Schulz nor in Buttimer, Relph, Seamon, Mugerauer, nor most of the other thinkers who are involved in the first appropriations of Heidegger's thinking of *Wohnen* into English-language discussions of architecture and geography, is dwelling taken to relate only, or even primarily, either to rural or pre-modern modes of living. And that, as it happens, is also true of Ingold's work, even though this is partly because his focus is on the non-human world as much as the human, and even though Ingold himself seems implicitly to assume that it is not true of Heidegger's.

For the most part, the claim that Heidegger's account of dwelling is specifically rural and dissociated from, even opposed to, modernity cannot readily be supported by the text of 'Building Dwelling Thinking'. Indeed, in many respects, the claim simply repeats a standard and quite general characterization of Heidegger's thinking that appears in Adorno (whose thinking is also clearly influential in Heynen's analysis),[20] and that is common among thinkers associated with the Frankfurt School. The fact that Heidegger was born a Catholic in the small town of Messkirch, lived almost his entire life on the other side of the Black Forest in Freiburg, and, in his writings, calls upon ideas and images of landscape and countryside (notwithstanding the larger context in which he does so) readily reinforces the Frankfurt characterization. But it is, in many respects, a stereotype that is at work here (one also ideologically driven), and as such it tends to override any more careful or nuanced engagement. Obrador-Pons's assertion, that 'contemporary urban life' was not intended to be encompassed by the original formulation of dwelling, seems itself to reflect such a stereotypical approach. Certainly, it is difficult to sustain, whether on the basis of Heidegger's 'Building Dwelling Thinking' or of the writings of those who first took up his work in architecture and geography. And it is similarly difficult to substantiate the idea, whether in Obrador-Pons, Heynen or Cacciari (despite the latter's rejection of any 'nostalgic' reading), that Heidegger holds 'dwelling' to be a notion inapplicable in the contemporary context.

The necessity of dwelling

The latter conclusion might be thought already to be suggested by some of the comments earlier, including the considerations concerning the German *Wohnen* and the English 'dwelling'. Although talk of dwelling in English may bring with it connotations of some special mode of being in the world, *Wohnen* refers to something ordinary and everyday, something from which one begins rather than at which one must arrive. It is certainly possible to question, even in ordinary German, the way the character of one's ordinary living in the world is altered by contemporary conditions – such that one's preconceptions about such living no longer hold – still there remains a sense in which, notwithstanding such alterations, human beings never cease to live in the world in some way, never cease 'to dwell'. Karsten Harries points out that the way Heidegger characterizes dwelling is such that it is '"the manner in which mortals are on the earth", or the being of man, or "the basic character of Being in keeping with which mortals exist"', and Harries therefore draws the obvious inference that 'we cannot help but be in accord with what is constitutive of our being. In this sense we cannot help but dwell.'[21] That means that human beings cannot help but dwell even, as Obrador-Pons puts it, 'under the conditions of modernity'.

In noting this point, however, Harries also sees a difficulty. Heidegger claims that 'only if we are capable of dwelling, only then can we build', but Heidegger gives us, says Harries, an ambiguous answer as to how this should be understood. Although dwelling is something to which human beings are already given over, and so there can be no choice as to whether or not one dwells, 'so understood dwelling cannot be a task', and yet 'again and again the lecture seems to call us to an essential dwelling'. Dwelling thus appears as both an inevitability and a demand. Harries is right to note an ambiguity here, yet that ambiguity, although important, represents a key feature of the kind of philosophical analysis in which Heidegger is engaged. Heidegger's question 'what is it to dwell?' is intended to ask after the basic character of human being in the world. This means that dwelling, *Wohnen*, does not name *one* mode of being as opposed to *another*, but instead refers to *the* way human being, in an unqualified sense, is 'in' the world. Thus there will be a sense in which human beings will continue to exemplify 'dwelling' – will continue to find themselves in a situation of inhabitation – no matter the circumstances of their situation, since their being human is the condition on the basis of which they encounter and respond to those circumstances. Yet, that human being has such a character does not mean that human being always realizes itself in a way that is in accord with what it is. The point can be illustrated using a more conventional set of ideas: human being is often characterized by its rationality, and yet this does not mean that human being cannot, in some sense, be irrational; human being is often characterized by its sociality, and yet this does not mean that human being cannot, in some sense, be asocial; human being is often characterized by a particular mode of linguisticality, and yet this does not mean that human being cannot, in some cases, be without language. So, too, human being may be fundamentally given over to 'dwelling', and yet this does not mean that human being cannot also, in some sense, fail to dwell.

Here it is worth going back to the claim that Cacciari makes as to the homelessness of human being in modernity. That claim involves the idea that, whatever may have been its character in the past, the fundamental character of human being now is its homelessness. One implication of this, although never made clear, is the abandonment of any claim that dwelling is part of how human being fundamentally *is*, or, perhaps, its replacement with the claim that the fundamental way human being is can change according to its historical situation. On this basis, dwelling will name just one mode of being among others, and a mode that, as it happens, is no longer possible. One consequence of this, however, is that dwelling can really be of historical or antiquarian interest only. It will be, on such an account, something irretrievably *past*, and therefore of no necessary relevance to the contemporary situation. It will certainly have no role to play in any *critical* engagement with that situation – with modernity – and certainly not such as to any *normative* force. It will be no criticism of modernity, then, that the mode of human being that belongs to it is a form of 'not-dwelling', of homelessness, since there will be nothing that could require that things be otherwise. The lack of dwelling will not, in other words, license any critique of modernity.

Part of what this brings out is a point about the nature of *critique*. Even when it advances no alternative to that against which it is directed, critique always requires *grounds* (a point made by the originator of the idea of 'critique' as it appears in modern thought, Immanuel Kant[22]). Without grounds, without some basis in what *is* (for there *is* nothing else that can offer such a basis), critique also lacks force, and as such is, in the end, empty. Even the rejection of foundationalism (which is present in both Heidegger and Adorno[23]) does not result in the setting aside of this requirement. If, as Cacciari argues, 'homelessness' did indeed name the fundamental character of human being in modernity, then there would be no compelling reason why such homelessness should not simply be embraced. Homelessness would, on such an account, be the inevitable fate of human being in the world – it would be the form of life, as it were, that belonged to modern humanity. Of course, to a large extent, this is exactly Cacciari's claim, which he also attributes to Heidegger. But such a claim offers no basis on which one can argue that such homelessness is genuinely problematic – there is not even any point to characterizing the 'laying bare' of such homelessness as 'pitiless', since what could be the basis for either pity or the lack of pity in such a situation – especially when the situation described is one's own. Inasmuch as homelessness is the issue here, then the lack of 'home' becomes a problem only if there is a 'need' for home in the first place, but there can be no such 'need' if such a lack of home characterizes contemporary human being in its entirety. There is no lack where what is lacked could never even be possessed. Heidegger makes this very point himself when he writes, as he does in "' ... Poetically Man Dwells ...'", of the way only one capable of sight can become blind,[24] and, elsewhere, of how only that which can support growth can lie fallow, how only one who can hear can become deaf, and how only one who thinks can be thoughtless.[25]

Cacciari's reading of Heidegger, as committed to the idea of a fundamental homelessness that afflicts modernity, is not based in 'Building Dwelling Thinking' alone, nor does it give any special primacy to the essay. Cacciari's reading is a quite general one. It is significant, however, that, if one does focus just on 'Building Dwelling Thinking', and notwithstanding the other comments already made, then the sort of reading that Cacciari advances has much to recommend it. Although Heidegger's essay is routinely treated as expressive of a 'nostalgic' desire for home in the midst of the homelessness of modernity, there is almost nothing in the essay itself that directly supports such a nostalgic reading – not even the example of the Black Forest farmhouse, which is indeed acknowledged to be irretrievably past.

What disrupts Cacciari's reading as adequate to 'Building Dwelling Thinking' is not the persistence of a problematic 'nostalgia', but something quite different in the essay's conclusion.

At the end of 'Building Dwelling Thinking', Heidegger talks about the plight of dwelling as an ancient one: it is 'older than the world wars and their destruction, older than the increase of the population of the earth and the condition of the industrial workers'.[26] So, although the plight of 'dwelling', or homelessness, is a plight that is experienced today, it is specifically *not* a plight that belongs to this time, to 'modernity' or the contemporary world, *alone*. It is also, of course, not a plight that is obviously resolved by any return to the past or, indeed, any escape from the current situation. It is notable that, not only does 'Building Dwelling Thinking' not restrict its considerations to the contemporary situation alone, but neither does it contain any explicit critique of contemporary modernity – and although there is such a critique elsewhere in Heidegger's work, it is not a critique that is unequivocally based on the impossibility of dwelling in modernity (indeed, there is an important sense in which modernity blocks or effaces even the appearance of homelessness as a genuine issue[27]). This does not mean that there is no sense in which homelessness is a problem for modernity, only that, inasmuch as it is such, it is in addition to the homelessness that has always been and always will be a part of human being and that remains even when human being is most 'at home'.

The question of homelessness, and with it the question of home – understanding this as one way of characterizing the question to which *Wohnen* refers – is a question that arises only because human being is already given over to a mode of being in the world that is itself configured in terms of home (this, whether recognized or not, underpinning all critical engagement with home – including that which is suspicious of the notion). Even though human beings may be threatened with homelessness, both empirically and ontologically (as Heidegger himself reiterates), the loss of home only threatens inasmuch as it stands within the frame of a mode of being that nevertheless always stands in a relation to home.

The general structure that appears here – a structure in which a loss or absence always arises in relation to an ongoing presence – is evident throughout Heidegger's thinking. In a passage that emphasizes the way in which human being is always a being among and in relation to things, and so also within the fourfold, Heidegger writes:

> The loss of rapport with things that occurs in a state of depression would be wholly impossible if even such a state were not still what it is as a human state: that is, a staying *with* things. Only if this stay already characterizes human being can the things among which we are also fail to speak to us, fail to concern us any longer.[28]

Heidegger's point is that, only if one remains with things, can one also experience an apartness from things. Similarly, only if one remains in a relation to home, can one experience homelessness. Homelessness is a *loss* or *lack* of home (something evident in the very term), and so carries home within it as just such a loss or lack. At the same time, however, home also contains homelessness within it, as both a possibility and a presence. Indeed, one should perhaps say that home carries within it two modes of possible relatedness. The first is that of being at home, and the second is that of being estranged from home. Home and homelessness are thus not two separate modes but one – *homelessness itself being a mode of home*.

That home always includes homelessness within it (so that being already given over to home is the condition of homelessness) is part of what might be thought of as the multivocity or, to use a term Heynen employs of modernity,[29] the 'ambivalence' of home. However, it is important to note that, unlike Heynen's use of 'ambivalence', what is at issue is not an ambiguity between nor a mixing of two different modes – as 'ambivalence' tends to suggest. This also marks a key point of difference between Heynen's account of modernity as itself ambivalent with regard to home and homelessness (so that Heynen is critical of both the approaches associated with Norberg-Schulz and Caciari), and the account of modernity that seems to be present in Heidegger. Being at home is not *impossible* in modernity, as Heidegger sees it, but modernity does render such being at home *problematic*. This is because being at home remains that to which human being is given over, even though the specific historical circumstances constantly efface and obscure such being at home – not only effacing being at home as a possibility, but also effacing the perduring character of human being as just such a being at home, and thereby also effacing human being as *a being-in-place* (rather than merely in an extended and unbounded 'space').

This is why the analysis of the relations between human being, space and place is so central an element in the argument of 'Building Dwelling Thinking', and why the essay is so important for architecture. What it offers is an account grounded in an analysis of the topological character of human being – one that itself draws on the topology *of being* – and it is this that determines Heidegger's treatment of both home and homelessness, whether in relation to the present, the past or the future. Homelessness, in Heidegger, is a modification of home, in the same way that placelessness is also a modification of place, and in neither case is it a matter of a simple opposition between states that are otherwise independently constituted. Among the ideas at work in Heidegger's thinking, home and place are not unusual in having this sort of complex, multivocal, structure. Indeed, part of what makes Heidegger's thought, especially his later thought, difficult for many readers – and gives rise to so many problematic readings – is the way it typically involves the holding together of multiple and often differing strands at one and the same time, often with respect to one and the same idea.[30]

Dwelling and thinking

Heidegger's emphasis, in 'Building Dwelling Thinking', on the way homelessness and the *plight* of dwelling belong to human being as such – just as 'dwelling' itself belongs to human being – echoes something that is present in Heidegger's thinking almost from the very beginning, something already remarked upon; namely, the character of human being, or of that which is 'essential' to human being, as always 'in question'. In the language of *Being and Time*, human being is that mode of being, *Dasein*, whose own being is always an issue for it, whose being is also, in the terms of *Introduction to Metaphysics*, essentially uncanny, not 'of the home'. It was this idea that appeared in the discussion of Ingold, in relation to the character of human being as both 'in' the world, and so always engaged with it, and nevertheless as also separated from the world. At one point, in a lecture given in 1941, ten years before 'Building Dwelling Thinking', Heidegger puts the issue in terms that emphasize the tension at work in human being in the world – the tension that makes 'dwelling' both inevitable and yet also an ever-present task – at the same time as they draw attention to its ontological and topological character:

> We belong to being, and yet not. We reside in the realm of being and yet are not directly allowed in. We are, as it were, homeless in our ownmost homeland, assuming we may thus name our own essence. We reside in a realm constantly permeated by the casting toward and the casting-away of being. To be sure, we hardly ever pay attention to this characteristic of our abode, but we now ask: 'where' are we 'there', when we are thus placed into such an abode?[31]

Another way to put this is to say that human being, although it is conditioned in certain important ways, is never settled, never 'completed', but always remains to be worked out – the space that dwelling opens up is thus a space of possibility.

Indeed, if this were not the case, then, at a more immediate and concrete level, there would be no task for architecture (nor for many other disciplines). What sets the task for architecture, and underpins its significance, is the need to respond to the uncertain and questionable nature of human being, and so also of human dwelling, as this arises in the specific content of certain forms of human building. In this respect, the architectural task is indeed a specifically human one, arising directly out of that uncertainty and questionability, and so out of the lack of any complete determination – which is to say out of the freedom or openness – that characterizes the mode of being of the human. In contrast, there is no task for architecture in addressing the modes of living in the world of non-human beings. This is not because the non-human is irrelevant to architecture, but because the mode of living of non-human beings is not in question in the way it is for human beings. As a result, architecture's role in such cases is typically one of replication or redress (for instance, in finding ways of artificially replicating habitats or living conditions, or of trying to find ways to reconstitute those habitats or conditions).

For something to be 'in question' does not mean, however, that it has therefore been lost, or that what is at issue cannot be addressed. As Harries emphasizes, and contrary to Cacciari's emphasis on the inescapability of contemporary homelessness, Heidegger talks explicitly of the possibility of the real plight of dwelling as one that can, at least potentially, be overcome. The way he suggests this is possible is both important and readily overlooked. It appears in one sentence near the end of the essay: 'As soon as man *gives thought* to his homelessness', Heidegger declares, 'it is a misery no longer'.[32] The emphasis on 'giving thought' is Heidegger's, and it does not mean that the plight of dwelling, the problem of homelessness, is simply resolved as soon as one gives philosophical attention to it. 'Thinking' is itself an important term for Heidegger – around the same time as 'Building Dwelling Thinking', he devotes an entire lecture course in Freiburg (over the semester from 1951–2) to the question 'what is called thinking?'.[33] 'Thinking' is also included, of course, in the title of 'Building Dwelling Thinking' as the third term at issue, yet there is remarkably little direct comment upon it in the essay itself. Although there remains a question as to what it means to 'give thought' to the plight of 'dwelling' (a question to which the discussion will return), such 'giving thought' is not ruled out as a possibility, and so neither is the possibility of 'dwelling', not even under contemporary conditions. 'Rightly considered', such 'giving thought' is, adds Heidegger, 'the sole summons that *calls* mortals into their dwelling'.[34]

'Dwelling' is something that Heidegger takes to be fundamental to human being. It is because human beings dwell that dwelling can be an issue for them – that the question, 'What is it to dwell?', can even be asked. But as it is an issue, so dwelling is both a mode of being and a form of life to which human beings – *mortal* beings – are always already given over, *and* it is something that has to be accomplished, that cannot be simply assumed. Although Harries sees this as a difficulty that is specific to Heidegger's account, it is, in its general form, characteristic of any situation that involves both a prior and continuing commitment at the same time as that commitment also requires realization or accomplishment. Friendship, for instance, involves a commitment to being a friend – to a certain mode of being – and that commitment is arguably a condition of the friendship. Yet the friendship is also something that has to be *realized*. It is not simply given as already accomplished, and it is also something with respect to which one can fall short.

The same point holds, more generally, for a whole range of normative situations or phenomena. Indeed, it may even be said to hold in respect of the ethical as such. It can reasonably be argued that, if the genuine normative or imperatival force that is central to the ethical is to be maintained, then the ethical life cannot be a life that is simply available to be chosen or not chosen. The unethical life is thus a problematic life, on this account, because it is a life lived either in ignorance, neglect or refusal of that which is nevertheless a condition of that very life. Of course, such a construal of the ethical or the normative cannot be assumed (although the grounds for such an account indeed lie in the imperative character of the ethical and normative – in the nature of the 'ought'), but it is not an implausible construal either, and nor is it an uncommon one. It is just this sort of structure that is at work in Heidegger's account of dwelling, and in this respect, Heidegger's account has a form that is not at all uncommon. Inasmuch as it exhibits a structure that is characteristic of a form of normative or ethical reflection, so this aspect of Heidegger's thinking (which is evident in many places other than 'Building Dwelling Thinking') also suggests the extent to which there is indeed an important normative or ethical dimension to Heidegger's thinking, despite the claims that are frequently made regarding its absence.[35]

But what of thinking here? What might thinking have to do with the task of dwelling? How could 'mere' thinking resolve the misery of homelessness? Significantly, the idea of a task applies to thinking itself, as Heidegger sees it, no less than it does to dwelling (which is why the relation between thinking and thoughtlessness arises as an example, used earlier, that parallels the relation between dwelling and not-dwelling). Neither dwelling nor thinking is something already given such that its accomplishment is assured, and both are constituted as activities that never reach any final completion. Thinking, here, also does not mean something purely 'mental' or narrowly 'rational'. It is a fundamental mode of relatedness *in* and *to* the world. Heidegger says that thinking 'itself belongs to dwelling in the same sense as building, although in a different way', and both are necessary for dwelling but insufficient for it.[36] In other words, both thinking and building are required as part of the way dwelling is articulated in the world, yet both building and thinking depend upon dwelling for their own possibility; that is, building and thinking arise on the basis of dwelling rather than being the ground for it. One might take issue with the seemingly simple contrast between building and thinking that appears in 'Building Dwelling Thinking' except that, as always with Heidegger, what may seem simple, at first, always presages a greater complexity. That is true of the relation between building and thinking, since it is clear that what Heidegger means by building – which really encompasses almost the entire range of materially productive activity by which human being articulates itself in the world – is not separate from thinking. Building, if it attends to dwelling, must also attend to thinking – building must be itself thoughtful – and this underlines the extent to which, even though building and thinking both belong to dwelling 'in the same sense', they each also belong 'in a different way'.

The question of thinking runs throughout almost all of Heidegger's later essays and lectures – not surprisingly, given the extent to which so much of the later thinking is itself a thinking about thinking and about the place of thinking. In "' ... Poetically Man Dwells ... '", the question of dwelling is approached once more, and although thinking only briefly makes any direct or explicit appearance, it is nevertheless centrally at issue, insofar as the essay addresses the relation between dwelling and the poetic. Poetry and thinking come to be entwined closely together in Heidegger's later work – thinking finds its own origin, in an important sense, in the poetic, in *poiesis* (the Greek term that Heidegger translates as 'making',[37] and that he also takes as referring to the original emergence or presencing of things) – and in "' ... Poetically Man Dwells ... '", Heidegger argues that dwelling is itself poetic. In saying this, he does not mean that dwelling is therefore something conducted in verse form or as part of some literary exercise. The title, "' ... Poetically Man Dwells ... '", is taken from a poem by Friedrich Hölderlin that addresses the character of human life as a dwelling 'on this earth', and that also asks after the 'measure' of such a life, and so after the measure of man, of the human. 'Is there a measure on earth?', asks Hölderlin, and he answers, 'There is none.'[38] The question of measure leads Heidegger, once again, to a discussion of the spatial and topological, but now specifically in relation to the poetic. Poetry is revealed as itself a 'taking of measure'. Such taking of measure is not about the determination of things in any quantitative sense – 'no mere gauging with ready-made measuring rods for the making of maps'. Put simply, it concerns the assigning of things to their proper place or perhaps better, the letting be of things in the places to which they belong – a letting be in place that is also a 'letting be' of things in their relation to the dimensionality that belongs to the world, and is opened up in and through the complex compositional unity that is the happening of the fourfold.

Thinking is not identical with this poetry, or 'poetizing', but it does stand close to it – so much so that, for Heidegger, thinking and poetizing are two sides of the same engagement with the world, which is also attentive and responsive to the complex and unitary relationality of the world. Significantly, the brief discussion of building that appears in the course of " … Poetically Man Dwells … " distinguishes building 'of the usual kind, often practiced exclusively and therefore the only one that is familiar', from a mode of building as itself a grounding for dwelling: 'Man is capable of building only if he has already built, is building, and remains disposed to build in another way.' This other way is 'the poetic taking of measure', and Heidegger adds that genuine building 'occurs so far as there are poets, such poets as take the measure for architecture, the structure of dwelling'.[39] Building is here tied to poetry, but also, thereby, even if implicitly, to thinking.

At the end of " … Poetically Man Dwells … ", Heidegger asks after what makes for 'genuine' or 'real' poetry.[40] For his answer, he turns back to Hölderlin and also to Sophocles. The taking of measure that is poetry, in its proper sense, occurs with the arrival of kindness[41] – *Freundlichkeit* in Hölderlin's German, *charis* in Sophocles' Greek. Such 'kindness' echoes the idea, from 'Building Dwelling Thinking', that 'the fundamental character of dwelling is … sparing and preserving'.[42] Heidegger also associates such kindness with the heart, it being, one might say, a form of 'heartfeltness' or, perhaps better, of attentive responsiveness (Heidegger describing what is at issue as 'the claim and appeal of the measure to the heart in such a way that the heart turns to give heed to the measure'[43]). Just such a connection to the heart is also evident in Heidegger's discussion of thinking in 'What is Called Thinking?' – a work that, as pointed out earlier, comes from around the same time as 'Building Dwelling Thinking' and " … Poetically Man Dwells … ", and appears in the same context in which dwelling and measure are also at issue (and in which Hölderlin is invoked as well).[44] Dwelling and thinking are bound together. Both are tied to a felt and embodied mode of being in the world that is already involved with the world but has still to respond to the world. When human dwelling and thinking are constituted as a responsiveness that is appropriate to the world – and so in a way that is 'measured', which is to say, in a way that takes allowance of the world in its compositional unity – then it remains true to its own character as 'dwelling' and as thinking. The responsiveness at issue here is a responsiveness that is fundamentally attuned *to* place, just as it also arises *out of* an attunement to place.

The details explored in this discussion go beyond anything to be found in the work of many of those who have taken up the idea of dwelling and its relevance to architecture – beyond anything in Norberg-Schulz or Cacciari, or in Keiller, Heynen or Leach – and much of the analysis necessarily operates at a level of philosophical detail that seems not to have any direct architectural relevance. Nonetheless, the fundamental ideas at issue point towards a way of thinking about architecture that is of contemporary significance and can be played out in relation to more specific architectural contexts. What the discussion does not do, however, and what it cannot do, is to offer what Heidegger himself declared (as already noted in the Introduction) was not something to be gained from his discussion, that is, 'architectural ideas', in the sense of ideas that are specific to architecture alone, or 'rules for building'. At issue is an account of human being in the world that lays bare the very conditions of such being – opens up the place of its possibility, its limit and ground – and, in doing so, allows entry into the thinking of the place of architecture, into the 'topology' of architecture.

Chapter 3

AUTHENTICITY AND ESSENTIALISM

'What is it to dwell?', asks Heidegger, and this question must now be seen as asking not after some strange form of mystical relation to things, but as instead concerned with the mode of human being in the world – and so with the nature of 'inhabitation' or, as one might also say, with how human beings find themselves 'at home' in the world. The use of the English term 'dwelling' turns out to be a misleading term in the context of Heidegger's question but as it is the term that has become firmly entrenched in existing discussions, it cannot easily be avoided. The question concerning dwelling, or inhabitation, goes beyond any mere question of what sorts of houses one should design, or what techniques are appropriate to architectural practice. Yet the question is fundamental to the very possibility of building and design, since it concerns the basic mode of situatedness and orientation of human being in the world in which such building and design are grounded, and by which they are, therefore, also shaped and conditioned.

Heidegger's own answer to this question does not consist in any specification of rules or principles, but instead involves a turn towards the elucidation of the fundamentally topological character of what is at issue – an elucidation of the nature of place, space and world, and of the human relation to these. Dwelling is relational. It is not founded in some entity or principle that underlies or transcends, but, instead, in the mutual constitution or composition of elements within a bounded yet open regionality. Whilst dwelling exists just so long as human being is, it is the relational structure of dwelling in which the human is enmeshed that makes such human being possible. As it is a relation in and to place, dwelling necessarily involves the human, and yet is not grounded in the human. The human finds its ground, its place, in and through dwelling. It does this through attending and responding to (making allowance for) the larger ordering of things that together constitute the world. In this respect, dwelling is indeed a matter of attending and responding to place in its complex relationality. Moreover, although dwelling characterizes human being as such, because this mode of being is a mode of being 'in possibility' (so that its actual realization is never fully determined), one of the possibilities it encompasses is its own obscuring or effacing. Human beings dwell, and yet their dwelling is such that it is readily forgotten or ignored, even refused. It is thus that homelessness, the failure to recognize one's own being in the world as one's own, is commonplace, although it also takes on a special and more extreme character in the contemporary world – in modernity. Homelessness, here, is also a form of thoughtlessness, and the overcoming of homelessness is the task of thinking – thinking being understood as just the attending and responding to place, to dwelling. Such thoughtful dwelling is a releasing of both self and thing – a releasing of and to the world – which is to say it is a 'freeing' or 'letting-be'.[1]

Many of the broad features of this account appear not only in the work of writers like Norberg-Schulz, but also in that of others such as Buttimer, Relph, Seamon and Mugerauer, and its *critical* aspect is certainly recognized by Cacciari. Yet this is not the reading that dominates in most of the contemporary architectural discussion of 'Building Dwelling Thinking', or of Heidegger's more general position as exemplified in that essay. Indeed, as has been evident from the start, among many architectural theorists, as well as those from other disciplines, Heidegger's approach has most often been characterized, not only as 'nostalgic', 'provincial' and anti-modern, but as regressive, reactionary and *exclusionary*. Moreover, the exclusionary nature of Heidegger's thinking is seen as tied to the ideas of place and 'dwelling' as well as to Heidegger's emphasis on the 'essential' and the 'authentic' in the thinking of these ideas. As Adam Sharr summarizes matters: 'Heidegger's thinking, including that on architecture, is easily challenged from the perspectives of critical theory. The philosopher perceived the "essence" of building and dwelling in authentic attunement to being, unapologetic about the tendencies of essentialism and authenticity to exclude people.'[2] This sort of highly general claim undoubtedly reflects a reading of Heidegger that is heavily determined by assumptions deriving from his Nazi involvement during the 1930s.

There is no doubt that there are places in Heidegger's work where spatial and topological language is used in a way that is indeed exclusionary and politically regressive – and where that language seems to converge with the language of Nazism and to reflect Heidegger's own involvement with the movement. Heidegger's lectures from 1933–4 (the period of his time as the Nazi-appointed rector at Freiburg University), published in English as *Nature, History, State: 1933–1934*, certainly contain passages that appear as, to use Sharr's phrase, unapologetically exclusionary.[3] There are also passages in Heidegger's *Notebooks*, from the 1930s to 1940s, primarily anti-Semitic in character, that can be read in a similar light.[4] Yet, even if one accepts that Heidegger did commit himself to such problematic forms of thinking on specific occasions, that by no means settles the question as to whether that same commitment extends to his thought as a whole. Moreover, there is very little, if anything, in 'Building Dwelling Thinking' or any of the later essays (which are the explicit focus for Sharr's own discussion) to support the claim as Sharr makes it, and there is much that actually runs directly counter to it. Nevertheless, that Heidegger's approach to dwelling and place does indeed have an exclusionary character is a commonplace assumption across a great many contemporary discussions. Indeed, the emphasis on the 'essential' and 'authentic' is frequently seen as part of the sort of topological thinking Heidegger exemplifies, and so the very ideas of place and dwelling are often taken to be exclusionary in themselves.

The problem, or apparent problem, is one that has already been touched upon at various points in the discussion, and is directly tied to the focus on the ontological as well as the question of the 'grounds' of critique. However, the central issues at stake here – including issues of authenticity, essentialism and the supposedly exclusionary nature of place – have not yet been properly addressed. Moreover, they do not appear only as possible problems for the reading of Heidegger or for the notion of dwelling. Problems around ideas of identity and belonging, both of which are tied up with the idea of the 'essential', the bounded character of place and the notion of authenticity, all appear within architectural discussion in ways that also stand apart from any connection to Heidegger. This is especially true of the last of these: authenticity. And although the aim of this chapter is to take up all these ideas, to a greater or lesser extent, it is 'authenticity' that will be addressed first.

The problem of authenticity

In a series of lectures in 1991 – lectures that make no reference to Heidegger or dwelling[5] – Peter Blundell Jones offers an extensive consideration of the way authenticity appears in architectural thinking. His discussion highlights both the ubiquity of the notion and its significance, as well as its potential to provoke fierce controversy – though not for quite the same reasons assumed in Sharr. Blundell Jones writes:

> Authenticity is an emotive word. Ask a group of architects to lecture on it, and some boldly nail their colours to the mast: Ian Ritchie has … made it his rallying cry … Smithson even went so far as to declare it a biological necessity. De Carlo found it in a response to *genius loci* and cultural history, St John Wilson in the connection between aesthetics and ethics. Others were more doubtful; perhaps authenticity lies less in the architecture, more in the eye of the beholder. Ahrends … had grave doubts about whether it can be attained, and whether ABK is even trying to attain it. Evans found the word easier to apply to a pizza where clear reference can be made to the Italian original, but considered it too problematic to be useful in architecture. He illustrated his point elegantly with an analysis of Le Corbusier's Ronchamp and the rich mythology that has arisen round it: authenticity is clearly a teasing problem there. Most dismissive of all was Reid, who sees architecture as a constant borrowing and rehashing of past elements, thus inevitably impure: those who think they escape the cycle are kidding themselves.[6]

'Authenticity' is a term that will resurface in the discussion in Chapter 5, when it will come up again in relation to the question of truth in architecture. Indeed, the most basic and common sense manner in which 'authenticity' is used in English is to refer to the quality of something as being 'true to' the way it appears or presents itself – what will be referred to here as the 'weak' sense of the term. In this sense, 'authentic' functions almost interchangeably with 'genuine' or 'real' and can also be used to mean 'sincere', 'honest' or 'having integrity'. In his discussion, Blundell Jones uses the term in the sense of 'being true to' (at one point he talks about authenticity in terms of the 'impression of self-evidence'[7]) as this applies in four realms: 'one, truth to the material object; two, truth to form or arrangement; three, truth to place or context; and four, truth to use and the meaning of use',[8] and his discussion explores authenticity in architecture as it relates to memory and time, to materials and construction, and to society and human institutions.

Authenticity is frequently appealed to in heritage architecture, where questions arise as to how existing buildings should be addressed in ways that are consistent with ('true to') their historical character, and in ways that do not distort, damage or misrepresent that character, especially when it comes to modifications or additions.[9] It also appears, however, as an issue in relation to new buildings that attempt to replicate or draw upon historical features and forms, as well as how and to what extent the features and forms of buildings, whether historical or not, should express or reflect their underlying character. These are essentially the areas that Blundell Jones first addresses. Sometimes the idea of the 'real', the 'genuine' or the 'honest' that is at work in 'authenticity' is used, in architectural as well as other contexts, to refer to the vernacular, 'native' or rustic – mainly, it would seem, because they are assumed to carry no suggestion of pretence or superficiality. This carries over into industrial and other utilitarian buildings and forms that are similarly seen in having an 'honesty' that is directly related to their utilitarian or 'functional' character.[10]

Authenticity has also been appealed to in discussions of urban planning and design, where it is seen as a positively valued feature of urban experience tied, once again, to notions of honesty and genuineness (although the exact content of the notion often remains vague and unspecified).[11] Although there is contemporary debate over whether 'authenticity', in this sense, is 'objective' or 'constructed',[12] much of this debate appears ill-conceived – less about authenticity as such, and more over differences in what authenticity is taken to be and the shifting contexts and judgements that surround it. How authenticity is experienced and understood, like almost any and every phenomenon, depends on the situation in which the question of authenticity arises. Consequently, variation in the way in which authenticity arises in many ordinary contexts is to be expected – such variation providing little insight into the notion itself. As a positively valued feature of urban experience, authenticity – whether used in the urban context or, for instance, as it is used to described the 'unvarnished' character of the vernacular or rustic – is often tied to the idea of a 'sense of place' (as it is in many heritage contexts). Places that are authentic, in this context, are also places that have a character and identity that belong, or are taken to belong, to those places. Again, this sense of authenticity seems to draw upon the idea of the 'genuine', the 'real', the 'honest' (even if what is taken to be 'authentic' in this way fails to be so). This sense of authenticity appears in Norberg-Schulz's work as well as in Relph's discussion of 'place and placelessness'.[13] It is often championed by urban conservationists, who look to preserve existing and historic features and landmarks (hence the connection to heritage discussions), but it is also taken up by city managers, businesses and tourism boards, for whom such authenticity, whether 'real' or 'constructed', is an important element in the commodification of urban landscapes in relation, for instance, to tourism and the property market.

Yet, although authenticity is indeed a commonplace notion, and can be used to mean something quite familiar and ordinary, even if sometimes contentious, there is also a sense that attaches to authenticity that is more immediately problematic. Originating in the nineteenth century, this sense is connected with a certain sort of 'expressivist' view of the self that emphasizes the importance (even the imperatival necessity) of one's actions and appearance being a direct manifestation or expression of one's *inner* feelings and commitments. This sense of authenticity will here be referred to as the 'strong' sense. It goes beyond mere genuineness, sincerity, honesty or integrity and is often associated with a refusal of collective conventions or mores. This strong sense actually draws more directly (though usually unknowingly) on the original Greek term *authentes*, meaning both one who acts with authority and one who acts by their own hand, and having the connotation, especially in the Greek, as Lionel Trilling emphasizes, of a murderer and even a self-murderer.[14] This idea of authenticity as tied to a sense of self-making and self-mastery, and so to the idea of powerful and direct action or agency, is what emerges as a theme in the modern *sui generis* sense of the term, especially as it differentiates itself from the 'weak' sense.

The appeal of strong authenticity lies in the idea of some direct connection to the 'reality' of the self in its absolute individuality, and of that 'reality' as immediately expressed in appearance and action and as its only genuine basis. Such an idea goes well beyond the idea of authenticity as it designates the 'genuine' as opposed to the fake, beyond authenticity as a form of sincerity, honesty or integrity, and even beyond authenticity as residing in some form of self-evidence – the sense employed by Blundell Jones. This is so, even though one can also see how authenticity, in its weaker forms, could provide the kernel from which the strong sense of authenticity might arise – although it is probably better to say that the weak form is a dilution of that original Greek sense that then re-emerges in modernity. There are obvious problems with authenticity in its strong form; not least, the way it seems to depend upon a similarly strong notion of the individual self.

Even though it goes largely unrecognized in most architectural discussion, the strong sense of authenticity does appear in architecture, and in a way that has a connection back to the original appearance of the strong notion in the nineteenth century, in the idea of the authenticity of creative 'genius'. In Ayn Rand's own *paen* to authenticity – her 1943 novel, *The Fountainhead* – the main protagonist is the architect Howard Roark, for whom Rand took Frank Lloyd Wright as the model.[15] Roark is portrayed as strongly individualist and uncompromising in his determination to impress his genius on the world around him. In the defence of himself and his actions that he offers at the end of the book, Roark describes the creator who aims at the 'conquest of nature' and who has always 'held his truth above all things and against all men' (echoing Wright's own family motto; 'The truth against the world'). Roark goes on:

His vision, his strength, his courage came from his own spirit. A man's spirit, however, is his self ... The creators were not selfless. It is the whole secret of their power – that it was self-sufficient, self-motivated, self-generated. A first cause, a fount of energy, a life force, a Prime Mover. The creator served nothing and no one. He lived for himself ... Men have been taught that it is a virtue to agree with others. But the creator is the man who disagrees. Men have been taught that it is a virtue to swim with the current. But the creator is the man who goes against the current. Men have been taught that it is a virtue to stand together. But the creator is the man who stands alone. Men have been taught that the ego is the synonym of evil, and selflessness the ideal of virtue. But the creator is the egotist in the absolute sense, and the selfless man is the one who does not think, feel, judge or act.[16]

Roark not only embodies Rand's ideal of the authentic individual, but has also come to exemplify a common image of the architect that fits closely with the original notion – itself tied to the idea of 'strong' authenticity – of the creative genius who refuses to abide by the rules of conventional society and acts only on the basis of their own inner vision and desire. Moreover, whilst Rand's picture of Roark may have been modelled on Wright, it might well be taken to fit, to varying degrees, the image of those many 'star' architects (or 'starchitects') whose buildings today dominate so many cities around the world.

Here, then, is a model of strong authenticity that does indeed seem to be at work in recent and contemporary architecture – although one might ask to what extent it is evident in architectural form, whether as designed or built, rather than merely in the persona of the architect. In fact, the 'signature' or 'iconic' building might itself be seen to embody a certain form of architectural authenticity in something like the strong sense. Such buildings gain much of their significance and notoriety from their character as an expression of the individual architect (even if their actual construction is less so) and, in many cases, the design intention often seems to override any consideration other than those pertaining to the design itself, with the iconic building seen as putting its stamp on the urban landscape in which it is located, rather than the other way around. Even if the exact character of the design may vary – and, in the specificity of its form, may even embody different architectural ideals – the way the design, and typically the building itself, is seen in its connection to the architect, as well as in its relation to the existing locale, does indeed seem to instantiate a form of strong authenticity.

It might be supposed that it is this strong form of authenticity that is at issue in the sort of criticism of Heidegger that Sharr exemplifies. Certainly, 'authenticity' is a term that appears throughout the English editions of *Being and Time* (along with related terms such as 'inauthenticity', 'authentic' and 'inauthentic'). Moreover, Heidegger can indeed be read as insisting on the importance of *Dasein*, in some sense, being 'true to' its own being, and he is also critical of the inevitable tendency for *Dasein* to lose itself in the conventionalities of social life. Yet Heidegger's account, in his 1927 *magnum opus,* is also strongly opposed to any narrow individualism, since *Dasein* always articulates itself in and through the world – including the world as it is given collectively and historically – and Heidegger is critical, too, of any substantive account of the self. Moreover, although Heidegger does not reject the idea of some form of 'inner life' that is fundamental to the existence of *Dasein*, such 'inner life' is not such as to allow construal in terms of some substantive and essential reality of which 'outer' life must be a direct expression. Howard Roark does not fit the model of 'authentic' *Dasein*, and Heidegger's position, as set out in *Being and Time*, is certainly far removed from Rand's. In fact, whilst versions of a philosophy of authenticity focused around the 'heroic' individual self and the importance of self-determination and creative self-expression are often attributed to Heidegger, such a philosophy owes more to popular forms of existentialist thought (and, to some extent, the work of thinkers such as Sartre) than to the details of Heidegger's own writings.[17] And when one looks to essays like 'Building Dwelling Thinking', one finds an account that actually runs directly counter to any notion of strong authenticity. The emphasis there is on an attentive responsiveness to place and to the world, rather than on the realization, against the world, of some inner 'truth'. In its concern with 'measure', it tends towards moderation rather than extremity.[18]

In fact, Heidegger does not employ the German term, *Authentizität*, that directly translates into the English 'authenticity'. Perhaps somewhat ironically, that term is more properly associated with Adorno's aesthetics than with anything in Heidegger. The term that is translated as 'authenticity' in *Being and Time*, and elsewhere in Heidegger's writings, is *Eigentlichkeit* (the term that also figures in Adorno's *Jargon of Authenticity* – *Jargon der Eigentlichkeit* – in which Heidegger is a central target). One of the problems surrounding almost all discussion of authenticity, in English, is the conflation of the two German terms into the one English term – something to which even native German speakers seem readily to fall prey.[19] *Eigentlichkeit* is a technical term in Heidegger's early thinking, formed from the common German adjective *eigentlich*, which means real, actual or *proper*, and deriving from the German *eigen*, meaning 'own'. Indeed, the literal translation, if 'own' is understood as it is operative in 'proper', is not far from 'appropriateness'. In English, the connection of 'own' to 'proper' is reflected in the idea of 'property' as that which is 'owned' or 'belongs to', and this is reflected in the German, where *eigen*, or 'own', is related to *Eigentum*, meaning 'property'.

Heidegger introduces *Eigentlichkeit*, in *Being and Time*, to refer to the particular way in which Dasein relates to itself such that it acknowledges what is indeed proper to it; *Uneigentlichkeit* refers to the way Dasein relates to itself such that what is proper to Dasein is effaced or hidden. So, for instance, Dasein's mode of being is *eigentlich* ('owned' or 'appropriate') when it faces up to its own character as being-towards-death; it is *uneigentlich* ('unowned' or 'inappropriate') when it effaces or denies this character (when, for instance, it treats death as always something that happens to 'other people'). Although Heidegger's Introduction of *Eigentlichkeit* as a proper noun is unusual, as is the contrast with *Uneigentlichkeit*, his use of *eigentlich* is not. As a term that picks out, for instance, what something 'properly is' or what 'is proper to it', *eigentlich* is commonplace. Indeed, when Adorno writes, as he does in the passage from *Minima Moralia*, quoted in Chapter 1, that 'dwelling, in the proper sense, is now impossible', the German term translated as 'in the proper sense' is *eigentlich*. Typically, when 'authentic' appears in translations of Heidegger's later essays, what it is being used to translate is a use of *eigentlich*, which is not at all far from that which appears in Adorno,[20] and which, incidentally, is appealed to no more frequently than in Adorno. By the time of the Heidegger's late essays, *Eigentlichkeit* has also largely ceased to operate as a significant term in the way associated with *Being and Time*.

It is true, of course, that the sense of 'proper to' that is at work in the ordinary use of *eignentlich* can be seen to converge with 'authentic' in its weak sense, as meaning 'genuine', 'real' or 'true'. As a person's actions may be said to be 'true to' their commitments, for instance, so those actions will also be 'appropriate', given those commitments; that is, when something really is as it appears, so its appearance is proper to or 'belongs to' what it is. This reflects the fact that what is at issue here is the making of distinctions between what things are and what they appear, or are taken, to be. Such a distinction is commonplace in ordinary discourse – 'the house seemed abandoned, but in fact it was just badly maintained', 'the food looked appetizing, but turned out to be inedible'. However, it is fundamental to philosophical, critical or reflective thinking, and is hard to see how one could engage in any such thinking without drawing on something like a distinction between what is *eigentlich* and *uneigentlich*. The very mode of reading on which writers like Sharr and Leach draw, and that effectively argues for a danger that is concealed within Heidegger's texts, cannot avoid the appeal to what is indeed a distinction between what is and what appears, between the genuine and the 'fake', between the 'true' and what is merely claimed to be true. The problem with the distinction (leaving aside the problems that may arise from its unfounded or unsubstantiated application) is not its use as such – whether in the form it appears in writers like Sharr and Leach or in Heidegger – but, rather, the way in which specific instances of the distinction are absolutized so as to become metaphysical (the elements of the distinction being thus treated as two distinct and fundamental modes of being – 'Reality' and 'Appearance' or some analogue of these[21]).

Understood simply in terms of what is 'proper', 'appropriate' or 'owned', Heidegger's use of the language of the *eigentlich* is itself directly connected to the term that becomes so central in his later thinking, *Ereignis*. This latter term is most directly translated as 'event', taking account of the ordinary meaning of the term in German, but in its earliest appearances in English translations of Heidegger's work, it is often given as 'appropriation' or 'event of appropriation'.[22] The complex interplay of the fourfold is also *Ereignis* – a drawing together and setting apart within a complex bounded unity. The process of architectural design and construction can be understood as just such an appropriative happening – though in being such it is more something that happens to the architect, and in which the architect is taken up, rather than a process the architect directs or controls.[23] Just such a shift in how one understands architectural and other forms of practice is, of course, just the sort of shift that Heidegger himself suggests needs to be made in the understanding of building, as it relates to dwelling, in the argument of 'Building Dwelling Thinking'. Notice, too, how this notion of being 'taken up' stands in contrast to the strong sense of 'authenticity' as a matter of some form of pure 'self-expression' or as an assertion of the reality of the individual self over and against the world. If there is any sense in which exclusion is implied here, it is in the strong sense of authenticity rather than in the 'appropriative' relation involved in the notion of *Ereignis*.

Rand's philosophy of extreme individualism, and the idea of authenticity that goes with it, finds few champions among contemporary philosophers. Nevertheless, there are many who do aim at a retrieval of the notion of authenticity, arguing that there is a 'moderated' form of authenticity that allows the articulation of what is at issue in the weak sense, which is therefore distinct from the strong form exemplified in Rand but ethically significant in its own right. Charles Taylor is probably the most important representative of this approach, and Taylor, like other contemporary proponents of an 'ethics of authenticity', argues that the idea of authenticity can be separated from the individualistic notion of the self with which the strong form is associated. How convincing is the attempt of thinkers like Taylor to retrieve authenticity as a viable ethical notion is debateable – a key problem, indicated already, is retaining a sense of authenticity that has significant content over and above notions of truth, honesty or integrity.[24] It is important to note, however, the extent to which such attempts very often take Heidegger as one source for such a 'moderate' notion of authenticity – this is especially true, for instance, in Charles Guignon's work.[25]

There are reasons for being suspicious of the language of authenticity when it is used in a way that goes beyond the usual, more limited, constrastive senses in which the genuine is differentiated from the fake, the sincere from the duplicitous, the actual from the apparent. The term has such a chequered history philosophically, as Trilling demonstrates, that it may well be better if it were avoided altogether. It is not at all clear that talk of 'authenticity' adds much more than does talk of 'sincerity', 'integrity' or 'genuine', whether in an architectural or any other context. When 'authenticity' does add something, what it often adds remains ambiguous or tends towards forms of extremity that are indeed problematic. Authenticity is treated, even in its weak forms, as a determinate state belonging to the subject that can somehow be 'achieved' and should certainly be striven for.[26] Such an idea stands quite apart from what appears in Heidegger's account in *Being and Time*, where 'inauthenticity' is a structural element in Dasein's being that Dasein can never escape – 'authenticity' is thus not an achievement for Dasein, but one of the two modes between which its being constantly moves. It is important to note, moreover, that, so far as Heidegger is concerned, the way 'authenticity' enters into the discussion is, like 'dwelling', as the result of a particular translational choice in the history of the English reception of Heidegger's thinking that turns out not to be especially well-tuned to the complexities of that thinking and, indeed, that readily gives rise to misunderstanding and misreading. The situation is exacerbated by the way in which so much of the critical reading of Heidegger, in architecture as well as other disciplines in the social sciences and humanities, has been determined by Adorno's critical-theoretic approach – an approach that is driven more by Adorno's own particular preoccupations than by any close engagement with

Heidegger's texts (and, here, the proximity of the two thinkers, a proximity that remains despite Adorno's criticisms, becomes an additional complication).[27]

Essentialism and identity

Authenticity, as should now be evident, is a complex notion, yet Sharr offers little or no substantiation of what might be at issue in what he terms 'Heidegger's problematic authenticity claims'.[28] And that is not unusual: authenticity has become, like dwelling, a notion that is taken to be so much a part of Heidegger's thinking that it requires little or no comment, nor does it require any interrogation or explication. But, like dwelling, authenticity cannot be used in relation to Heidegger without potentially giving rise to significant misunderstanding – the term is, after all, not one that Heidegger uses even in its German form. However, 'authenticity' is not the only term that figures in Sharr's claim concerning the 'exclusionary' character of Heidegger's thinking, where such 'exclusion' is said to follow from Heidegger's supposed essentialism. Indeed, Sharr uses 'authenticity' and 'essentialism', together, in a way that suggests a connection between them, and this is often how authenticity is treated, even in its weak form. Thus, to say that something presents itself as being 'true to' what it really is seems to imply, in the very idea of what something 'really is', just the idea of that which is 'essential' to that thing – and the etymology confirms this, since the English 'essence' comes via *essentia,* from the Latin *esse,* meaning 'to be', and is also tied to the idea of the 'real'. Regardless of what one might say about authenticity, then, it might well be thought that there is still more to be said about essence and the essential – and not only these, but also related notions of identity and belonging, as well as their connection to place.

In Heynen, the critique of Heidegger's 'essentialism' is tied back directly to Adorno. Heynen writes:

> For Adorno ... it is clear that Heidegger's treatment of the question of dwelling is symptomatic of what is wrong with his philosophy. Heidegger attempts to reduce the idea of dwelling to an original essence, but this ontological approach disregards the question of concrete dwelling for concrete people and also ignores the banal but very real question of actual housing needs caused by social conditions. An approach like Heidegger's, in Adorno's view, is not capable of giving any impulse for change; rather, it implies an acceptance of historically determined conditions as if they were 'eternally human': 'No elevation of the concept of Man has any power in the face of his actual degradation into a bundle of functions. The only help lies in changing the conditions which brought the state of affairs to this point – conditions which uninterruptedly reproduce themselves on a larger scale.'[29]

Once again, a closer consideration of Adorno, of Heidegger and of the relation of the one to the other reveals a more complex position than Adorno – or

Heynen – suggests. The idea that Heidegger's philosophy is problematic because of its attempt to reduce dwelling to an original essence appears both argumentatively weak (too much would need to be specified before such a claim could be made meaningful, if it could be made meaningful at all) and to depend on a peculiar misconstrual of the Heideggerian position.

What appears to be assumed is that any talk of the 'essential' must imply 'an acceptance of historically determined conditions'. Yet, not only is the assumption manifestly false, quite independently of the case at issue (liberation theology providing a striking example of an essentialist position that is also revolutionary), but Heidegger's own position demonstrates the falsity of that assumption. Although not strongly evident in 'Building Dwelling Thinking', Heidegger's analysis of dwelling, and of the character of human being, plays a key role in the critique he develops elsewhere of the historically *realized* (if not, as Heidegger would see it, entirely historically *determined*) conditions of the contemporary world; that is, of modernity (a critique, as already noted, that also converges in many respects with Adorno's own). Moreover, the claims that Heynen approvingly quotes from Adorno rely on what can only appear as a rather simplistic opposition between philosophy as against applied social critique, and an unargued preferment of the one over the other that is extremely hard to sustain. One might also wonder where, in any of Adorno's works, there is any positive programme for the amelioration of actual conditions of housing for specific individuals or communities. Adorno was, like Heidegger, neither an architect nor a planner, and his writing on the questions of dwelling and housing contains little more in the way of specific recommendations or concrete proposals than does Heidegger's. Both of them, one might say, adopt an ontological approach, one doing so explicitly and the other doing so without acknowledging the fact. In fact, if 'ontology' refers, in one sense, to the basic structure that grounds a way of thinking – and so is operative even in thinking that argues against any form of determinate 'foundation' (the idea of a non-foundational ontology need not be an oxymoron) – then ontology is inescapable. The issue is not whether one thinks ontologically but whether one does so reflectively or unreflectively – whether the grounds of one's thinking have been addressed or simply assumed. And this is just the question that bedevils Adorno's work.

Essentialism is typically seen as standing in contrast to constructionism, and to consist in commitment to the idea that membership of a specific category implies the possession of a determinate and unchanging set of features or properties that together make up the 'essence' of the category or of what belongs within it. Constructionism, on the other hand, implies that there is no such determinate and unchanging set of features or properties that make up categorial identity, and that such identity, and so also the categories with which identity is associated, is 'constructed' – which means is a 'conventional' or socially determined notion that may vary according to circumstance and context. Undoubtedly, it is this sort of contrast between the essential and the constructed, between the unchanging and the changeable, that is at work in Adorno's criticism of Heidegger, but the contrast is much less straightforward than it may seem.

Constructionism finds itself in difficulty, as noted earlier, when it is treated as an absolutized position. The same is true of traditional forms of 'essentialism' that look to take certain underlying structures, entities or processes as completely determinative of what is (such a position being what Heidegger pejoratively refers to as 'metaphysics' but also as 'nihilism'[30]). In fact, rather than being diametrically opposed, the essential and the constructed, or perhaps better, the 'socio-historical', are necessarily related as part of a single continuum. Construction depends on pre-existing and 'essential' structures (even if only those of underlying causality), just as what is essential always has to be worked out through contingent processes of 'construction' (a relationship that parallels that between the inherited and the environmental in developmental theory). Indeed, one might argue that it is partly this dynamic that underlies the possibility of the same mode of being appearing in different ways – as dwelling might appear as homelessness. Such a possibility is also central to the idea that, to take an especially important example, human beings can be understood as fundamentally committed to an ethical mode of life, and yet human beings can nevertheless fail to live ethically. It is at work, too, in the tension between the structures within which the engagement with built form must operate and the ways in which that engagement is worked out, not only in differing architectural visions, but in differing forms of building and differing built forms.

Significantly, what this shows, once again, is the way in which genuine critique cannot do without some notion of the essential, precisely as this is understood in terms of the notion of what is proper to or appropriate, that is, without some notion of what Heidegger also refers to as the possibility of 'measure'. As a result, however, the discussion of essentialism turns out to recapitulate, if in a different way, much of the discussion of authenticity, and as before, part of what creates difficulty for the sorts of purportedly critical readings of 'Building Dwelling Thinking' – found in such as Sharr, Heynen and even Adorno – is simply a failure to attend to the character of Heidegger's own use of terms and to the specific structure and direction of his arguments.

The way some notion of the essential might figure in the possibility of critical discourse is indicative of the fundamental role that ontological inquiry has in Heidegger's own critical engagement. Moreover, Heidegger's employment of the idea of the 'essential' cannot readily be assimilated to most traditional conceptions, and he is critical of the traditional notion of essence and its tendency to reduce the being of a thing to a collection of properties.[31] For Heidegger, 'essence' – the term he uses is *Wesen* – can only refer to that which is proper to a thing, so that the essential is also the 'proper' or the 'ownmost'. What is *wesentlich* is also *eigentlich*. So although there is a connection between what is often referred to, in English translations of and commentaries on Heidegger's work, as 'essential' and 'authentic', the relation cannot be assumed to mirror either the way those two terms relate or the connotations they bring with them in English.

The idea of the essential is, as already noted, tied up with notions of identity and, so, also belonging (since belonging can be seen to be a function of identity). That which is essential may not entirely determine identity, but inasmuch as identity is tied up with being, so essence and identity seem to stand together. Although it can also carry connotations of uniqueness or singularity, identity often means 'same' (as in 'identical'), making the question of identity also a question about the nature of the 'same'. Here, one can readily see how a focus on this cluster of notions might also be tied, depending on how these notions are understood, to forms of exclusion. A preoccupation with what is the same can also lead to the exclusion of what is different, especially if such 'sameness', and the identity associated with it, is seen to be threatened by difference. Heidegger's use of the language of the essential, especially as it occurs in essays like 'Building Dwelling Thinking', does not easily fit this exclusionary model. Indeed, in "' … Poetically Man Dwells … '", he is explicit in emphasizing the way in which sameness always implies difference.[32]

This issue is at the centre of one of Heidegger's most important later essays, 'The Principle of Identity', from 1957.[33] In an argument that develops the ideas of "' … Poetically Man Dwells … '" in more detail and at greater length, Heidegger distinguishes between two ways of understanding identity. The first takes identity to be a matter of the self-sameness of a thing with itself (a self-sameness most simply and succinctly expressed in the formula 'x=x') and, so, to be a matter of the thing taken alone. Identity is, on this account, autonomous and non-relational, a matter of a thing's own self-sufficient being. The second way of thinking moves away from the thing as understood in such an autonomous fashion, and towards the thing as already placed in relation. Identity emerges, not out of the being of the thing as static and separated, but rather in terms of the dynamic play of things and world, of concealed and unconcealed, of sameness *and* difference. It is a way of understanding identity that is entirely in accord with the 'compositional' or relational account of dwelling and world set out in 'Building Dwelling Thinking'. It is also a way of understanding identity that is directly connected to the idea of appropriation that is at work in Heidegger's talk of the event, or *Ereignis*.

The question of identity, as it arises here, is not some merely peripheral issue in Heidegger's thought. Instead, it is a question that lies close to its very heart (and relates directly to the issue concerning the multivocal character of so much of his language as noted in Chapter 2). It is central to Heidegger's thought just as it is also a central issue in philosophy more generally. The question of identity is directly connected with the issue of difference, but rather than being exclusionary, it moves in exactly the opposite direction. As Heidegger understands them, identity and difference each implicate the other as part of unitary but also pluralized structure that is what appears, in one important form, in the complex and dynamic structure of the fourfold. Heidegger thus contests the conventional understanding of identity in a way that is itself directly tied both to his thinking of the question of being and to the topological frame within which that thinking proceeds. It is all the more striking, then, to find Heidegger so often read – by those who are sympathetic as well as antagonistic – in ways that take for granted a conventional understanding of identity, thereby attributing to Heidegger a view of identity that he explicitly eschews.

Place, home and exclusion

Ian Hacking notes of 'essentialism' that the term 'is not purely descriptive', and he adds that 'most people who use it use it as a slur word, intended to put down the opposition'.[34] Certainly, in the absence of any reasoned argument, the charge of essentialism made against Heidegger turns out to be fairly empty (much like Sharr's related claim about 'authenticity' and the frequent claims elsewhere concerning the 'totalizing' character of Heidegger's discourse). Moreover, once one looks, not only to the way Heidegger employs the language of the essential, but also to his thinking of the related notion of identity, then it becomes very clear just how far removed from Heidegger's actual position is the charge of 'essentialism' that Sharr and others like him so frequently advance.

Already the analysis of Heidegger's supposed essentialism and the brief consideration of his account of identity ought to cast significant doubt on the claim concerning the exclusionary nature of Heidegger's thinking, particularly as it is developed in the later essays, like 'Building Dwelling Thinking'. Moreover, there is much in Heidegger's own account that itself operates against exclusionary forms of thought precisely because of the conventional and problematic ways in which they construe both identity and difference. This is a point to which the discussion will return. For the moment, there is another possibility to consider; namely, that, even if one allows that there is no commitment to authenticity or to essentialism of a sort that makes for exclusion, the very way in which Heidegger gives priority to *place* as well as to *home* is exclusionary simply because these terms are themselves exclusionary. It is so, on this account, because place always requires the setting – and, one might say, the 'policing' – of boundaries (it is worth noticing the implicit way in which a notion of the 'essential' seems to be in play in such a claim). This is especially evident in the notion of home as the place that is one's own, and so the place from which others are excluded.

When 'Building Dwelling Thinking' was first presented in Darmstadt, the strongest criticism came from one of Karl Jaspers's ex-students, the political philosopher Dolf Sternberger whose comments during the discussion are included in the original volume of *Mensch und Raum*.[35] Sternberger did not address any supposed essentialism in Heidegger's presentation, nor any appeal to authenticity (or even *Eigentlichkeit*), and neither, it should be noted, did he contest Heidegger's focus on *Wohnen*, or dwelling, as such. Nevertheless, Sternberger advanced a reading of Heidegger's position that (although undoubtedly influenced by Adorno) is effectively the first public iteration of the critical response to Heidegger's account of dwelling that has since become commonplace. In a lengthy set of comments that followed Ortega y Gasset's presentation (which came after Heidegger's), Sternberger argues that Heidegger's account relies on a problematic understanding of dwelling as tied to the idea of home or 'homeland', in German, *Heimat*. The latter notion is one Sternberger interprets as meaning 'the place of the final settling of the human being in himself, the fortification in a home of one's own, sedentariness as groundedness on one's own land, and so forth, however modest the dimensions'.[36] Sternberger thus reads Heidegger as offering an account of dwelling in terms of the same sort of 'settled' mode of being in the world that Keiller also criticizes.[37] Whilst Sternberger acknowledges the attractions of such a notion, he warns against the danger with which he takes it to be associated.[38]

The German term *Heimat*, on which Sternberger focuses, is the same term that figures in *Heimatlosigkeit*, one of the topics that Bartnig specified as central to the Darmstadt meeting. *Heimat* is often translated as 'home' and as 'homeland' but is more concrete and evocative notion than the English terms. *Heimat* is distinctively German, and cannot be exactly translated, often being taken to refer to a certain way of being oriented in the world, rather than to a specific place (the German -*at* ending usually indicates a state or condition). There is an enormous literature – both positive and negative – that surrounds the term, and *Heimat* has been drawn upon by those from both the left and the right. It is a term that was made use of by Nazism,[39] yet it is also a term employed in the utopian project of Ernst Bloch,[40] and has been drawn upon in progressive discourses elsewhere.

If one accepts the rough equivalence, notwithstanding their differences, between *Heimat* and the English 'home', then *Heimat* is just as complex and polyvalent a term, and just as resistant to being appropriated in only one fashion. There is no doubt that both *Heimat* and 'home' have been drawn upon in extremist conservative political discourse, but that alone does not demonstrate the inherently problematic character of the terms, rather their centrality and significance. The language of the 'just' and the 'right' is also drawn upon in right-wing politics, but that alone does not mean such notions should be abandoned. Indeed, there is a significant political project that consists in the retrieval of such key notions, whether of 'home', or of the 'just' and the 'right', from problematic political appropriation and association; the rethinking of 'home', no less than 'dwelling', thereby appearing as an important task. Thus, when a writer such as Mark Wigley takes up the language of 'home' in Heidegger's work as indicative, because of its use in Nazism, of a hidden violence within Heidegger's text,[41] he ignores the centrality of the terms that leads to their Nazi appropriation. In addition, however, he also entirely neglects the way in which Heidegger, and especially the later Heidegger, is involved in a rethinking of those terms – a rethinking that is demanded precisely because of those terms' centrality, and because of the way they are therefore bound up with a clutch of key philosophical issues concerning self, place and world.[42]

One reason why such rethinking and retrieval are important and necessary tasks is that both *Heimat* and home are closely tied to the self. The home is a mode of the self, the self as it first finds itself in the world. *Heimat* is that idea of home as articulated in explicitly topological fashion. Home is a mode of place, and *Heimat* is the home as given in a specific locality or region, with all of its communal as well as personal associations and memory. The way the self is tied to place, evident in the importance of home as well as of *Heimat*, is not merely a function of some conventional or socio-culturally determined association. Instead, it reflects the underlying character of human being as fundamentally topological in character. Heidegger's approach, especially as set out in 'Building Dwelling Thinking', exemplifies such a topological understanding of the human, something that was already evident in the discussion in Chapter 1. The 'compositional', or relational, account of place and world that Heidegger develops also entails a 'compositional', or relational, account of the self – one that takes such relationality as worked out in and through the concrete places in which the self finds itself, and in which it acts and is acted upon.

The overall approach that is evident in Heidegger – and the 'externalized' or 'extended' understanding of human being that it involves – is not peculiar to Heidegger alone. Nor is it peculiar to the broadly phenomenological (or hermeneutic) tradition in thinking about place in disciplines like architecture or geography. One of the reasons why Heidegger's approach has been so significant in contemporary philosophy has been its articulation – in works like 'Building Dwelling Thinking' but also, much earlier, in *Being and Time* – of exactly the idea of human being, and so of the self and the 'mind', as extended into the world (although Heidegger's reservations about the language of the mental and the subjective mean that he avoids the latter terms along with talk of 'consciousness' or 'cognition'). Such is now commonplace in cognitive science and philosophy of mind, where it is often known as the 'extended mind' thesis (EMT).[43] However, it is not an idea restricted to technical work in the sciences of mind, having also become influential within almost all areas of the human and social sciences, even though it sometimes takes on philosophically less rigorous forms, including, for instance, the range of 'new materialisms' that have appeared across many different disciplinary fields.

It is often said that Heidegger neglects the body, and it is certainly true that he does not give primary attention to the body as it figures in many psychoanalytic, feminist and deconstructive approaches. In *Being and Time*, he notes that '[Dasein's] bodily nature hides a whole problematic of its own, though we shall not treat it here'.[44] Elsewhere, Heidegger warns against any approach that would take the body as already given.[45] But there is also an important sense in which the body has a central role in Heidegger's account, inasmuch as that account understands human being as necessarily externalized, or extended, into the world – as essentially emplaced – and as such it is also necessarily embodied. Thus Heidegger's comment in *Being and Time* concerning the problematic that is hidden in the question of the bodily nature of *Dasein* comes in the midst of a detailed discussion of the spatiality that belongs to *Dasein* in which the question of embodiment is already implicated. Heidegger's point is that the body cannot be assumed here, and even that it cannot be approached directly. Moreover, not only is the body already at issue in the question of spatiality, but Heidegger's emphasis on activity also draws the body into view, and does so in a way that enables the body to be understood as itself given *in activity,* just as space and place are themselves dynamic. Building is itself an activity of the body and a working out of embodiment – a 'bodying' – and even thinking has to be understood as tied to the body, as a mode of embodied being that has a worldly comportment belonging to it.

In philosophy, the extended view of self and mind stands in contrast to the Cartesian understanding of self and the mind as constituting an internalized realm separated from the world – a realm of pure 'subjectivity'. And it is this Cartesian conception that seems to be reflected in the very understanding of *Heimat* that

Sternberger criticizes – the idea of *Heimat*, of 'home', as a closing off from the world in an attempt to find some self-settled, internalized form of security and familiarity. The latter idea echoes Walter Benjamin's characterization of *Wohnen*, or dwelling, as connected to 'the image of that abode of the human being in the maternal womb' and given, in its 'original form', as 'existence not in the house but in the shell'. Here a certain way of understanding 'home' and 'dwelling' comes to appear as the topological equivalent of the Cartesian view of subjectivity to which Heidegger was so opposed. In Descartes's own writings, this view presents itself in the story of his famous interrogation of the basic principles of philosophical thinking as having been undertaken in the self-contained comfort of a stove-heated room (called in French a *poêle*)[46] – the room seeming to express, even if implicitly, the self-containment of mind and self. In this way one finds topology written into the text of philosophy even in those thinkers, like Descartes, who might otherwise be assumed to give a secondary role to place. Moreover, just as Heidegger is critical of the Cartesian notion of the self that appears here, so his account in 'Building Dwelling Thinking' and elsewhere in the later essays represents an effective repudiation of the parallel understanding of dwelling expressed in the characterizations of such as Benjamin and Sternberger. As Heidegger presents matters, dwelling is not a matter of closed-off containment within a secure and self-sufficient domain,[47] but an engagement in the world in its complexity and multiplicity. This point is at the very heart of the Heideggerian understanding of the constitutive, or productive, character of the boundedness that belongs to place – the very boundedness that enables openness and in which the world has its beginning.

The form of place and home that is implicit in Cartesian thinking about the self is widespread in many modern approaches to subjectivity – the internalized and closed-off character associated with place and home mirroring the separated internality of self and mind. Indeed, it is just such a conception of the self, or one closely related to it, that is at work in the strong sense of authenticity explored earlier. The idea of the authentic self that appears in Rand, for instance, is of a self that is autonomous and self-sufficient, and that imposes its will upon the world rather than allowing the world to impose upon it. In general, leaving the specific issue of authenticity to one side, one might say of the modern view of the self as it appears in Cartesian thought, and in the work of someone like Rand, that it involves just the idea of the self as autonomous, not only with respect to the world (or in Rand's case with respect to others), but also with respect to place. Such a view of what might be called the topological autonomy of the self is widespread, and although it may well be said to extend beyond what are usually taken to be the main tenets of Cartesian thought, probably ought to be seen as implicit in them.

An especially pertinent example is found in the work of Emmanuel Levinas. Although Levinas draws heavily on a language of space and home as part of his ethics of hospitality – an ethics that emphasizes the face-to-face encounter with the other – Levinas is also deeply opposed to what he characterizes as the 'paganism' of the Heideggerian commitment to the centrality of place in the understanding of human being. 'One's implementation in a landscape, one's attachment to Place, he writes, ' ... is the very splitting of humanity into natives and strangers. And in this light technology is less dangerous than the spirits [*génies*] of the Place.'[48] In contrast to Heidegger, Levinas applauds the achievement of Yuri Gagarin, who made the first human flight into space.[49] As Levinas sees it, Gagarin freed himself, even if only 'for an hour', from the 'spirits' of place, thereby existing, temporarily, in a 'geometrical space' that is 'beyond any horizon'.[50] Levinas does not deny the human connection to home, nor the importance of 'home' as such or even of 'dwelling',[51] but for him, that connection is one established by the act of an exilic or displaced subject. In *Totality and Infinity*, Levinas declares, directly repudiating Heidegger, that 'the chosen home is the very opposite of a root',[52] but what is crucial to note is that the home at issue is indeed *chosen*. The subject thus *makes* its home rather than its home being already *given* to it. Here homelessness and displacement are taken as primary. Human beings are first cast out in the world, in exile within it, and then must find a home. Since to be human is to be in a state of exile, so the act of hospitality – of extending one's home to the other – is one required of all and an act of which all are in need. Indeed, the choice that constitutes a home is a choice that is unfounded, except inasmuch as it allows the act of hospitality to the other, an act that can be seen as an obligation or responsibility that follows from one's own being-at-home.

A similar emphasis on the primacy of exile or displacement is also present, if in more abbreviated form, in Sternberger. Taking Heidegger to be one of a group of thinkers who think of human beings as dwelling in a sort of cosy *Heimat*, as if it were a 'Paradise', Sternberger reminds his audience that the earth is not the Garden of Eden and, in any case, that garden is one from which human beings have already been evicted. Moreover, rather than being already a home for us, Sternberger insists that this earth is, as it is simply given, not 'absolutely uninhabitable [*absolut unwohnlich*]' but 'not livable [*wohnlich*] enough'.[53] Rather than being already possible, dwelling must be established as a possibility by human beings. In other words, on Sternberger's account, building comes prior to dwelling. The emphasis on the priority of displacement and even of homelessness is not uncommon in contemporary discussions, although it is seldom argued for in the way that is evident in Levinas, or even Sternberger. Sometimes it seems to be derived from the fact that it is displacement that typically brings place and home to the fore as issues – the idea of home, and especially of 'homeland', thus appears as that to which one would return, but with respect to which such a return is impossible. In this way, the very idea of home is seen as irretrievably bound up with the 'nostalgic' – the latter being understood in terms of the persistent desire for an impossible return.

Levinas aside, at least for the moment, these sorts of readings of the relation between place and displacement, and so also of home and exile, overlook exactly the character of Heidegger's thinking of place and home that was arrived at in Chapter 2: the idea that home encompasses both homelessness and being-at-home. In this respect, the idea of homelessness that is often valorized in many contemporary discussions is no less an ideal than is the notion of home that is taken to be the object of an impossible longing. The Heideggerian point, already made in Chapter 2, is that home is always affected by uncertainly and instability – home is that which allows the emergence of the self into the world, but for this very reason, home is that which opens up the possibility of being not at home, of homelessness. And so, as Heidegger says in the passage quoted earlier, 'we are ... homeless in our ownmost homeland'. This is a central point for Heidegger, not only because of the way he takes human being to be given over to questionability, but also because of the way the very openness of the world, and connected to this the possibility of freedom, is taken by him to reside in a fundamental mode of being-in-place or, as might also be said, of being at home. That also means that the possibility of otherness emerges out of the first placing of self in the world such that the world and one's own place in it are at issue for one. Significantly, the way Heidegger refuses any simple univocal characterization of these key ideas of place and home can be seen to reflect his own resistance to the conventional reading of identity – the way identity always encompasses difference is carried over into the essential or necessary indeterminacy and complexity of thought and idea.

Place, bound and relation

Central to much of the discussion in these first three chapters – and central also to those yet to come – is the idea of place as a *sui generis* notion that is not reducible to time and space, even though it is intimately related to both. With place also comes the idea of bound – as Aristotle says, place is a kind of bound[54] – and this is partly what distinguishes it from mere space. Much of the critique of the Heideggerian account of dwelling comes, in the final analysis, to rest on the notion of place on which that account depends, and especially on the boundedness of place. This reflects a broader antagonism to place, beyond the Heideggerian discussion, that reflects an antagonism to the notion of bound (something characteristic of modernity), and a tendency to understand boundedness as restrictive more than productive. The task of rethinking dwelling necessarily requires the thinking and rethinking of place and, therefore, of bound (see especially Chapter 10). That rethinking also extends to ideas like those of sameness and difference, and part of what is significant about Heidegger's treatment of those notions in 'The Principle of Identity' is the way it moves in a similar topological direction to that which is so clearly evident in 'Building Dwelling Thinking'.

A detailed analysis of the topology at work in 'The Principle of Identity' is beyond the scope of this volume. However, what can be noted is that the interplay of sameness and difference within the structure of identity and being is an interplay that is only possible in and with respect to the bounded regionality of place. In this respect, it is the 'same' event at work in the interplay of sameness and difference that is also at work in the interplay of the differing elements of the fourfold that makes for the happening of world. This event always occurs with respect to what appears or 'comes to presence' – this thing, this life, this person, this encounter, even this building – and within an encompassing horizon or bound that gives 'room' to that appearance or presencing. When Heidegger uses the language of 'peace' [*Frieden*] and 'freedom' [*Freiheit*] in his account of dwelling, he does not mean that the realm of dwelling is a realm of security or unfettered liberty. Rather he indicates the way in which dwelling is tied to a freeing that is the opening of the world, and this freeing is a 'letting be' – and so a withdrawal from any constraint or violence – of things, others and the self. It is, however, a freeing that occurs, not in some indeterminate and unlimited space (certainly not in the unbounded 'geometrical space' that Levinas extols, which, even in the case of Gagarin, is an abstracted ideal rather than a reality[55]), but only within a bounded place.

Adorno is, as has been evident throughout the preceding discussion, one of the central sources for much contemporary criticism of Heidegger. However, the other source (although less prominent in architecture) is Levinas, and in many respects, it is Levinas who is much more important in making salient the key issues here. This is not because Levinas is more consistent or more effective in his critique than Adorno – there are problems of consistency that affect both thinkers, and both also misconstrue important elements in Heidegger's position. But Levinas's thinking is much more directly engaged than is Adorno's in a topological or spatial exercise of its own. The subtitle of *Totality and Infinity* (perhaps the book that engages with Heidegger in the most sustained fashion) is *An Essay on Exteriority*, and this is indicative of the centrality of a set of topological, or spatial, ideas in Levinas's thought.

From the perspective of the topological, of course, space is encompassed by place, and from that perspective, Levinas's work is indeed topological. But, from another perspective (although one that the argument advanced in this volume contests), the spatial is seen as prior to and independent of the topological. Even though he nowhere makes it explicit, Levinas is of the latter view. This not only means that he is critical of the supposedly imprisoning effect of place, as he makes plain in the argument of 'Heidegger, Gagarin, and Us', but also that he is critical of the primacy accorded to place over space, to the bounded over the unbounded, to the finite over the infinite. On this basis, Levinas's position is better characterized, at least from its own perspective, as *spatial* rather than *topological* in its basic orientation. The Levinasian account thus draws closer to traditional ethical accounts that emphasize the abstract universality of ethical engagement (with all of the difficulties to which such abstract universalism is vulnerable) and that also rely on an essentially spatialized understanding.

Again, this is not the place to go into a detailed analysis of the way space, as opposed to place, operates in Levinas's thinking, but one can note that it is evident in the Levinasian rejection of the importance of horizonality,[56] as well as in his emphasis on the character of the face-to-face encounter as occurring independently of socio-historical situatedness, independently of the concretely embodied circumstances, and independently of place (it is thus in the pure extendedness of space, outside of any situation, that the human face is allowed to 'shine in all its nudity'[57]). What is crucial here is the centrality of Levinas's prioritization of space as it operates both critically and constructively. The extent to which such a spatialized mode of thinking and the modern idea of the autonomous self are tied together has not been adequately explored – either in discussions of Levinas or elsewhere. However, the Levinasian position is deeply Cartesian in its basic orientation, dependent both on a similar spatialized understanding to that at work in Descartes and on what is essentially a mode of Cartesian subjectivity (even if developed in somewhat different terms).[58] It is this difference – between a spatialized and topological mode of thinking and an autonomous or relational mode of subjectivity – that underlies the real opposition between Levinas and Heidegger. Moreover, this is not merely an opposition between two thinkers, but between two fundamental modes of thinking.

It thus becomes evident that what is at issue in the discussion of the Levinasian position as against the Heideggerian – as well as of the evaluation of the Heideggerian position as such – encompasses issues that are of quite broad significance within the philosophical tradition and are not restricted merely to questions of ethics or to the philosophy of self and mind or, indeed, to the philosophy of architecture. They are issues that are only obscured by the often facile tendency, on the one hand, to treat Heidegger, and with him almost any thinking that accords significance to place, as inescapably aligned with conservative and even fascist politics, and to treat Levinas, on the other hand, as the unique exemplar of a genuinely ethical mode of thought. The tension between the abstracted mode of thinking towards which Levinas tends and the emplaced thinking exemplified in Heidegger is fundamental, so much so that it may even be viewed as irresolvable. But to acknowledge the fact of that tension – its fundamental character, and the way it plays out across many different forms of ethical, political and philosophical thinking, regardless of their conservative or progressive character, and in relation to a wide range of concepts (including those of freedom, knowledge and the good) – is also to recognize the significance of what is at issue here, a significance that goes well beyond Heidegger's discussion in 'Building Dwelling Thinking'.

If one were to mount a Heideggerian critique of the Levinasian position, it would be in terms of the limitations of the spatialized understanding to which Levinas is committed. Such limitations include Levinas's failure to take up, in any explicit fashion, the spatiality that is operative in his thinking, including its relation to the topological (which means, to a large extent, a failure to attend to the place, and so the bounds, of his own thinking). That means that Levinas never really addresses the question as to the nature of the spatial or the topological, whether and how the former could indeed take priority in relation to the latter, and what implications the prioritization of the spatial over the topological might have for Levinas's understanding of relationality (in fact, the very framework of Levinas's approach would seem to render this almost impossible). Of course, Levinas is not unusual in this regard. The direct engagement with issues of place and space is rare in the philosophical tradition. Levinas's work is notable for the attention that it gives to the spatial, despite its relative lack of any direct thematization of the issues this raises. Still, what marks out Heidegger's thinking, in contrast to Levinas, and to much of the preceding tradition, is that the issues of place and space that are at issue in the discussion here, and their relation to the understanding of the human and the world, are indeed the focus of direct and sustained consideration. And it is partly because they are – because Heidegger takes so seriously the explicit focus of the Darmstadt meeting as set out by Bartning – that Heidegger's work has such relevance to the architectural. Moreover, Heidegger's own prioritization of place, so criticized by Levinas, is what positions his work in such a crucial way within contemporary architecture, since that prioritization is indicative of an emphasis on the qualitative, the responsive and the embodied – on the architectural as always 'taking place' amidst the complex gathering of world. The implied exhortation to escape from place, which is present in Levinas, becomes even more obviously problematic when it comes to architecture than it is when formulated philosophically or ethically. Architecture has no escape from place, or, at least, any attempt at such escape can result only in an architecture that has lost sight of its own grounds.

What Adam Sharr describes as Heidegger's 'unapologetic' commitment to the exclusionary notions of 'authenticity' and 'essentialism', and the wider critique along these lines that is evident in the architectural literature (and elsewhere), typically relies more on the prior assumptions of Heidegger's critics than on any close engagements with the arguments or ideas advanced in essays like 'Building Dwelling Thinking'. But Heidegger has always been a complex and demanding thinker, whose work is also spread over many different writings, and the very fact that his work also contests many conventional ways of thinking means that he is all the more prone to being misread. Perhaps more important is the fact that many of the problematic ideas that are often attributed to Heidegger are ideas that he himself argues against – and often in powerful and insightful ways. Essays like 'Building Dwelling Thinking' and 'The Principle of Identity' contain critiques of the very ideas of authenticity and essentialism, and even of certain readings of dwelling, that are so prominent in the criticism of Heidegger by writers like Sharr.

In the chapters that follow, many of the underlying issues that have appeared in the discussion here will be more directly taken up in relation to specific topics. But the position that has been reached and, in particular, the contrast between a topological approach, which takes place as being central, and a spatial approach, which largely abjures place, is crucial to understanding both Heidegger's account of 'dwelling', including the critiques of it, and the broader approach to the architectural that can be said to follow from Heidegger's thinking. Rethinking dwelling means not only looking again at the account Heidegger offers in 'Building Dwelling Thinking', but also exploring the way a rethought understanding of dwelling, which really means a re-thought understanding of place – and so, too, of space, relationality, identity and other such key notions – plays out in relation to issues in contemporary architecture. That is what is undertaken in Part II. The issues that have been dealt with already will all be relevant to that task, even if they will sometimes remain in the background.

Part II

ARCHITECTURE AS TOPOLOGICAL PRACTICE

Chapter 4

DESIGN AND THE HUMAN

At the same time as 'Building Dwelling Thinking' was starting to be read in English-language circles, Heidegger's essay apparently caught the attention – 'to an unusual degree' according to Heidegger's friend the art historian Heinrich Petzet – of the Finnish architect, Alvar Aalto, undoubtedly one of the great figures of twentieth-century modernism. As Petzet tells it:

> On Aalto's writing desk, friends noticed the volume containing the text of this lecture and reported this back to Freiburg. When I was coming back from Finland, I ran into some young Finnish architects who were likewise talking about that lecture. When soon thereafter I reported this to Heidegger, he was very pleased; and he gave me the assignment of taking his greetings to Aalto when I repeated the trip as planned the following year. But the death of the great architect kept me from making a connection between the two men, which I would have only too happily have done.[1]

There is, however, something a little strange about Petzet's remark here. The incident can be dated to 1975 or 1976, since Aalto died on 11 May 1976. But Heidegger also died in 1976 – on 26 May. Even had Aalto lived, the additional two weeks would hardly have provided Petzet with much more of an opportunity to make the connection to Aalto. Did Petzet misremember the incident or perhaps the timing of it? Petzet's account is also tantalizingly brief. He offers no more detail than is given in this one passage, and there seem to be no other sources, from Heidegger's side or Aalto's, that offer any additional corroboration or elucidation.[2] Thus nothing is known of the extent of Heidegger's knowledge of Aalto, or of Aalto's of Heidegger. It is not even clear what weight should really be attached to the presence of that volume on Aalto's desk.

Nevertheless, the main point of the anecdote – namely, that the philosopher and the architect might each have had an interest in and even respect for the work of the other – is in accord with a widespread understanding that associates both with a similar mode of architectural and design thinking that is phenomenologically attentive and situationally responsive, and one that takes, as a central focus, the relation between human being and its environmental context. Yet for all that it is commonplace to assume such convergence, there is little in the existing literature, by way of any direct and detailed investigation, of that in which such convergence might be said to consist. And often, when Heidegger and Aalto are spoken of together, it is as part of a much broader treatment,[3] rather than in terms of a more direct focus on the work of each in relation to the other. Why might Heidegger have thought Aalto's work to have any special significance in relation to his philosophy? And what might such a seminal figure as Aalto have seen in Heidegger's work that could have made it relevant to his own thought and practice as an architect, and especially to his work as it involved architectural design?

Dwelling, home and design

'Building Dwelling Thinking' does not, as has already been noted, aim to advance anything like a 'theory' of architecture, nor does it directly address the issue of design. The standard English translation of the essay might suggest otherwise, however, at least in relation to one brief passage towards the end of the essay, where Heidegger employs the term *Entwurf*, which, in German, can mean 'design' or 'draft'. The passage reads:

> Building ... is a distinctive letting-dwell [*Wohnenlassen*]. Whenever *it is* such in fact, building already *has* responded to the summons of the fourfold. All planning [*Planen*] remains grounded on this responding, and planning in turn opens up to the designer the precincts suitable for his designs [*den Entwürfen für die Risse die gemäßen Bezirke öffnet*].[4]

The difficulty with this translation is that *Entwurf* (of which *Entwürfen* is the plural) also means 'project' or 'projection' as that refers to an anticipatory 'throwing forward' of a particular way in which things are or might be.[5] Moreover, the reference to 'the designer' that appears in the translation is not present in the original German – in fact, Heidegger seems not to be referring specifically to architectural design here, but to any form of 'design' where that is understood as just the advancing, in anticipatory and guiding fashion, of a particular form of activity, in other words, of building, in the broad sense. For that reason, the crucial last sentence of the passage is probably more closely rendered (though still somewhat awkwardly) as follows: 'All planning remains founded on this responding [to the fourfold], and in its own turn [planning] opens up the domain appropriate to what is projected.' Yet although there is no reference to 'design' here, in the sense that is so common in contemporary architectural circles, still there is a broad notion of 'design' that clearly is at issue in the idea of planning and 'projection' (in the sense indicated above), and that properly belongs to building. Significantly, in Heidegger's early thinking, the idea of what might generally be termed "projection" is much more important than in the later. In *Being and Time*, for instance, it is through Dasein's projection of possibilities that the world is opened up. The later thinking gives priority, as this passage from 'Building Dwelling Thinking' demonstrates, to *responding* over *projecting* – and this emphasis on responding and responsiveness is, as was noted in the discussion in earlier chapters, a central theme in that essay and throughout Heidegger's later work. Yet regardless of whether the passage is taken to be specifically about design, or about a more general notion of planning or projecting the key point is that such activity is not simply a matter of the opening-up of a space that belongs only to that activity nor is it achieved by that activity alone. Instead, the space of design, of plan and of project is opened up in the original responsiveness that is involved in dwelling and in letting-dwell – which is to say, through an original responsiveness to the character of human life and being as always placed, always standing in relation to home, and so also through a responsiveness to place as such.

The way place, home and dwelling appear as connected issues here, and as related to the issue of design, is not only important because of the light it might shed on Heidegger's account of dwelling, but also because it is quite clear that these issues, and their interconnection, are also of concern to Aalto – although this is most often expressed, not surprisingly, through a more particular focus on residential construction and design as that arises architecturally.[6] The concern with residential design is, of course, something central to all architecture, but especially so in the work of many modernist architects. This is partly a reflection of the urgent need to address issues of mass housing in the wake of the destruction following the Second World War – the very context in which Heidegger's lecture was presented – and also as a response to the rapid pace of industrialization and urbanism from the nineteenth century onwards (Le Corbusier's longstanding interest in residential design, evident well before 1945, being one example). However, it also reflects the idea of architectural modernism as itself constituted around a revisioning of the nature and possibilities of human life (something evident in Le Corbusier's much-quoted characterization of the house as a 'machine for living in'[7]). This is especially true in Aalto's case for whom residential design (including, significantly, *interior* design) is indeed a focal point for a larger question about design as it relates to human life and existence.

The turn to residential design does not imply a turn to a narrow concern with home only as instantiated in a specific built form – with the house as residence or *dwelling* (to use the term in its most common English form). Certainly, from the perspective already set out above, the problem of home, and of dwelling, is not only a problem concerning the design of houses. When Heidegger says that the truck driver is at home on the highway, but does not make it his home, Heidegger is not suggesting that the only concern should be with residential dwellings as opposed to highways, and that only the latter has any relevance to the form of human living in the world. Both are encompassed by Heidegger's notion of what it is to build, and so also by what it is to dwell. Heidegger's concern is to emphasize the way in which the 'being at home' that may seem to be immediately evident in one's ordinary coming and goings, one's ordinary activities, is not the same as the 'being at home' that provides the ordering of one's mode of living as such – the sort of 'being at home' that is at issue in dwelling, and that was the focus of discussion in Part I. Moreover, although one can distinguish between the individual places and regions within and with respect to which one's life is articulated and also between the places in which one lives and those with which one is merely familiar, one's dwelling, and even one's sense of home, is not restricted to, or expressed in, only those places that belong to the realm of the intimate, the personal or the familial. The question of dwelling, of the manner in which one finds oneself at home, is raised also by forms of building and design beyond the privacy of the residential, and can therefore be seen as extending out to encompass more public forms of building and design – including highways, power stations and spinning mills.

Although the question of home may arise through an initial concern with the home as residence, it does not end there, but instead leads on to a more encompassing concern with the ways in which human living is given form across the entire range of human activities. In Aalto's case, this means that the question of living – of home – should not be seen as a question relevant only to his residential projects; Aalto's thinking about design and its relation to the human encompasses hospitals, libraries, schools and concert halls, as well as larger built configurations, from the housing complex to the city, no less than it does individual dwellings. The breadth of his interest here is evident in his emphasis on the importance of attending to the human and the 'humanistic' as expressed in quite general terms – and even as expressed from within the frame of architectural modernism. Thus, he writes that 'true architecture exists only where man stands in the centre. His tragedy and his comedy, both.'[8] Elsewhere, he observes that architecture is that which 'most closely strives to realize a true humanism in our world, to create the very limited happiness one can offer man.'[9]

'Humanism', functionalism and relationality

Aalto's willingness to talk of 'humanism' might seem to be at odds with what is commonly assumed to be Heidegger's rejection of the same in his famous 'Letter on "Humanism"', from 1946. However, Heidegger's critique is specifically directed at humanism in its *metaphysical* and so, for Heidegger, also its *nihilistic* form.[10] Heidegger leaves open the possibility that his position can be seen as embodying a more fundamental and radically different mode of humanism, one that more properly attends to the essential character of the human (which means, in Heidegger's case, to its essential finitude). Similarly, for Aalto, 'humanism' implies an attentiveness to the actual character of human living and to a mode of architecture that is similarly attentive and attuned. This does not mean, of course, that it is exclusively concerned with the human alone, or, to reiterate a point made earlier, that the focus on the human is meant to rule out a concern with what might ordinarily be thought of as going beyond the human. Just as Heidegger's notion of the fourfold encompasses earth, sky and divinities, as well as mortals, so, too, Aalto understands nature, in all its forms, as that to which the human stands in an essential relation, and as having a value and significance that go beyond mere utility or instrumentality. Aalto's attentiveness to the human also means thinking of architecture, not in purely aesthetic terms, nor in terms of formal or technical considerations alone, but rather through what he terms its 'functional' character. Function, as used here, however, is not to be understood in some narrow sense – the way a floor plan is set out or the extent to which a building serves certain designated activities associated with it. Instead it relates to the larger structure of human living in the world.

In this respect, Aalto's conception of 'function' is not to be construed in the manner that was common among many of his contemporaries. Aalto undoubtedly shared, especially early on, some of the 'functionalist' concerns that underpinned the work of Le Corbusier, Mies van der Rohe and Walter Gropius (to name the three other great European modernists[11]) but, for Aalto, those concerns came to be embedded in a much broader and encompassing conception. As Aalto wrote in 1940:

> During the past decade, modern architecture has been functional mainly from the technical point of view … But, since architecture covers the entire field of human life, real functional architecture must be functional from the human point of view. If we look deeper into the processes of human life, we shall discover that technique is only an aid, not a definite and independent phenomenon therein.[12]

It is worth noting that the functional conception at work here implies not only a conception of architectural *design* as constrained by a set of both holistic and relational considerations (functionalism is a form of relationalism, and in this context, where there is not one function but a unitary complex, it must also be understood as holistic) that goes beyond the built form alone, but also a conception of the human that is similarly holistic and relational.

Why should the building be ordered in functional terms? By Aalto's account, because the mode of human living is itself functionally, that is holistically and relationally, ordered – a mode of ordering that is also exemplified in the natural realm where it is associated with a multiplication of form:

> Nature, biology, is formally rich and luxuriant. It can with the same structure, the same intermeshing, and the same principles in its cells' inner structure, achieve a billion combinations, each of which represents a high level of form. Man's life belongs to the same family. The things surrounding him are hardly fetishes and allegories with mystical eternal value. They are rather cells and tissues, living beings also, building elements of which human life is put together. They cannot be treated differently from biology's other elements or otherwise they run the risk of not fitting into the system; they become inhumane.[13]

Implicit in Aalto's approach is a conception of human living – of dwelling – as expressed and articulated in spatialized, materialized and also built forms.[14] Thus Aalto writes, in a discussion of art and technology, that 'the most important thing is always how the whole community is formed, what we make with our own hands of the material through which our lives are finally to be channelled'.[15] Such an idea might seem obvious from an architectural perspective such as Aalto's – but the point is also at the heart of Heidegger's focus on the connection between building and dwelling, and, with them, space and place, as developed in 'Building Dwelling Thinking'.

The functional approach to architecture, seen in Aalto's work, bears comparison with a similarly functional conception that is present in Heidegger's analysis of the Black Forest farmhouse in 'Building Dwelling Thinking'. There, the different aspects of human living in the world are seen reflected within the building – the ordering of the building thus gives a material form to the ordering of life and world as it is also part of that same ordering. This encompasses the way the house is sited ('on the wind-sheltered mountain slope looking south, among the meadows close to the spring'), the way its external form is structured to meet the challenge of the elements ('the wide overhanging shingle roof whose proper slope bears up under the burden of snow and ... shields the chambers against the storms of the long winter nights'), and the way the internal arrangement of the building accommodates the different stages and activities of human life ('It did not forget the altar corner behind the community table; it made room ... for the hallowed places of childhood and the "tree of the dead" ... and in this way it designed for the different generations under one roof the character of their journey through time').[16] If Heidegger does not present us with a critique of the social arrangements that are themselves encoded within this building (he does not acknowledge, as is often pointed out, its patriarchal character – something of which, with respect to older building forms, Aalto was well-aware[17]), then one reason is simply that this is not germane to the point of the example.

What Heidegger aims to show by reference to the Black Forest farmhouse is the manner in which the form of the building is grounded in the form of dwelling or living – and so, too, of course, the way the form of dwelling or living, in its own turn, is embodied, materially and spatially, in built form. Consequently, Heidegger says of his use of this example, as noted earlier, that it 'in no way means that we should go back to building such houses; rather it illustrates by a dwelling that *has been* how it was able to build'.[18] That the farmhouse illustrates this so clearly is partly because the built form, evident here, is so directly derivative of a specific mode of living in the world, of a specific mode of 'home'. It is also a mode of living in which the home itself encompasses almost all of the activities relevant to that mode of living, since the homeplace is also the primary workplace and is situated at the heart of the larger landscape that supports that living. Indeed, the same is true of many other vernacular, and also 'indigenous', built forms – in each, the same direct relation is discernible between building and living. It is not that this relation does not exist in 'modern' forms of building (there is an increasing turn to accommodate combined live/work arrangements whether for small businesses and entrepreneurs or 'work-at-home' employees), but that the relation is often more complex, more mediated, and therefore less easy to discern and to delineate.

Aalto is also concerned, as Heidegger is not, with the direct investigation of the functionality of particular built forms – something that Aalto views as possible, not only through scientific inquiry into the biological and other constraints on human being, but also through architectural experimentation. In this regard, one of the examples to which Aalto frequently refers is his design for the Paimo Tuberculosis

Sanatorium. The considerations at work in this case involved, as Aalto describes it: 'the relation between the single human being and his living room ... [and] the protection of the single human being against larger groups of people and the protection from collectivity'.[19] A similar experimental mode of inquiry, though one less constrained, is exemplified in Aalto's design of the explicitly designated 'experimental house' at Muuratsalo on Lake Paijanne (see Figure 4.1). Here Aalto emphasizes the role of play in architectural design, although, since he also warns

Figure 4.1 Muuratsalo Experimental House 1952–4. Patio. Photo: Eino Makinen, © Alvar Aalto Museum. Approximately 1953.

that a reliance on play alone would be to treat architecture as if it were a 'game' played 'with form, structure and content, and finally, with people's bodies and souls', he insists that 'we should unite our experimental work with a play mentality and vice versa'.[20] He goes on: 'Not until architecture's structural elements ... and our empirical knowledge are modified by what we seriously call play, or art, will we be proceeding in the right direction. Technology and economy must always be combined with life-enriching charm.'[21] The Muuratsalo house thus combines a series of experiments that relate to matters of construction, spatial sequencing and siting, as well as to internal plan and functional arrangement, set against a proximity to nature that is both a source of inspiration and relationally encompassed within the building itself. It is significant that Aalto views his experimental investigations as always tempered by a spirit of artistic playfulness, and this is indicative of the extent to which even his experimental inquiries do not take his thinking completely away from a proximity to Heidegger's more philosophical concerns. Indeed, even when concerned with the 'scientific' or experimental investigation of the 'functionality' of the built, Aalto retains a focus on the larger and more encompassing questions that also preoccupy Heidegger – questions concerning what Aalto refers to in terms of the human 'soul' – although always approached, in Aalto's case, from the specific mode of engagement of architectural design.

In this latter respect, the holistic or organicist elements that are evident in Aalto's *reflective* engagement with architecture and design, and that underpin his concept of functionalism, are equally evident in his practice, including his experimental practice, and in the built forms of his designs. Not only does he make use of certain patterns and forms from nature – including the curved form of the famous Aalto wave (in Finnish, *aalto* means 'wave') – but his buildings also exemplify modes of organizational and structural unity that depend, as in nature, on the interplay between otherwise independent and sometimes counter-posed elements. The result is a dynamic view of design that rejects any idea of a single uniform conception to which all else must rigidly conform.[22] This view of both the human and the architectural as having a relational, holistic or 'organic' character undoubtedly derives in part from Aalto's early interest in vitalist philosophy, especially the work of Bergson, as well as his acquaintance with elements of anarchist thinking, particularly ideas deriving from the life and work of Pyotr Kropotkin (a thinker perhaps best known for his emphasis on mutuality as a key element in social and political life).[23] It is also partly derivative of Aalto's artistic interests, as evident in his own endeavours in painting and sculpture, as well as in his engagement with art and artists more generally, not only within Finland, but also with contemporary figures such as Léger (with whom he shared a friendship), and figures from the history of art, of whom the most important is undoubtedly Cézanne.[24]

Space, place and things

The role of art in Aalto's design thought and practice is particularly noteworthy[25] – all the more so when one considers this in relation to Heidegger. Petzet and others have drawn attention to Heidegger's interest in art, especially painting (also of particular importance to Aalto), and Heidegger, like Aalto, had a special regard for, and interest in, Cézanne – 'if only one could think', said Heidegger, 'as directly as Cézanne painted'.[26] Göran Schildt argues that in Aalto's case, Cézanne is especially influential in Aalto's understanding of architectural space. Schildt writes:

> If we look at a painting by Cézanne […] we see how the space grows directly out of the forms placed on the canvas; individual elements with volume spread out towards the sides from an intensely modulated central zone. There is no abstract space here, merely concrete relations between forms and volumes, surfaces forming partly overlapping solids, creating an impression of space which is neither uniform nor unambiguously coherent.[27]

As Schildt sees it, Cézanne also showed Aalto that architectural space, especially interior space, could be treated in a similar fashion, enabling the opening up of space within a building in a way that allows both its openness and boundedness, and the indeterminacy that belongs with both, to be present at one and the same time.[28] Space thus appears as itself dynamic (and so as already entwined with time) – and, if perhaps less obviously, it also appears in direct relation to place: 'Spaces receive their being from places', Heidegger reminds us,[29] which is to say that the openness that belongs to space (its character as 'room' – *Raum* in German, *Rum* in the Swedish that was familiar to Aalto) only appears within the boundedness of place (space can thus be understood, in its primary sense, as the openness of place).

Obviously, these ideas are not exclusively accessible via Cézanne, but the point here is that Cézanne is an important, if not the primary, route by which they were accessed by Aalto – and it is likely that Heidegger too saw Cézanne as offering an important source or exemplification of those ideas. One might add that Cézanne also shows that what painting achieves is done not by beginning with the attempt to recreate a realistic representation, but rather by attending to the complexity of things in their placed, and so spatialized, appearance[30] – thus Schildt comments that 'Cézanne showed how to paint pictures without starting from stereometric abstractions'.[31] In Cézanne, especially in his late painting, this means that things appear as things, not through being present as clearly defined 'objects' – nor as mere 'views', or visual 'representations' – but rather through their partial dissolution into bounded relations of surface, colour and form – invoking, as they also extend into, the larger horizonality in which they are placed and that grounds their appearing.[32] What Cézanne demonstrates and exemplifies is also evident, though articulated conceptually rather than concretely, in Heidegger's treatment of the thing as it stands within the gathered relationality of the fourfold, which he sets outs not only in 'Building Dwelling Thinking' but also elsewhere, and especially in 'The Thing'.[33] Here, the thing is understood as standing in an essential relation to space, and so also to place. Space and place, in their own turn, stand in relation to the thing, and so to the larger structure that Heidegger understands in terms of the fourfold, and that appears more ambiguously and variously in Aalto in terms of the ideal of the harmonious unity of the human, and of the human with nature.

While more general notions of holism and organicism undoubtedly bring with them ideas of relationality and unitary complexity of the sort that are present in Aalto, and to some extent in Heidegger also, taken on their own, such notions can also lead away from a focus on the concrete and the immediate, away from things, away from the human (which is why they are sometimes taken to be associated with forms of political authoritarianism). Cézanne's work demonstrates how such relationality and unitary complexity is itself articulated in and through the concrete spatiality and placed-ness of things. Only by attending to things, in their indeterminate and multiple unity, can humankind attend to the larger unity of the world, and its human mode of living.

The focus on the thing, which must now be understood as also entailing a focus on complex structure of space and place, is evidenced by Aalto's work in several ways. It is surely connected with his close attention to materiality and to the sensory and experiential qualities of building. Not only does this mean that Aalto is not seduced by the idea of architecture as some form of 'textual' or discursive practice, but it also means that he is especially attentive to the potential for materials to themselves function in ways that, through their materiality, and the sensory complexity that brings, to draw other elements into relation with them. The combination of material and formal elements is thus understood, not only in terms of their functionality in technical terms, but also in terms of a sensory and experiential richness that plays a role in the spatial and topological functioning of a built form. This is especially evident in the house that Aalto built for his friends, Harry and Maire Gullichsen, the Villa Mairea (see Figure 4.2) – a building that exhibits a complex interplay of elements, both within the formal and material elements of its construction and in its sensory, experiential and affective character.[34]

Aalto's focus on spatialized form in its concrete complexity is also evident in the character of his practice. Schildt comments that, when Aalto began a new building, 'he would not start by drawing the floor plan or elevation, but by looking at it as an object in space and depicting it as a reality'.[35] Of course, this 'looking at' is inseparable from the *sketch* and *the act of sketching* – from that specific form of drawing that explores the reality of the thing through the vitality of the drawn line. Here, a sense of the spatiality that is at work in such a superlative way in Cézanne can also be discerned in the sketches by which Aalto's own practice was advanced – sketches that also demonstrate something of the essentially spatial character of the engagement with things that is integral to design practice as such. The spatialized character of Aalto's practice in architecture and design also seems to be reflected in Heidegger's philosophical practice – certainly as exemplified in essays such as 'Building Dwelling Thinking'. What appears there is a thinking that, no matter its density, nevertheless operates, not only through an attempt to stay close to things, and so to respond to the circumstances of thought, but also by means of an active *visualizing* and *imagining*. A thinking that engages, not merely with ideas in their abstraction, but rather with a ideational field articulated in terms of concrete figures and experienced forms – the fourfold, and its gathering of earth, sky, mortals and divinities, being a particularly clear example.

Figure 4.2 Villa Mairea, Alva Aalto, 1938–9. Living room windows and main entrance. Photo: Martti Kapanen, © Alvar Aalto Museum. 1980.

In Heidegger and in Aalto, the understanding of things in their located and spatialized concreteness, in their indeterminacy and complexity, can be seen to connect directly with the two thinkers' common concern with the human and, with that, the human mode of living in the world to which the idea of home refers us. To reiterate a point already made, that concern does not depend on a prior and substantive definition of the human, nor does it imply some notion of human superiority or excellence. It consists in a much simpler and more fundamental point; namely, that it is out of human being in the world, and only thus, that the need for building comes, and that building, both in its generality and in its specific architectural form, arises as an issue. It is only thus that there is even a question about what it is to dwell or to live in the world, about what it is to find a sense of home. Moreover, the way the human appears here is inextricably bound to place and therefore to bound or limit, *and it is here that the proper limit of design itself appears*. The limit of design is given in and through its human character, which is to say, its *placed* character, and in design as a responsiveness and attentiveness to that placed-ness.

Neither for Heidegger nor for Aalto can the question of what it is to dwell, or to live in the world – which is the question of home – be resolved by reference to any single overarching frame. That question can only take its bearings, can only appear as a question, from within the place and space in which it is opened.

The question of home, of living, of dwelling and so of building is thus always and only a question that arises within a singular horizon, with respect to a concrete situatedness, in and through the unitary multiplicity of what is given *here*, within these *bounds*, in this *place*. In this way, too, the question of the possibility of the human, of a human mode of living, is indeed seen to be a question inseparable from the question concerning the *being* of things – a being that is no less material than it is 'ideal' such that one might say that its ideality is given in its materiality – for it is only in and through the engagement with the concrete and the material that human living is shaped in its own *being*. The question of the human, of living and of home, and the question of things, of building and so, too, of architecture and of any and all forms of design, thus arise together, within the same, though complex and expansive, place.

It may be that, in dwelling and building, the aim is, as Aalto says of architecture, to create a certain paradise (thereby seeming, perhaps, to step into that domain against which Sternberger warned in his Darmstadt comments), but any such paradise remains always an aim and never an achievement. As Aalto recognizes, it is a 'very *limited* happiness' that architecture, and so also building, offers. It is thus that, in Aalto's work, and increasingly so towards the end of his career, a key task of architectural practice is to strive against what Aalto saw as the 'dehumanizing' effects of technology and rationalization – an idea often expressed in terms of his injunction to 'protect the little man',[36] as well as in his ever-present concern to maintain a role for art in architecture, and in design more broadly, where art goes beyond any mere aesthetic concern and moves us into the wider sphere of the interconnectedness of things, of nature, of the human and of the world. In fact, the younger Aalto expressed something of what is at issue here in a comment on the character of the built form of the home. 'If you want my blessing on your home', he writes, 'it must have one further characteristic: you must give yourself away in some little detail. Your home should purposefully show up some weakness of yours', and he adds 'no architectural creation is complete without some such trait; it will not be alive'.[37]

Thinking and design

Despite Heidegger's own reluctance to make specific claims about architecture or about design, his thinking is not without implications for those domains, and has the potential to open out to an account that in many respects converges, as Heidegger himself seems to have thought (if Petzet's report is correct) with that of such a key practitioner as Aalto. On the basis of Heidegger's account, one can view design as operating within a domain opened for it out of the active engagement in the world that is building, and as standing in a close relation to the mode of living in the world. Design is predicated, and indeed arises out of, that more fundamental mode of orientation. The question is whether this is something to which humankind attends – either in terms of attending to the larger context in which a particular design task is situated, or to the broader dependence of design that is also at issue here. Attending to that dependence means adopting a different attitude to design – one that sees design as responding to the task of building and of living as that takes on a singular and concrete form.

The measure of design cannot be simply an aesthetic or technical one. It cannot, as Aalto so often emphasized, be one of mere economy. The only real measure comes, in the terms Aalto uses, from 'the general attitude towards life',[38] from the mode of living within which any specific design is embedded. In this respect, design in general must be understood, as Karsten Harries has argued, to have a fundamentally 'ethical' function[39] (something further explored in the Epilogue). This is all the more so if proper attention is given to the idea of the ethical as concerned with the realm of human action as it shapes human living, with human action as always standing within a certain *ethos* (and so also a certain bounded place or *topos*). Such an ethical emphasis is evident in Heidegger, even if it is not named as such,[40] and is explicit in Aalto, as he writes: 'The architect's task is to restore a correct order of values.'[41]

Much contemporary architecture, and especially the broader field of design practice, operates in a way that seems divorced from such ethical concerns – divorced, that is, from the concern with human living that preoccupied Heidegger and Aalto. This is evident, although it may sometimes seem otherwise, even in the recent fashion for so-called 'design thinking'. On the face of it, such thinking may seem to exhibit many of the features that are suggested by Aalto and Heidegger's accounts of building and design practice (the emphasis, for instance, on what are often referred to as 'non-linear' forms of thinking, and on the need to address multiple considerations at one and the same time).[42] Given the contemporary rhetoric around the notion, perhaps one could even be led to suppose that design thinking moves in the direction of the thinking that figures as the third element in Heidegger's 'Building Dwelling Thinking'.

Yet it is worth taking a closer look here. While the idea of design thinking undoubtedly encompasses many different things (and there are forms of design thinking that may be thought close to the view of design found in Aalto and Heidegger), there is also a sense in which what it refers to is a mode of practice that is firmly embedded within contemporary forms of economic and political organization (in this sense, the idea has almost taken on the status of a design 'product' in its own right), and thereby often serves exactly the forms of technological and rationalistic ordering that Heidegger and Aalto find so threatening.[43] It is a form of thinking that typically understands itself as a means for the more effective solution of already given 'problems' – even if complex (or 'wicked'[44]) in character – rather than of attending to the larger place, its openness and its bounds, in which such thinking arises. In this respect, one might ask to what extent some of the celebrated exemplars of current design and 'design thinking' match up to the conception of design found in Heidegger and Aalto.

Moreover, whereas the phrase 'design thinking' may suggest that it is *design* that leads thinking, in fact, as Heidegger would urge, it can only be *thinking* that leads design – that grounds design, that opens up the proper domain of its activity (which is to say that design, properly understood, is itself embedded in thinking, may even be understood as itself the expression of a fundamental mode of thinking). The thinking at issue here, however, is a thinking that itself stands in direct relation to human living, and so also to the placed mode of being in the world to which Heidegger's thinking can be seen to direct us. Only on that basis is it possible to think design, and only on that basis can design, through its role in relation to human building, contribute to thinking. On this basis, one can well imagine, as Petzet seems to suggest, that Heidegger and Aalto might have come together in a fruitful meeting – if only such a possibility had not itself been cut off by the limit to which their own lives were brought in such coincidental fashion.

Chapter 5

ARCHITECTURE AND TRUTH

What does it mean to talk of 'truth' in relation to a building, or to a design? The question is not an uncommon one in architectural contexts,[1] and briefly appeared in Part I in relation to the issue of authenticity in architecture. The latter notion is often invoked in discussions of Heidegger, even though it has a problematic role in such discussions – 'authenticity', as it is usually understood in English, is not an idea that can be applied without qualification to Heidegger's thinking whether early or late. The treatment of truth in architectural contexts often draws on ideas of authenticity, but not only on that, and it also connects with issues concerning how architecture itself is to be understood, in what form it might be practiced, and how buildings themselves might function. Significantly, Heidegger's thinking of truth is developed in ways that have architectural relevance through the way they engage with space and the topological. But before coming to truth as is taken up in Heidegger, there are two other more familiar senses of truth that are at work in architectural discourse: truth as tied to *assertion* and as tied to *appearance*.

Meaning, truth and assertion

The most familiar and seemingly straightforward sense of truth takes it to be essentially a property of statements or claims (or derivative of this, of beliefs). Since statements or claims are given in the form of sentences, truth also belongs to sentences, or more specifically, to assertoric sentences, or more simply, to assertions (which is another way of referring to the idea of a statement or claim). For a sentence to be true is for the world to be as the sentence says it is – and so truth appears as a matter of correctness or, it might be said, of correct representation (since a sentence is a form of representation). Depending on how it is developed, the idea of truth as representational correctness can be relatively anodyne, but it can also be quite problematic.

Philosophers argue as to what more can be said about truth: whether, for instance, the relation of correctness can be clarified by reference to any more basic concept, with the usual candidate being some notion of *correspondence* (suggested by the idea of correct representation); whether anything else might be an indicator of correctness or a surrogate for it, where appeal is often made to *coherence*; or whether truth as a substantive notion, beyond some *pragmatic* or *disquotational* sense, should simply be given up on altogether.[2] However, there is good reason to suppose that, no matter what else is said about truth, some sense of truth as correctness cannot be abandoned. It is certainly the sense of truth that appears in most everyday contexts. It also seems to be at work in Aristotle's well-known characterization that, 'to say of what is that it is not, or of what is not that it is, is false, while to say of what is that it is, and of what is not that it is not, is true',[3] as well as being what is expressed in the commonplace idea of truth as just a matter of 'telling it like it is' (the difficulty is when one tries to develop such ways of speaking into a fully fledged 'theory' of truth). Even Heidegger, who is critical of the idea of truth as nothing more than correctness (as well as of truth as belonging primarily to sentences or assertions), nevertheless accepts, like several other key thinkers on this matter, that the sense of truth as correctness is where one must begin in trying to think about truth. Accepting, then, that *one* sense of truth is indeed of truth as a matter of correctness and as attached to assertions, then there is an immediate problem in making sense of truth in many architectural contexts, since how can a building, or an architectural design, be 'correct' – or, more specifically, how can the notion of correctness of assertion or of representation be applied to a building or a design?

If this sense of truth is indeed to be applicable to architecture, then one must make sense of the idea of a building or design having some assertoric content – of making some statement or claim. Sometimes, of course, buildings do include statements – they may appear as features of a façade or a portico, chiselled into stone, painted onto wood, or in the form of signs or placards themselves fixed to some feature of the construction. For the most part, such explicit forms of statement are not integral to the design of a building, although modern advertising is such that one might be led to think that at least some buildings are less important than the messages they carry. There are some interesting questions that might be pursued concerning the role of advertising in building, or indeed, of the role of building in advertising, as well as in commoditization and consumption.[4] Yet it is not so much the appearance of statements *on* buildings that is at issue, but rather the idea of the building as itself, in some sense, assertoric or declarative.

It is worth clarifying what this might involve, because it is easy to misunderstand the way in which the assertoric or declarative may be at work here – and so to misunderstand the way truth could be at issue. Strictly speaking, even though a statement may have the form of a declaration or assertion, that it is a declaration or assertion is for it to be asserted or declared. Statement and assertion are *uses* of language rather than being simple features of sentences apart from use. This is especially evident when one considers the possibility of the lie – to lie is to make an assertion, knowing it to be false, but presenting it as true. Strictly speaking, the sentence at issue does not engage in the lie (although it is common to talk as if it did), instead the speaker does. The same would be true of buildings, supposing that they could indeed carry some declarative or assertoric content. Making or seeming to make a claim to truth depends on being located within some discursive practice. This is a small point of clarification, and often it does not make a huge difference to the discussion. But it is a clarification worth keeping in mind, since it indicates the extent to which the truth claim, in the case of the building no less than the sentence, only arises in a larger context of discourse – which means in a context in which claims to truth can be made, considered and even contested. Neither buildings nor sentences engage, in a strict sense, in any such discourse, or, at least, they do not do so apart from 'speakers' and communities of 'speech' (here 'speech' includes the written, spoken and signed, not merely oral communication alone, and 'speaker' has a similar breadth).[5] The upshot, of course, is that buildings say nothing, and that, strictly speaking, is true. The same is also true, however, of marks on paper, and sounds in the air, and movements of the body. These things take on meaning – become speech – only in certain contexts, and for the most part, only in the context of language.

'Meaning' and 'content' are often used quite broadly, however, and in ways that result in both terms appearing across many different contexts and with a high level of generality. When 'meaning' is treated as identical with 'information', for instance (as it frequently is), then, since any state can be treated as an informational state, so every state will be a meaningful state. When 'content' is just a matter of differential behavioural response (so that a different presentation provokes a different behaviour), then there will be 'content' wherever there is behaviour (and then, one can ask, what is to count as 'behaviour'?). Although one might treat buildings as having meaning or content in either of these senses, such construals are so broad as to be unlikely to be especially meaningful or contentful in themselves. Of course, buildings are often treated as having *symbolic* content as a result of their belonging within larger systems of images or symbols – the Gothic cathedral being an especially salient example – but this does not imply that such content arises independently of a context of discourse, which can be understood, in such a case, as referring to the symbolic system in its socio-cultural, and especially linguistic, context. The same is true of more broadly semiotic approaches that treat buildings as parts of larger systems of meaning production. Moreover, although symbolic and semiotic analyses do not focus directly on the issue of the assertoric or declarative content that may be associated with an object or activity – in this case with buildings or designs – one can still generate such content on the basis of the way the object in question operates within particular contexts and towards certain outcomes or effects, since these are also mediated by or connected with systems of linguistic meaning.[6] Meaning and content arise within larger systems of meaning and content, and those systems invariably involve forms of linguistic articulation that are embedded in the activities of communities of speakers.[7]

The idea that a building or design may be associated with some assertoric or declarative content requires that one be able to associate some meaningful content with the building or design such that the content in question can indeed function assertorically or declaratively – more specifically, that it can take the form of sentences or statements. This means one has to be able to think of the building or design, even if viewed purely spatially or graphically, as being capable of operating as a sort of 'text' or as an instance of 'speech', and so as being able to be used *to say something*. One can still distinguish the question of the truth *of the building* from the truth of ordinary utterances *about buildings*, but one effectively extends the realm of the 'textual', or to some extent the linguistic, so that it encompasses more than just the usual kind of utterances (instances of ordinary speaking, writing and so on). Such 'textuality', as applied to buildings, may seem odd to some, but it connects with a language that is often used of built form in relation to ideas of fabric, weave and textile (as in talk of the 'built fabric' of the city).[8] It also connects directly with what is often taken to be the post-structuralist assertion of the ubiquity of textuality (so that there is nothing that is not textual[9]), and this is certainly involved in many of those instances in which buildings and designs are taken to have a specific assertoric content.

What is central here is not some general claim to the effect that a building *can* be construed in textual terms, or that it *could* be interpreted as connected with some assertoric content (that would be all too easy), but rather that it is already part of such a textual, discursive or assertoric practice, and, perhaps more strongly, that it is indeed intended and consciously read in a way that takes up a specific representational and assertoric content. Certainly, inasmuch as architecture has entered into and become party to what may be thought of as a broader socio-cultural and political discourse, and as making contributions to such discourse, then one might well be inclined to attribute to architecture, that is, to particular architectural constructions or designs, the capacity to make assertions and to therefore make assertions that can also be judged to be true or correct – or as false or incorrect. For the most part, the claims made by buildings in this regard turn out to be rather banal and so are often trivially true, if true at all. The idea that the use of glass in a government building – a notable feature of some of Norman Foster's designs for public buildings (e.g. the Greater London Council Building and the Reichstag Dome) – is an assertion of the 'openness' and 'transparency' of democracy (which might be interpreted either symbolically or declaratively) is one example of an assertion that seems to have become so commonplace as to be almost empty.[10] Indeed exactly what assertion is being made remains unclear – perhaps just 'democracy is about transparency'? Whether the declaration such buildings attempt to make may show something else about the real *opacity* of contemporary democratic claims, since the reflective and refractive properties of glass mean that glass can obscure as much as reveal, is another question. One suspects that if there is indeed more to be seen here, then it is more likely to be an unintended consequence of the materiality of the building in its context, than anything the designer may have explicitly in mind.

The use of glass to make a claim about democratic politics surely involves a rather banal level of assertion. But there are many other examples of seemingly more sophisticated sets of claims that architects take their buildings to express. One of the narratives Daniel Libeskind has offered of his Jewish Museum in Berlin ties it to Walter Benjamin's essay 'One-Way Street',[11] and the building can be construed as containing a complex set of textual elements within it. At the other side of the world, the National Museum of Australia, in Canberra, itself partly indebted to Libeskind's work (or frequently presented in that way), is also supposed to carry a declarative content relating to the history and nature of the country whose museum it is. The building works, so it is claimed, as a set of knotted ropes that pull the various elements of Australia together (and to do so in an almost literal fashion inasmuch as the building contains those elements of Australia within it).[12] It also contains explicit textual elements throughout, including a set of messages in Braille on its walls. The latter are oddly contradictory, since though they are *in* Braille, they cannot be read *as* Braille – the symbols cannot be *touched* – and so must instead be read purely *visually* (after the building was completed, these messages were also seen to be politically contentious, and so were later deliberately garbled by the addition of randomly inserted dots[13]). The use of graphic elements on the exterior surfaces of buildings is a common feature of contemporary design and is often intended (by the designers) to be connected to some assertion, symbolic or metaphoric content that is frequently articulated (or as one might also be tempted to say, 'fabricated') as part of some background narrative or 'story' – a phenomenon discussed further in Chapter 6. Yet typically the content is not evident from the building itself but must be explained independently (the graphic element often appearing as a more or less randomized and extraneous patterning), thereby underscoring the tenuous nature of the connection between the built form and the purported content.[14]

The idea that a building may carry some declarative or assertoric content is particularly evident in much contemporary architectural theory and criticism, and in many architects' own exegeses of their work (sometimes in terms of the often rather facile 'story-telling' noted above, but also in more theoretically sophisticated fashion). Often, as in Libeskind's case, this is part of a conception of architecture as driven by a specific conceptual content, such that the aesthetic quality of the building is itself determined by that content.[15] This seems especially true in much of Peter Eisenman's work, but also in that of Rem Koolhaas. Their works are often meant to convey a set of argumentative claims and forms of contestation expressed in the design or form of the building – challenging the expectations of the users of their buildings at the same time as they also seem to assert the autonomy of the design over and above any claims of functionality or utility, and of architecture as a purely conceptual activity quite apart from any activity of 'making'. Indeed, in the writing about these buildings, one commonly finds claims being made about the assertoric content of the buildings as a whole, or about certain features of those buildings – about, for instance, the connections between spaces, or the role of and nature of elements of architecture itself.

The assertoric content at stake here is typically conveyed in and through the elements of the design as these are given in representational form. Eisenman has commented that 'the "real architecture" only exists in the drawings' (by which he means, presumably, sketches, plans, elevations and sections), and he goes on to assert that, 'if there is a debate in architecture today, the lasting debate is between architecture as a conceptual, cultural and intellectual enterprise, and architecture as a phenomenological enterprise – that is, the experience of the subject in architecture, the experience of materiality, of light, of colour, of spatiality, and so on'.[16] In fact, this emphasis on conceptuality is not, it should be noted, one that stands apart from every form of experiential engagement. If, as Eisenman claims, architecture exists 'in the drawings', more so than the building, this cannot mean that architecture as it exists in that way is thereby disengaged from the experiential or the sensory, but rather that it involves a different mode of engagement than as it does in relation to the building (even if this remains implicit). And although drawing, as representational, is not thereby always visual (as is noted in Chapter 6), Eisenman's talk of drawings does suggest an emphasis on a specific mode of visuality, and this is itself often taken to be part of (both deriving from and contributing to) an emphasis on the conceptual and textual.[17]

The prominence of visuality in architectural thought and practice (which is not restricted to approaches like Eisenman's) is frequently cited, not only as a feature of recent and contemporary architecture, especially Modernist architecture,[18] but also as a problematic feature.[19] Yet, for the most part, if there is a problem here, it is not to be found *in visuality as such,* nor even visuality alone, but rather in the same highly spatialized understanding that was already identified as present in Levinas at the end of Chapter 3. It is this spatialized understanding, an understanding that also tends towards *abstraction*, that is given expression in the emphasis on the conceptual, the textual, the representational, and that is partly evident in the way certain modes of visual representation are taken up in architectural thought and practice (not just the drawing, but more importantly perhaps the photograph – something that critics have identified as a feature even in Norberg-Schulz's work[20]). The abstraction that appears here does not arise primarily or solely as a result of visuality (even though it may be connected to it), but is exactly the abstraction that is achieved through the separating out of space from place.

In contemporary architecture, the tendency towards abstraction can itself be seen to give rise to a certain *aesthetic* turn (although more of the *conceptual* than of the sensory), that itself leads, not only to the treatment of the architectural object in aesthetic terms, but to the assimilation of architecture to the discourse of aesthetic theory. The tendency is not an explicit one, nor is it absolute or universal, and it exists alongside other tendencies that can run counter to it, but it is significant, nonetheless. The general tendency towards such aestheticization, and towards treating architecture as primarily a conceptual and discursive practice that depends on an abstracted mode of the spatial, has become widespread across much of contemporary architectural discourse (and especially across that discourse as it appears in an academic context and so in architectural education). It is no accident that contemporary architects so often talk about the 'proposition' that a building or design may put or the argument it might advance. Architecture has become saturated with 'theory' imported from a wide range of other domains, and there is barely an architectural discussion that does not make reference to some philosophy or philosopher (though most often, nowadays, Gilles Deleuze, or even Peter Sloterdijk, rather than Heidegger). Buildings now seem to have become embedded in dense clouds of narrative and discursive analysis and articulation to such an extent that the sorts of functional concerns identified by Aalto, and that, *pace* Eisenman, remain central to architectural practice across the vast majority of its instances, might easily be treated as of only secondary relevance, if they are relevant at all. At stake here is not merely the relative interest, or lack of interest, in questions of phenomenology, but the very content of architecture and its practice, as well as the aims and purposes that it might properly be said to serve. The question of truth in architecture, which here comes down to the question as to whether truth in architecture is primarily to be understood in terms that tie it to the conceptual, the discursive or the textual – and so to the assertoric or declarative[21] – is thus itself tied up with fundamental questions about the nature of architecture. It is especially significant, therefore, that the sense of truth associated with the conceptual and assertoric is not the only sense.

Truth, appearance and opening

Although truth is commonly talked of in terms of the correctness of statements or claims, truth can also be used in a quite different fashion to refer to things and even persons. When one says of someone that they are a 'true' friend, or that some sample quantity of orange-yellow metal is 'true' gold, a sense of truth is invoked that is other than that of assertoric or representational (or even epistemic) correctness. Instead, the sense of truth at work in such cases is of a certain convergence between how something *appears* and what something *is* so that its appearance *shows* what it is, without dissembling or hiding. It is just this sense of truth that is often referred to as 'authenticity'. The problems associated with certain *strong* notions of authenticity were already discussed in Chapter 3. As it appears here, however, what is at issue is authenticity in the *weak* sense of the term – the sense (discussed by Peter Blundell Jones[22]) in which something does not dissemble or pretend (or is not intended in a way that dissembles or pretends); authenticity as indicating what is 'real' or 'genuine'. And the idea of truth as authenticity, in this latter sense – perhaps better understood as honesty or even 'integrity' – does seem, in fact, to be the way the notion of truth, at least when directly invoked, has most often operated in architectural discourse. Thus, Adrian Forty, for instance, in his *Words and Buildings: A Vocabulary of Modern Architecture*, distinguishes three senses in which truth is used in architecture – truth as expressive (true to essence), as structural (true to structural principles), as historical (true to a time), [23] and all seem to be variations on the same idea of truth as honesty or (weak) authenticity.

It is this sense of truth as honesty that appears in John Ruskin,[24] and a similar notion of truth as honesty can be seen in the association of form with function that developed among American artists and architects in the mid to late nineteenth century – most notably in the work of Horatio Greenough (though also found in Walt Whitman), and later in that of Louis Sullivan, who, in an essay from 1896, declares that 'form ever follows function'.[25] Much the same idea continues (though with some important differences also[26]) in the emphasis on functionality and the rejection of ornamentation that is famously associated, in the first part of the twentieth century, with the work of Adolf Loos (who spent time in the United States in the early 1890s)[27] and the German Bauhaus movement. Interestingly, one can also connect this conception of truth as honesty (which is really an honesty related to an intention in what is shown or appears) to the idea of truth as correctness, since the idea of truth as honesty depends on the idea of a correlation between the appearance and what underlies the appearance that is analogous to the correlation, in the case of correctness, between the representation and that which it represents. The 'honest' building, or the building that is honestly intended, is therefore the one that *looks* as it really *is* – its structural and material character is neither deliberately hidden nor denied. This leaves aside the question as to whether any *specific* claims to honesty in architecture, whether made by such as Ruskin or Loos or anyone else, are indeed honest in the way claimed. There is always the possibility that the claim to honesty conceals its own dissemblance, that is, that it effectively lies (and the fact that the lie always conceals its own character as a lie is part of the very essence of its own dishonesty).

That truth as honesty might have an important role in architecture has widespread acceptance, although it is seldom given any clear justification (aside, that is, from the sorts of more specific arguments that one finds around ideas of ornamentation). So why is honesty so important and what is wrong with the building whose character, or that of its materials and structure, is somehow hidden, a simulation or a fake? Of course, it would be a mistake to assume that there are no legitimate cases in which a building or some aspect of a building may hide its real character or be designed so as to appear other than as it is. The stage set has just this character, and there are some buildings that, although not stage sets in the usual sense, may nevertheless function in a similar fashion – the architectural folly being, perhaps, such an example, the pleasure house, and most obviously the amusement park. Of course, in most such cases, one does not take the buildings at issue necessarily to be 'dishonest', since their character as appearances – as 'artful' presentations – is usually made evident by the larger setting. Similarly, the incorporation of *trompe l'oeil* effects into a building need not be, nor is it always taken to be, a problematic form of deceit. Nevertheless, there is a tendency in some quarters to demand more honesty in a building than is perhaps reasonable or possible – every building contains an element of artifice, operating through the creation of certain effects, and buildings have always to be considered in their contexts. Total honesty (whatever that may mean) in all spheres of speech and action would be an impossible and foolish ideal – what counts as honesty depends on the situation, and in some situations, honesty can be damaging, dangerous or hurtful. Honesty is thus an important presumption of speech and action, but it is not the only or over-riding consideration, and the same is true in architecture.

That honesty is indeed a presumption derives from the fact that widespread dishonesty undermines the very possibility of speech and action. To speak and to act depend on what is said and on the world being more or less the way it appears (even delusional behaviour is possible only because the delusion does not affect *everything* that one says or does). To suppose a situation in which most sentences uttered are false is to suppose a situation in which no meaningful sentences are uttered at all (meaning being closely dependent on truth); to suppose a situation in which most actions are predicated on things being completely other than they are is to suppose a world in which action itself is impossible, *pace* Descartes and the Wachowskis,[28] since even the attempt at action would be other than it appeared. There is a deeper level of reflection at work here that is indicative of the limits to certain forms of philosophical scepticism, solipsism or relativism (reflection that itself leads back to considerations of the placed character of knowledge and experience). But at the more prosaic level of the architectural, what this also indicates is the importance of built forms being consonant with or true to their appearances. This need not hold absolutely, in every case or in all respects, but it must hold in general and for the most part. For the built environment to be such as to appear in ways too much at variance with the real nature of that environment would not only be a violation of some aesthetic ideal, but would also threaten the very possibility of being properly oriented and situated. In fact, the common reaction against dissemblance or simulation in architecture, which is often taken to be based in the *aesthetic*, is much more grounded in the *ethical* and *ontological*.

Within architectural discourse, the sometime appearance of the notion of truth as honesty might be thought to present another instance of the seeming prioritization of visuality that is sometimes taken to be an issue in relation to the emphasis on conceptuality or textuality and so in relation to truth as associated with the assertoric. But even if one were to assume that there is a prioritization of the visual evident in both truth as tied to assertion and truth as tied to appearance, what is at issue in the former is a visuality of *represented* form, whereas in the other it is a visuality of *built* form. The same point applies, in fact, regardless of whether one focuses on visuality or on spatiality. It is this difference between the focus on the represented or the built that is crucial here – quite aside from any question of visuality – important, since even though figures such as Ruskin, Sullivan and even Loos did not disregard the drawing, they would likely not have assented to Eisenman's claim that architecture properly resides in the drawing more so than the building. Indeed, if one focuses on the idea of truth in architecture as a matter of honesty in both materiality and form (so that materials show themselves as what they are and form does indeed relate to function broadly understood), then it is hard to see how one can avoid giving prominence to architecture as it is embodied in the built. This focus on the built, and so on the way architecture operates 'in the round' as it were (which here means as it is given through a range of senses, and therefore as it is given both spatially and topologically), also opens up a path towards an a third sense of truth that goes beyond the idea of truth in terms of either correctness or honesty (although it is connected to the latter). This third sense is of truth as that which *enables* the grasping or appearing of anything as true (or indeed as false). This is a sense of truth as revealing or bringing into the light, or better, as *opening* – an opening that is always also a *placing*.

Truth as opening

What is at issue in this idea of truth as 'opening' is the way in which, prior to any particular instance of assertion that may be true or false, prior to any question concerning the consonance of something as it is intended to appear with the thing as it is, there must already be the opening up of a domain in which that to which the assertion refers, or the thing as implicated by its appearance, is already made available. What must already be given is a domain in which the possibility of questioning is itself enabled and freed up – a domain in which things are brought into a play of relations with other things. That is, of course, just what is at issue in the account of the fourfold at work in 'Building Dwelling Thinking'. Truth is then understood as a form of opening closely aligned with the opening of the world itself. Understood as opening, truth occurs always against a background of what is closed off or concealed, and so, just as it is an opening, truth is also an 'unconcealing', a revealing or dis-closing.

It is just this notion of truth that, as briefly noted earlier, is to be found in Heidegger, in the idea of truth as unconcealment[29] – *aletheia* in the Greek[30] –

Figure 5.1 Aerial view of the Piazza del Campo, Siena. Photo: Stefano Marinari/Shutterstock.

which he understands in relation to the German term *Lichtung*, meaning a 'lighting' or 'clearing'.³¹ What is at issue here is not just the idea of light or illumination, however, but specifically of a lighted or open space – which is to say, an open but bounded region, as exemplified by a clearing in a forest, where the underlying structure is much the same as that which is at work in the open but bounded space of a town square. The Italian *piazza* provides a exemplary instance of this – the term *piazza* itself being the Italian equivalent of the French and English 'place' as it is used to refer to the same urban form³² (see Figure 5.1). *Lichtung* also carries a sense of 'lightening', in the sense of releasing or 'freeing', and this closely relates to the way Heidegger understands being as itself tied to finitude and bound (the opposite of the Levinasian position, as was seen in Chapter 3) – the openness, even the infinity, of being arises only on the basis of the boundedness of place.

Truth itself is thus understood as tied, not just to space, but more fundamentally to place, namely, to the bounded open of the 'here/there'. Truth as revealing or unconcealing is thus essentially topological – an event that is always itself placed. The sense of truth at issue here appears throughout many of Heidegger's writings, but it tends to remain in the background of later essays such as 'Building Dwelling Thinking'. The reason for this is largely that the investigation of truth, in the sense at issue here, occurs on the way towards the more explicit development of the topology that is so evident in Heidegger's later thinking. Thus, if one looks to an essay like 'The Origin of the Work of Art', in which the idea of truth as a fundamental mode of revealing or disclosure is set out in detail, then one finds an account that is reliant on an essentially topological understanding, even though it does not take up that topology in direct fashion.

'The Origin of the Work of Art' nevertheless has a special relevance here, since one of its central examples is a building – a Greek temple (see Figure 5.2):

> A building, a Greek temple, portrays nothing. It simply stands there in the middle of the rock-cleft valley. The building encloses the figure of the god, and in this concealment lets its stand out into the holy precinct through the open portico ... Standing there, the building rests on the rocky ground ... The temple's firm towering makes visible the invisible space of air ... It clears and illuminates, also, that on which and in which man bases his dwelling [*sein Wohnen gründet*]. We call this ground the *earth* ... The temple-work, standing there, opens up a world and at the same time sets this world back again on earth ... The temple, in its standing there, first gives to things their look and to men their outlook on themselves.³³

Heidegger's account of the temple finds an echo in Vincent Scully's famous work on Greek sacred architecture, *The Earth, the Temple, and the Gods*:

> The mountains and valleys of Greece were punctuated during antiquity by hard white forms, touched with bright colors ... These were the temples of the gods ...

the temples were not normally intended to shelter men within their walls. Instead they housed the image of a god, immortal and therefore separate from men, and were themselves an image, in the landscape, of his qualities ... the temples and the subsidiary buildings of their sanctuaries were so formed themselves and so placed in relation to the landscape and to each other as to enhance, develop, complement, and sometimes even to contradict, the basic meaning of what was felt in the land ... But ... in order to act to the full ... [the temple] had to become an embodiment, not merely a construction, or an abstractly perfect shape, or a pictorial element.[34]

Scully's account is worked out through an analysis of a large number of temple sites showing how, in each case, general principles of temple construction were adapted to the specific characteristics of the god and of the place. Scully, of course, is interested in the character of the Greek temple, and of Greek sacred architecture more generally, as well as what it shows about the character of Greek religion and experience; Heidegger is interested in what the temple shows of itself *as a work* and thereby the relation between the work and truth. What Scully emphasizes in a way that converges with Heidegger is the character of the temple as embedded in the landscape, on the earth and beneath the sky, in a way that is also an embodiment of the world to which it belongs. This is also partly expressed in Heidegger through the emphasis on the temple as a work, and of truth as *at work* in the work. Truth

Figure 5.2 Temple of Apollo Epikourios at Bassae before restoration in the early 1970s. Photo: Tuh de/Wikimedia.

here being a matter of the way the work relates, *in and through its being-placed*, to world, the way it opens up the world – hence the idea of truth as itself an opening or clearing, or even itself a placing.

It is this idea of truth as opening that is at work in 'Building Dwelling Thinking', even though truth is not explicitly mentioned in the text. The later essay also involves a similar emphasis on the way the 'work' or 'thing' – the bridge for example – functions to bring other things into salience (as the bridge does with the banks of the river),[35] and the fourfold that is so central to the later essay can be seen as adumbrated in the twofold structure of earth and world that appears in the earlier.[36] The way the two essays are connected, and especially the shift from what is essentially a topological account of truth (in which place and dwelling figure but are not directly taken up) to a more direct focus on topology as such, and so on place and dwelling, is very much in accord with the broad trajectory of Heidegger's thinking from the earlier to the later. As Heidegger himself characterized it in the Le Thor Seminar of 1969 (referred to earlier), it is a trajectory that moves from the meaning-focused investigations of *Being and Time*, to the truth-oriented inquiry that is evident in 'On the Origin of the Work of Art', and culminates in the explicit concern with place that is so important in 'Building Dwelling Thinking'. The sense of truth as opening provides a way of thinking about truth that is of special relevance to the architectural – and not only because of the architectural example that Heidegger uses in 'The Origin of the Work of Art'. It is a way of thinking about truth that does not depend upon notions of the correctness of assertoric content nor the honesty of intended appearance, but instead relates, more fundamentally, to the character of architectural form, especially when realized in building, as opening up relations and possibilities, and as itself opened up by those relations and possibilities – especially the opening up of possibilities for action and movement.

The focus on the latter is particularly important, since it is essentially in and through action and movement, whether potential or actual, that space is ordered (something noted already, but also discussed further in Chapter 7). The problem with the purely representational engagement with space – with space as given through the diagram or photograph (though less so in the hand-drawn image) – is that it can easily lead away from the active character of space and towards either a static conception (exemplified in what Benjamin calls 'the attentive concentration of a tourist'[37]), or else to a form of abstracted and idealized space that is actually given over to a form of aestheticization (as one may argue is the case with Eisenman).[38] The sense of truth as correctness, and even of truth as honesty of appearance, is all too readily associated with a distanced or partially 'disengaged' approach to architecture – one that effectively stands off from the building and looks to its formal or surface properties. The sense of truth as openness lends itself to a different and more basic understanding of the spatiality of the built as given in and through the possibilities for active engagement – which need not be only in relation to action and movement, but also to the full range of sensory modalities, to bodily orientation, mood, emotion and affect. And while this does involve a shift towards an emphasis on what Eisenman characterizes as the phenomenological in architecture, and away from his own focus on architecture as primarily a conceptual or textually oriented inquiry, it is not a shift towards the phenomenological understood only as an attentiveness to specific experiential features of built form, but towards the phenomenological as it encompasses the orientational and topological (which always involves more than can be given in any single representation).

Truth and the topological

Understanding architecture orientationally and topologically means understanding the way architecture is given in and through a complex sensory engagement and in terms of capacities for action and movement, rather than through merely some narrowed-down mode of conceptual or representational engagement or a framed 'viewing'. The everyday experience of and interaction with the built environment exhibit just such complexity and dynamism, even though frequently going unnoticed, but often brought powerfully to salience in certain kinds of buildings, and often in buildings that are exemplary of past architectural forms. The Gothic cathedral, to return to an earlier example, is a building specifically geared to the functions of ritual; to a specific mode of bodily orientation and comportment; to the experience of the visual, the acoustic, the haptic, even the olfactory; and to specific structures of memory and narrative. One cannot really appreciate the character of such a building independently of the way it affects one's own embodied being-there in that place.[39]

It is indicative of the complex character of architectural Modernism that, as exemplified in Aalto and in the form inherited by many contemporary designers, it retains what can be understood as a form of humanism – although one understood specifically in terms of what is also at the heart of Heidegger's thinking in 'Building Dwelling Thinking', namely, an attentiveness to the space of building as indeed a *human* space or, better, a human *place*.[40] Of course, the way 'place' appears here is not just in terms of some notion of subjective affectivity that a building may generate, but of a much more encompassing mode of being that founds experience (across all its modalities), in which both spatiality and temporality are embedded, and that is the fundamental ground on which any sort of being in the world depends (including that of the abstracted, narrowly spatialized being that seems to be so common in many forms of contemporary architecture). Attentiveness to the role and significance of place in this regard makes evident the way in which architecture works through the configuring of those multiple elements that are together experienced in the sense of the place to which a building responds, but which building also brings into the open. And in this way the discussion of truth is directly connected to the functionality of architectural design that, as was seen in the last chapter, is so central to Alvar Aalto's work, as well as to Heidegger's talk of 'dwelling'.

It is precisely in relation to the *topological* character of built form that one finds the primary sense in which truth operates architecturally – and this reflects Heidegger's claim that truth as unconcealment or opening, truth as itself topological, is the fundamental sense of truth that makes possible even truth as correctness.[41] All architecture can be understood as standing in an essential relation to truth in this sense, since all architecture stands in an essential relation to place and to the opening of place, but not all architecture opens in the same way, and not all architecture engages with place in a direct or explicit way or understands its own topological character. To some extent, this might be understood as itself reflecting the character of truth (and of place) as an unconcealing or revealing that is specific to its place – always taking the form of a bounded clearing. The point is not to overcome the boundedness within which truth arises, which is impossible, but rather to understand the fact of that boundedness, to be attentive and responsive to it. In this respect, truth, like dwelling, is not something simply achieved, but is instead a constant demand, a task that always lies before.

Chapter 6

BUILDING AND MEMORY

The aim of Heidegger's discussion in 'Building Dwelling Thinking' is 'to think about dwelling and building'. But as has already been seen, this does not involve the uncovering of 'architectural ideas' or 'rules for building' or an investigation of building as 'an art or as a technique'. Rather, it takes the form of a moving back to that in which building has its proper ground – its beginning, its 'first principles' (*archai* in the Greek) – and it is in just this sense that the inquiry is ontological in character. The essay 'traces building back into the domain to which everything that is belongs', as Heidegger puts it, and it does this by showing how building is tied to dwelling. The reference to 'the domain to which everything that is belongs' indicates that what is at issue here is already a question that has a distinctly topological character – it is a moving or tracing back to a specific domain. The topological character of this language, as has been emphasized already, is not to be dismissed as merely metaphorical – what is at issue is indeed a certain sort of place. Moreover, the moving back to this place is a movement of retrieval – and so can be construed as a form of 'homecoming' (though a form in which home does not remain unquestioned). It is a movement back to a place that has never properly been left and, as such, it takes the form of a re-finding of place, a reorienting to place, even a *remembering* of place.

The connection between place and memory is especially important for Heidegger's account of thinking – even though this has received surprisingly little direct or detailed discussion in the existing literature.[1] Heidegger claims that the history of philosophical thinking is a history of forgetting (and specifically a 'forgetting of being'). This means that thinking, as Heidegger approaches it, must always be a form of the overcoming of such forgetting – a form of recollection or remembrance. Writing specifically of the way such recollection is at work in the philosophical engagement with the origins and history of thinking, Heidegger says that it 'is no historiological activity with the past, as if it wanted to make present, from outside and from what is later, what earlier thinkers "believed" "about" being'. Instead he insists, in a way that echoes some of the discussion in Chapter 3:

> Remembrance is placement into being itself, which still presences, even though all previous beings are past. Indeed, even talk about placement into being is misleading because it suggests we are not yet placed into being, while being

yet remains closer to us than everything nearest and farther than all that is farthest ... Hence it is not first a matter of being placed into being, it is a matter of becoming aware of our essential abode in being, and becoming genuinely aware of being beforehand.[2]

This is just, of course, what is at issue in 'Building Dwelling Thinking' – 'a becoming aware of our essential abode in being', that is to say, a becoming aware of being already given over to 'dwelling', to a mode of inhabitation or being at home in the world that comes 'before' (in the sense that it already shapes and directs) any specific activity in the world.

The character of thinking, as a mode of reorienting that is also a remembering or recollecting, indicates how, for Heidegger, thinking is always embodied in the world rather than somehow standing apart from it, and this is so even given the contemplative, which is to say the 'theoretical', tendency that is also essential to thinking ('theoretical' coming from the Greek *theoria* meaning 'to watch' – having the same etymological root as 'theatre'). Even though thinking retains an interiority that is essential to it, the interiority of thinking should not be understood as the interiority of some realm apart from the world – an idea that only appears even remotely plausible if one treats the topology that is at work in thinking about thinking as 'metaphorical' rather than 'real'. Instead, the interiority of thinking derives from the character of place itself. Place is constituted precisely in terms of the relation to a boundary, and so in terms of the relation of interior to exterior. When given topologically (or as one might also say, when it is experienced from the perspective of being already placed), that relation to a boundary is experienced as a relation to a horizon (broadly understood). The relation of interior to exterior thus occurs as one that is given as much within the horizon (through the structure of the near and the far), and so within the place, as in relation to what lies beyond the horizon – outside the place. Here then, subjectivity can itself be rethought as part of the complex interiority of place – the body, too, is to be understood as it belongs to this topological structure rather than as apart from it. Embodiment, as noted earlier, is tied to place, and the body does not constitute any sort of independent founding principle or structure apart from place.

The relation between place and memory, which is evident in the character of thinking, reflects a deep connection between place and memory as such, and not only as these may be operative in Heidegger or in historical-philosophical thinking alone. There can be no place without memory nor memory without place – and so, as human being is always a placed being, it must also be always a remembering being, and as remembering, human being must also be placed. On this basis, topology itself must be, in an important sense, mnemonical or recollective. The fundamental character of the relation between place and memory carries over into architecture no less than other domains. However, in the case of architecture, the connection is especially significant. If there is no place without memory and no memory without place – and if it is also the case that there is no architecture that is not engaged with place, even if the exact nature of that engagement is contested – then neither is there architecture that is not engaged with memory. Appreciating the nature of such claims, however, requires attending more closely to the considerations that support and articulate them, as well as the consequences that follow from them.

Place and memory

The connection between place and memory is evident in almost every tradition and from all parts of the world. It is evident in oral cultures, through the narrative articulation of landscape in story and song, as that by which knowledge is retained. 'Wisdom sits in places', affirms an Apache elder to Keith Basso, in the same-titled book, and for the Apache, memory is similarly seated, similarly placed.[3] This sense of the intimacy of the connection between place and memory, place and knowledge, is also present in Australian aboriginal culture – memory and knowledge are held in 'country', in the land itself. In European thought, the connection of place and memory is famously exemplified in the Classical *ars memorativa* (the art of memory) and the associated 'method of places' (or method of *loci*), according to which memory is enabled through the connecting of particular images or ideas – those to be remembered – with specific locations.[4] It is also a connection that appears in the work of many twentieth-century thinkers.

In Bachelard's *Poetics of Space*, for instance, memory is explored as it is given in the intimacy of domestic places.[5] In the writings of Walter Benjamin (and most notably in Benjamin's unfinished *Arcades Project*), memory appears in its embeddedness in the materiality of things, and especially in the materiality of the city – in its buildings and streets. The exploration of memory is central, not only in the work of Marcel Proust,[6] but also, more recently, in that of W. G. Sebald[7] – the one surely standing in an essential relation to the other – as it arises in the form of public history and private recollection, and as it is formed in and through specific locations and locales from Combray to Paris, Norfolk to Vienna. Yet, although the connection of memory to place is clear in these thinkers and writers (and in the work of many others, including those working within what is now known as 'material culture studies'),[8] the exact nature of that connection, and whether it is a necessary or a contingent one, often remains much less clear. Moreover, in spite of the work of writers and thinkers like Proust, Sebald, Bachelard, Benjamin and others, there is also a common tendency to assume that because memory is 'of the past', so memory is primarily a *temporal* phenomenon rather than having any connection to the topological, that is, to place.

Even were memory taken to have a special relation to time, still this would not itself imply the priority of that relation over the relation of memory to place. The reason is simple: time does not stand apart from place any more than does space. Indeed, time and space, even though they may sometimes be treated as opposed to one another, should both be understood as grounded in place, and may even be thought as abstractions from it. Nonetheless, the tendency to think of memory as primarily temporal is undoubtedly one of the factors that encourage a forgetfulness of the essentially topographical character of memory. This tendency is in turn underpinned by a certain 'temporalist' prejudice within modern thought according to which subjectivity is itself understood as essentially temporal in character. Temporality, and so also memory, is thus viewed as tied to the subjective interiority of human existence, whilst spatiality is tied with objective exteriority. There is a much longer story to tell here, but even leaving aside the complication that comes simply from the dependence of time on place, still the prioritization of the temporal gives rise to a problematic conception of memory. Edward Casey makes the point that the focus on temporality leaves out the need for embodiment, and embodiment requires emplacement.[9] More fundamentally, as memory is *meaningful* or *contentful*, so memory is only constituted through the embeddedness of the one who remembers in place, while the necessary interdependence that obtains between self and place, coupled with the essential role of memory in the formation of the self, means that memory and place are thereby also brought into intimate relation.[10] To suppose that memory is tied primarily to temporality is thus to neglect the place-bound character of content itself, including the content of memory.

The key point at issue here is very similar to that sketched in Chapter 3 regarding the idea of the mind or the self as 'externalized', or as 'extended' out into the world. Although there are various considerations that lead towards such an 'extended' view, one particularly important consideration stems from the interrelated, or 'holistic', character of meaning or content (already mentioned in Chapter 5), not only as this applies to the elements of mental life, such as beliefs, desires, actions and so forth, but also to memories. Specific meanings and contents are always embedded within networks of attitudes and states, which are also networks of memory. But such networks are, in turn, embedded in, and interrelated with, the objects and entities in the world that cause them and that are also their objects. The very idea of meaning or content thus depends essentially on the connectedness of those who remember – and who also act, think, believe and experience – to the world, and so to objects and entities in the world.

Thus, one is indeed led to the idea of the mind as 'externalized', or as 'extended' out into the world, and meaning and content as given, not in some separate, 'inner' realm, but only in the space of worldly engagement. Inasmuch as it is constituted through dynamic integration, even if always impartial and incomplete, of memories, beliefs, actions and the rest, the self is also constituted through its worldly involvement – *who* and *what* one is being thus partially dependent on *where* one is and has been. Memory cannot be prised away from the world any more than can the self, but more than this, memory is also given *in* the world, in the concrete materiality of things, since it is there that self and identity, meaning and content, are jointly constituted and articulated. In this way, memory is only to be found through the placed materiality of the world, and this is equally true of both private and public memory. In its own turn, place appears as that which gathers self, others and things in a way that opens them both to the world and to each other (in much the way that is evident in 'Building Dwelling Thinking').

The placed materiality of memory that appears here has several consequences, the first of which is that memory is not 'subjectively' determined, nor does it belong to the 'subject' alone. This means that memory is not something that is to be understood as merely a product of subjective experience. Certainly, memory is an essential element of the 'interior' life of the mind, but it is not constituted only in terms of such interiority (and nor, strictly speaking, is the life of the mind so constituted either). Memory arises through interactive engagement with the world – an involvement that does not come *after* the formation of the self but is the very means *by which* the self is formed. In this respect, the self is formed through its continuously developing engagement in the world, including both perception and action – which also has the consequence that the self is not autonomous in relation to the world, but a function of the world in which it is engaged.

Moreover, as memory is not 'subjective', neither is it socially 'constructed' – despite the prevalence of such social constructivism in contemporary thought (including its prevalence, as noted in Chapters 1 and 3, in relation to ideas of place, space and even 'dwelling'). In its original formulations, and so as it arose out of what might be thought of as a form of 'social phenomenology' (particularly as associated with Schutz), social constructionism is based in the idea that social phenomena arise, as do any and all phenomena on this account, through processes of meaning constitution (such processes being the focus of phenomenology in its original Husserlian form). What most contemporary social constructionism does, however, is to understand that process of constitution as operating within the domain of social and political processes, structures and activities. Much depends on the nature of the processes, structures and activities that are taken to be at issue here. Sometimes social constructivism can be read as entailing no more than a fairly weak claim concerning the social context of meaning. Almost all human activity depends upon language, and inasmuch as language is social (and not merely contingently so), then one might also say that almost all human activity is 'constructed' socially, merely in virtue of the fact that it is 'constructed' linguistically (though what 'construction' might mean here is not clear, but then, what it means in many versions of social constructionism is not clear either).

Constructivism of this weak sort is relatively unproblematic, but it is also lacking in content – little more than a reformulation of what might be taken to be an obvious truism concerning the ubiquity of linguistic formulations in experience and discourse. More often, however, social constructivism, which here includes the supposedly socially constructed character of memory, involves the stronger idea that memory is *determined* by the social (and by the social as it extends beyond the linguistic alone, although just what the social means here often remains obscure), that is, in effect, a product of the social. One of the difficulties with such strong constructionism, however, is that if the social constructs memory, then it is also true that memory constructs the social; that is, only in and through memory is sociality even possible.

More broadly, and given the interconnection of memory with place, one ought to say, not that memory is determined by either the subjective or the social (or the 'intersubjective'), but rather that subjectivity and sociality (and also objectivity) emerge only within the overarching structure of place. Place is just that within which self and the social are reciprocally constituted, and in which they are both constituted in essential relation to the materiality of the world. Memory, one might say, itself begins in place, although in saying that, it is important to note that place never appears but as already imbued with memory. To be in place is already to remember, even if the memories that attach to any specific place are fragmentary, associative or recent. Moreover, only on the basis of memory is one oriented, and only if oriented is one also placed. Being in a place is a remembering in which the grasp of a place and one's own bodily situatedness in relation to it are necessarily dependent on one's prior familiarity with that place. So, to be in a place is to be attentive to some aspect of the place (an attentiveness tied to the specific focus of activity), but it is always also to be dependent on a retained awareness and knowledge of the place in its entirety, and so of features that lie outside of that current focus of attention. One thus finds oneself in the world, which means one only finds oneself at all, in and through placed memory and remembered place. To reiterate, there is no place without memory and no memory without place.

In an important and often overlooked sense, memory is always *nostalgic* – and so always *melancholic*. This is so, not in the sense that memory involves a desire to regain what cannot be regained (what is sometimes termed 'restorative nostalgia'), but rather in the sense that memory always involves a sense of loss (hence the melancholia) – to remember is to attend to what is past, what is no longer present as it was, or if present still, then present in a different way. To attend to what is remembered is thus to attend to the dynamically unfolding character of place. The nostalgia that is associated with memory – and as genuinely nostalgic so it combines a sense of 'home' (for the loss at issue here is also a loss directly related to the self) with the pain that comes from the inevitable estrangement from home – is thus an essential feature of human engagement in the world. It cannot be escaped any more than one can escape the world or oneself. This is where a form of nostalgia does indeed become evident in Heidegger's approach (notwithstanding Cacciari's claims to the contrary), but not a nostalgia of mere reconstitution. The 'pain of the return home' (the literal meaning of the combination of the Greek terms *nostos* and *algos*) that is at issue here is a reflection of the way the task of recollection, or retrieval, is as difficult as it is necessary – not a turn back to some secure resting place, but rather a turn back into a fundamental questionability and even a sense of loss. The nostalgic is that which marks the dynamic opening of the world in place, in terms of both freedom *and* limit – and so, too, in terms of the character of human beings as both active and acted upon, as capable of a degree of self-determination and yet as also possessed of an existence that is finite and fragile. From an ethical perspective, it is here that the idea of responsibility has its essential origin.

Bachelard asserts, and Casey repeats the claim, that memories do not move.[11] Yet even if this is so, memory is always at the beginning of movement, containing the possibility of movement within it. Casey argues that the supposed immobility of memory is given through its connection to place. Thus, places *fix* memory.[12] Yet, as it is only in and through places that memories have form, so places are themselves given form only in and through memory. The idea that places fix memory seems to presuppose an asymmetry in which it is place that has determinacy and fixity. However, neither memory nor place has a fixity that belongs to either of these alone – memory always carries multiple possibilities that accord with the multiple possibilities of the places that memory opens up, and in which memory is itself opened. This point is an important one, since it is often assumed that memory and place possess, if not a fixity, then a perduring character or even a determinacy that is alien to both. Precisely because of the relationality that characterizes memory and place, as well as the self, none of these have an absolute determinacy, either over time or at a time. Place and memory and the self with it are dynamic structures – neither those who remember nor their memories are fixed in place like insects in amber, and places are not static structures that stand as the unmoving backdrops to human lives.

The latter is indeed one reason to be wary of those appropriations of Heideggerian thought that emphasize the character of place as a source of determined and determinate identity or 'authenticity'. As was emphasized in Chapter 3, the character of the turn back to place on which Heidegger is so insistent is always a turn back to the indeterminate and the questionable. This does not mean that there is nothing at issue in the idea of a human 'need for roots', as Simone Weil puts it, or for 'home' (something taken up, for example, by Jean Améry[13]), or in Heidegger's own emphasis on 'groundedness', *Bodenständigkeit*, but only that such 'need' demands a more careful and complex examination than it is usually accorded. Moreover, although home is a place primarily characterized in terms of the possibility of rest and repose, of internality and intimacy, it is never wholly so. Its 'homely' character is never secure and may contain within it the very deepest of melancholy. Home is always 'uncanny', but care must be exercised in considering what that is taken to mean. The 'uncanny' has become such a common term with which to conjure the spirits of modernity, and perhaps nowhere more so than in relation to architecture, that the term is in danger of losing any real meaning. The 'uncanny' is now used – as in Anthony Vidler's discussion of 'the modern unhomely'[14] – to encompass a wide range of different, even if related, moods, attitudes, tropes and dispositions. Moreover, not all of these are specific only to the modern – and here the tendency to view the modern as in some sense 'exceptional' (as indeed 'new') is indicative of the same disregard of ontological considerations alluded to above. Certainly, the modern is different, but its difference has to be understood against the background of that which is constitutive of the possibility of historical existence as such. Inasmuch as 'home' contains within itself the capacity for its own disruption *as* home, then this does not show that home is therefore 'unhomely', but rather that home is indeed a mode of *place*, and as such, contains an essential indeterminacy and openness within it, even an essential fragility and tendency towards loss. Home is never *just* home, just as no place remains utterly self-contained within its boundaries.

Memory is impossible without forgetting, just as the salience of place is impossible without its withdrawal. As the coming into salience of something within the space opened up in place is also a withdrawing of other things into the background (a phenomenon familiar from phenomenological analysis as well as studies of sensory perception), so memory and forgetting are not separate, but two sides of the one process. To forget is to remember, and to remember is to forget. This is one reason why the idea of an 'absolute' or 'complete' memory in which there is no forgetting – the sort of 'memory' that one finds exemplified and explored in Borges,[15] as well as Luria[16] – is perhaps best understood, not as memory in any genuine sense at all, but rather as a distorted form of memory in which all that is left is a debilitating retentiveness that undermines the capacity for action and the sense of self.

No memory is completely private, because all memory is placed, and the placed character of memory means that every memory has some dimension that is accessible to others, even as it also has a dimension that resists such access. In part this reflects the fact that memories are related differently to different modes of human identity and narrative – to identity and narrative as personal and as collective. Memory is also given in ritual and event – it is performed – and the performance of memory connects modes of personal and collective life. This can be seen in forms of collective celebration – both on those occasions where people celebrate together as part of community-wide festivities and when they celebrate in more localized or intimate settings, among family, with friends and colleagues, or as part of institutional and organizational groupings, but in ways that are shared across the community. Once again, the performative character of memory relates directly to the dynamic and indeterminate character of place and memory both, and so also, one might say, with the performativity of built form. If place is not static, but dynamic, then neither is the built. Indeed, it is largely through the dynamic and performative character of place, memory and building that these are bound together. The ontology that appears here is thus an essentially relational and dynamic one, and it is this ontology that belongs to place, to memory, to building and to architecture. It is, moreover, an ontology that remains irrespective of whether it is recognized or represented. What *grounds* and *limits* existence is often just that which is forgotten, or even denied, within existence – so that existence is a forgetting of its origins.

The 'romantic materiality' of the architectural

The relation between memory and place, sketched here, can be characterized as a form of 'romantic materialism'. It is *romantic* in that it holds that materiality appears as material only through being taken up in and through the meaningful and the remembered, whilst it is *materialist* in that it holds that meaning and memory are, in turn, given in the very materiality of things. If one turns back to architecture, and particularly to a consideration of the built form of the architectural (since what is at issue here is the materiality of memory as given in and through place), then such 'romantic materialism' suggests that one should think of buildings, not as inert structures that stand apart from remembrance, from felt experience, sentiment or affect, but as constituted *romantically* and *materially* at one and the same time. In terms of memory, buildings carry memory as an essential and inevitable part of what they are, and they do this in several ways.

The very sensory properties of built forms – their shapes, structures and materials – have a memorial character. This is not only true of the sensory properties of buildings as they may be given visually (although this is certainly important), but also in terms of other modes of sensory presentation. The smell of a building, the touch of its surfaces and shapes, the acoustic properties of its spaces – all of these contribute to memory but also serve as the carriers and triggers for remembrance. Sometimes, the relation to memory may be direct – this specific angle in a wall, this juxtaposition of doorway and window, this fall of light may immediately evoke a memory of one's own. Sometimes, the relation to memory may be via certain archetypal forms or schemas that are typically felt and recognized through generalized modes of bodily engagement and responsiveness.

The complex interplay of memory in building, as well as the role of the body, is given explicit recognition in Peter Zumthor's work and writing, so much so that, for Zumthor, architecture might be seen to be constituted in terms of bodily remembrance (especially of certain archetypal forms: hollows, mounds, caves, platforms, nests and tents).[17] Memory is given, not only in the felt or sensed qualities of a building – in the concrete qualities of its presencing – but also in its symbolic and semiotic elements, whether they belong to the particularities of site, orientation, ornament or style. In one sense, such elements are not strictly the material of memory – at least not insofar as they remain at the level of the abstract or generic – but, since they are invariably embedded in, and evocative of, collective as well as personal history and remembrance, and so also given specific materiality, they never stand wholly apart from the memorial or from the shared understanding of forms and structures that are part of materialized cultural memory and tradition. Often, the forms of memory that are at work here are so mundane and commonplace that they are readily overlooked. The remembered narratives that are encoded in the floor plan of a building and the arrangement of rooms within it, or that differentiate different aspects of a building's relation to the street, play a basic role in the functioning of buildings and in the human ability to engage with them. Memory is given, too, in the inscriptive and dynamic elements of building – in the effects of weathering, of decay and renewal, of extension and re-use. The ruin, or the evocation of ruination, provides an extreme instance of this mode of presentation of the built as the concretization of its own history, and so of the history of a place, but also of building as itself the operation of the historical.

Built form is always *remembered* form. The opening up of place through building that occurs in the architectural engagement with place is thus also an opening up of memory. Consequently, memory is itself formed in and through building. The infusing of building with memory and memory with building means that building is never just 'objective', and never just 'subjective' either – it always operates between the two and in the space in which both are themselves opened up. At the level of Australian domestic architecture, Richard Leplastrier's own 'Lovett Bay House' at Pittwater, NSW (see Figure 6.1), built on the site of an earlier dwelling destroyed by bushfire, provides a striking illustration of a mode of

Figure 6.1 Lovett Bay House, Richard Leplastrier, 1998. Photo © Leigh Woolley.

architectural practice that consciously draws on memory, building memory into the forms it constructs, allowing memory to emerge in and through the site – and doing so on a multiplicity of levels. Here memory also means a memory of continuity of settlement – the memory of a belonging that is not and cannot be proprietorial. As Leplastrier writes:

> The house continues a history of simple living on the site, which I suspect has continued for thousands of years: small shells that litter the place give testament to that fact. The form of the building is simple – its central core room restrains a broad cantilever roof that surrounds the building, the lack of columns allowing the line of the landscape to continue unbroken. Being inside the house is like sitting under a strong over-hanging tree.[18]

For all this, however, the contemporary practice of building, and of architecture, often remains enmeshed in a 'presentism' that refuses memory as it frequently ignores place. Such 'presentism' can be discerned in the material forms of many modern and contemporary buildings.

Presentism and the refusal of memory

Memory is given in and through sensory quality, which means that it is given in and through the materiality of things. Such materiality is always given through *surface* and the interplay of surfaces. The surface, as the boundary that is constitutive of a thing (a sense at play in the original Greek sense of *topos* that is at work in Aristotle[19]), is that by which the thing is in the world and which mediates between thing and world (between interior and exterior); it is that by which the thing is brought into contact with other things and, in particular, by which it comes into contact with the senses. It is in the encounter with its surface, therefore, even if the encounter is at a distance, that a thing is touched, seen, heard, even smelt and tasted. The surface is thus that by which a things *shows* itself – surface *is* appearance and appearance is, in this sense, always 'superficial', but not, therefore, in the sense of some 'mere' appearance, but in this sense of a genuine showing in and through the surface (echoing the sense of truth as appearance that was at issue in the last chapter). Moreover, as the surface is the boundary by which the thing shows itself *and* by which the thing is brought into contact with other things, so the surface is also that which also records, in varying degrees, the history of that contact. Time accumulates both in and through the surface. It is that accumulation that is sometimes referred to as weathering, sometimes as patination and sometimes simply as age. Memory thus resides in the surface because of the way memory resides in materiality, but this relates to both the 'memory' that belongs to the thing and the memory that the thing may hold for one who remembers.

The capacity of a surface to show itself, including its showing of its capacity for memory (as something recorded and also evoked), might be understood in terms of a certain *depth* of surface. This is not a matter of some physical quantity, but of the character of the surface as such. In the case of buildings, depth of surface may be understood in terms of the capacity that the surfaces of built forms have to respond to the surrounding environment and to sensory engagement. Such responsiveness is usually the result of a complex of factors including the material constitution of the surface, the manner in which the surface has been constructed and the way in which it is formed or deployed, the inter-relation and interaction between surfaces, and the way the surface is situated or positioned. A surface with the same material constitution may exhibit a rich depth in one context but not in another.

One of the features of many modern and contemporary buildings, however, is their tendency towards the effacement or loss of materiality, and thereby also the effacement and loss of memory as well as of the capacity for a richness of sensory engagement. This occurs not only through the tendency towards the homogenization of built forms and their surface appearances through the use of standardized modes of construction and materials geared to such standardized modes, but also through a reduction in the complexity or depth of surface in the sense at issue (which is sometimes itself a result of the standardized character of contemporary construction). Many modern materials are used such that they often seem intended to disappear 'behind' the formal structure of the building as a whole or even to conceal more basic elements of the structure – the use of highly finished surfaces can also tend away from a sense of the building in its materiality, and towards a more homogenized and even idealized presentation of the building as a whole. Rarely, in contemporary buildings, is there consideration of the specific ways in which surface materiality might relate to memory or a breadth of sensory and situational engagement. There has also been a powerful tendency – noted by Mohsen Mostafavi and David Leatherbarrow – to look to materials, and combinations of materials, that will resist the surface effects of weathering, or more particularly will not show such effects, and thereby also exhibit a resistance to time[20] – itself a very clear form of 'presentism'. Of course, what is crucial here is less the material itself – since every material has the potential for greater and lesser depth of surface – but of the way materials are *used*. And this is why methods of construction and architectural style are so important. Moreover, this is not only a matter of *how* materials may be utilized in specific cases, but also of *when* they are utilized and how *often* – materials that might well have powerful effects when used in certain situations may cease to be effective when their use becomes ubiquitous.

The capacity for materials, and their surfaces, to connect with memory, to hold memory and to elicit a complex of sensory effects is itself tied to the way those material surfaces are topologically, rather than merely spatially, embedded, and so also to the way in which they are encountered topologically rather than merely spatially. In this respect, the tendency towards the loss of what is here referred to as depth of surface is itself associated with the tendency towards abstraction, and so towards a spatialized rather than topological mode of architectural engagement, that was discussed in the previous chapter. Part of what was at issue there, of course, was also the tendency towards a prioritization of represented form over built form. Yet one might also argue that even within the built form itself there is a certain tendency towards the prioritization of the representational.

In part, this prioritization of the representational in the built has been encouraged by the way architecture has itself interacted with representational modes as these operate through photography and other media. Beatriz Colomina writes that 'emerging systems of communication that came to define twentieth-century culture – the mass media – ... are the true site within which modern architecture is produced and with which it directly engages'.[21] This site is one in which both architecture and buildings are taken up into the realm of the representational – one might also say, of the image[22] – and in which the representational has a tendency to suffuse the realm of the built, affecting even the engagement with materiality and surface. The building thus becomes bound up with its own reproduced form – just as architectural photography has become bound up with architecture. Colomina goes on to argue that this means one must think about modern architecture differently:

> It will be necessary to think of architecture as a system of representation, or rather as a series of overlapping systems of representation. This does not mean abandoning the tradition architectural object, the building. In the end, it means looking at it much more closely than before, but also in a different way. The building should be understood in the same terms as drawings, photographs, writing, films, and advertising ... because the building is a mechanism of representation in its own right.[23]

Here then, it is indeed a matter, not of prioritizing the representational *apart* from the building, but of prioritizing the built *as it is* representational. Yet although it is true that buildings can and do function as representations, especially so in the case of many modern and contemporary buildings, such a way of understanding buildings cannot be adequate to *all* that the building is nor even what building is in the most basic sense. Moreover, understanding the building as a 'mechanism of representation' does not rule out the building also being something else besides, but actually implies the contrary: for the building to be a representation, it must also be something more than just a representation. Representation is a property of things and not something that exists independently of things, and consequently, whatever functions representationally also functions non-representationally (a simple point, and one that ought to be uncontroversial, but nevertheless frequently overlooked or denied).

Although focussing on 'reproduction' rather than specifically on representation, the representation nevertheless being a form of reproduction, Walter Benjamin writes that:

> Even the most perfect reproduction of a work of art is lacking in one element: its presence in time and space, its unique existence at the place where it happens to be. This unique existence of the work of art determined the history to which it was subject throughout the time of its existence. ... The presence of the original is the prerequisite to the concept of authenticity [*Echtheit*] ... The whole sphere of authenticity is outside technical – and, of course, not only technical – reproducibility.[24]

What is here translated as 'authenticity' (*Echtheit*) has a meaning similar to the weak sense of authenticity discussed previously[25] – a sense of *genuineness*. Such authenticity is closely tied to (and grounded in) both the placed being of the work[26] and the work's capacity to bear the marks of time, or as one might also say, to act as a sort of repository for memory. Such authenticity or genuineness is what belongs *to the work* – or more generally to any immediately present thing – in contrast to its reproduced image, facsimile or representation. It is the work in this sense that is also the focus of Heidegger's discussion in 'The Origin of the Work of Art', but much of the character of the work as explored there is also evident in his account in 'The Thing' where his focus is on the ordinary and everyday – it is thus not just the work of art that is at issue here, but the way memory and presence, and also (harking back to Chapter 5) truth, are intimately bound up with the thing *as it exceeds anything given in its representation*.

It is in the thing, rather than the representation alone, that memory is founded; and it is in relation to the thing, rather than the representation, that the world is configured. Of course, since the representation is always more than a representation, every representation will indeed have the capacity to 'hold' memory and to draw together elements of the world (hence the capacity of, for instance, the photograph, to operate in ways that do indeed direct attention back to the singular and the placed), but that capacity is underpinned by the fact that the representation is not merely a representation. Where the focus is on the representational content of representations (as it all too often is), the tendency is for that content to take precedence, and thus the underlying singularity that belongs even to the representation recedes in the face of the generic or the abstracted. The result is also an effacement of the thing, of memory, of place and of world. And thus one arrives at something like the world as simulacra that is not only prominent in the work of contemporary thinkers such as Jean Baudrillard,[27] but is replicated in contemporary socio-cultural forms and practices, and in the structures of contemporary technologized capitalism, whether in its 'liberal' or more authoritarian modes (and so in the United States as well as Russia, in China as well as in the European Union).

Benjamin's identification of the way technological reproduction erases or hides the singular character of the thing – and so erases or hides both memory and place – is itself an indication of a form of presentation that belongs, in the context of Benjamin's account, to contemporary technology. In contemporary architecture, something similar is evident in the tendency for the building to be lost amidst the representational – both through the frequent use of representational modes in built forms (apparent in the idea of the building as having its own representational content) and through the way the representation often dominates over the building. The character of the building as a building is thus readily merged with or submerged in its representational character, and the subsequent erasure or obscuration of memory and place constitutes a form of architectural presentism. Such presentism is not encouraged only by tendencies in design or construction nor by the practices of architectural photography, but also by architecture's predilection for certain forms of narrative and storytelling. There can be no doubt that story and memory are related – as are narrative and place – but there are stories and stories, and not every story secures or is secured by memory, just as not every story told about a place belongs to it. Many (although certainly not all) of the stories told about buildings, and the designs that supposedly underpin them, seem to depend on taking the built form as something other than it is – not as a concrete form that does indeed engage with a certain place, but instead (in a way that recalls Chapter 4) as almost a piece of text, carrying a script that is to be read in some specific fashion. Understood thus, the building as 'text' or as 'image' is no longer constituted by its materiality, but rather becomes that which determines its own materiality through being inscribed into it (the materiality of the built being almost entirely taken up into the building as text). It is thus that the materiality of so much built form recedes, in modernity, in the face of the primacy of the image, the text, the representation. It can indeed seem as if there is nothing outside the representational, and the representation has become the form of the architectural.

The dominance of what is here called 'storytelling' – which is actually the dominance of a certain form of narrativist textualism or representationalism – and the problematic character of that dominance, should not be confused with the centrality of narrative form in the constitution of meaningfulness more generally. There could be no design, no building, no engagement with place, were it not for the narrative. Yet, to repeat, there are narratives and then there are narratives.

The centrality, even indispensability, of narrative, does not license any and every narrative or any and every narrative practice. The question to be asked of every narrative is the extent to which it is indeed embedded in that which it also aims to narrate – to what extent does the story belong to the material and the material to the story. In many cases, the connection at issue is tenuous at best, and the materiality of the built is lost in the narrated fabric with which it is clothed.

The materiality that is obscured or forgotten in so many architectural narrations is not only the materiality of the built as it evades any and every narrative (even as it also comes to appearance in and through narrative), but also the materiality of the built as it contains and sustains memory. In this respect, however, the fabricated narrative that has no genuine foundation in the material and the concrete is unlikely itself to be remembered. There is something especially ironic here, since often the design intention that is encoded in a particular architectural narrative is one that it is usually expected will continue to shape the life of the building even after construction. In some cases, this can signify another form of architectural presentism in terms of the idea that a present narrative (regardless of the strength of its embeddedness in the materiality of a building) might be able to determine the future narratives, and so the future uses and meanings, that accrue to a particular built form. Yet the only narrative that can reliably continue to have power in the life of a building is the narrative that the building itself remembers, that the building itself embodies and contains – the narrative that is given in the singular materiality of a specific built form and the place it occupies (a point that follows from the general character of the relation between creative intention and creative work).

Memory in architecture

The implication of memory with building concerns the very nature of building, as well as of the human. It provokes several questions. How, for instance, is one to build in a way that acknowledges the implication with memory? What memories and forms of memories pertain to different forms of building? What difference would it make to the built environment if memory were to become an explicit element in architectural thinking and making? There is, however, another matter that comes to the fore once one begins to take seriously the connection of place with memory, and of both with building and architecture: the matter, not only of ontology, but of ethics. As used here – and throughout this volume – ethics is not about some theory of the 'good' or the 'just'. Instead it essentially concerns an attentiveness to the remembered place and the placed memory – an attentiveness to the *placed-ness* of the human and the *humanness* of place. Once the essential interconnection of the concepts at issue here is understood – and likewise the materialized, placed character of human being – then the task of building, and of architectural design, becomes a task from which the ethical can never be excluded, and that is fundamentally tied to matters concerning the very formation of the human.

To build is to build memory, and every building carries memory within it. What this means, however, is that to neglect the memorial character of building, and so the way memory must also enter into building construction and design, is to neglect an essential element of what it is to build. And, to misunderstand building is also to misunderstand oneself. The implication of the self in architectural practice is, of course, part of a larger hermeneutic structure of self-implication that characterizes all modes of understanding, inquiry and creation. Yet such self-implication takes on a particular form in architecture, since the working out of the self that occurs in architecture is also externalized and concretized – it is a reciprocal shaping of self and built form as that occurs in and through the engagement with place. Here, once again, is a reaffirmation of one of the key reasons for the importance of the investigation into the ontology of architecture that is to be found in Heidegger's discussion on 'Building Dwelling Thinking'. Such an investigation cannot but force us back to an investigation of the properly human context of architectural practice, since it is that which is at issue when inquiring into the character of architecture as an engagement with place. The engagement with place is also, by its very nature, an engagement with the human, just as the engagement with the human also implicates the topological – even when that is ignored or neglected. The human dimension of architecture is something that the presentism of modern architectural theory and practice often effaces. That it does so is no accident, for the effacing of memory is indeed an effacing of the human. It is also, by the same token, an effacing of *both* the ontological *and* the ethical. It is a fundamental mode of forgetting and of self-forgetting.

Chapter 7

THE LINE AND THE HAND

Memory, as is evident from the last chapter, is no mere 'inner' state, but is always embodied in the world, in place and so also in the built forms by which human being-in-place is articulated. Understood as remembrance, thinking is related to memory, and this itself implies the embodiment of thinking in the world, as well as indicating the way in which thinking and building do not stand apart but are intimately entangled. Although it is not directly addressed in 'Building Dwelling Thinking', this means that the character of human being is given an important expression in the character of the human body. Indeed, the structure of the body reflects the structure of place and space, that is, the differentiated and oriented character of the body (most immediately evident in the sense of difference between the left and right side, between face and back, between the crown of one's head and the soles of one's feet), which is tied to differential capacities for perception and movement, connects with the differentiated and oriented character of place and space given in terms, for instance, of earth and sky, east and west, above and below, near and far.[1] Even the space into which Levinas's cosmonaut hero, Yuri Gagarin, found himself was a space similarly differentiated and oriented – though, in his case, determined in terms of the direction of orbital movement, the relative positions of sun and earth, as well as the internal ordering of his spacecraft. And, of course, Levinas draws attention, even if indirectly, to bodily orientation and differentiation in his emphasis on the face as the focus for the human encounter with the other.

For Heidegger, the way human being relates to the world in and through bodily orientation and differentiation, and especially through the activity and capacity for activity to which it is directly tied, is already indicated in *Being and Time* (despite the commonplace claim, already noted in Chapter 3, that the body is neglected in that work) through the emphasis on the ordering of the world in terms of the ordering of work and tool in which human being as *Dasein* is essentially implicated. It has a particularly important bodily expression in the primacy that Heidegger gives to the hand in the idea of 'handiness or readiness to hand', *Zuhandenheit*.[2] The emphasis on the hand is, however, something that appears even more clearly and directly in other works.[3] In a lecture from 1942–3, Heidegger comments:

Man (*Der Mensch*) acts [*handelt*] through the hand [*Hand*]; for the hand is, together with the word, the essential distinction of man. Only a being which, like man, 'has' the word (*mûthos, logos*), can and must have the hand. Through the hand occur both prayer and murder, greeting and thanks, oath and signal, and also the 'work' of the hand, the 'hand-work', and the tool. The handshake seals the covenant. The hand brings about the 'work' of destruction. The hand exists as hand only where there is disclosure and concealment … Man does not 'have' hands, but the hand holds the essence of man, because the word as the essential realm of the hand is the ground of the essence of man.[4]

Here, reference to the 'word' implicates speaking and writing, but more broadly it also implicates thinking. 'Only when man speaks, does he think', says Heidegger in his recapitulation of the 1942–3 discussion that appears in another set of lectures, *What Is Called Thinking?*, from 1951. And he goes on to stress the way in which the work of the hand itself runs through language and through thinking.[5]

The relation Heidegger identifies between the hand and the word reflects the way in which he understands productive activity, or 'building', as tied to language and to thinking, but also the way in which speaking, writing and thinking (all of which are bound up together) are worked out in the world, as forms of 'hand-work' or, indeed, of 'building', and so too as they are embodied in voice and script. In the specific case of writing (though the argument is clearly intended much more widely), Heidegger argues that the move away from writing by hand – evident, in his time, in the use of the typewriter – represents a movement that conceals the importance of this relation between hand and word, and so conceals the way in which hand and word belong together. One might say that, in the increasing operation of language by means in which the involvement of the hand is hidden – nowadays through the use of the keyboard, mouse and screen – language itself comes to appear as disembodied and displaced, even as formalized and abstracted, even as mere 'information' available to be digitized, stored, transmitted and analysed.

These lectures, from the 1940s and 1950s, are an important point of reference for Friedrich Kittler's discussion of the mechanization of writing, something that is also taken up by other theorists and that feeds into issues concerning computerization and digitization (partly addressed in Chapter 8).[6] It is important to notice, too, that what concerns Heidegger here – the disappearance of the hand in relation to the word – is not a change in the character of hand or word as such. Just as modernity does not alter the fundamental character of human being in the world – of human 'dwelling' – neither does it alter the fundamental relation of hand and word. The word as articulated on screen is still accessed by the hand, but now in a different way. Moreover, the way in which it is accessed is such as to hide or obscure the relation at issue. Consequently, it is no response to Heidegger to claim that, because the hand is still implicated even when writing is done by means of a typewriter or keyboard, Heidegger's account is thereby mistaken.

In the 1942–3 lecture, Heidegger talks of the way action has, within it, a certain potential for concealing or obscuring, but he emphasizes how this comes to the fore in the obscuring of the relation between hand and word that occurs as the word is articulated through the typewriter (and so, by extension, although Heidegger's discussion largely predates them, through the keyboard and the screen). What occurs is not a change in the relation as such, rather 'the typewriter veils the essence of writing and of the script'.[7] This is problematic for the same reason that the loss of home was seen to emerge as a problem in Chapter 2. There, the point was that the seeming loss of home arises only in relation to a continuing presence and that presence is itself a condition for the seeming loss. Home is thus denied at the same time it is implicitly affirmed. The same is true of the relation between hand and word. It is veiled or effaced and yet it remains – and remains as essential even in its veiling or effacing.

There is more to say about the way the hand and the word become problematic in the face of modern technology (an issue that recurs in Chapter 8). But the way Heidegger draws attention to the hand, particularly when understood in connection with his discussion of 'building' and 'dwelling' in 'Building Dwelling Thinking', raises the specific question of the role of the hand, and so of embodied action, in architectural practice, and not merely in relation to the process of construction. The hand – and so, too, the body – is an essential point of reference for architecture, from the very start, for the simple and obvious reason that it determines a basic set of constraints that are operative on building design. Built form thus relates to bodily form (including the form of action) – even if sometimes indirectly. Thus, one of the ways in which the hand is evident in architecture is in the way the building is designed so as to be fit for human occupancy and use. But, just as in Heidegger, the hand is that by means of which the word is articulated as script, so the hand is also that by means of which architecture is realized in the process of design (and, in fact, the latter is properly an instance of the former – 'design' being essentially a form of the 'word'). Nowhere is this more evident than in the practice of architectural sketching and drawing, in which the connection to the hand is itself so self-evidently present.

Drawing and the line

Despite the advent of computer-aided design techniques, the practice of drawing continues to have an important role in architectural design – and, one might argue, in design in general. Whilst design ideas may arise in a great many different forms, and in a range of different ways, still the drawing constitutes one of the key modes by means of which a three-dimensional design concept begins to take concrete form as something to be shared, worked upon and developed. Through the drawing, ideas can be illustrated and communicated, explored and tested out, given shape and direction. Moreover, even though most drawing takes the form of a visual presentation, not all drawing does so – tactile drawing is a mode of drawing that typically relies on the hand, not only for its creation, but also for its apprehension.[8] From the very first, then, the drawing should not be assimilated to any purely visual mode of engagement. This will be an important point in the discussion here, just as it indicates a point of connection back to Heidegger's emphasis on the significance of the hand in human engagement in the world.

The continued relevance of drawing to architecture does not mean, of course, that it might not be possible to dispense with the drawing in design practice, but only that its being completely dispensed with would likely change the character of that practice in important, if not crucial respects. The importance of the drawing, and its continuing role in architectural practice, lies not merely in the way the drawing is constituted as an artefact in its own right, and so as a means of giving concrete form to an idea, but also in the particular way in which the act of drawing engages the hand and eye of the designer in the design itself. The drawing is the record of that engagement as it arises in and through the movement depicted by the drawn line, and this is true, even in computer-aided design. Leaving aside the abstract lines of geometrical hypothesis, every line begins at one point and leads to some other point, and, especially as drawn by the hand, the line is therefore an image *of* movement created *through* movement. The drawing begins in the line – whether as the hand-drawn imprint of carbon on paper or as the computer-generated image on a screen – and the line is both that which forms the basis of the drawing and that through which the act of drawing occurs. One might argue that the importance of drawing is, in fact, derivative of the importance of the line as such, because it is the line that connects points in space and delimits different parts of space, and so it is the line that enables, and indeed constitutes, the formation of a design *in* space.

Understood as both that which connects and delimits, as well as that which moves,[9] or represents movement, the line is integral to the very structure of space. Contrary to the conception of physical space as an empty container, a featureless void, which gained currency in the Renaissance (appearing most notably, perhaps, in the writings of Giordano Bruno) and came to prominence in the modern period of Descartes and Newton, the lived and experienced spaces in which human beings find themselves are spaces that have a shape and character, a form, that belongs to those spaces as such. The form of a space is given in and through the connection between parts of that space. Such connectivity is a connectivity evident, first and foremost, in movement, and in the shape of that movement, but also in the orientational properties of the space.

From an architectural perspective, the role of movement and orientation in the shaping of space is something evident in Baroque planning and design – famously in the re-design of Rome undertaken by Pope Sixtus IV in the 1580s.[10] It is also evident, to take an especially notable and more developed example, in the designs and design principles of Le Corbusier. Echoing some of the comments here, but referring to the *axis* rather than the line (the one being a form of the other), Le Corbusier thus writes:

> An axis is perhaps the first human manifestation; it is the means of every human act ... The axis is the regulator of architecture. To establish order is to begin to work. Architecture is based on axes ... The axis is a line of direction leading to an end ... Arrangement is the grading of axes, and so it is the grading of aims, the classification of intentions. The architect therefore assigns destinations to his axes. These ends are the wall (the plenum, sensorial sensation) or light and space (again sensorial sensation).[11]

Le Corbusier's Villa Savoye, in which the promenade leads one through the various spaces of the building, offering various perspectives on those spaces, to the open space of the rooftop garden (see Figure 7.1), provides an illustration of certain key aspects of the principles that Le Corbusier enunciates in this passage, although it operates other than in strictly axial terms. The line through the building, which

Figure 7.1 Villa Sovoye, Poissy, France, Le Corbusier, 1928–31. Top, exterior view; bottom, view to the rooftop garden. Photo: Algie Said/dreamstime.com.

moves in ascending fashion, switching back on itself, provides the central focus around which the various axes are ordered.[12] In Villa Savoye, the line thus opens up to other lines and so to other spaces, and not only within the building, but also outside.

In this respect, and understood more generally, the line orders the building internally, but it also orders and so orients the building in its surroundings. Le Corbusier viewed such lineal and axial connections of the building to its surrounds, not in terms of an abstracted linearity imposed from above (though they may be presented in that way), but as given through situatedness *in* a building, environment or landscape. Using the example of the Acropolis in Athens (which does indeed allow a very clear sense of axial structure, though largely in virtue of its elevation from the plain), Le Corbusier thus argues:

> A birds'-eye [*sic*] view such as is given by a plan on a drawing board is not how axes are seen; they are seen from the ground, the beholder standing up and looking in front of him. The eye can reach a considerable distance and, like a clear lens, sees everything even beyond what was intended or wished. The axis of the Acropolis runs from the Piraeus to Pentelicus, from the sea to the mountain. The Propylae are at right angles to the axis, in the distance on the horizon – the sea.[13]

The point here is the contrast between the bird's-eye view, which enables a view of space as a relatively flat expanse, landmarks reduced essentially to points, compared to the view which, even if from an elevated position on some rocky outcrop such as the Acropolis, is still a view that looks along and towards rather than from above, and so allows landmarks to be salient as landmarks, retaining a certain sense of embeddedness in a landscape. The way the axial structure works out in a larger landscape is clearly evident in Le Corbusier's urban designs – notably his design for Chandigarh, with its avenues and linear configurations.[14]

As examples like that of Le Corbusier (or sixteenth-century Rome) make clear, the understanding of space and place that is at work in this idea of the connection established by the line, and its relation to design, is not new or unprecedented, and one might argue that, in some form or another, it is, in fact, foundational to architectural practice – even if it is not always explicitly recognized as such, and even if it is not always well-integrated into that practice – and is especially clear in urban and landscape design (partly because both require the integration of elements across distance). Indeed, one might reasonably argue that the way in which spaces, and also the places that hold such spaces within them, are shaped and formed, and so are experienced and understood through the movements and orientational possibilities that they afford, is actually fundamental to any form of spatial design (and so, one might argue, for all design), as well as for any form of spatial representation (including the architectural drawing) or spatial mapping.

The way in which this idea appears in spatial representation, in particular, is exemplified in an especially interesting way in early maritime charts – so-called portolan charts – that connect points along the coastline (usually ports or anchorages, hence the name 'portolan' or 'portulano') by direct lines that represent compass bearings and also, therefore, lines of sail (see Figure 7.2). Here, the otherwise featureless space of the ocean is rendered navigable, and given a shape, through the connections between the destinations at its edges. The space of a portolan chart is essentially a space of connectivity. However, although portolan charts give rise to patterns of intersecting lines, it is not the connections between lines that matter (the points of the intersection between lines can be almost entirely ignored), but rather the connections between locations that the lines indicate. Each line represents a direction of movement from one location to another along a particular compass heading. The space of connectivity that the portolan chart delineates is thus a space depicted specifically in terms of a set of linear elements: first, the lines that make up the compass rose that is a key element in all such charts (see, again, Figure 7.2, top left-hand corner); second, the multiple lines that extend outwards from each significant point on the chart to connect that point up with other such points; and third, the delineation of coastlines (portolan charts, being entirely maritime, typically contain no details concerning the interior of the land).

The multiple and intersecting lines that make up a portolan chart appear in a different form in topographic mapping, where the aim is to delineate, not merely pathways between points, but the face of the landscape as such. The lines that

Figure 7.2 Map of the eastern Mediterranean Sea from a Portolan atlas (*c.* 1544) dedicated to Hieronymus Ruffault, Abbot of St. Vaast. Agnese, Battista, 1514–64. Library of Congress Geography and Map Division – https://www.loc.gov/resource/g3200m.gct00001/?sp–11

enable such a mapping do not appear on the map but are part of that by which the mapping is achieved. Thus, the topographical surveyor takes sightings from one landmark to another, measuring the angles between sightings and the distance between landmarks (a distance that, in the days of theodolite and chain, was measured by means of the surveyor's actual journey across that distance), so as to triangulate between them and thereby plot their relative positions. In that manner, through the repetition of such triangulation, a picture of the entire landscape is built up. Here, the key point, once again, is the idea of the line as both indicating movement between locations and orienting at a location, which is to say, as that by means of which a place or space – in the case of topographical surveying, a stretch of country – is articulated, re-presented and understood. Moreover, the lines that the surveyor uses in the articulation of a landscape are not merely lines imposed onto that landscape, but are, rather, lines that can also be found within it (in the same way that the pathways that connect towns and landmarks are not impositions onto the terrain that they traverse, but are themselves part of that terrain). To put the point more generally, the connections between the elements in a landscape are themselves part of that very landscape.

The use of the line here emphasizes the line as an axis of movement or journey, but it is quite clear that the line also constitutes a line of orientation – a sighting, a line of vision, a view – that is not too far removed from the line of orientation that, together with the surveyor's measured movement between landmarks, enables the topographic understanding and representation of a stretch of country. The line is thus both path or journey and sight or view – the potential of movement and orientation together. Indeed, only thus could the line be said to shape space and assist in the forming of a response to a place, or even in the formation of a place as such. Movement, if it is directed or meaningful, is impossible without orientation; and, in turn, orientation is always and only in relation to movement or possible movement.

The line establishes certain pathways of movement, not only through the connecting of elements within a building, a site, or between building, site, and surrounding locale, but also by virtue of the line's own shape and direction. One of the key forms that exemplifies this is the spiral, particularly as it appears in the labyrinth – a typically doubled structure that takes us into the centre, but also takes us out again (the labyrinth being, in this respect, distinct from most modern *mazes*, although the terms 'labyrinth' and 'maze' are often used to mean the same). The structure is clearly evident in the famous labyrinth (dating from the thirteenth century) in the floor of the cathedral at Chartres (see Figure 7.3).[15] The inward curve of the spiral gives a dynamic character to the line that turns the line constantly inward, and the curve and the spiral nevertheless emerge through the combination of sequences of lines (each of which delimits and demarcates a separate space) set end to end, with each at an angle to the other. The curve and the spiral thus emerge from the movement established by the inward turn of each lineal segment of the journey into and through the larger structure. Although the movement of the labyrinth is both inwards and outwards, which is made self-evident in the double spiral figure,

Figure 7.3 Labyrinth, Chartres Cathedral, Chartres. Photo: © Sylvain Sonnet.

that doubled movement is also possible, of course, with a single spiralled line – and, in that form, one can see the labyrinth also at work in the form of the architectural promenade that appears in Le Corbusier's Villa Savoye where the pathway takes us upwards towards the sun.

Line, surface and space

From an architectural point of view, the line is both a means for the analysis of a site and a building – and so for the articulation and development of a design – as well as a central element in the functioning and form of the completed building. The line is an integral feature of the built structure, not only evident in the way that structure orients itself to the landmarks around it, and so enables the experience of those landmarks and the surrounding environment, but also in the physical plan of the structure – most obviously in the arrangements of corridors, stairways, doors and windows – and in the composition of the spaces by which it is constituted, and which it also constitutes. Once one moves to understand the role of the line in the physical form of the building, however, one is also forced to recognize the way in which the line cannot be separated from other elements of that built structure, and, indeed, of the site, but is interdependent with those elements, modifying and being modified by them.

If, however, one attends to the spaces at issue as volumetric rather than merely in terms of their linearity, then it would seem that the organizing principle would not be the line, but rather the interlinking of adjoining or overlapping spaces, and the key idea would be the use of the surface as that which constitutes the boundary between spaces. The omission or removal of a section of that bounding surface allows a disturbance of the spatial separation that otherwise obtains – whether that disturbance is of the relation between an external and an internal space (in the case of a window), or of the relation between two internal spaces (through the use of cut-out sections of wall that might form a door or passageway, or simply a connecting space). Yet to treat the design as determined in this fashion (and the determination that is at issue is not that of the designers' intention, so much as that of the 'inner' principle governing the design as such) is to treat the building as a static, rather than dynamic, formation. But how exactly are the overlapping spaces at issue here interlinked? The interlinking cannot be purely geometrical, that is, two spaces that are each composed of a section of space that also belongs to the other. Instead, the interlinking has to be an interlinking that is constituted through the way in which each space is somehow oriented towards the other, opens into it, allows movement towards or through it (this connects with the question of interiority as always involving an entry 'into' that is the focus of Chapter 10). Here the line reappears as that by means of which two places or spaces are able to be connected, either by movement or by orientation, and so can be seen as operative even in a design that might otherwise appear to prioritize a different design principle.

What is evident here, of course, is the way in which the line functions as a fundamental element in the very structuring of a space. The shape of a space is a matter of the dynamic that is inherent to that space, and that dynamic is determined by the possibilities of the movement, as well as the orientation (which need not always be a matter of visual orientation alone), that it affords. Such possibilities of movement and orientation can be understood, as already seen, in terms of the specific lines that connect different parts of a space, or that connect parts of that space with other spaces.

The preference, in so many buildings, for orthogonal structure might be thought to stand somewhat at odds with this emphasis on the dynamic character of space – purely geometrical forms, whether understood in terms of two- or three-dimensional figures (square, cube, rectangular prism), appear to exemplify the static and the fixed, rather than the dynamic or the mobile. It is not so much geometric form alone that must be attended to, but the way in which those forms, in their concrete realizations, operate within the larger structures of which they might be part, that is, as they stand in relation to other elements of those structures and to the surrounding environment. Understanding those forms in this 'functional' manner does not mean understanding them only in terms of the dynamic of the line that connects spaces, however, but also in terms of the bounding surfaces that are themselves constitutive of spaces.

The role of the bounding surface is directly tied to the role also played by the connecting line. Indeed, one might say of the surface that it is a form of the line or is generable out of it – it is the line as drawn out and expanded into the plane (imagine the line stretched at right angles to its length). Typically, the line connects (joins or mediates), but the line can also be used to dissect (as it cuts across and separates, and thereby also delimits), though in this latter form it operates primarily as surface. One could, of course, also treat line and surface as they appear here as distinct. Yet however the relation between them is understood, surface always implicates line and line always implicates surface. Line and surface appear together, and together they mark out the shape of a space. While the line marks out a space through the way it marks out possibilities of movement and orientation in and through that space, it is the surface that determines and directs the possibilities for such movement and orientation through the way in which it bounds and contains, and so also constitutes, the space itself.

The surface, whether placed vertically or horizontally, whether functioning as wall, ceiling, roof or floor, can be seen to operate in a way that highlights its character as delimiting boundary – almost as the skin that shapes that space, that holds it together, although a skin that forms both an inner and an outer space at one and the same time. The role of the surface here is one recognized in Aristotle's definition of the *topos* of a thing as 'the innermost motionless boundary of what contains it'.[16] *Topos* is the inner surface that encircles and contains the thing – its horizon, one might say – and thereby gives to that thing its particular place or location. Aristotle can therefore be said to understand place and space (*topos* encompassing both, somewhat as does the French *espace*) as essentially a matter of containment. There is no doubt that this is an important element in any topological structure. Yet, although to be in a place (or in a space as it is understood in connection to place) is to find oneself 'within' that place or space, to have a sense of being in this space or place rather than another – of being just 'here' – is also to have a sense of what might lie without that place, which is to have a sense of 'there'. That is why the surface does, indeed, have to be seen as a 'skin' that belongs to two spaces at once, so that, from one side, it may be seen as the skin of an outer space into which the inner space pushes and, from the other side, as the skin of an inner space pushing outward (which also means that in its very character as delimiting the surface also joins or mediates, and so the initial distinction made above between line as connecting and surface as separating is underlain by a greater degree of complexity).

The relation that appears here – described by the phenomenological psychologist Erwin Strauss as 'the relation of within and without'[17] – is central to any topology and it is part of what sets the topological apart from the merely spatial. The latter point holds despite the tendency to think of containment according to the way one space can be included *within* another – the reference to 'within' indicating how the topological (at work in this 'within') is already presupposed. This relation of 'within and without' and, with it, 'interiority', is a topic to which the discussion will return in Chapter 10. What is important, here, is to see how the structure of a place, and so of space as derivative of place, is differentiated rather than uniform, and is organized in a way that, as Strauss also argues, is dynamic and active, rather than inert and passive. Place and space do not exist merely as some stretched out expanse that awaits the intervention of an agent, but already contain movement and activity – even, one might say, already structure such movement and activity.

Strauss puts this point by claiming that the boundaries at work in the structure of 'within and without' are 'relative to the action system of the bound person',[18] and that 'the relation of within and without is not a spatial phenomenon ... [but] a phenomenon of the scope of action'.[19] This threatens, however, to make the structure of a place and space into something dependent on the structure of agency or, even, of subjectivity – as if agency or subjectivity came first. This is especially problematic in relation to subjectivity which is not something apart from the place in which it finds and articulates itself but something more like a function of that place, intimately and inextricably bound up with it. Agency, meanwhile, must be understood as also a part of that place – as belonging essentially to it. In this respect, one might say that the bounding surface and the line of movement appear together, as part of a single topology, and together they can be seen as determinative of the shaping of space, as well as being primary elements in the design and analysis of spaces. Spatial design draws out and draws upon these elements, and in doing so, draws out and draws upon their role in spatial formation, thereby also drawing out and drawing upon the lineal and topological character of such architectural forms (which encompass both forms of opening and enclosure) as window, door, corridor, pathway, wall, roof and ceiling. Thus, the wall, for instance, appears as a form of bounding surface, and so as integral to the space that is a room, rather than as an architectural feature that could be grasped apart from that space.

Place, space and movement

As a principle of design, the integrated operation of line and surface is not a principle that is geared merely to the *visual* appearance, or 'look', of the building, but rather to its *dynamic* appearance – to the forms of movement and orientation that the building enables. Indeed, on this account, the building is the concrete realization of a certain set of dynamic and orientational possibilities that already lie present in the landscape in which the building is situated.[20] This means too that the integration of building with environment is not primarily or only based in its visual integration (although such visual integration is not unimportant) but rather in the various forms of connectivity and disconnectivity established by means of the line as well as the bounding surface. The connection and disconnection, at issue here, is that which comes through being able to move from one place, space or thing, to another – a bodily movement that may involve the body's moving (in the passage from one place to another) or the body's being moved (by the way in which a certain place opens up to a view and to a mode of bodily comportment that accords with that).[21]

The fact that a design may be driven by its dynamic, rather than purely visual, character does not mean, however, that the visual is therefore a neglected element in the design, or in the design process. The question is how the visual is understood and how it relates to the design as such. What role does it play in the design, and how do visual elements emerge in the design process and become evident in the design as such? – a question that is also related to the matter of ornamentation or decoration that was briefly considered in Chapter 5. Ornament and decoration are not primarily elements added to a building, but can be seen to reside, in Semperian fashion, and from the very first, in the way the elements of the built form are ordered and configured, including, for instance, in the use of colour and texture. The latter are part of the very surfaces that constitute spaces – whether interior or exterior – rather than being mere additives to surfaces and spaces already fully constituted (and so, for instance, a change in colour is itself a change in surface). This coheres with the way the surface functions, and with the way the surface is itself brought to the fore. Decoration and ornament can, of course, perform many different functions – some of them symbolic, some purely aesthetic (in the sense of a certain sort of sensory 'pleasure') – but decoration and ornament can also serve to draw attention to, or to make salient, certain elements or features within the structure of a design. The use of decoration and ornament enables the bringing to salience of surface and of line. In this way, decoration and ornament serve to bring out elemental features and forms that are integral to the design as such. The surface and the line can thus be seen as ornamental, not through being additions to a structure, nor through having elements added to them, but rather through the way in which they can themselves function ornamentally as essential elements of the structure. Moreover, they operate as forms of ornamentation or decoration, not only through the way in which they draw attention to their own topological and linear character, but also through the way in which they are used to draw attention to the relation, integration and separation between different elements of a design.

Places and spaces are not constituted, however, only, or even primarily, in terms of the visual image they present to a viewer. Instead, places and spaces are constituted in terms of the movement that is possible within them, and closely tied to this, the orientational possibilities they also afford. The employment of the line and, with it, the surface (whether understood as a form of the line or additional to it) embodies this conception of the fundamentally dynamic character of spaces and places, and so, too, of the necessity for any response to place, in the form of built space, to operate in a way that is attentive to, and draws upon, the lines that delineate a place, and give shape to a space. The drawing is constituted through the movement of the line, but the line itself gains meaning only in relation to the drawing that it enables. In similar fashion, the line that is integral to a place, and opens up a space, becomes evident as significant, as a pathway to or from somewhere, only in relation to that place and space. In a certain sense, then, the line does not exist prior to the drawing, but, rather, both appear together; and neither does the line come before the place or space to which it belongs. Movement and orientation are integral to places and to space, and places and space are given in and through movement and orientation. In the text of 'Building Dwelling Thinking', this emphasis on the dynamic character of place and space, and so, too, on the role of the body, is not something to which Heidegger draws attention.

Yet that does not mean it is absent from his account. Indeed, the fundamentally relational character of the fourfold, which includes the place of human being in it, ought to be indicative of exactly the same sort of dynamic, moving character that is so salient in the discussion of the hand and of the line. That means that 'dwelling', too, is a kind of movement, not a mere staying, but already something active, even if it is also receptive in that activity. This is partly why Heidegger can say that '*dwelling*, insofar as it keeps or secures the fourfold in things, is, as this keeping, a *building*'.[22]

Chapter 8

PLACE AND PARAMETRICISM

Although not an architectural treatise or manifesto, 'Building Dwelling Thinking' nevertheless situates architecture in direct relation to 'dwelling' and, thereby, to place. It is thus that the essay has become a key text in 'place-oriented' thinking about architecture and design. This is true, not only in terms of the role Heidegger's essay plays in the work of such as Norberg-Schulz, Relph, Mugerauer, Seamon and others like them, but also, even if indirectly, in a contemporary understanding of architecture, among many theorists and practitioners alike, as essentially constituted in and through the engagement with place. And whilst the idea often appears in a simple and even superficial form – sometimes little more than in the idea that architects should pay attention to 'site' – it also appears in more sophisticated articulations. Critical Regionalism (the Frampton manifesto) provides one important example of this (even though it offers little insight into the concept of place on which it draws), as does, perhaps even more so, the phenomenologically oriented approach to design found in the work of architects and architectural theorists such as Peter Zumthor and Juhani Pallasmaa. And despite the infrequency of its explication, the appeal to place is commonplace in many contemporary institutional and policy contexts. In Australia, for instance, the architecture and design policy for the state of New South Wales (administered through the office of the Government Architect) not only invokes the idea of place in its very title, *Better Placed*, but also talks of the creation of 'good places' as a primary aim of architecture and design.[1]

If a focus on 'place' (or at least appeal to the idea) is evident in many areas of contemporary architectural and design discourse, it is by no means widespread nor is it the most salient feature of such discourse. Indeed, many would argue that the language of parametric design, or 'parametricism', along with the general shift to forms of digitality, has a much higher profile in contemporary architectural discourse, being associated with some of the best-known of recent and contemporary architectural practitioners such as Frank Gehry and the late Zaha Hadid (whose practice has continued under the direction of Patrik Schumacher). To a large extent, at least in terms of the realities of concrete architectural practice, the placed and the parametric seem to stand quite apart from one another. Place-based design tends not to engage with the parametric, while parametric approaches often seem not to draw on ideas of place in any integral way that goes beyond the merely symbolic. Thus, a building such as Hadid's Heydar Aliyev

Figure 8.1 Heydar Aliyev Center, Baku, Zaha Hadid Architects, 2007–12. Photo: Elnur Amikishiyev/Meashots.com, 2014.

Center in Baku, Azerbaijan (see Figure 8.1), purports to connect with previous architectural and cultural forms native to the region, but its dominant character is little different from that of Hadid's designs elsewhere – a distinctive parametric form dominates over any local character. And on the other hand, a building such as Peter Zumthor's famous Therme Vals spa (see Figure 8.2) eschews the sculpted curvilinear surfaces often associated with parametricism looking instead to more regular forms and emphasizing a connection to human habitation rather than to formal complexity alone. Yet, if place is an important notion in architecture and design, then it seems reasonable to ask to what extent place can be taken up within the frame of the parametric; and if the parametric is so important and transformative of contemporary architectural and design practice, then to what extent can the parametric be accommodated within any place-based approach. How one answers such questions depends, however, on what the terms at issue are taken to mean – on what is taken to be at issue in talk of both 'place' and the 'parametric' – something that cannot simply be assumed.

Parametricism and the parametric

Parametricism is a controversial term. To some, notably Patrik Schumacher, the one who is credited with inventing the term and who was also Zaha Hadid's

Figure 8.2 Therme Vals, Peter Zumthor, 1996. Photo: cjreddaway/Flickr, 2011.

collaborator, it designates a style or movement.[2] To others, it names any approach to design that gives priority to the use of parametric techniques.[3] Although terms can certainly be appropriated to different uses, the emphasis on parametricism as characterized by technique rather than style seems the more reasonable if only because it ties parametricism and the parametric back to that which is certainly invoked in the terms themselves – namely, the idea of the parameter as such. Indeed, the fact that approaches to design that draw upon parametric techniques can, in principle, give rise to a wide range of different design forms (and have done so in the past even if, in contemporary architecture, they often give rise to much that is similar) and can also be applied to many different design tasks (not only in architecture) would seem to reinforce the characterization of parametricism in terms of technique. Understood in this way, parametricism, or parametric design, can be said to be a mode of design practice according to which design outcomes are generated through the manipulation (frequently, but not always, using computer design tools) of sets of quantities that can be varied within a certain range and whose variation is often interlinked. The degree of variability, over which those quantities range, indicates and is set by the parameters (or what might also be thought of as the boundary conditions or defining limits) of the design, and the final outcome will be the result of the fixing of those quantities in a way that satisfies those parameters overall, according to the preferences of the designer.

This characterization of parametric design, and of the idea of the parametric as such, does not, of course, touch on the possibility of parametric techniques and the outcomes of those techniques being deployed and made use of in a wide variety of ways. So, for instance, parametric techniques, when allied with forms of computer visualization, allow the construction of models that can enable both the virtual realization of design ideas and the testing out of variations on those ideas, as well as offer an environment in which multiple participants in a design conversation can access and contribute to a developing design process. This may well be an important feature of the way in which parametric design is employed in many digitally oriented design situations – and it is especially significant for the way in which it allows the handling of complex bodies of information and the enormous variability in potential outcomes that may result from different design approaches that may draw on or respond to that information. Nevertheless, the way parametric approaches may, in this way, facilitate forms of communication and collaboration is more a feature of the complexity and power of contemporary digital and computational technology in general than of a specific mode of parametric design as such. Moreover, the fact that parametric approaches can also lead to unanticipated outcomes – something that may be especially important in design – is a function, not merely of the parametric, but of complex systems in general. Certainly, parametric design calls upon algorithmic and mathematical processes that are also at the heart of many digital and computational technologies, but this does not mean that digital and computational technology can be taken to be identical with (or as an instance of) the parametric as it is at issue in contemporary design practice.

Parametric design is frequently treated as a relatively new phenomenon – as essentially an outcome of contemporary digital approaches to design – and as such one can already see how it might provoke questions concerning the relation between parametricism and the critique of technology that Heidegger advances (and that have been alluded to, if not fully explicated, at various points in the discussions so far). But there is an important sense in which what lies at the heart of parametric design is something basic to all design and, indeed, to almost any attempt at explanation or understanding. Parametric design can be viewed as a form of optimization process that begins with a set of general optimization conditions that can be fulfilled in more than one way. This situation is one that can obtain specifically in design, but it also obtains in every problem-solving situation involving multiple variables that must be solved together, and so where the constraints on solution are holistic rather than atomistic. Consider, for example, a translation problem focused on a specific text. There will be no single solution to the problem of translation that is uniquely determined by the text. There will be a set of parameters within which the translation must operate, but essentially those parameters are set by the text itself. The translation must be adequate to fix the values (where such 'fixing' is relative to the translation) of all the terms that the text contains, and so the assignment of translational values to each term must be consistent with all of the other terms. In the practice of translation, one typically varies the values assigned to parts of the text until one arrives at an overall assignment that is deemed satisfactory.

The major difference between the translation case and that of contemporary parametric design is that the variation in assigned values is not a variation that ranges over quantities – the variation is over semantic values which might be seen as qualitative rather than quantitative. However, that has not stopped attempts to develop approaches to translation that draw, like contemporary parametric design, on computational and algorithmic approaches (although how adequate these approaches are or can be remains controversial). Of course, in design, one can also employ parametric techniques without explicit appeal to computation or algorithms. A designer who sketches variations on a basic design form using paper and pencil may effectively be operating parametrically even if not in any formalized fashion. The basic idea of the parametric is just that of a set of parameters that allow for variation among a range of outcomes. Significantly, neither the decision regarding the setting of the initial parameters, nor the decision that governs which outcome is to be preferred, can be determined parametrically – at least not from within the parameters of the original parametric process (although any specific parametric process can be embedded within other such processes, so one might have a parametric process that operates to deliver both settings and decision outcomes for other such processes). It is important to recognize the way contemporary parametricism in design is connected both to the character of problem-solving in general (as a specific form of problem-solving) as well as to earlier and especially non-digital design practices. Doing so allows what is at work in parametric design to be better understood, revealing the basic structure of parametric design and its limits. In other words, it allows a better understanding of the parameters within which such design operates, and which also constitute it. In Heideggerian terms, one might say that what this allows is a shift, even if limited in scope, to an ontological perspective – to allow the question as to the nature and grounds, as well as the limits, of parametric design to become evident.

The distinctiveness of place

Unlike parametricism, 'place' is, as should be evident from the discussion in previous chapters, a much broader and more complex term. Although place is often invoked by architects and designers, what is meant by place in architecture or design is seldom explicitly explained or interrogated. Often invoked as if its meaning were already self-evident, the way place is used suggests that it is frequently taken to be identical merely with a particular spatial location or some spatially demarcated area.[4] In this respect, there is a strong tendency for 'place' to be treated as almost interchangeable with 'space'. Yet even though the *terms* can overlap (and in some languages the same term can be used to refer to both place and space), the *ideas*, and place and space themselves, are nevertheless distinct. That place is *sui generis* and not simply identical with space, and certainly not with the reduced notion of space *as extension* that is common in modern thought, has underlain much of the preceding discussion. It has also come explicitly to the fore at various places in the discussion so far (most notably in Chapters 3 and 7) and will do so again (in Chapter 10). Nevertheless, the issue is one that requires attention here since it is so directly relevant to the discussion of parametricsm and the parametric.

The most significant point of distinction between place and space, as noted several times already, relates to bound or limit (the latter terms being used here more or less synonymously[5]). Place is essentially bounded. However, there is nothing in space, *as such*, that requires boundedness or limitation. One can thus begin with the idea of a delimited space as might apply to the space of a particular object or site (often a notion of volume or area), but if one then removes the limits of that object or site, extending the space outwards indefinitely, one has not thereby undermined the idea of space that is at issue. An *unlimited* space still makes sense *as space* no less than does a *delimited* space. Indeed, in many respects it is the idea of a delimited space that more immediately gives rise to difficulties, something evident in the problem – given especially concrete formulation by Lucretius – of whether one can make sense of an edge to the cosmos. Lucretius imagines a spearman, standing at the supposed edge, who throws a spear outwards. Either the spear flies past the supposed edge, in which case it is no edge at all, or it bounces back, in which case it must have been stopped by something, some sort of wall, that is itself in space, and so exists on the other side of the edge, in which case, once again, the edge is no real edge at all (and one can repeat the same argument with respect to any edge that is postulated further out beyond the original supposed edge).[6] Contemporary thinking has dealt with this problem through forms of geometry that allow us to understand the absolute boundedness of a space without that boundedness appearing as an impossible boundary that occurs within the space. But this does not impugn the basic point at issue here; namely, that neither the idea of space, nor space as such, contains within it (either as a phenomenon of the space or a component of the idea) the idea of any non-arbitrary and transgressible boundary. This is not so in respect of place. Place can be entered into or departed from, and so places are essentially tied to ideas of boundary and boundedness. Thus, if one removes the bounds or limits of a place associated with an object or site, then one is not left with an *unlimited* place, but with *no place* at all – one loses the here/there that is the heart of place – and what is left, if anything, is just the idea of pure extension, or *space*.

8. Place and Parametricism 141

The lack of any intrinsic limit to space or the idea of space is tied to the character of space as amenable to quantification – something indicated by the etymological connection of the Latin term *spatium*, from which modern forms of the term in many European languages derive, to *stadium*, a unit of linear measurement as well as a place measured out to a certain length, and to the Greek *spadion*, which has similar meanings. Quantification is tied to number, and much the same problem in trying to formulate the idea of a boundary *in* space appears in relation to trying to formulate the idea of an upper boundary in the sequence of natural numbers, because, for any number that is supposed to represent an upper limit to the sequence of numbers, there is always another number greater than it (and the same might be said to apply to any additive quantificational sequence). Unlike 'space', 'place' has no such quantitative connotations in its etymological derivation, instead having its origin via the Latin *platea*, in the Greek *plateia*, meaning 'broad way', and which itself comes from *platus*, meaning 'flat' or 'broad' (as in the broad-billed platypus). Although space is tied etymologically to notions of span or stretch, essentially to the idea of measurable extension, and place also carries a sense of breadth or openness (so that every place gives space within it), what marks off the notion of place is just the idea of an openness that is also bounded. Place is essentially a *bounded openness* – something nicely captured, as noted in Chapter 5, in 'place', as it appears in English and French, and as *plateia* itself is used in contemporary Greek (the Italian *piazza* coming, via Latin, from the same Greek root), in reference to an open but bounded area, a 'square', within a town or village (see earlier image – Figure 5.1).[7]

This understanding of place not only differentiates place from space, even while it acknowledges a connection between them (since every place allows space within it), but it also distinguishes place from mere position or simple location. This is significant since it means that place cannot be construed in geometrical terms – neither as tied to any sort of positional array, nor as a point in a system of coordinates, nor as a geometrical projection. In addition, place cannot be construed as some sort of construction, whether geometrical or social. In this latter respect, place cannot be a product of subjectivity, since subjectivity only arises in a place, and is itself always placed – and the same is true for the social and for the political. The standard understanding of place, ubiquitous in modern social theory, as essentially space plus subjectivity is not only false but also naïve, since it treats subjectivity as prior to place and as therefore somehow unplaced. The tendency in many areas of architecture and design to treat place, in similar fashion, as *essentially* a function of subjectivity is problematic for the same reasons. Place undoubtedly stands in an important relation to subjectivity (and to the human), but it is not determined by subjectivity. Indeed, properly speaking, it is subjectivity that is 'determined', in the sense of being made possible, by place.[8]

None of this is to deny the fact that the terms 'place' and 'space' (and 'time', too, for that matter) can be used in a wide variety of ways. At issue here is not how the terms may sometimes be deployed, but what concepts are at work in talk of, for instance, place-based design. If such talk is to be genuinely contentful, and not arbitrary, then it must involve the idea of a mode of design that does not mistake place for space or reduce place to some subjective construct or geometrical projection; that does not treat place as a mere quantity, but that is also attentive to the bounded openness that is place, and so is attentive to both the boundedness *on* which the act of design is focused and the boundedness *within* which it operates.

Measure, quantity and limit

If the parametric is treated in its broadest sense, the sense that does not tie it exclusively to the computational, the algorithmic or the quantitative – the broad sense of the parametric, indicated earlier – then the parametric displays an important point of convergence with the placed. The idea of the parametric is the idea of the bounded, since the parameter is a bound, and place is also constituted by its boundedness. But the parametric also carries with it the idea of a bounding *measure* (*metron* in the Greek). How the latter notion is understood – to what extent measure is taken as *quantitative* – will determine how the parametric is understood, and so how it is understood in relation to place. Understood as *quantitative*, measure implies the prioritization of space, as quantifiable, over place, as irreducibly qualitative (quantity being itself tied to the spatial). If measure is understood differently – as, for instance, Heidegger treats 'measure' and, more specifically, the 'taking of measure' in "' ... Poetically Man Dwells ... '" (discussed in Chapter 2) – then a different path of thinking is opened up. In Heidegger's case, where the 'taking of measure' is a matter of the proper assigning of things in their relations to one another, then measure (which now brings with it connotations of appropriate *judgement*) is itself tied to place – to the letting things be in the places proper to them. This, however, seems a sense of 'measure' that is far removed from that at work in most contemporary discussions of the parametric.

If the question of the extent to which the parametric is tied to the quantitative is nevertheless put as a genuine question here, then it is partly in order not to forget or overlook the point, made earlier, regarding the way the parametric connects with general forms of problem-solving as well as those unique to architecture or design. This would still be consistent with also recognizing the way the parametric connects with measure and, given the tendency to construe measure in terms of quantity, with recognizing the way the parametric itself tends towards the quantificational, the computational and, so, also the spatial. But it would allow us to see that connection as it stands against a more complex conceptual background, and thus provide some insight into the complexities of the parametric itself. Yet the fact that the emphasis on the parametric as quantificational already tends the parametric towards space, and away from place, may be thought to have begged the original question – to have already assumed, in the way place has been characterized, the incompatibility of place and the parametric. Is it really the case that place is so resistant to quantification? What exactly is it about place that could set it apart from quantity in this way?

A large part of the answer lies in the nature of limit itself – or in the different forms of limit at work in the spatial and in the topological. Spatial limits always demarcate a spatial domain in such a way that the space on either side of the limit is essentially the same. Thus, space can be divided up, without changing the nature of the space that is so divided – the divisions being like the divisions of a measuring tape or ruler or, even, of a map. One might say that the limit at issue in spatial terms is purely quantitative or numerical because this is also the nature of quantity and number. The quantitative is just that which allows itself to be divided up or added to without any intrinsic alteration. Topological limits or bounds – the limits or bounds that constitute places – are quite different in this respect, as are the places themselves. The bounds of a place mark out quite different regions on each side of the bound, which is to say that the bound is always asymmetrical in structure – what lies on each side of the boundary is not the same, and this is captured in the difference between inside and outside. That difference is not a difference merely of quantity or number and cannot be expressed only quantitatively or numerically.

At this point, a brief diversion may be in order, since one of the features of Patrik Schumacher's treatment of parametricism (mentioned earlier) is his assimilation of the parametric to the *autopoietic*, and the autopoietic also brings with it a notion of bound or limit. The notion of autopoiesis, which has become fashionable in many contemporary domains, originates in discussions of biological systems.[9] Literally translated from the Greek, it means 'self-making' (*auto-poiesis*). It refers primarily to processes of self-realization and self-maintenance. Biological systems are the paradigmatic examples of autopoietic systems or entities because their development is governed by principles and structures internal to the system or entity that also maintains the integrity of the system or entity. Autopoietic systems are bounded systems, since both the maintenance and development of the entity or system are tied to the bounds or limits that are constitutive of it. The role of bound or limit in autopoietic systems is not always explicitly thematized, and it is not thematized in Schumacher's account.

Schumacher's focus seems to be on the parametric as autopoietic, strictly in the sense of being self-realizing and self-maintaining. The difficulty, however, is that the parametric is not autopoietic in this sense – or at least not in any especially meaningful way. The parameters within a parametric design framework operate in such a way that changes in assigned quantities always bring adjustments in the overall structure, but this simply reflects the character of parametric systems as indeed systematic and holistic. Autopoietic systems are also systematic and holistic, but autopoiesis is not identical with systematicity or holism. Significantly, autopoietic systems need not be conceptualized as systems that operate over quantities. Aristotelian biology understands living things autopoietically (in fact, one might argue that, whilst Aristotle does not use the term, the idea of autopoiesis is essentially the reformulation of an Aristotelian notion, though, in Aristotle, expressed in terms of entelechy and function), but it does not, therefore, understand living beings as determined quantitatively. Perhaps most significantly, as self-realizing and self-maintaining, autopoiesis is a temporal notion as well as spatial. It involves the idea of an entity or system developing and maintaining its integrity within the limits proper to it over time. Parametric systems need exhibit no such capacity for temporally – or spatially – extended self-maintenance or self-realization.

To return, however, to the main theme, it is the distinctive character of the limit or bound associated with place that presents an insuperable limit to attempts to treat place, or the bounds and limits of place, in quantitative or numerical terms. Indeed, this underlies the difficulty involved in any attempt to treat experience, meaning, mind or any such 'contentual' notions quantitively and numerically. The claim advanced here is that it is the character of place that underlies this non-reducibility, but the fact of such irreducibility is evident in many different domains, often without any reference being made to the notion of place at all. The idea that one could treat place parametrically, by looking to quantitative 'measures' of place, is already ruled out by the character of place – and so of experience, meaning and mind – as intrinsically qualitative.

This should not, in fact, be a terribly surprising conclusion. It is evidently the case, for instance, that variations in an agent's mental life – in experiences, thoughts, emotions and so on – cannot be mapped in any direct linear fashion onto physical variations in the agent's environment (even in the immediately surrounding environment). This is not just because of individual or 'subjective' difference. Instead it arises, first, because of the way in which individuals are embedded in environments 'holistically' (which means that the assigning of values to elements within any individual-environmental structure, even were it possible overall, would be subject to the same variability – what in other contexts might be called indeterminacy – as is evident within parametric systems. It arises, second, because of the complex way in which mental states depend (or 'supervene') upon physical states (so there is no significant type-type identity between those states that reliably carries across from one instance to another). There is another level of difficulty here, however, that relates to a fundamental difference specific to the situation of architectural design.

Language, place and narrative

In one of several allusions to the limitations of parametric design in his *Attunement: Architectural Meaning after the Crisis of Modern Science*, Alberto Pérez-Gómez writes:

> The obsession with algorithmically generated form thrives on a distrust of the capacity of words to recount the experiential qualities of a site and to propose meaningful, attuned environments for human cultures, a distrust justified by the inherent opacity that always operates in the gap between the words we speak and the things we make.[10]

8. Place and Parametricism

Language permeates human experience. Even when one does not speak or cannot find the right words, language stands always in the background, surrounding and supporting us. Places are structured by and opened up by language. The most obvious way this is evident is in the way places are suffused with stories and narratives. Many of those stories and narratives are of the simplest kind – stories and narratives of how to get from here to there, or of how to do this or that – but there are also stories and narratives of a more complex and emotionally charged character, stories and narratives of identity and self-formation, that connect to memory and anticipation, to hope and fear, to desire and belief, that enable and express communication and community, as well as alienation and loss. Without stories, and so without language, there are no places. How then does a quantitative approach to design that aims to engage with place also manage to engage with language and with story?

The problem is even more complex than it might first appear since architectural design, including the techniques of parametric design, is so much oriented towards the production of three-dimensional designs in visual form. But how are language and story to be encompassed by means of three-dimensional visual presentations? Contrary to the old saw, pictures do not tell stories – neither one story nor many stories. Stories live in language and not in pictures, and it is only through being embedded in language that one can suppose that there are stories to be found in pictures in the first place. The stories found in pictures are stories that emerge as the picture is given linguistic articulation. If there is a limit to parametric design in its capacity to engage with place, then it is not only in the limit of the quantitative and the spatial, but also in the limit of the story, of the narrative and of language (a limit, it might be added, that is directly connected to the way language and place are intimately tied together).

Although he does not focus so directly on story, narrative or language, Richard Coyne also draws attention to certain features of parametric design that are evident visually:

> It's no wonder that parametric design flourishes in the production of elegant sweeping building facades and continuous organic roof structures, rather than floor plans, circulation routes, and subtle spatial interventions. With skins, surfaces and sculptural abstractions, the constraints and their interdependencies are more amenable to algorithmic control, unencumbered by issues of use, history, culture, politics, and the complexities of human inhabitation.[11]

Part of Coyne's point is that the very quantitative nature of contemporary parametric design practices tends to give priority to certain more abstracted and even aesthetic aspects of building design and the forms associated with them (although the aestheticism is more an aestheticism of the conceptual than the sensory), and such abstraction can be seen, once again, as tied to a particular prioritization of the visual. Moreover, in alluding to 'issues of use, history, culture, politics, and the complexities of human inhabitation', Coyne can also be seen to be drawing attention to the complex narratives that are embedded in places, and in which places are embedded, as well as to the way these narratives are an inevitable and inextricable part of any design, both in plan and in built form. To assume that all of those can be encompassed within the frame of a single parametric design system is already to have left out much of what is essential – and that is true even without explicit recourse to the complexities introduced by ideas of place.

Significantly, many of the elements that Coyne suggests are overlooked by parametric approaches are also elements that are more directly related to the way in which built forms interact with human life and activity. On the other hand, those features in the production of which parametric design often 'flourishes', as Coyne puts it, are, in their very abstraction and formality, already removed from such life and activity. In this way, the tendency of parametric design, in its commonly realized contemporary forms, not only stands apart from the complexities of language and narrative, and of 'use, history, culture, politics, and … human inhabitation', but also from the complexities of the human as such (and this is surely what underlies a large part of Pérez-Gómez's critique).

To reiterate a point that runs throughout the discussions in this book, place and the human are inextricably bound together. Human existence is always an existence *in place*, and not merely in the sense that it is spatially located. Human existence is first of all relational, which means that is constituted through the multiple ways in which it is connected, causally, affectively and rationally, with respect to the internality of the self, the commonality of others and the externality of things. Such relationality does not ramify in some unbounded and homogenous space but arises only within the bounded but open heterogeneity of place. The world, as it is open to human engagement in all its multiplicity and alterity, begins in that place, and in the placed-ness that belongs essentially to the human. Just as place resists any reduction to the quantitative, the numerical or the merely spatial, so, too, does the human also resist such reduction. For this reason, the more the parametric is tied to the quantitative, the numerical and the spatial, the more it is untethered from any genuine connection either to place or to the human. It should be no surprise, then, to find many parametrically oriented designers focused on forms of design that seem to operate independently, not only of the complexities of 'human habitation', but even of human capacity,[12] or of human scale (design comes to be a matter of pure form unrelated to *any* scalar frame, including the human). One may then ask to what extent this also constitutes an untethering of this form of design practice from any previous tradition, and so whether it constitutes a completely different form of design practice – perhaps even a new and different disciplinary configuration.

The parametric and its limits

Whatever else it might be or become, it seems clear that parametric design cannot directly take up place as something to be defined parametrically, in the sense in which the latter term is most often used today. And the reason this is so is that place resists reduction to quantity or number. Moreover, not only is this true of place in general, but also of the elements of place – the movements that are an integral part of it, the stories entwined in it, the organizational configurations that it enables, the atmospheres and experiences to which it gives rise. Parametric design will always remain with that which can be given quantitatively, and so also formally, even though that may also be in forms that are aesthetically elegant – indeed, their elegance is a function of their mathematical manipulability and indicative (once again) of the parametric tendency towards the prioritization of form.

One conclusion that might be drawn, here, is that parametric design can operate only as an adjunct to place-based design, along with other design techniques, rather being that in which such design is based or founded. The danger, however, is that the way in which so much contemporary parametric design privileges the quantitative, as well as the abstracted and purely conceptual-aesthetic elements in design, may mean that, even when employed in an explicitly place-based design approach, parametric design will have to be used with caution, just because the tendencies with which it is associated run counter to what is at issue in place. It will be all too easy for the quantitatively parametric to take over, with the likely result being what we so often see in parametric design around the world, namely, the production of buildings whose forms are determined more by the design tools by which they have been formed than the places in which they are actually situated – hence the globalized character of much contemporary design (globalism itself being a feature that Schumacher takes to be characteristic of parametricism as a style).

Of course, parametric design, as noted earlier, does not, itself, generate the parameters with which it operates. Those parameters must have their origins in some existing artefact, site or design idea. The parameters that parametricism employs thus always lie outside of the parametric. This would seem to reinforce the point, already made above, that parametric approaches can only be an adjunct or a tool in design, rather than being constitutive of design, and this must be so even given the design tendencies that parametric design may itself bring with it. If there is a style associated with contemporary parametricism, then, it will be a style grounded in the more basic choices made by parametric designers and that themselves set the parameters of that mode of design that is then termed 'parametricism'. Recognizing this general point is a part of grasping the proper place of parametric design, which is to say, it is part of grasping the limits of parametric design.

Despite the tendency for the parametric to be identified with quantitative and numerical approaches, and so for parametricism to be taken to be more or less convergent with computational (or digital-computational) approaches in design, it remains important not to treat parametricism as simply identical with computationalism. Although it has become dominant in many areas of contemporary architectural design, computation is not always parametric in character. Thus, not only does the parametric extend beyond the computational (as already noted, parametric modes of design and design-making existed even before the advent of digital computation), so does the computational extend beyond the parametric. If computational and parametric are brought together at all, it is only in virtue of the tendency for parametricism, in its narrower contemporary form, to privilege quantity and number, a tendency that is, of course, central to the computational. But inasmuch as parametricism and the computational can be distinguished, then there is also the possibility of thinking of parametricism more broadly, and so in ways that do not rule out the possibility of a real connection between place and the parametric – one that goes beyond the mere technical usefulness of parametric techniques.

To take place as the key notion in architectural design is to take place as having the central conditioning role in the making of design. On this approach, architectural design should, from the very first, be constituted as a response to place. Another way of putting this is to say that it should be place that is the proper *measure* of design (where 'measure' is here understood not as a quantity, but as that which is 'proper to', is 'moderated', is 'within limits'). In this sense, the parametric can be understood as already invoked in the idea of place, since place must here function as that which sets the parameters within which architectural design, in general and in particular, must operate (place will thus be what provides the measure in the sense of moderating, 'appropriating', limiting). Here, finally, there appear to be two answers to the question of the relation between place and parametricism. On the one hand, parametricism always concerns place, since, in one important sense, the parameters of any architectural design can only be the parameters set by the place itself. On the other hand, if the parameters at work in parametric design are understood always to be set quantitatively and numerically, then parametricism will be, at best, a tool or technique available to place-based design (as to any design), or, at worst, may operate to obscure the placed, which is to say, the properly bounded character of design.

There is an obvious irony in the way in which, when understood narrowly as focused on the quantitative, numerical and so also the spatial, parametricism does indeed have a tendency to neglect or overlook the idea of limit or bound. It does so, however, just because of the way in which the bounds that arise within the purely quantitative, the numerical or the spatial can only be arbitrary in character (for this reason, it is also subjective, which is to say that it operates always as something *posited* or *projected* by a subject). The notion of limit or bound at work in the idea of place is not arbitrary, but relates directly to the very nature of place and is constitutive of it (therefore also not a subjective posit or projection). The irony, then, is that parametricism, in this sense, itself stands opposed to a certain form of the parametric – to the parametric as referring to the bounds that belong to place itself. Recognizing this does, however, reinforce the possibility (already briefly indicated above) of rethinking the parametric, quite aside from its role as a design technique, in a way that takes the idea of the parameter, of the 'proper measure', as indeed a fundamental notion. In that way, parametricism would not only be compatible with place-based design but would have to be recognized as identical with it.

Such a reading of parametricism would, however, require a quite radical shift in the dominant understanding of parametricism in contemporary architecture and design. So long as that shift is not accomplished, then parametricism will appear as another of the forms in which the quantitative and spatialized mode of engagement, so characteristic of modernity, continues to operate. The question is whether such a shift is indeed possible. That question is one that Heidegger seems to put in terms of what he says is the 'world-question of thinking' (the answer to which will decide 'what will become of the earth and of human existence on the earth'):

> May we give up what is worthy of thought in favor of the recklessness of exclusively calculative thinking and its immense achievements? Or are we obliged to find paths upon which thinking is capable of responding to what is worthy of thought instead of, enchanted by calculative thinking, mindlessly passing over what is worthy of thought?[13]

What Heidegger takes to be at issue here is the question of being and the human relation to being. But what is at issue in that question, and so what is itself 'worthy of thought', is what is also at issue in the question of place and of limit, perhaps even what is at issue in the very idea of the 'parameter', understood as the 'proper measure' that belongs with dwelling.

Chapter 9

VERTICALITY AND THE STREET

Central to Heidegger's account in 'Building Dwelling Thinking', and throughout many of his later essays, is a point that should now be extremely familiar; namely, that human being is articulated in and through the engagement with place (which includes space and time but exceeds both). Human being is fundamentally a *placed* being – its specific spatiality being directly connected with this. Although Heidegger's later thinking is notable for its explicit focus on place, and so on the relation between place and the human and between place and being – something captured in Heidegger's talk of his thinking as taking the form of a topology of being – such a topological approach is present in Heidegger's work almost from the start, even though it is not always directly thematized. *Being and Time* is thus as much a work of topology as is 'Building Dwelling Thinking' or '" ... Poetically Man Dwells ... "' (something evident, from the perspective of the former work, in Heidegger's critique of the Cartesian understanding of space, even as he also advances an account of his own in which a certain mode of spatiality is nevertheless central).

As noted in Chapter 3, part of the significance of Heidegger's topological account of human being is the way in which it adumbrates – and to some extent also influences – contemporary approaches to self and mind that emphasize their embodied and extended character. Thus, the 'extended mind thesis' (referred to in Chapter 3), although presented in the terms of contemporary cognitive science and analytic philosophy of mind, can be seen as arising out of a larger context of thinking in which Heidegger's work, as well as that of Maurice Merleau-Ponty (alongside a range of other thinkers, including those from within the pragmatist tradition broadly understood), plays a key role. However, it is not just its impact upon thinking about the mind that makes Heidegger's topology so significant. The so-called spatial turn in social theory – though that names quite a diverse range of approaches, not all of which are entirely consistent with one another – is a turn that is heavily indebted to Heidegger, even if it is more often the Heidegger of *Being and Time*, than of 'Building Dwelling Thinking'. Often, that indebtedness is indirect, running through other thinkers including, most notably, perhaps, Michel Foucault. As Stuart Elden emphasizes, in the case of Foucault, 'his understanding of space, and his use of a spatialized history, is indebted ... most importantly, to his reading of Heidegger'.[1] What Foucault develops, in a way that is never directly taken up in Heidegger's work (even though it follows directly from it), is the way in which social, and especially political, structures and processes must, given the primacy of the topological and the spatial, be articulated in topological and spatial terms. As Elden puts it, 'politics is inherently spatial',[2] and this is indicative of a direct relation, as Foucault makes clear, between place and space and structures of *power*.

It might be objected that, unlike Heidegger, Foucault's work (like much of the work in the 'spatial turn' to which both Heidegger and Foucault's thinking has contributed) does not focus on place but only on space – and, certainly, the subtitle of Elden's *Mapping the Present* invokes a *spatial* history, not a *topological* one.[3] But French, unlike English and German, tends to combine the spatial and topological rather than separate them. There is thus not the same distinction, in French, as that between the English terms 'space' and 'place' (even though 'space' can also be used equivocally), and the French *espace* carries the sense of both – which is why an essay such as Foucault's 'Des autre espaces', usually translated as 'Of other spaces', appears to move between a range of notions encompassing the spatial and topological. This point applies quite generally across many of the thinkers who have influenced the contemporary discourse about place and space, especially given the fact that, Heidegger aside, so many of those thinkers have written in French – not only Foucault but also, for instance, Marc Augé, Gaston Bachelard, Pierre Bourdieu, Michel de Certeau, Guy Debord, Henri Lefebvre and Maurice Merleau-Ponty.

Space, place and power

The relation between place, space and power has always been part of thinking in and about architecture, even apart from any 'spatial turn'. Usually, however, this has been in ways that assume an understanding of power as identical with the exertion of control. Power is then seen to be embodied in architecture, and so in architectural places and spaces, through the use of built form by governments, organizations and individuals as a means to express and reinforce their attempts to exert and maintain social, economic and political control. The focus is most often on architecture as a purposive expression of state power and authority – something evident in the construction of capital cities[4] – but also on the architecture of the corporation, or of capitalism more broadly. Sometimes, the focus is on the way in which built forms exert control directly, but frequently, the focus is also on the way in which built forms serve to enable and reinforce control by more indirect means (though not necessarily any less purposively), through symbol and representation. Inasmuch as the relation between place, space and power, at issue in these cases, is one that is taken to operate in ways amenable to purposive direction, so it is seen as part of the deliberate use of architecture as a political instrument. Adolf Hitler saw architecture in just this way, as a tool of the state and leader,[5] but he is certainly not unusual in holding to such an idea.

There is, however, a deeper, if perhaps less obvious, sense in which power and architecture are related – although it is a sense that underlies the connections referred to already. This is the sense in which architecture is not merely a means by which power is deliberately exercised and expressed, but rather part of the very structure by which it is constituted. Here, power is understood, not merely in terms of control or the attempt to exert control, but, more fundamentally (and in a way that is also evident in Foucault), as that which is productive of differentiation and ordering – including orderings of authority and subjectification but not only these. In this latter sense, power is at play in any and all forms of architecture, and it is so because the primary mode in which power is articulated is that of materiality, which is to say through the ordering of place and space (as well as time), and this is just what is at issue, in a quite explicit way, in architecture.[6]

It is indeed only in and through the material and spatial, and often through the sensory affectivity that belongs to the material and spatial, that the representational and symbolic operate. Once the question of the relation between power and architecture is understood as a question concerning the inevitable materialization of power, power being itself understood in relation to ordering (which is not to make any judgement on the character of the ordering so produced), then one can begin to ask after the nature of this materialization as it occurs in architecture *as built form*, both in general and in particular cases. One can also ask after the way architecture, *as a practice*, participates in this materialization – how it participates in the materialization that is architecture as built form (in this latter way, the question of the relation between architecture and power is seen as a political and ethical question).

It is commonplace, as was evident in some of the discussion in previous chapters, to think of built form as having a significatory or meaningful content – as itself embodying larger discursive, and so, in some sense, 'linguistic' structures. On this basis, the productivity of power, and so the structure of differentiation and ordering that is identical with it, is often taken to consist in the production or articulation of meaning.[7] Aside from the difficulties associated with the broadened sense of 'meaning' at work here, there is also a certain ambiguity in this way of proceeding. Although meaning and power may be said to be articulated spatially and materially, it may not always be clear whether the character of the spatial and the material is nevertheless entirely determined by the structure of meaning or of power, or whether power and meaning are themselves shaped, in their own character, by the spatial and the material. Does space 'make' power, it may be asked, or does power 'make' space?

The answer to this question, at least in most contemporary theoretical circles, is usually that it is power that makes or produces space (an answer that may well be encouraged by a framing of the issue in terms of meaning). Yet although this answer is often assumed, it neglects the deeper structures that are operative. If power is indeed taken to have primacy over space, then this means that, although space may be that in which power is articulated and is materialized, it is nevertheless power that shapes space, power that takes form in space. The structure of space is thereby understood as a function of the structure of power – or, as it is often put, space is *constructed* by power – and so also a function of the social and political structures and processes with which power is immediately connected. This account is often read into Foucault, and taken to be explicit in Lefebvre,[8] another key thinker who exemplifies a mode of spatial-topological thinking (but, once again, Lefebvre's work should not be construed as unequivocally being about *space* alone, despite the standard translation of *La production de l'espace* as *The production of space*[9]). Although it is true that the spatial is that in which power is materialized, the spatial cannot be taken as itself merely constructed – as 'made' by power. Indeed, to suppose that it is so is to overlook a basic and simple truth; namely, that the spatial and so, too, the temporal must provide the very frame within which any form of construction takes place. This means that the structure of spatiality, and even prior to that, the structure of place (since it is indeed place that underpins the structure of space as well as time), is what itself determines the discursive articulation of power, or indeed of meaning. Consequently, the first step in understanding the way power is shaped in buildings is a matter of understanding the structures that belong to space and place – a matter, in other words, of attending to the character of the topological.

Understanding power topologically

A fundamental notion in any topology – and a point that has recurred throughout the preceding discussions – is that of the boundary, or bounding surface, and its productive rather than merely restrictive character. The ordering of space, and so the materialization of power, operates first and foremost through the establishing of such boundaries. Even those forms of power that depend on treating another person as an object – slavery, for instance – depend on forms of material and spatial demarcation, often in relation to the body, the latter being a spatialized form. Distinctions between persons, those at work in gender, for instance, as well as 'race', are also realized through forms of material and spatial forms and boundaries. The boundaries at issue here are not merely *constrictive*, but also *constructive*, and they involve the establishing of possibility through delimitation. Such possibilities can be tied to forms of oppression – as is most obviously so in the case of slavery and in relation to gender and race – that is, to modes of ordering that are identified, rightly, as politically problematic. However, such establishing of possibility does not operate with respect to forms of oppression alone. Instead, it is operative with respect to any and every form of ordering – to any and every form of difference – and so to any and every form of possibility. This reflects the productive character of power noted earlier, but what is now evident is that the productivity of power is more fundamentally grounded in the productivity, the 'making possible', of the boundary.

The most obvious and basic way in which the boundary operates is through the establishing of the relation between inner and outer – something discussed further in the next chapter – where the focus is on the boundary as a specific architectural form and its role as realized in that form, in ordering and differentiating. It is thus that the wall (and secondarily the foundation or floor and the canopy or roof), no matter how realized, is architecturally so important, especially when the focus is on the way architecture relates to power. The relation between inner and outer, which the boundary establishes by means of the wall, is always an asymmetrical relation, that is, a relation directly tied to power and ordering. In marking off an inner from an outer space, the wall establishes forms of inclusion and exclusion – and this, one might say, is the most basic form in which spatialized power operates. One might also add that such demarcation is that which establishes the real space and structure of the architectural, and thus interiority itself emerges as a key architectural element so that, as architect Louis Kahn says, 'the room is the beginning of architecture'.[10]

The nature of the relation between inner and outer, in any specific case, is directly tied to the nature of the relation between built forms and their surrounding spaces or environments. How the inner space of a building relates to its outer space is mediated by the walls (as well as by canopies and floors) that are its very fabric, and which might also be called its constituting surfaces, as well as by the way those walls determine the interaction between inner and outer spaces. What is at issue in such interaction is the possibility of communication – in other words, *movement* – between spaces, where such movement may consist in the flow of information, of action or of bodies. In terms of human experience, such communication is primarily a matter either of sensory or bodily movement. It involves the capacity, from one space, to see, hear, smell or feel what is in the other; from one space, to act upon what is in the other; or from one space, to move bodily to the other. The movement and communication between inner and outer spaces is that which underpins the articulation and constitution of power – the materialized ordering and differentiation that is thereby established – as it is given in built form.

Admittedly, the centrality of the distinction between inner and outer has not gone entirely uncontested within architecture. Famously, Piranesi's *Le Carceri d'invenzione*, or *The Imaginary Prisons*[11] (see Figure 9.1), can be viewed as presenting a visual argument to the effect that there can be architectural forms in which the distinction is almost entirely lost. And there are certainly design approaches, and concrete design interventions, in which interior spaces are treated as if they were exterior, and *vice versa*, or in which exteriority and interiority intersect, overlap or blend into one another. But all of these approaches, including Piranesi's, depend on taking the distinction and then complicating it, or rendering it indeterminate in specific circumstances and by means of specific interventions or techniques. Thus, none of these approaches contest the distinction as such, but do indeed depend upon it.[12]

Although the account sketched here applies to built forms as they appear anywhere, including, for instance, built forms as they may appear in rural or semi-rural landscapes, the focus in this discussion is with built form in *urban* settings – with architecture in the contemporary city. Part of the reason for this is that such a focus draws attention to the way power is materialized, in architectural terms, in relation to modern technological capitalism, and it is in the contemporary city that this is directly evident (although certainly not exclusively). If what is at issue is the relation established by built forms, between their inner spaces and the outer

Figure 9.1 Giovanni Battista Piranesi, Le Carceri d'Invenzione, plate VII: The Drawbridge, 1761, Princeton University Art Museum, Gift of Frank Jewett Mather Jr.

spaces surrounding them, then, in an urban context, the primary focus (though certainly not the only possible focus) must be on the relation between the building and the street. One way of understanding the relation between inner and outer, in general, is in terms of a relation between that which is common and that which is apart, and certainly the street appears as a space of commonality, even a public space, in contrast to the internalized space of the building which, in virtue of its very internality, is also that which is apart from the common.

None of this is to deny that it might be possible for the street to itself become internalized, so that some buildings might contain common spaces (perhaps one might argue that this happens, almost literally, in the case of the Parisian *passage*, or arcade, which so obsessed Walter Benjamin), or even that different spaces might lose demarcation, so that, although it is no longer clear what is the street and what is not, there will always be the possibility of demarcating spaces that allow different degrees of accessibility and movement, and the street will always represent a level of accessibility available to all. It is precisely the character of the street as a space of commonality that underlies Jane Jacobs's famous valorization of the street in *The Death and Life of Great American Cities*,[13] and even if *all* that Jacobs has to say about the role of the street in the life of the city is not endorsed, still it can be said that the street constitutes the common space in which the life of the city is indeed founded. As Kahn says: 'A city is measured by the character of its institutions. The street is one of its first institutions', and, he adds, 'today, these institutions are on trial'.[14] If what is at issue is the way power is materialized in the contemporary city, then the relation between the street and the building, as that is realized through the dominant forms of contemporary buildings, will be a crucial point of inquiry. One of the most salient features of contemporary cities is the increasing tendency for high-rise construction – especially so in the case of newer cities, and evident even in the case of many older cities, like London, which have previously been relatively low-rise in character. Against that background, the question of the relation between street and building comes increasingly to concern the relation between the street and the high-rise tower – between, one might say, the horizontal and the vertical planes.

Verticality in the contemporary city

The modern tower is directly tied to modern technological development, not only in its construction methods and materials, but also in its dependence on the elevator. Without the latter, development beyond a few stories (five being about the highest) would be impracticable at least for commercial purposes (though to cite an ancient example, Roman apartment buildings, or *insulae*, were sometimes as high as ten stories, and so, too, were some medieval towers, though the latter often combined defensive with other functions). High-rise development includes buildings designed for commercial as well as residential use, and sometimes a combination of both. In residential terms, high-rise construction has, of course, been used both for luxury and also for low-income housing.

The large high-rise estate development that was common in the 1950s and into the 1970s, and that was designed to provide relatively inexpensive housing, can be viewed as undermined by what was also, in effect, one of its aims – the concentration of the poor into spatially segregated communities. Such concentration may have been seen as allowing more efficient provision of services and support, but often gave rise to ghettoization and frequently intensified disadvantage. It provides a very immediate example of the way power operates spatially, through the establishment of forms of inclusion and exclusion (sometimes, architecturally, contrary to any explicit design intention), even if the way that operates in the low-income tower block can be seen as a form of exclusion of the poor from the realm of the public and the common. This does not mean that large-scale public housing projects are always doomed to failure, nor does it imply that such projects should be abandoned (though many have been), but the other problematic features that often attend on such projects – poor construction and maintenance, inadequate planning, failure of support services – are exacerbated by the spatial concentration that the tower, in particular, brings, and at the same time, that spatial concentration and, with it, the spatial dynamics of the tower are seldom directly addressed.

Although it is often said that the origins of the modern high-rise lie in the increasing cost of urban property and the consequent need to maximize the development value and opportunity of any given site, this seldom seems borne out by the facts of the case – neither in the past nor now. Tower construction is often a difficult and expensive enterprise, and the provision of services becomes more costly the higher the building, so that there is no simple relationship between increase in height or concentration and increase in value or return.[15] Hirst points out, in relation to the design of military fortifications, that the nature of the design is never driven by strictly utilitarian defensive considerations, and the same applies to the supposed economic drivers of high-rise construction. There are instances where property values contribute to the way developments proceed. Cost and profitability are factors in the design decisions around tower construction, and high-rise residential buildings can enable higher-density living with consequent benefits in the concentration of urban infrastructure (which can be read as indicative of a cost imperative). Nevertheless, the reality seems to be that tower building is underpinned, as it has always been, by a complex of factors, many of which have little or nothing to do with the cost of land, and sometimes not even with the direct profitability of the building, but which are more often connected with the way the tower or high-rise functions to articulate other forms of power.

Vertical development has become a commonplace sight in cities around the world from Doha to Djakarta, Mumbai to Manchester, Sydney to Shanghai. Many of the greatest concentrations of high-rise developments have occurred in areas outside of, even if somewhat adjacent to, the central city – in areas where land is less of a driver – and where placement of buildings at some distance from one another actually results in medium-density land use. In this latter respect, the rise of the high-rise has often been part of a withdrawal from the city centre as development has focused on areas that offer greater latitude for large-scale building projects – usually areas of dilapidated factories, warehouses or low-income housing. This is notably true in several instances: Canary Wharf in London, the Pudong New District in Shanghai (situated across the river from old Shanghai) (see Figure 9.2), the Docklands area in Melbourne (situated two kilometres to the west of the CBD, and much lower-rise and less extensive than Pudong) (see Figure 9.3) and La Défense in Paris (the more established development, often taken as a model

Figure 9.2 Pudong, Shanghai. Photo: dibrova/Shutterstock.

Figure 9.3 Docklands, Melbourne. Photo: Gordon Bell/ Shutterstock.

Figure 9.4 La Défense, Paris. Photo: pisaphotography/Shutterstock.

for others, located three kilometres from the city centre) (see Figure 9.4). In these cases, high-rise architecture has been a key element of urban redevelopment that also emphasizes commercial occupancy, even if it is mixed, as in the Docklands example, with its high level of residential usage.

What also typifies many of these developments, to a greater or lesser extent (La Défense being less exemplary of this tendency), is a distanced relation to the street. Indeed, in areas like Pudong, but also Docklands, the street has become little more than a conduit for vehicular traffic with few pedestrians or very much of anything that might encourage pedestrian activity. The buildings themselves – in contrast to many older high-rise buildings (and, especially, the first generation of modern towers that appeared in late nineteenth-century Chicago) – are generally closed off from any public access. The ground floors, like the rest of these buildings, are frequently visually impenetrable and inaccessible to anyone who does not have appropriate authorization. Rather than there being a lobby that might allow a degree of public movement between building and street, these structures often prevent access at the edge of the building itself and sometimes in its surrounding forecourt, if not at the very edge of the site.

The modern tower can often present an almost defensive orientation, its ground floor and lobby, if it is open to the public at all, frequently becoming little more than a security space for the screening and surveillance of visitors before granting access to the elevators. Significantly, these buildings not only cut off access to the street, as they withdraw their activities into the building and away from ground level, but they also, and for the same reasons, generally do not contribute to the street. In some cases, notably in many of the Pudong buildings as well as in Docklands, there is only limited bodily interaction between building and street as the buildings themselves contain internal parking levels that allow the buildings' inhabitants to enter and exit by vehicle, rather than having to do so on foot. In many ways, the dominant interaction between building and street comes to be one of visuality, as the building strives to dominate the surrounding landscape in which it sits (though invariably in competition with the other buildings around it), or in the way the building surveys the street and surrounding landscape both through its security systems and by means of the views afforded by its height and omnipresent glass.

The relative lack of interaction between building and street is readily evident. Consider almost any of the tall buildings that make up the streetscape of Pudong, Docklands, or, to a lesser extent, La Défense, and one finds buildings set, each in its own area of open space, amidst a network of roads, with little or no integration at ground level and, typically, little or no pedestrian or other activity at the base. In Melbourne's Docklands, the inhospitable character of the neighborhood at the street level is reinforced by the way the towers function to funnel winds in and around the buildings, and in Pudong, large areas of fairly undistinguished open space, often raised above the normal street level, provide the main routes for pedestrian access in those few areas of pedestrian concentration. No wonder that Docklands has been seen, in spite of various attempts at improvement (some more and some less successful), as something of an urban desert, and Pudong has often been described as exemplifying the spatial configuration that goes with a centralized and controlling politics. Even La Défense exhibits a similar reduction in activity and engagement at the street level, especially in newer constructions, and a similar tendency towards an almost defensive isolation of the building from the street. In recent years, especially, that lack of penetration is driven by concerns of security. Increasingly, the aim is to protect the building from any possibility of attack or incursion from the street level, and this becomes all the more important for corporate buildings and for those buildings that are representative of national or globalized interests – exactly those that often proclaim their status and significance in the wider urban landscape by means of their salience, usually in height and singularity of design.[16]

The withdrawal from the street – even a form of isolation from the street – is readily evident in the architecture of areas like Pudong (there are areas of Pudong especially that retain some low-rise mixed usage,[17] but this is not what dominates in the area, even if it does show the extent to which areas like Pudong are never entirely consistent in their character). To some extent, these sorts of developments, so often set to one side of the city's existing centre (across the river from the historic Bund, in the case of Pudong) and in which towers stand in relative isolation from one another within a network of roads, can be seen as quite specific urban phenomena. But many of the features that they display, particularly the character of their relationship with the street and surrounding landscape, are also evident in other high-rise tower constructions, including those set in denser urban locations and in buildings that are more multi-use than are the towers of Pudong or Docklands. London has the example of Canary Wharf, but it also has the Shard, western Europe's tallest building and a multi-use construction that combines office, retail stores, a hotel and restaurants – and, of course, the inevitable viewing platform. The Shard, like many similar projects around the world, was presented as the key element in the regeneration of the London Bridge area in which it was built, and it has certainly attracted tourists and commercial activity. Its architect, Renzo Piano, is the designer of another development that has ambitions to similarly revitalize the area around Paddington Station. Of the projected building – the 'Paddington Cube' – Piano has said that it will create 'a wonderful sense of place which Paddington greatly needs'.[18]

Talk of 'sense of place' seems to invoke issues concerning precisely the relation of the built form to the locale – the street and wider landscape – in which it is sited, something that seems poorly articulated in projects like those of Pudong or Docklands. But in the case of the Paddington project, which has been the focus of considerable local opposition, the building makes few, if any, concessions to the existing place. Indeed, much of the opposition to the building has been on heritage grounds – the design being seen as incompatible with the low-rise heritage character of the area, not least because it requires the demolition of an existing heritage building.[19] So, 'sense of place', in the case of a building like the Piano design in Paddington, seems to refer more to the availability of opportunities for commercial and consumer activity and display than to any richer or more complex sense of topological character. One might well argue that the 'revitalization' accomplished by the Shard similarly has more to do with the stimulus of commercial and consumer activity than any genuine contribution to a more vital sense of locale.

In New York, the increasing proliferation of high-rise towers, often for residential apartments, has led to concerns about the loss of amenity on the streets below. As Fred A. Bernstein notes – making an explicit contrast with the towers of Pudong as well as Dubai – New York's new high-rise projects are 'crowding into already dense neighbourhoods where light and air are at a premium, and quality-of-life issues are on the minds of everyone ... The buildings are making the city less pleasant for anyone who cannot afford one of the condos in the sky'.[20] The withdrawal from the street occurs, here, as part of the consolidation of urban wealth in the upper levels of the city proving a physical instantiation of contemporary inequality that places the privileged above and the less privileged below. As Bernstein puts it: 'Think of it as the new Upstairs, Downstairs, but on an urban scale.'[21] Here, the street becomes that from which one withdraws, from which one aims to escape, and merely something to be viewed as well as defended against.

Even in the case of multi-use buildings, the relation to the street remains problematic. Thus, the Shard, for all its claims to regeneration and revitalization, makes no concession to the articulation of its base, either in relationship with the street or with the wider urban landscape in which it sits. The same point holds with respect to many other high-rise developments that have become such a feature of the London cityscape. Rowan Moore's comments in relation to St George Wharf Tower, also known as Vauxhall Tower (and designed by the firm of Broadway

Malyan[22]), seem to typify the character of many of the buildings at issue: 'It makes no apparent effort to form any kind of relationship with its surroundings, neither a Georgian house behind it, nor even St George Wharf, an existing development by the same architects ... It does not relate to the river in any particular way or, in longer views, to the Palace of Westminster. It is just there, sullenly uncommunicative.'[23] More generally, the very character of multi-use towers, as essentially spaces dedicated to the concentration and representation of globalized wealth and status – to residential exclusivity and to high-end consumer activity – means that they essentially function as self-contained islands of privilege, within what are often barren urban landscapes at the street level.

It might be argued that the withdrawal exemplified by the contemporary highrise reflects a more general tendency in modern urban design, one also seen, for instance, in the organization of many low-rise suburban developments. A major factor here – also evident in areas of high-rise development like Pudong and Docklands – is the prevalence of the private car as a primary means of transport. Where there is a reduced use of public transport, and where the primary use of the street is to enable the flow of vehicular traffic, then the relation between building and street will always be reduced. Yet while this is a factor in developments like Pudong and Docklands, as well as in places like Dubai and Doha, it is less so in the case of La Défense, and not a significant factor in most London or New York highrise constructions. The private home may be said always to have been characterized by a high degree of withdrawal – the private space of the home mirroring the private space of the self (a key point in Gaston Bachelard's topo-poetics of interior, domestic space[24]), and recent decades may even have seen an increased withdrawal into the space of the home. Nevertheless, the withdrawal of the inner city high-rise has a very different character and significance from the withdrawal evident, for instance, in suburban areas. This is partly because the former is a phenomenon of the city itself, and partly because it so often reflects the transformation of cities under the impact of globalized capital and its technological instantiations.

The problematic relation of the high-rise tower to the street is, indeed, a function of the very character of the tower and was evident as a problem very early on in the development of the typology. If it was less of a problem early on, as, for instance, in the case of early high-rise development in Chicago, and later in Manhattan, that was partly because it occurred in the midst of an urban landscape that was already much more active at the street level, and in which the street remained an important site of public engagement and exchange. As the character of the urban landscape has changed, and the street with it, so the problem of the articulation between the high-rise and the street has also become more difficult. The attempt to address the problem is a feature of some notable high-rise projects over the course of the last century, particularly in Manhattan. The Citicorp Building (later renamed Citigroup Center, and now called 601 Lexington) and the Rockefeller Center exemplify different solutions to this problem. In the case of the 1977 Citicorp Building (designed by Hugh Stubbins and often credited to its chief engineer, William LeMessurier), the attempt is almost to physically disconnect the tower from the street level, through its elevation on large columns, thereby leaving space for other constructions beneath (including a Lutheran church – space for which was a project requirement). The elevation, however, merely serves to exacerbate the sense of withdrawal and disconnection. The Rockefeller Centre, a much older construction – from the 1930s – incorporating several buildings, maintains a much stronger level of integration with the street through concourses and outdoor public spaces. Setting the pattern for many New York towers, the iconic and influential Seagram Building – designed by Mies van der Rohe with Philip Johnson – has a relatively utilitarian lobby providing access to the building's lifts (consistent with van der Rohe's modernist form of functionalist aesthetic), but it is also significantly set back from the street, which allows it to open onto a large plaza at its front. If the articulation with the street is minimal here, one might also argue that the building retains a degree of modesty. It is not overbearing in its relation to the street, and so the element of withdrawal may also be said to be, to some extent, minimized.

The articulation between building and street is an issue for all buildings, precisely because it concerns that most basic of architectural relations: the relation between interior and exterior. In the case of the tower, that relation becomes especially problematic simply because the tower necessarily involves a more restrictive, or as indicated earlier, a more defensive relationship to the street. The concentration of space within the tower form sets up issues in relation to the means of access to the building, both vertical and horizontal, and its tendency to dominate its site sets up issues concerning the way the tower relates to the immediately surrounding landscape, as well as to that which is set further apart. The very nature of the tower is such that it always involves a degree of withdrawal from and of surveillance over, and this reflects, in fact, the role of the tower as such an important feature of much military architecture (though how it operates militarily has changed with changing weaponry). There is reason, then, to suppose that, wherever the tower or high-rise appears as an architectural form, it will also exhibit these same features of withdrawal and surveillance. It should also be unsurprising to find the tower so frequently employed as a feature of contemporary architecture. The significance of the tower as a symbol of power, and so also of status and wealth, is directly tied to the spatial and topological formations with which it is associated. That is even more so given the way the tower is so enmeshed within modern technological systems and devices.

The convergent and connected character of contemporary technology, which is to say, the character of that technology as tending towards increasingly complex and interconnected systems of operation (the so-called 'Internet of Things' being one example of this), is a character also evident in the contemporary high-rise. Not only are such constructions impossible without modern technologies, but they are also thoroughly integrated with those technologies and with the economic systems with which they are in turn enmeshed. From the communications devices and helipads that may be found on their roofs, to the complex systems of cabling and ducting that supply services and infrastructure, and to the high-specification cladding and windows that make up their walls, contemporary tower buildings are intimately linked to the globalized world of modern technological capital.

The very space that they contain is itself a thoroughly technological product, a genuine example, one might say, in which space is indeed 'produced', in which it has become a purely created commodity. In this way, the contemporary tower, with its extreme internalization and its withdrawal from the realm of common public engagement, also exemplifies the increasing turn in modernity, away from the realm of human commonality and towards an increasingly technologically connected and mediated mode of largely individualized interaction – a mode of interaction that gives the illusion of increasing control, and yet remains bound to the same spatialized, materialized and topological structures in which is embedded any and every form of being or appearance.

What does all of this imply for the realities of architectural practice? What does it mean for the possibility of future high-rise design and construction? As in Heidegger, there is no theory of architecture being advanced here that tells decisively against the high-rise, and so such a mode of building cannot simply be ruled out of account from the start. The point is, rather, to understand the bounds within which the high-rise necessarily operates and to be able to acknowledge and take account of those bounds. That is the real problem of so much contemporary high-rise design and construction; not that it occurs, but that it does so in a way that ignores or refuses the bounds that make it possible, that it ignores or refuses the place in which it arises.[25] This, however, is not a problem restricted to the architecture of the high-rise alone. It is a problem and a challenge for architectural practice as such. It is a challenge that arises once one begins to consider what architecture may be, that is to say, when one considers the domain in which it arises and from which it comes.

Chapter 10

SPACE AND INTERIORITY

Louis Kahn's assertion that 'the room is the beginning of architecture'[1] is indicative of the importance attached to interiority in architecture by many Modernists. The same basic idea that appears in Kahn thus also appears, to name three notable instances, in Aalto, Le Corbusier and Wright.[2] The issue of interiority has already been touched on in previous chapters, but not in any sustained fashion and largely as it arises in relation to other matters; thus, interiority as such has not, so far, been a primary focus of discussion. Yet interiority is not only an important topic in Modernist architecture, in the work of such as Kahn or Aalto, but as was evident in the last chapter, interiority is central to the understanding of place. It is closely entangled with the *boundedness* of place, with its *differentiated* character and with its fundamental *relationality*. Moreover, interiority is also implicated in a particularly significant way with the question of space, and so with the connection, as well as the contrast, between space and place. This final chapter (or penultimate, depending on how one views the Epilogue) directly addresses the issue of interiority and of space with it. Because interiority brings the issue of exteriority with it, the distinction between interior and exterior – between inner and outer – will also be at issue, and so too will there be a focus on the interiority that belongs even to what is conventionally regarded as exterior, including, most importantly, landscape. And whilst Heidegger's thinking has often been less central in many of the previous chapters, the discussion here will hark back to Part I in its more direct engagement with Heidegger as a key element. The way space and interiority come together in this discussion involves a consideration of landscape, as well as the 'room', but also brings to the fore questions of boundary, entry and threshold.

Topological and non-topological space

It is easy to suppose that what is at issue in the 'room', as it is invoked by Kahn, can be taken to be simple and self-evident and, so, to assume that interiority is something already well-understood. The latter term, which comes from the Latin for 'inner', is often used outside of architecture to refer to subjectivity and the self, also carrying connotations of intimacy and privacy. But this is already to understand interiority and, so, the 'inner' (as well as self and subjectivity) in a particular way, even though it is a way that often carries over into contemporary architectural discussion.³ Peter Eisenman acknowledges that 'the interiority of architecture might not be something stable and already known'.⁴ One can readily see that this is so, in fact, by considering, if not the term 'interiority' as such, then certainly the term Kahn uses, 'room'. The latter, as noted previously, carries connotations of a certain sort of boundedness or enclosure, and so seems to stand in contrast to that which is unbounded and open, but which can also be taken to carry a sense of openness and space. This is particularly evident in the German *Raum*, which means both a 'room' and 'space' (Heidegger comments that 'a space is something that has been made room for, something that is cleared and free'⁵), but a similar equivocity pertains to the English 'room', even if not in quite such a strong form (so one speaks about having *room* to move when what one has is *space* in which to move). The way the idea of the 'room' brings the issue of space to the fore is indicative of the important connection between interiority and spatiality – and so too of the fact that interiority can no more be taken to be a self-evidently understood notion than can space or spatiality. In twentieth-century architecture, the importance of interiority has often been taken to derive from just this connection with spatiality. The connection, however, is one that can also lead away from the concern with interiority, or with interior space as such. There is thus a curious pathway that moves from a focus on *interiority*, and so on the space *of* interiority, to a focus on space *apart* from interiority.

The pathway is one that moves by way of a process of abstraction. Imagine a box of cherries. Remove the cherries and one is left with the empty box that now contains just a space. Remove the sides, top and bottom of the box and one is left with the space alone. Since there is nothing that contains the space that is left, there seems no reason why this space cannot be extended in all directions indefinitely.⁶ One might argue that something like this process of the thematization of a purified form of space through the emptying of interior spaces has been made possible in architecture over the last hundred years or so through the photographic representation of buildings, and especially their interiors, as largely devoid of people and activity.⁷ Once a built form appears as empty in this sense, then, even if one retains an idea of its form, it is easy to image it as a purely *spatial* form. What is brought to the fore, in this way, is space as it might be understood independent of interiority, and so, architecturally speaking, space as it might be at issue in the *exterior* of buildings as much as in their *interior*.

Interiority, on this basis, becomes merely an instance of a more generalized spatiality – a spatiality more or less identical with extension – and the difference between interiority and exteriority, between inner and outer, becomes merely conventional (a matter of what is usually designated as interior or exterior), so that one can as easily be 'in' an exterior space as an interior one (although what 'in' might mean here is not at all clear – a point to which the discussion will return). The example from Piranesi, discussed in the last chapter, of the way the centrality of the inner-outer distinction may be contested, itself partly depends on this assumption of a generalized spatiality that underlies forms of interiority and exteriority. It is thus that, despite the emphasis on interiority in the work of such as Kahn, interiority, in any genuine or *sui generis* sense, often tends to be neglected or overlooked in contemporary architectural thought and practice. Robert McCarter claims that contemporary architecture is characterized by what he calls 'our obsessive focus on the exterior form and our concomitant blindness to interior experience'.[8] But one might also say that this lack of attention to interiority is itself a function of the dominance of a certain mode of space and spatiality.

That it is indeed a *mode* of space and spatiality, rather than space and spatiality as such, that is at issue here is a key point. In his discussion of axial structures in architecture, Le Corbusier emphasizes the way in which axes are seen, not in terms of 'a birds'-eye [sic] view such as is given by a plan', but 'from the ground, the beholder standing up and looking in front of him'.[9] The difference between these two 'ways of seeing', one of which, it should be noted, is itself tied to a mode of representation, can be understood in terms of two different modes of space and being in space. The first is the mode of space that is associated with the disappearance of interiority – space as pure extension – and this space is also readily amenable to being understood in an abstracted and representational form (and also, recalling the discussion in Chapter 8, quantitatively and formally[10]). It is space as given in terms of a 'view' that is *apart* from any specific locatedness in the landscape (which is why Le Corbusier ties it to the plan). The second is the mode of space that is embodied and concrete – space as given in terms of a view that is tied *to* locatedness in the landscape (hence the emphasis on the 'beholder' standing up and looking forwards).[11] One might designate this second sense of space as *topological* space, since it is space as given in the openness of place. Such a space will always be evident from *within* place – it is, indeed, the space of interiority, a space that is bounded, anisotropic and heterogenous (as places themselves are). In contrast, the first sense of space – space as pure *extension*, evident in the plan and the representation, is indeed a *non-topological* space. Such a space is one that sets itself apart from the bounds of place (effectively reducing place to a location within space), a space that is typically isotropic and homogenous, and also, therefore, a space that is apart from interiority. The space of extension is not a space that has any interiority that properly belongs to it nor does it properly have any exteriority either – within such a space, interiority and exteriority can be nothing more than different parts of a single space differentiated only according to convention.

The two views that Le Corbusier identifies, and the modes of space and spatiality that go along with them, have been at work, if differently expressed and sometimes implicitly, throughout much of the discussion in the preceding chapters. Moreover, both play important and indispensable roles in architecture. Architecture would be impossible without the idea of space as given in the bird's-eye view – extensional and representational space – just as architecture would be impossible without the capacity for abstraction, without extension and without representation (and this is true more generally: human being in the world requires a capacity to engage with space as extensional and as representational). But topological space is also essential here, since, without it, architecture has no proper subject matter, nothing properly to address or to which it can respond, and no ground on which to situate itself (and this too applies more generally). Moreover, it is only on the basis of an embeddedness in topological space, which is to say, in place, that the grasp of space as extensional, or as representational, is itself possible. The bird's-eye view is thus not a view that can arise independently of the view from within the landscape.[12] Many of the tensions within contemporary architecture, and in other disciplines also, can be traced back to the failure to attend to these two modes of space, and to the tendency to prioritize extensional or representational space over the topological (or, sometimes, if less frequently in architecture but more commonly in other disciplines, to the attempted refusal of any role at all for the extensional or representational).

Being in and being here/there

Le Corbusier's characterization of the two views – the bird's-eye and the located – is useful, not only for the way it highlights the different modes of space at issue here, but also because it indicates how topological space, given in terms of the view 'from the ground, the beholder standing up and looking in front of him', has an essential interiority as opposed to what might appear to be the exteriority – the bird's-eye view – associated with space as extensional or as representational (although it is less a genuine exteriority than it is an *apartness*[13]). Interiority is thus exhibited as tied to place, or as it might also be put, 'in-ness' appears as itself connected to 'there-ness' or 'here-ness'.[14] This connection is one that also appears in Heidegger, although less in 'Building Dwelling Thinking' (where it is addressed in different terms) than in *Being and Time*. And its appearance in the latter work is in the same discussion in which Heidegger first makes significant reference to *Wohnen,* or 'dwelling'.

Being and Time aims to address the question of the meaning of being. It does this through an inquiry into the being of the specific being for whom being arises as a question, namely, *Dasein,* 'being here/there'. What characterizes the being of *Dasein* is that it is essentially 'being-in-the-world', *In-der-Welt-sein* – which is why world is such a central issue – and so *Da-sein* is also *In-sein*. But what is the nature of this being-in? From the start, Heidegger is clear that being-in cannot be assumed to be a matter of simple spatial 'containment' (the sort associated with the way cherries are 'in' a box – or, to use Heidegger's examples, the way water is 'in' a glass or clothes 'in' a cupboard).[15] 'Being in', and so also the interiority, or in-ness, that is at issue here, is thus tied, not to *spatiality* in this sense, but to *dwelling*. In a dense passage whose etymological excursions make it difficult to render into English, Heidegger begins with a set of comments on 'in' (the German, apart from its declined forms, is the same as the English, so also *in*) and 'at' or 'next to' (the German *an*), and then he moves on to explain further what is at issue:

> 'In' stems from *innan-*, to live [wohnen], *habitare,* to dwell [sich aufhalten]. 'An' means I am used to [ich bin gewohnt], familiar with, I take care of something. It has the meaning of [in Latin] *colo* in the senses of *habito* and *diligo* ['to reside' and 'to set apart']. We characterized this being to whom being-in belongs in

this meaning as the being which I myself always am. The expression '*bin*' I connected with '*bei*'. 'Ich bin' ['I am'] means I dwell [ich wohne], I stay near ... the world as familiar in such and such a way. Being as the infinitive of 'I am': that is, understood as an existential, means to dwell near [wohnen bei] ..., to be familiar with ... *Being-in is thus the formal existential expression of the being of Dasein which has the essential constitution of being-in-the-world.*[16]

Most readers, unless they are already immersed in Heidegger scholarship, are unlikely to follow all that is at issue in this passage. The recurrent appearance of the various verb forms of *Wohnen* is an obvious point to notice, however, as is the way in which the passage prefigures, in highly condensed form, elements of the argument that appears in 'Building Dwelling Thinking'. But most important is indeed the focus on being-in, and so on interiority, as tied to dwelling, and of dwelling as itself connected with being-familiar with, caring for, staying near. Dwelling does not figure much in *Being and Time* outside of this passage. However, Heidegger does have more to say about the specific mode of spatiality that belongs with dwelling and so with being-in or interiority – a mode of spatiality that he calls *existenziale Räumlichkeit*, existential spatiality (an analogue of topological spatiality) – and that is quite distinct from the (non-topological) mode of spatiality as extension that is part of the modern Cartesian understanding of space as well as world.[17]

The existential spatiality associated with dwelling does not consist in some statically juxtaposed positioning within a spread out and homogenous field but, rather, is essentially *active* and *relational*. This is where the idea of the ready-to-hand, *Zuhanden*, comes into play.[18] Heidegger's account of being-in, as worked out through the notion of the ready-to-hand, looks to forms of activity and the ordering of things that goes with it (an ordering, as noted earlier, in terms of work and tool). It is through participation in this structure that the world is opened up for *Dasein*. And it is this structure that, in the terms of *Being and Time*, provides the basis for the more developed articulation of what it is to be 'in', and so of interiority or 'in-ness'.[19]

The ready-to-hand, which is tied to the practical, is contrasted by Heidegger with the present-at-hand, associated with the theoretical. The distinction, which can also be seen as playing out between existential spatiality and the Cartesian spatiality of extension, is analogous to that which is apparent in Le Corbusier's two 'views' – the bird's-eye view and the view from the ground. Heidegger is explicit, however, in taking the two modes as standing in a necessary relation to one another, with the ready-to-hand coming before the present-at-hand (hence the tendency to see Heidegger as prioritizing the practical), and existential spatiality coming before Cartesian spatiality. Heidegger's account is also significant in drawing attention to another point made earlier, namely, the difficulty in making sense of any genuine 'in-ness' or interiority associated with the space of extension. At one point, Heidegger suggests, echoing a claim similar to one also made by Georg Simmel,[20] that things that are merely positioned 'in' space, things that are merely 'present at hand', can never stand in any genuine relation to one another, writing that 'when two entities are present at hand within the world, and furthermore are worldless in themselves, they can never touch each other nor can either of them "be" "alongside" the other'.[21] But, if there is no genuine relationality neither can there be any genuine sense of being 'in' that applies to such entities. To repeat the point made earlier, strictly speaking, there can be no interiority within the non-topological space of extension.

The interiority of landscape

The distinction of topological from non-topological space is thus already evident in *Being and Time*, and so too is the character of interiority or being-in as itself belonging to the topological and thereby also to dwelling. And following further from this, it is also evident that the primary sense of space is not that of the bird's-eye view, or of Cartesian extension, but the sense of space that goes with the view from the ground (with which, it turns out, the bird's-eye view is itself bound up), the view that is always interior. The primary sense of space, in other words, is that which is given in and through place.

If the latter point is not completely clear in *Being and Time*, then it is partly because Heidegger never really names place in the course of his analysis – and it is notable that the explicit language of place that is so characteristic of the later essays is largely absent from the earlier work. As noted previously, this does not mean that place is not at work in the early Heidegger, but only that it often remains implicit, and, as a consequence, that the focus on place is often less evident or more easily overlooked (as it has been and continues to be by many commentators). But the fact that the topological character of *Being and Time* is not so directly to the fore as in the later thinking also means that some aspects of Heidegger's analysis turn out to be incomplete, limited and, sometimes, misleading. This is true of the focus on the idea of the ready-to-hand, which can itself lead to space (and place) being seen as functions of Dasein's own way of configuring the world – functions of Dasein's 'projecting' of possibilities, tied to Dasein's practical activities and concerns, and so, potentially, 'subjective'. Heidegger recognized the extent to which the analysis that is based around the distinction of the ready-to-hand from the present-at-hand could be misconstrued. In a lecture from 1929–30, he draws attention to the fact that his account was never intended to encompass the entire structure of the world in which *Dasein* has its being but, rather, was an attempt only at a 'preliminary characterization', adding that 'it never occurred to me … to try and claim or prove with this interpretation that the essence of man consists in the fact that he knows how to handle knives and forks or use the tram'.[22] If the structure of the ready-to-hand gives only a partial picture of the 'essence of man' – which is to say, of *Dasein* – then it also gives only a partial picture of the nature of being-in, or of interiority.

The partiality of the account is particularly evident in the way the focus on the ready-to-hand and present-at-hand seems to leave out the appearance of nature and, especially, of nature as given in landscape. The latter appears only briefly in *Being and Time*, in a famous passage that indicates that the simple dichotomy of ready-to-hand and present-at-hand cannot encompass all that is at issue in the idea of being-in-the-world.[23] But landscape appears more prominently in Heidegger's thinking and writing in the period after *Being and Time* (especially after 1933 and even more so after 1945), and, of course, it is partly the prominence of ideas and images of landscape and countryside in the later work that is often taken as evidence of Heidegger's provincial and rural proclivities. That landscape, and the experience of landscape, might be significant philosophically, and especially for the philosophical engagement with place, is not, however, peculiar to Heidegger alone. It has, for instance, always been important in Chinese and Asian thought,[24] notwithstanding the presence of urban modes of life. And although it might be argued that philosophy begins in the city (and certainly this is true of philosophy as it is identified with that form of thinking that originates in Greece and has its first great flowering in Athens), it is by no means restricted to remaining within the city walls, or to finding its fundamental ground and impetus only in the phenomena and experience of urban life.

In 'Why Do I Stay in the Provinces', from 1934 (already briefly discussed in Chapter 2), Heidegger talks, in a way that echoes some of Nietzsche's writing, of a certain solitariness in the landscape that has, he says, 'the peculiar and original power not of isolating us but of projecting our whole existence out into the vast nearness of the presence [*Wesen*] of all things'.[25] The theme of solitariness is one that recurs in many writers – it is also present, for instance, in Rousseau and Thoreau – but the role of landscape here (which need not always mean the 'natural' landscape[26]) should also not be overlooked. What is at issue for Heidegger is an encounter with a presence that is not restricted to the human alone. And, although that is not impossible in the urban context of city and town, it often more immediately and readily occurs away from the denseness of human habitation, in places in which human activity takes place against a much larger and more encompassing domain. It is for this reason that landscape looms so large in many contemporary forms of topological thinking, and why such thinking often converges with aspects of environmental thought.

Relatively few discussions of landscape take up interiority as a key theme.[27] Yet to think interiority in relation to landscape, and landscape in relation to interiority, requires that the very phenomenon of interiority be thought in a more basic way than is usually the case when interiority in its more conventional form – most often the interiority of built spaces – is taken as the starting point. More specifically, interiority as given in landscape tends to be less readily amenable to the move from interiority to pure spatiality that is evident in the way the interiority of built spaces is taken up in so much modern and contemporary architecture. And, although landscape can give rise to its own modes of abstraction – especially in more expansive and seemingly empty landscapes (the desert, the plain and even the sea)[28] – this is less so when understood in terms of its own essential interiority.

One of Heidegger's closest engagements with place as a central topic occurs in relation to the *Feldweg*, or 'country path' (literally, 'field way'), that runs from the castle garden in his hometown of Messkirch out into the nearby countryside, and along which Heidegger frequently walked (see Figure 10.1). The path is the subject of a short piece Heidegger wrote in 1949, titled *Der Feldweg*,[29] or 'The Country

Path' (or just 'Pathway' as one of the English translations has it), and it is also the likely setting for the 'Conversation on a Country Path' that he completed in 1945 (appearing in an edited form in 1959),[30] whilst staying at Wildenstein castle, some sixteen kilometres northwest of Messkirch. It is in the encounter with *landscape* that Heidegger's own thinking about place seems to be shaped in key ways, and it is also in relation to the character of place as given in landscape (often as given, poetically, in the work of Hölderlin and others, including, notably, the French poet René Char) that the structure of place appears in especially salient form in Heidegger's work – and in a way that necessarily encompasses the structure of interiority. Significantly, the country path that is both the background to and an important focus of Heidegger's thinking, in 1945 and 1949, is no track into the wilds. It is very much a path that moves from a place of inhabitation, Messkirch itself, and out into a wider landscape that – although it opens into the embrace of earth and sky, and so of the world as 'nature' (the path borders a wood and also looks out over a much wider landscape) – is never entirely apart, even if it does lead away, from the ordinary places of human activity. This relates directly to a point already made; namely, that human engagement with the world is neither with the world as completely other nor with the world as completely human either. The world is both near and far (and when Heidegger talks of *nearness*, *Nähe*, in relation to the world, he means the very possibility of the near and the far, the two being given together[31]).

Set as the day is settling into night, the dialogue of the 'Conversation on a Country Path' begins with its participants apparently already on the path.

Figure 10.1 The country path – *der Feldweg* – that runs from Messkirch into the surrounding countryside. Photo: © Ilona Schneider, 2017.

And, even though the path itself is not to the forefront in what is discussed, the conversation is nevertheless very clearly placed *on the path*, and the conversation's own movement is mirrored in the movement of the participants along the path. The country path conversation thus takes the form of a journey – one that makes direct reference to the landscape in which it is placed and takes place, and, as such, it is also a movement into and within a space and place that opens up in that journey. The 'Conversation' is framed as a conversation about thinking, in broad as well as more specific terms, and the movement of thinking is bound up with the movement along the path and of the conversation. The focus on thinking means, too, that the relation between the human, thinking, place and world is also at issue. The conversation is one that constantly reflects back upon the situation of the participants as they are indeed *in* the landscape, *in* the conversation, *in* the world. Although, at the same time, as the conversation moves away from human habitation, and, at one point, into the forest, the focus moves increasingly away from the human and onto the happening (the event or *Ereignis*, to use a key Heideggerian term from elsewhere in his writings) of landscape, place and world. What is centrally at issue in the conversation – that in which the possibility of the journey along the path, of the passage of the conversation itself, of the movement of thinking – is the character of that in which the participants find themselves: a surrounding open that opens itself within the bounds of a horizon (though 'horizon' will turn out itself to be too limited a term here[32]). This open is described 'as something like a region' (*Gegend* in the original German – a term that carries a sense of that which surrounds but also of directional movement[33]). The use of the term 'region', here, is intended to capture the idea of boundedness that is also at issue in the idea of horizon, but the region is also open and free. Heidegger talks of it as having the character of an expanse (*die Weite*) and an abiding while (*die Weile*); as something like, to use language closer to *Being and Time*, both a spatializing and a temporalizing. The region is dynamic – Heidegger describes it as gathering 'each to each and everything to everything else, gathering all into an abiding while resting in itself' – but, in gathering, it also allows things to come into a rest which is 'the hearth and the reign of all movement'.[34]

It might seem as if the path of Heidegger's 'Conversation' not only leads far away from a focus on the human alone but also far away from anything to do with architecture. Yet, although much of the discussion here does indeed operate at a highly philosophical level, what is central to the 'Conversation' is a set of issues that are also central to the investigation of being-in in *Being and Time*, that are central to the question of topological spatiality, and that underlie what is at issue in interiority, including the way that interiority arises within architecture. The question of interiority, whether in architecture or elsewhere, is inextricably bound to the questions of space, place and world. And what the path of Heidegger's 'Conversation' does is to engage in a rethinking of the key notions that are at issue – a rethinking that also occurs in conjunction with a certain sort of re-experiencing that occurs on the path, in and through the landscape of the 'Conversation'. This rethinking can be understood as a rethinking of interiority, or of what is essentially at stake in interiority and, so, of the fundamental notions of being-in, of topological spatiality, of place and of world.

Inasmuch as Heidegger's 'Conversation' begins with its participants already on the path, they begin having already moved beyond the idea of interiority (using that term to name the complex of issues involved here) as just a matter of some sort of static enclosure. But the path of the conversation also takes them beyond the idea – evident in Kantian as well as phenomenological thinking – of interiority as a matter even of engagement within some sort of horizontal field. Just as the movement into the landscape takes the conversation into a region that is both related to human being and extending beyond it, so the thinking of place, which the conversation essentially enacts, is one that leads towards place in its own originary happening, as a 'regioning' into which human beings come, but also as a constant going towards, a constant nearing, rather than as something ever finally and fully realized or realizable. This is partly why the guiding word of the conversation is the strange term from Heraclitus that figures in the original title and is invoked at the very end – Αγχιβασιν, or *Anchibasie* – which Heidegger suggests can be understood as 'coming into nearness'.[35]

Place and liminality

What Heidegger's 'Conversation' makes evident (if it were not so already) is that the question of interiority – of being-in, of topological spatiality, of place and of world – is not about some 'state' of in-ness already arrived at, but is rather of movement-towards, nearing, entry into. What is at issue in the question, and the clue to its answer (which is really given in the rethinking of the question), appears in the very idea of the path that opens the way into the landscape. And whilst the approach to landscape, and the interiority that belongs to it, turns out to be an especially valuable way of bringing this to the fore, the same point applies more generally and, so, also to the question of interiority as it arises in relation to the built. Although Louis Kahn's claim that architecture begins in the room draws attention to the importance of interiority – given this rethought understanding of what is at issue in interiority – it is perhaps better to say that architecture begins not so much in the room as in the door and the threshold;[36] *in the entry across and into*, in the *liminal* and *liminality*.

The *limen*, from which 'liminal' comes, is the Latin for threshold, but the term is also related to the Latin *limes*, meaning boundary, border or limit (the last of these itself coming from the Latin). For the Greeks, the threshold belonged to both Hermes and Hestia – the one, male, being the god of coming and going, of messages, of strangers and thieves, of the path and the street, and the other, female, being the god of the hearth and the home, of family and familiarity, of domesticity and the settled order of things.[37] The two were essentially joined despite their seeming opposition, since both place and region (as the latter term appears in Heidegger) stand in an essential relation to the boundary or the limit. Massimo Cacciari says of place, in a way that draws directly on Aristotle and connects to *limen* and *limes*, that it is 'nothing else but the limit', and, later, that it 'persists-consists in its limit; it is, so to speak, only conceivable *eschatologically*'.[38]

The way liminality appears, here, is not only significant because of the way it draws attention to the character of what has been dealt with in terms of interiority as tied to the entry into – and so to door, gate and threshold – but also because liminality brings with it the idea of a constituting boundary, a boundary or limit that is not merely restrictive but productive. This is a central idea in Heidegger, especially, as has been seen already, in the discussion in 'Building Dwelling Thinking': 'A space is something that has been made room for', he says, 'something that is cleared and free, namely within a boundary [*Grenze*], Greek *peras*. A boundary is not that at which something stops but, as the Greeks recognized, the boundary is that from which something begins its presencing. That is why the concept is that of *horismos*, that is, the horizon, the boundary'.[39] Here, it is worth noting how Heidegger plays on the way the German *Raum* encompasses both room and space, but also his use of the term 'horizon' (despite his comments about the term in the 'Conversations'), although emphasizing its Greek origin. Heidegger does not deny that the boundary restricts or constrains, but it does not *merely* restrict, and its restriction also enables, opens, *frees*.

Elsewhere, in a discussion that is explicitly focused on the door and the bridge, Georg Simmel also addresses the character of the boundary, emphasizing, in similar fashion, the way the boundary, as realized in the door and the bridge, *separates* and also *connects*.[40] Simmel's discussion prefigures elements of Heidegger's, including Heidegger's own characterization, in 'Building Dwelling Thinking', of the way the bridge functions to establish differentiation within space. Heidegger writes that the bridge:

> does not just connect banks that are already there. The banks emerge as banks only as the bridge crosses the stream. The bridge designedly causes them to lie across from each other … With the banks, the bridge brings to the stream the one and the other expanse of the landscape lying behind them. It brings stream and bank and land into each other's neighbourhood.[41]

The idea is already present in Simmel, for whom it is directly related to the character of human being:

> Because the human being is the connecting creature who must always separate and cannot connect without separating – that is why we must first conceive intellectually of the merely indifferent existence of two river banks as something separated in order to connect them by means of a bridge. And the human being is likewise the bordering creature who has no border.[42]

Here, Simmel's final comment is also echoed by Heidegger. The human being, he says, is [the one] 'who walks the boundary of the boundless'.[43]

In the work of the seminal, twentieth-century, New Zealand painter Colin McCahon – one of whose works appears on the cover of this volume – the issues of entry into, of boundary and limit, even of the liminal, develop as key elements in his own approach to landscape, or, as one might also say, to place. And place is certainly at the very heart of McCahon's work. Writing of the experience of the New Zealand landscape, he says: 'I saw something logical, orderly, and beautiful belonging to the land and not yet to its people. Not yet understood or communicated, not yet really invented. My work has largely been to communicate this vision and invent a way to see it.'[44] And elsewhere, writing of one of his major works, *Takaka: Night and Day*, he comments that it 'states my interest in landscape as a symbol of place and also of the human condition'.[45] For McCahon, the question of entry is first a question of how to enter into landscape as it is given in the painting – how to enter into the open realm of the landscape through the flat painted surface. Indeed, this is a question *for* painting as well as for landscape *in* painting – it is partly why the issue of the frame has been such a focus for many modern and contemporary artists.[46] McCahon's solution is to employ differing views, movement, contrasting panels (as in his *Northland Triptych* – see Figure 10.2), which, like the paintings themselves, are both his gates and his journeys (hence the title of one of his most important and major retrospectives[47]).

The landscape that appears in McCahon's works is itself understood in terms of its essential relationality – a relationality that moves outwards (as well as drawing inwards) as part of the horizonal opening of and to the landscape. It is this relationality, and the openness that belongs to it, that is space, although a space that now has to be understood, not merely as static container, but as dynamic and, so, as itself temporal as much as spatial. McCahon writes that 'space is no longer tied to the Renaissance heresy of lines running back from the picture frame but is freed from these ties to reach out in all directions from

Figure 10.2 Colin McCahon, *Northland triptych*, 1959. Hocken Collections, Uare Taoka o Hakena, University of Otago, Dunedin, New Zealand. © Colin McCahon Research and Publication Trust. Courtesy of the Colin McCahon Research and Publication Trust.

the painted surface of the picture'.[48] As it is freed from this 'Renaissance heresy' (which is also the modern idea of space), so it is also freed from the idea of space as given purely in the emptied interior, from space as evident primarily in the diagram, the plan and the bird's-eye view. Of course, the space at issue here is nevertheless a space given in and through the painted surface, but that surface is itself opened up. As McCahon said of the paintings of Braque (whom he preferred, as did Heidegger, to Picasso): 'There is a gap there you can look through into infinity.'[49] The development of McCahon's work over the course of his career was, in the words of the catalogue for McCahon's 1961 *Gates and Journeys* exhibition, towards 'an even more "abstract" style in paintings whose forms, with their forceful antithesis of black and white, "earth" and "sky", often remain, in some mysterious fashion, "landscapes"'.[50] They are landscapes that are 'like revelation', as the poet Geoffrey Hill says of landscape in a different context, 'both singular crystal and the remotest things',[51] but they are also landscapes that draw attention to their own character *as* revelatory. Indeed, what is brought to appearance here is the revelation – the opening – of space, of landscape, of place. It is this opening, which is the opening of a form of interiority, but of interiority given in terms of a constant liminality – a happening of space, time and place – that Heidegger, and to some extent Simmel, too, directs our attention, and which McCahon lays bare in the illumination of canvas and paint. It is also that which architecture itself has the potential to bring forth.

EPILOGUE: RETHINKING ARCHITECTURE

Heidegger's opening question in 'Building Dwelling Thinking' – 'What is it to build?', 'Was ist zu bauen?' – asks after a certain sort of 'ethics' of building no less than it asks after the 'ontology' that belongs with it. The ethical dimension of what is at issue has come to the fore repeatedly in the preceding discussions, even though it has often been addressed only briefly. That dimension becomes evident as soon as one considers the way the question as to the *nature of building* leads on to the question as to how one *ought to build*, which can also be put as the question as to how building must proceed if it is to be consistent with its own character or nature, and indeed, with the 'function' that is embedded in that nature. This concern with 'function' is just the sort of concern that was explored in relation to Aalto's work, as well as Heidegger's, in Chapter 4, and that is centrally at issue in the idea of dwelling, or *Wohnen*.

'Function' is a useful notion in this context, so long as it is understood in a sufficiently broad fashion, since it provides one way of understanding how something like building can indeed have a certain 'task' to which it is committed, and by which it is shaped. Even if that task is never completed, but is constantly underway, and even if the undertaking of that task sometimes goes awry, still the task remains, and as such, the task, and so the function, remains as a defining feature of that to which it belongs. It is thus that the idea of function enables an understanding of the normative element at work in the notions of building and dwelling, and thereby of the ethical dimension in which they operate. Moreover, the way this 'functional' way of thinking does this, and so the way it connects to the idea of the ethical, is not through the elaboration of some 'system' of ethical conduct or a set of moral principles (the sense that is most commonly assumed, and also the sense most common in English-language discourse about ethics). Instead, it aims to draw attention to the proper orientation and situation, in a fundamental sense, of human being in the world. Like Heidegger's thinking in relation to architecture, his inquiry into the ethical does not aim 'to give rules' for living or for acting, for instance, but instead 'traces' such living and acting 'back into that domain to which everything that is belongs', which is to say, back to the *ethos* proper to them.

In the context in which 'Building Dwelling Thinking' was originally presented, the question of the ethical, and so the critical engagement that comes with it, was self-evidently to the fore, even if the language of 'ethics' was not explicitly drawn upon. Heidegger was addressing a group who were already concerned with the question of the built and the architectural as it relates to a set of human concerns – including that of homelessness – and his intention, clearly, was to open a space of questioning in relation to those concerns. His aim was to provoke his audience to thinking about both 'building' and 'dwelling' – and towards a more basic mode of thinking about what thinking itself might be also – as this arises in the only context in which it can arise, namely, that of human dwelling. His aim was not merely to uncover the character of contemporary building and dwelling – how building and dwelling currently are – but also to derive conclusions about what building and dwelling may properly be said to be, which is just the question of how they *ought* to be. As is so often the case in Heidegger, however, the way he aims to achieve this is by means of an exploration of the *topos* within which our thinking already moves – the place into which what is at issue already draws us as thinkers. In the case of 'Building Dwelling Thinking', that involves an exploration of the place within which building and dwelling appear as phenomena that are familiar even prior to giving explicit thought to them (and this, as was seen earlier, is why the translation of *Wohnen* as 'dwelling' already sets off on the wrong foot).

All thinking has this character of a movement back into its place, or an orienting and reorienting to that place (which means that *all* thinking is, in a sense, a *re-thinking*). And all thinking, when directed at things – no matter how they are understood – is a thinking of the place of those things. It is thus that thinking always looks to the elucidation and articulation of things in their relatedness, and so as they participate within a larger landscape. In 'Building Dwelling Thinking', Heidegger's aim is to turn back to the *topos* to which building and dwelling belong and so to turn back the *topos* to which architecture belongs also – which means to *think* that *topos*, to rethink, to recollect and remember. But this turn towards the *topos*, or place, of architecture, which is an ontological turn just as it is topological, is necessarily a turn in which the *telos* of architecture is implicated too. *Telos* here does not mean 'purpose' or 'aim', as usually understood. It is instead that to which something is oriented – and so again implicates a sense of place and being-placed – and, in being oriented, is configured according to that orientation. It is in this sense that the *telos* can be understood as the 'for the sake of which' or the 'function'.

An echo of Heidegger's question concerning the nature of dwelling can thus be heard in the title, as well as in the text, of Karsten Harries's seminal contribution to architectural theory, *The Ethical Function of Architecture*. If Heidegger moves from the question of what it is to build to the issue of what it might be properly to dwell, and what such dwelling might require of us,[1] thereby moving, one might say, from ontology to ethics, then Harries begins with an explicitly ethical perspective that nevertheless turns out to lead into the ontological. Harries's opening concern is with the question as to architecture's function, which is precisely to raise the issue of its *telos*. Harries rejects, or at least treats as secondary, two possible answers to this question: that architecture is primarily *aesthetic* and that it is primarily *utilitarian*. Although he never makes the point himself, the way Harries connects architecture, and so also building, to the ethical implicitly involves a reading of the question of 'Building Dwelling Thinking' that draws it into close proximity with Heidegger's 'Letter on "Humanism"' (written a few years before 'Building Dwelling Thinking'), and its own investigation of the ethical. But in doing that, Harries engages both in a thinking though, and sometimes a rethinking of, what is at issue in Heidegger's text – and so engages in a similar task to that attempted here – as well as a thinking and rethinking of what architecture might be. It is a rethinking that is directly undertaken through the focus on the ethical function of architecture, a topic seldom directly or seriously addressed, which, properly understood (especially in a Heideggerian context), is also a question that concerns the proper place *of architecture*.

The focus of 'Building Dwelling Thinking' is, as already seen, on the relation between building (and thinking) and that mode of being in the world that Heidegger refers to by the very ordinary German word *Wohnen*, which carries into English as 'dwelling'. What is at issue for Heidegger is, to repeat a now familiar point, no strange poetic mode of being, but that everyday mode of living in the world in which one also finds a 'home' in the world, in which one attends to the world and to one's place in it. In the 'Letter on "Humanism"', what is at issue in the question of dwelling is taken up in terms of the question of human being, and the relation between human being and being itself. Fundamental to the question of the human is the issue of ethics, but that question is one Heidegger understands in direct connection to the matter concerning the place of human being in the world, that is, to the question of *Wohnen*, or, to use the other term Heidegger deploys here, *Aufenthalt* – abode or 'dwelling place'. Explicitly connecting 'ethics' back to its origins in the Greek *ethos*, Heidegger writes:

> *Ethos* means abode [*Aufenthalt*], dwelling-place [*Ort des Wohnens*]. The word names the open region [*offenen Bezirk*] in which the human being dwells. The open region of his abode allows what pertains to the essence of human being, and what in thus arriving resides in nearness to him, to appear … If the name 'ethics', in keeping with the basic meaning of the word *ethos*, should now say that ethics ponders the abode of the human being, then that thinking which thinks the truth of being as the primordial element of the human being, as one who eksists, is in itself originary ethics.[2]

The 'open region', which is here identified with *ethos,* is indeed the place to which human being belongs, and not only human being, but since this place is also the place of the truth of being (*Wahrheit des Seyns*), so it is the place in which any appearing, any coming to presence, is possible – the place that belongs *to being* (*Ortschaft des Seyns*). What underlies both *Wohnen* and *ethos,* then, is indeed the idea of *place* or *topos.* Understanding the ethical function of architecture, which is to say its human function, is thus also to understand its *topological* function, but also its topological foundation and, with that, the essential relation between place and the human. The question as to what architecture is 'for' (which is not separable from the question as to what architecture 'is') is thus a question that cannot be answered apart from consideration of the placed character of the human, and that question, in turn, depends on a clearer understanding of place itself. In that case, to understand architecture, one must also understand place.

Place is not a central focus for discussion in *The Ethical Function of Architecture* (although it is addressed in one chapter – Chapter 11, 'Place and Space'). That is not surprising given that Harries's approach is indeed one whose first concern is with a set of problems that belong specifically to *architecture*, and inasmuch as place appears in the course of his development of that approach, it does so out of and in relation to that concern. Moreover, when place does appear, it is in a fashion deriving from an assumed view of place that treats it in a way such that the primary contrast is with a specific mode of space.[3] Place is associated with that which constrains and encloses, but which also shelters and affords intimacy, and so which offers a sense of home and belonging, whilst space is associated with freedom and openness, as well as the promise of the new and the challenge of the strange. The contrast between place and space at issue here is expressed in the contrast of earth with sky, of tradition with the futural and the utopic, of security with hope. One of the key themes in Harries's discussion is the need to negotiate between both place and space – for architecture to acknowledge 'both the sheltering power of place and the indefinite promise of open space'.[4]

One can well understand why Harries uses these terms as he does, and yet there is also an important respect in which that usage requires modification. The contrast that Harries presents between place and space actually obtains, as should already be evident from much of the discussion in preceding chapters, *within place itself*. This is because, to reprise the argument of Chapter 10, the openness that belongs to space is indeed only genuinely possible *within bounds* – something most evident in the way the openness of the sky appears only within the horizon. The two dimensions of boundedness and openness are already present in even the simplest of architectural forms – the hut, for instance, operates through a bounding that also opens, since the boundedness of walls and roof is what makes possible the open room within. It is easy to think of boundedness and openness as if these were simply identical with interiority and exteriority: the open is that which expands outwards into the world and the bounded is that which contracts inwards towards, ultimately perhaps, the self. Yet the contrast between interiority and exteriority arises only in relation to the bound or limit that itself belongs to place. If architecture must concern itself with both place and space, this is largely because space arises only within and with respect to place – just as time, which is the dynamic aspect of that openness that is also evident as space, arises in the same fashion (and so there is properly no time nor space outside of place). The idea that Heidegger appears to take from Simmel – namely, that the human is 'the one who walks the boundary of the boundless' – is worth repeating here. Inasmuch as that idea draws attention to the character of human being as essentially *placed* being – since to walk the boundary of the boundless is indeed to find one's way in place – so it captures a point that is as central to Harries's account as it is to Heidegger's.

The interplay of the bounded and the open that is at issue has a significance for human being that goes beyond the architectural alone. The very possibility of human knowledge and experience, which is to say, the very possibility of human openness to the world, arises only out of the singular finitude of human being, that is to say, out of its concrete situatedness, its placed-ness, its 'being here/there'. Yet the dynamic interplay of bounded and open that lies at the heart of place nevertheless has a special significance for architecture in virtue precisely of architecture's own concern with space and with place. The interplay of bounded and open founds what architecture *is* and what architecture is *for*. Architecture, and more broadly 'building', is a mode of engagement with the world and with the happening of world, as that occurs in and from out of place. Architecture does not 'make' the world, nor does it properly 'make' place, but in *responding* to place, in articulating the human mode of being-in-place, architecture participates in the world, becomes part of its happening, allows that happening to be revealed. Architecture is for nothing if it is not for this.

Much of what is said above, not only in this chapter but in those that precede it, is an explicit thinking and rethinking of place, and so also of dwelling, as it appears in Heidegger's later thinking – but it also, to some degree, involves wresting place from out of Heidegger's own grasp. Harries once commented (in conversation, rather than in print) that, if one is to think the role of place in Heidegger, one must attend more closely to the work of Meister Eckhart[5] – a comment that opens up the perhaps unexpected question as to whether the thinking of this thirteenth-century mystic might be relevant to architecture also (at least so far as Heidegger is concerned).[6] Heidegger's own engagement with Eckhart, though it often remains implicit, is at its strongest in the later thinking, in which the focus on place is also clearest – at a point at which Heidegger has moved beyond the existential analytic of *Being and Time*, as well as the history of being that characterizes his thinking during the 1930s and early 1940s, and towards what he calls the 'topology of being', the thinking of the place of being. The 1959 volume, *Gelassenheit*, published in English as *Discourse on Thinking*,[7] combines two pieces – the 'Memorial Address' (in honour of the Messkirch-born composer Conradin Kreutzer), given in 1955, and an abridged and edited version of what is there titled 'Conversation on a Country Path about Thinking' (the shortened version of the conversation discussed in Chapter 10).[8] Although the volume does not mention Eckhart by name, it nevertheless invokes him by its German title (*Gelassenheit* being a term taken directly from Eckhart). The volume stands in an intimate connection to Heidegger's home town of Messkirch, and the thinking that it sets forth is explicitly connected with the experience of place, as given in that place (and especially in connection with the *Feldweg* that runs from the town into the nearby countryside).

Undoubtedly, part of what is at issue for Heidegger, in *Discourse on Thinking*, is his own profound sense of indebtedness to the place of his childhood, the place to which he returned throughout his life, the place of which he talks as providing the sustaining ground of his thinking – precisely those aspects of place that Harries emphasizes in contrast to space – and, so, the opening words of the 'Memorial Address' with which the *Discourse on Thinking* itself begins are words of thanks to Heidegger's home town, to his 'homeland', to his *Heimat*. The fact that it is a particular place, and Heidegger's own relation to that place, that provides an important part of the background here, can certainly be seen to reinforce the common tendency to think of the focus on place as indicative of an introverted concern with a past and provincial origin and to reflect Heidegger's own personal affectivity. Yet there are a much broader range of considerations at play in *the Discourse on Thinking*, and what emerges there, both in the 'Memorial Address' and in the 'Conversation' that follows it, is a meditation on the nature and significance of place that goes beyond anything to do with personal affectivity or past origins alone, just as the discussions in the preceding chapters have not been concerned merely with the nostalgic, the past or the rural.

Heidegger emphasizes the importance of human being as grounded in a 'homeland', but in the 'Memorial Address', he also points to the way in which, 'for a truly joyous and salutory human work to flourish, man must be able to mount from the depth of his home ground up into the ether'.[9] Human beings thus find their place in the world 'between heaven and earth',[10] which can be understood to mean between the open and the bounded. The groundedness of human being,[11] which is a grounding in 'earth' as well as in the 'between' of heaven and earth, is something that Heidegger argues is threatened by the contemporary dominance of 'planning and calculation, of organisation and automation',[12] that is, by the dominance of modern technology. Heidegger proposes that the path to a way of being-in the-world that will enable us to find a ground in the face of such technological dominance is that of releasement (*Gelassenheit*) towards things. Such releasement is coupled with what Heidegger calls 'openness to the mystery',[13] an openness to the happening of revealing and concealing (what Heidegger elsewhere calls the happening of truth) to which human being is already given over. Significantly, the *thinking* that belongs with such releasement and openness is a thinking that is grounded in its own place (understood again in terms of both the 'earth' and the 'between') and so in a genuine engagement with the world as given in that place: 'It is enough if we dwell on what lies close and meditate on what is closest; upon that which concerns us, each one of us, here and now; here, on this patch of home ground; now, in the present hour of history.'[14] In the 'Conversation', releasement is again drawn explicitly into the discussion (though with the *caveat* that it is not to be thought 'as within the domain of will, as is the case with old masters of thought such as Meister Eckhart ... From whom, all the same, much can be learned'[15]), and much of the 'Conversation' can be understood as an extended meditative dialogue on the nature of the releasement invoked in the 'Memorial Address'.

The way the 'Memorial Address' characterizes human being, as 'between heaven and earth', can be seen already to gesture towards the character of place as it encompasses both the bounded and the open – a theme throughout many of the chapters here. In the 'Conversation', the idea of releasement is explored in terms of the relation to that open region – 'the region of all regions ... *the* region'[16] – that was the focus of discussion in Chapter 10. Releasement is a releasement to this region, but in being thus, it is releasement to that to which it already belongs – to which thinking and human being already belong:

> Releasement comes out of that-which-regions because in releasement man stays released to that-which-regions and, indeed, through this itself. He is released to it in his being, insofar as he originally belongs to it. He belongs to it insofar as he is appropriated initially to that-which-regions and, indeed, through this itself ... releasement consists in this: that man in his very nature belongs to that-which-regions, i.e., he is released to it ... Not occasionally, but ... prior to everything ....[17]

The way in which, in Heidegger, releasement is releasement to that to which one already belongs reflects the analogous way in which releasement, in Eckhart, also involves a return to God as the ground of our being. It is because one always already remains in an essential relation to God that the turn back to God – the 'rebirth of God in the soul' – is both possible and necessary.

Eckhart does not use the same topological language that one finds in Heidegger, although one might well argue that some such topology is implied (and not merely as a result of its inevitable presence in all thinking or understanding[18]). The very language of 'being released' (*gelassen*), for instance, is hardly to be grasped without a sense of the open domain in which such release is possible and into which something is let. Moreover, the way Heidegger connects releasement and place as region seems to depend and to draw upon the sense of released involvement that one finds in any genuinely self-aware being-in-place. To be in place is to grasp one's own being-somewhere as a belonging-to and an apartness-from. These very elements are already presaged in the idea of place as both bounded and open. Quite distinct from any way of grasping place that takes place as the object of possession or as the mark of exclusive proprietorship – which is really the assertion of subjectivity over place and, so, is exactly the sort of 'willfulness' that releasement is not – the thinking that gives priority to place is one that is also necessarily a relinquishing of will and, so, a giving up of claims to possession, determination or exclusivity. In the simplest of terms, releasement is a releasement to that to which one belongs and in which one's being is grounded – a releasement to one's own being-placed – and, as such, releasement captures something essential to such being-placed, and so to place itself. It also indicates the way which any genuine *ethics* does indeed have its own origin in place, and may even be understood as a releasement towards place.

Why might any of this be relevant to architecture? Quite simply, because architecture is a mode of thinking, as well as of making, that concerns itself with the places in which one finds oneself as these are worked out and articulated in and through concrete 'built' forms. Building, as Heidegger emphasizes, arises out of, but also for the sake of dwelling,[19] so building is that by means of which our living in the world is worked out, by means of which it takes on a certain form. Building is itself a bounding that opens, even though it is always dependent on and, properly understood, must be responsive to the more originary bounding in which the very possibility of architecture, no less than human being, is opened up. Architecture functions inasmuch as it allows our own releasement towards that originary bounded open, as it allows its own such releasement.

The danger for architecture is that it becomes dysfunctional through a refusal of that releasement – through the holding on to place, to the bounded and the open, as if place were indeed that which remains in the possession of architecture, as if it were the 'gift' of architecture, as if it were 'made' by architecture. But architecture does not possess, does not have in its gift, does not make, that to which it already belongs.

Because of the need to remember that prior belonging, there must always be a sense in which attentiveness to place will take the form, as it does so often in Heidegger and especially in *Gelassenheit*, of a return to a certain sort of origin, a turn back to place as that in which human being first finds itself, a 'coming near' or 'into nearness',[20] even a return home (although to a home that is itself revealed as uncertain and even uncanny). The open and the free – which is the worldliness of the world – do not emerge in an already boundless realm, nor in some place that is still beyond us, but always and only here, now, in this place. The function of architecture, what it is indeed 'for', must always be to return us to this place in a way that is attuned to that place and to the many differing ways in which it reveals itself, as well as to the possibilities that may emerge in and from it. It is, moreover, a return to that place that occurs only in and through *this* place – whatever its own singular character, wherever it may be. In this way, and only thus, can architecture remain attuned to its own origin in the belonging-together of the bounded and the open; only then can architecture fulfil the genuinely *ethical*, which is to say, *human*, function that, as Harries so rightly argues, is proper to it; only then can architecture be of the world and also adequate to it.

When one turns back to rethink what might be at issue in Heidegger's *Wohnen*, in dwelling, in place itself, one cannot escape a rethinking of what might be at issue in 'building', and so also in architecture. This rethinking does not lead in the direction of some new method, plan or formula that can uniquely determine either an architectural or ethical practice, any more than it leads in the direction of a method, plan or formula by which one might know in advance how to 'build' or 'dwell'. There is nothing that can direct in that way. Indeed, since the place to which all 'building' and 'dwelling' respond is always multiple and differentiated, so the responsiveness at issue here can never be determined or prescribed in advance. It is, in fact, always 'indeterminate', which here means always open to more than one mode of appearing, of being understood or of being engaged. That is just what it means, in fact, for thinking and building to be genuinely *responsive* – that is, for thinking and building to be *responses to* the very place in which they also arise, out of which they come, and on the basis of which they can be said to be *responsible*. It is in relation to such a responsiveness that architecture finds its proper function and *ethos*, its *telos* and its *topos*, its own place and ground. It is thus that its own mode of being in the world is worked out. Moreover, this is just what becomes evident through the thinking and rethinking of dwelling, and of place, that Heidegger's 1951 text has the potential to open up. What is required, however, is the same responsiveness and attentiveness to that text, and the matters it brings forth, that the text itself aims to explore.

NOTES

Introduction

1 There are, however, several volumes that take up the issue of a 'philosophy of architecture', including Michael Mitias, ed., *Philosophy and Architecture* (Amsterdam: Rodopi, 1994) and Christian Illies and Nicholas Ray, *Philosophy of Architecture* (Cambridge: Cambridge Architectural Press, 2014). Others take up philosophical issues in architecture in more specific ways, such as Tom Spector, *The Ethical Architect: The Dilemma of Contemporary Practice* (New York: Princeton Architectural Press, 2001) and Roger Scruton, *The Aesthetics of Architecture* (Princeton: Princeton University Press, 1979). Karsten Harries, *The Ethical Function of Architecture* (Cambridge, MA: MIT Press, 1997) is one of the best-known works that aims to address architecture from a philosophical perspective, and that also does so in a way directly influenced by Heidegger.
2 See Paul Wijdeveld, *Ludwig Wittgenstein, Architect* (London: Thames and Hudson, 1994). See also the discussion in Robert Mugerauer, *Interpreting Environments: Tradition, Deconstruction, Hermeneutics* (Austin: University of Texas Press, 2014), 2–14.
3 Arthur G. Wirth and Carl Bewig, 'John Dewey on School Architecture', *The Journal of Aesthetic Education* 2 (1968): 79–86.
4 See Brendon Wocke, 'Derrida at Villette: (An)aesthetic of Space', *University of Toronto Quarterly* 83 (2014): 739–55. See also Jeffrey Kipnis and Thomas Leeser, *Chora L Works: Jacques Derrida and Peter Eisenman* (New York: Monacelli Press, 1997).
5 See W. Julian Korab-Karpowicz, 'Schopenhauer's Theory of Architecture', in *A Companion to Schopenhauer*, ed. Bart Vandenabeele (Malden, MA: Wiley-Blackwell, 2012), 178–92; also Schopenhauer, *The World as Will and Representation*, trans. E. F. J. Payne (New York: Dover, 1969), 1:213–18, 2: 411–19.
6 Derrida remarked of the original *chora* text: '… it's a sort of philosophical essay. It has nothing to do with architecture', in Kipnis and Leeser, *Chora L Works: Jacques Derrida and Peter Eisenman*, 13. See Anthony Vidler's discussion, 'Nothing to Do with Architecture', *Grey Room* 21 (2005): 112–27.
7 But, see Mark Wigley, *The Architecture of Deconstruction: Derrida's Haunt* (Cambridge, MA: MIT Press, 1993).
8 Eisenman has also engaged with Elizabeth Grosz – see her *Architecture from the Outside: Essays on Virtual and Real Space* (Cambridge, MA: MIT Press, 2001).
9 See Jean Baudrillard and Jean Nouvel, *The Singular Objects of Architecture*, trans. Robert Bononno (Minneapolis: University of Minnesota Press, 2002).
10 Martin Heidegger, 'Bauen Wohnen Denken', first published in Otto Bartning, ed., *Mensch und Raum: Darmstädter Gespräch 1951* (Darmstadt: Neue Darmstädter Verlagsanstalt, 1952), 72–84. The original English translation was first published in 1971 – see Martin Heidegger, *Poetry, Language, Thought*, trans. Albert Hofstadter, 1st Harper Colophon ed. (New York: Harper Colophon, 1975), 143–62.

11 It is a major focus for Martin V. Woessner's discussion of Heidegger's influence on American architecture in *Heidegger in America* (Cambridge: Cambridge University Press, 2011), 230–62.
12 Heidegger's writings refer to various artists, most notably Cezanne, Van Gogh and Klee, but he also had a keen interest in art more broadly. He engaged with the Basque sculptor Eduardo Chillida, and was a great admirer of the expressionist painter, Paula Modersohn-Becker, as well as of Georges Braque, although he had an equivocal relation to the work of Picasso. See Heinrich Petzet, *Encounters and Dialogues with Martin Heidegger, 1929-1976*, trans. Parvis Emad and Kenneth Maly (Chicago: University of Chicago Press, 1993), 133–58 and Julian Young, *Heidegger's Philosophy of Art* (Cambridge: Cambridge University Press, 2001), esp. chap. 4, 'Modern Art', 120–74.
13 He also seems to have had some appreciation of Le Corbusier, visiting Le Corbusier's pilgrimage church at Ronchamp – see G. Neske, *Errinerung an Martin Heidegger* (Pfullingen: Neske, 1977), 136; Petzet, *Encounters and Dialogues with Martin Heidegger*, 150. Some, however, have seen 'Building Dwelling Thinking' as a direct counter to Le Corbusier's claim, first made in 1923, that the house 'is a machine for living in' – Le Corbusier, *Towards a New Architecture*, trans. Frederick Etchells (New York: Dover Publications, 1986), 107.
14 See Derrida's essay 'Khôra', in *On the Name*, ed. Thomas Dutoit (Stanford: Stanford University Press, 1993), 89–130. See also: Nader El-Bizri, 'On και χωρα: Situating Heidegger between the *Sophist* and the *Timaeus*', *Studia Phaenomenologica* 4 (2002): 73–98 and Malpas, 'Five Theses on Place (and some associated remarks): A Reply to Peter Gratton', *Il Cannocchiale: rivista di studi filosofici* 42 (2017): 69–81.
15 On philosophical topology (or topography), see Malpas, *Place and Experience: A Philosophical Topography*, 2nd ed. (London: Routledge, 2018), esp. 37–40. As used here, and in other works like *Place and Experience*, 'topology' and 'topography' are used to mean more or less the same. 'Topography' is an important term in David Leatherbarrow's *Uncommon Ground: Architecture, Technology, and Topography* (Cambridge, MA: MIT Press, 2000) – a work that also shares a similar sensibility (although it adopts a different language and approach) to this volume. However, Leatherbarrow's use of 'topography' is narrower than the use of 'topology' (or the implied sense of 'topography') at work here (see Leatherbarrow, *Uncommon Ground*, vi).
16 See Malpas, 'On the Reading of Heidegger: Situating the Black Notebooks', in *Reading Heidegger's Black Notebooks, 1931-1941*, ed. Ingo Farin and Jeff Malpas (Cambridge, MA: MIT Press, 2015), 3–22.
17 See Heidegger, 'Letter on "Humanism"', in *Pathmarks*, ed. William McNeill (Cambridge: Cambridge University Press, 1998), 239–76.
18 Neil Leach has talked previously of 'rethinking architecture' – see Leach, ed., *Rethinking Architecture: A Reader in Cultural Theory* (New York: Routledge, 1977).
19 See Heidegger, 'Memorial Address', in *Discourse on Thinking. A Translation of Gelassenheit*, trans. John M. Anderson and E. Hans Freund (New York: Harper & Row, 1966), 45.
20 See the discussion in Malpas, *Place and Experience*, esp. chap. 2, 'The Obscurity of Place', 23–47.
21 Christian Norberg-Schulz, *Genius Loci: Towards a Phenomenology of Architecture* (New York: Rizzoli, 1980), 5.
22 In his *Dwelling: Heidegger, Archaeology, Mortality* (London: Routledge, 2017), 11, Philip Tonner asserts that Heidegger takes as a basic theoretical premise throughout his work an understanding of 'dwelling' as applicable only to 'anatomically fully modern humans'

(referring, at the same time, to Heidegger's 'analogically deprivational bio-philosophy of poverty'). This is not a claim that is readily substantiated, but it does reflect an assumption, or type of assumption, that can be found in many readings of Heidegger's work.

23 *Being and Time,* or *Sein und Zeit* in its original German, was published by Max Niemeyer Verlag, Halle, in 1927, and almost immediately established Heidegger's reputation in Germany and beyond, becoming perhaps the single best-known and important philosophical work of the twentieth century. *Being and Time* is referred to at various points throughout this volume using the following English translations: *Being and Time*, trans. John Macquarie and Edward Robinson (New York: Harper & Row, 1962); and *Being and Time*, trans. Joan Stambaugh, rev. Dennis Schmidt (Albany, NY: SUNY Press, 2010) – the first unrevised edition having appeared in 1996. There are important differences between the two translations which is why both are included. Where relevant, the particular translation will be designated, but all page references to *Being and Time* are given using a number preceded by an H (thus 'H342'), which standardly refers to the pagination in the 7th German edition from 1953 (and all editions thereafter). The H number also appears in the margins of both English translations, enabling consistent reference to both German and English.

24 See, e.g., Heidegger's discussions, originally published in 1959, which appear in English as *On the Way to Language*, trans. Peter D. Hertz (New York: Harper & Row, 1971), esp. 'The Nature of Language', 57–110.

25 As Heidegger says in 'Art and Space', in *The Heidegger Reader*, ed. Günter Figal, trans. Jerome Veith (Bloomington, IN: Indiana University Press, 2009), 307.

26 Significantly, language comes increasingly to the fore in Heidegger's own thinking as topological themes also become more directly thematized. In the same way, Heidegger's later thinking also tends towards a more implicitly 'hermeneutical' stance – notwithstanding the fact that he almost never employs the term itself. There is a great deal more that can be said about the role of the hermeneutical, not only in Heidegger, and in its connection to topology, but also in relation to architecture. The tendency in the existing literature is to treat hermeneutics as largely about the question of *interpretation* or even *reception*. But as it develops through Heidegger and Gadamer, hermeneutics is less a 'theory of interpretation' than it is a mode of ontological inquiry that takes place and situatedness as fundamental to the possibility of understanding. In other words, hermeneutics is essentially topological – see, e.g., Malpas, 'Place and Situation', in *The Routledge Companion to Hermeneutics*, 354–66.

27 Heidegger, 'Building Dwelling Thinking', 143. Although Heidegger does not do so, various other writers have attempted to develop Heidegger's thinking in ways more specific to architectural theory and practice. This includes the work of Norberg-Schulz, but also, notably, Robert Mugerauer – see Mugeraurer's *Interpretations on Behalf of Place. Environmental Displacements and Alternative Responses* (Albany, NY: SUNY Press, 1994).

28 See *Oxford English Dictionary,* 3rd ed. (2004), s.v. 'ontology'. The Latin *ontologia* is derived from the combination of the Greek *on*, *ontos*, 'being', with *logia*, from *logos*, 'account' or 'story', but also 'principle' or 'reason'.

29 Thus Heidegger suggests, at one point, that his own thinking is 'neither ontic nor ontological' meaning that it is neither concerned with 'a connection of cause and effect nor the transcendental-horizontal relationship' – see 'Αγχιβασιν [Anchibasie]. A Triadic Conversation on a Country Path between a Scientist, a Scholar, and a Guide', in *Country Path Conversations*, trans. Bret W. Davis (Bloomington: Indiana

University Press, 2010), 90. Although Heidegger's concerns about ontology are not without foundation, the way those concerns have often been taken up has been such as to contribute not only to the suspicion of ontology within contemporary theory, but also to exactly the *refusal* of the sort of fundamental thinking that Heidegger himself undertakes. In this way, the critique of ontology has become part of the very forgetting of being and the effacement of place that were the basis for the Heideggerian eschewal of ontology in its traditional forms.

Chapter 1

1. Patrick Keiller, *London*, written, photographed, and edited by Patrick Keiller, narr. Paul Scofield (London: BFI and Koninck Studios, 1994; released on video, London: BFI Video, 2012), DVD, 85 min.; *Robinson in Space*, written, photographed, edited by Patrick Keiller, narr. Paul Scofield (London: BBC and Koninck Studios, 1997; released on video, London: BFI Video, 2012), DVD, 82 min.; *Robinson in Ruins*, written, photographed, and edited by Patrick Keiller, narr. Vanessa Redgrave (London: Royal College of Art/Illuminations Films, 2010; released on video, London: BFI Video, 2011), DVD, 101 min. (The latter film developed out of a collaborative project involving Keiller, the cultural critic Patrick Wright, and the geographer Doreen Massey).
2. Keiller, *Robinson in Ruins*, soundtrack; see also *Robinson in Ruins* [booklet accompanying DVD] (London: BFI, 2011), 2.
3. *Robinson in Ruins*, soundtrack.
4. Heidegger, 'Building Dwelling Thinking', 157. Heidegger goes on to note that 'Our reference to the Black Forest farm in no way means that we should or could go back to building such houses; rather, it illustrates by a dwelling that has been how it was able to build' (158). The definitive work on the Black Forest farmhouse is Hermann Schilli, *Das Schwarzwaldhaus* (Stuttgart: W. Kohlhammer, 1953) – Schilli founded the Black Forest open air museum, Vogtsbauernhof, dedicated to such buildings, in 1964.
5. Hilde Heynen, *Architecture and Modernity* (Cambridge, MA: MIT Press, 1998), 17–18. See also, Heynen, 'Worthy of Question: Heidegger's Role in Architectural Theory', *Archis* 12 (1993): 42–9.
6. Neil Leach, 'The Dark Side of the *Domus*', *The Journal of Architecture* 3 (1998): 31.
7. Leach, 'The Dark Side of the *Domus*', 39.
8. Both Heynen and Leach make reference to Jean-François Lyotard, 'Domus and the Megalopolis', in *The Inhuman: Reflections on Time* (Cambridge: Polity Press, 1988), 191–204, in which the 'mythic' realm of the domestic is set against the contemporary 'megalopolis' of modernity.
9. Leach, 'The Dark Side of the *Domus*', 31, 39.
10. Adam Sharr, *Heidegger for Architects* (London: Routledge, 2007), 114.
11. See Anthony Vidler, *The Architectural Uncanny: Essays in the Modern Unhomely* (Cambridge, MA: MIT Press, 1992), e.g. 7–8.
12. Mark Wigley, 'Heidegger's House: The Violence of the Domestic', *Columbia Documents of Architecture and Theory* 1 (1992): 91–121.
13. Christopher Alexander and Peter Eisenman, 'Contrasting Concepts of Harmony in Architecture: The 1982 Debate between Christopher Alexander and Peter Eisenman', ed. Lucien Steil, Brian Hanson, Michael Mehaffy and Nikos Salingaros, *Katarxis*, no. 3

(2004), accessed May 2020, http://www.katarxis3.com/Alexander_Eisenman_Debate.htm.
14 Heynen does try to encompass a wider range of readings and approaches, including differing readings of Heidegger's position, notably that of Massimo Cacciari (discussed further in Chapters 2 and 3).
15 Albert Borgmann reads all of Heidegger's work in terms of an oscillation between these two – 'Cosmopolitanism and Provincialism: On Heidegger's Errors and Insights', *Philosophy Today* 36 (1992): 131–45.
16 The volume in which the English translation of 'Building Dwelling Thinking' appeared (*Poetry, Language, Thought*, ed. Albert Hofstadter) brought together various essays from 1936 to the early 1950s, all of which touched on themes of art, poetry and language.
17 Otto Bartning, ed., *Mensch und Raum: Darmstädter Gespräch 1951* (Darmstadt: Neue Darmstädter Verlagsanstalt, 1952), 85.
18 The first colloquium, in 1950, was on 'The Image of Man in Our Time' – see Hans Gerhard Evers, ed., *Neue Darmstädter Sezession: Das Menschenbild in unserer Zeit* (Darmstadt: Neue Darmstädter Verlagsanstalt, 1951).
19 Heidegger, 'Building Dwelling Thinking', 161. It is sometimes said that Heidegger seems to pass all too quickly over the issue of the wartime destruction that would have been so evident in 1951. But that it was so evident also makes it less likely that Heidegger would have felt a need to draw attention to it, and, in fact, none of the other contributors in Darmstadt give extended attention to it either.
20 A view most often associated with Hubert Dreyfus – see his *Being-in-the-World: A Commentary on Heidegger's Being in Time*, Division I (Cambridge, MA: MIT Press, 1990).
21 See *Being and Time*, H358.
22 Closely tied to the question of being, the issue of world already implicates space and place, since the world is that surrounding region or domain *in which* things appear and *in which* human beings find themselves. This is more directly addressed, with particular reference to the issue of the 'in' (or as it appears there of 'interiority'), in Chapter 10.
23 See Malpas, *Heidegger's Topology: Being, Place, World* (Cambridge, MA: MIT Press, 2006), 256.
24 See Georg Simmel, 'Bridge and Door', in *Simmel on Culture*, ed. David Frisby and Mike Featherstone (London: Sage, 1997), 170–4.
25 Heidegger, 'Building Dwelling Thinking', 159.
26 See Malpas, *Place and Experience*.
27 See, for example, Heidegger, *Gesamtausgabe*, Vol. 15, *Seminare*, ed. Curt Ochwald (Frankfurt: Klostermann, 1996), 335 and 344; *Four Seminars*, trans. Andrew Mitchell and François Raffoul (Bloomington: Indiana University Press, 2004), 41 and 47.
28 Theodor W. Adorno, *Minima Moralia: Reflections from Damaged Life* (London: Verso, 2005), 38–9.
29 Walter Benjamin, *The Arcades Project*, trans. Howard Eiland and Kevin McLaughlin (Cambridge, MA: Harvard University Press, 2002), esp. 220–1, but also 865.
30 Although Benjamin does offer some reflections on *Wohnen* as such, writing of 'the difficulty' of such reflection, and remarking that 'on the one hand, there is something age-old – perhaps eternal – to be recognized here, the image of that abode of the human being in the maternal womb; on the other hand, this motif of primal history notwithstanding, one must understand dwelling [*Wohnen*] in its most extreme form

as a condition of nineteenth-century existence. The original form of all dwelling [*Wohnen*] is existence not in the house but in the shell [*Die Urform allen Wohnens ist das Dasein nicht im Haus sondern im Gehäuse*]. The shell bears the impression of its occupant. In the most extreme instance, the dwelling becomes a shell [*Wohnung wird im extremsten Falle zum Gehäuse*]'. See Benjamin, *The Arcades Project*, 220 (also 865). On the one hand, one can see what is at issue for Benjamin here, but as the play between *Haus* and *Gehäuse* indicates, there is also a certain obscurity here – the 'house' is a 'housing', and yet Benjamin sets the two in opposition. What, then, one might then be led to ask, does it mean 'to house'? Both Benjamin's comments and those of Adorno have been taken up in architectural and other contexts since their original publication, including English-language discussions of 'dwelling' and related topics.

31   Adorno, *Minima Moralia*, 38.
32   Adorno, *Minima Moralia*, 35.
33   Benjamin, *The Arcades Project*, 220 (also 865).
34   This is true of Norberg-Schulz's, *Intentions in Architecture* (Cambridge, MA: MIT Press, 1962). It is also true of that of Steen Eilar Rasmussen (although he also, very occasionally, uses 'dwell' as a verb) and Amos Rapaport – see, for example, Rasmussen, *Experiencing Architecture* (Cambridge, MA: MIT Press, 1962), and Rapaport, *House Form and Culture* (Englewood Cliffs, NJ: Prentice-Hall, 1969). The way the 'dwelling' is taken up in Norberg-Schulz, as well as Rasmussen and Rapaport, is indicative of a concern with the functional and environmental context of architecture, and so with what might broadly be termed its 'existential' relevance, that can be seen to presage some of the concerns that are evident in Heidegger. However, in the early work of Norberg-Schulz, and in Rasmussen and Rapaport, this remains oriented to the empirical rather than the ontological, and so does not extend to the same sort of fundamental analysis that Heidegger attempts.
35   'Dwelling' is a term that appears in two of the very first monograph-length treatments of Heidegger in English (also the first that address the later thinking): Vincent Vycinas, *Earth and Gods* (The Hague: Martinus Nijhof, 1961) – a ground-breaking work that was especially important for geographers such as Edward Relph and David Seamon, although (unfortunately) largely ignored by many contemporary Heidegger scholars; and William Richardson, *Heidegger: Through Phenomenology to Thought* (The Hague: Martinus Nijhoff, 1963). That these are indeed two of the earliest full-length treatments of Heidegger in English is an indication how long it took for Heidegger to be taken up in the English-speaking world – *Being and Time*, Heidegger's *magnum opus*, having appeared over thirty years before. For much of the 1950s, and even into the 1960s, there was relatively little engagement with Heidegger's thought outside of theological circles, and as Martin Woessner points out, the entry of Heidegger's work into the United States, in particular, was via theology. See Woessner, *Heidegger in America* (Cambridge: Cambridge University Press, 2011), 112. In English-language philosophy, dominated as it was by analytic thinking, there was widespread suspicion and ignorance of Heidegger's work as a whole, especially of the later thinking (although this was not restricted to analytic thinkers, as Woessner's recounting of Hans Jonas's attitude to the later thinking demonstrates; see Woessner, *Heidegger in America*, 114–16). Even as Heidegger's early work became more widely known, the later thinking continued to be viewed as having little philosophical relevance (many seeing Heidegger as having abandoned philosophy for poetry), and this remained so well into the 1990s and beyond. Outside of English, in languages

such as Spanish and Italian, and even French (see Dominique Janicaud, *Heidegger in France*, trans. François Raffoul and David Pettigrew [Bloomington: Indiana University Press, 2015]), although not German, the situation was different, with greater engagement of Heidegger, including the later essays, both within philosophy and outside, even in the 1960s.

36   Kenneth Frampton, 'On Reading Heidegger', *Oppositions* 4 (1974): n.p.
37   There is some brief reference to Frampton's essay in Woessner, *Heidegger in America*, 235. Heidegger's thinking is an important influence on Frampton's 'Critical Regionalism', but not in a way that leads Frampton to draw, in any significant way, on the notion of 'dwelling', nor to engage substantively or directly with Heidegger's thinking as such.
38   For a useful and insightful overview of the critical reception of Norberg-Schulz's work on Heidegger (although not in terms of the critique of Heidegger but of Norberg-Schulz), see Rowan Wilken, 'The Critical Reception of Christian Norberg Schulz's Writings on Heidegger and Place', *Architectural Theory Review* 18 (2015): 340–55.
39   Christian Norberg-Schulz, *Existence, Space and Architecture* (London: Vista, 1971); *Genius Loci: Towards a Phenomenology of Architecture* (New York: Rizzoli, 1980); *The Concept of Dwelling: On the Way to Figurative Architecture* (New York: Rizzoli, 1985). See also 'Heidegger's Thinking on Architecture', *Perspecta* 20 (1983): 61–8.
40   Norberg-Schulz, *The Concept of Dwelling*, 12.
41   Norberg-Schulz, *The Concept of Dwelling*, 16–20.
42   Norberg-Schulz, *The Concept of Dwelling*, 20–5.
43   See Norberg-Schulz, *The Concept of Dwelling*, esp. 26–30.
44   Buttimer's may well be the first explicit discussion in a geographical publication in English, but it was soon followed by several other important works, as indicated below (including Relph's *Place and Placelessness* in the same year). And although located within geography, work such as Buttimer's also extended out to a range of other disciplines.
45   Anne Buttimer, 'Grasping the Dynamism of Lifeworld', *Annals of the Association of American Geographers* 66 (1976): 277–92.
46   Buttimer, 'Grasping the Dynamism of Lifeworld', 277.
47   Edward Relph, *Place and Placelessness* (London: Pion, 1976), 16–18. Relph acknowledges his indebtedness to Vincent Vycinas's important 1961 work, *Earth and Gods,* in his reading of Heidegger. In *Rational Landscapes and Humanistic Geography* (New York: Barnes and Noble, 1981), Relph directly takes up issues of architecture and urban design, but without any direct discussion of dwelling other than in the sense of a built habitation.
48   See especially the quotation from Norberg-Schulz in Relph, *Place and Placelessness*, 28.
49   David Seamon, *A Geography of the Lifeworld: Movement, Rest and Encounter* (London: Croom Helm, 1979).
50   See David Seamon and Robert Mugerauer, *Dwelling, Place and Environment: An Introduction* (Dordrecht: Martinus Nijhof, 1985), esp. 3.
51   All of these figures – Buttimer, Relph, Seamon and Mugerauer continued to make important contributions well beyond their original ground-breaking work. See, for example, Buttimer, Buttimer, *Geography and the Human Spirit* (Baltimore: Johns Hopkins University Press, 1994) and Relph, *Modern Urban Landscapes* (Baltimore: Johns Hopkins University Press, 1987). Most recently, in the case of Seamon and Mugerauer, see Seamon, *Place: Phenomenology, Lifeworlds and Place Making* (London: Routledge, 2018); Mugerauer, *Responding to Loss: Heideggerian Readings of Literature,*

Architecture, and Film (New York: Fordham, 2015). From 1990 to 2018 Seamon also edited the *Environmental and Architectural Phenomenology Newsletter* – a key forum for interdisciplinary place-oriented thinking. Relph currently edits an important website on placelessness: https://www.placeness.com/, accessed September 2020.

52 Within geography, the work of Marwyn Samuels is notable for the way it focuses specifically on existentialism as a source for thinking about the spatial character of human existence (although Samuels does not thereby ignore phenomenology) – see Marwyn S. Samuels, 'Existentialism and Human Geography', in *Human Geography: Problems and Prospects*, ed. David Ley and Marwyn S. Samuels (London: Croom Helm, 1978), 23–40.

53 To talk of a determining structure here is not to imply any specific determination in advance, as if ontology makes necessary that things will be exactly thus and so in their concrete details. What is at issue is the structure that establishes the framework of determination – that in respect of which existence becomes determinate and what constrains or directs the mode of such determination.

54 Most notably from its occurrence in Husserl, *The Crisis of European Sciences and Transcendental Phenomenology*, trans. David Carr (Evanston, IL: Northwestern University Press, 1954). However, as Carr points out, the term first appears in Husserl's work, in 1917, in a supplement to *Ideas II* – see Carr, 'Husserl's Problematic Concept of the Life-World', *American Philosophical Quarterly* 7 (1970): 332.

55 The term appears infrequently, usually in the earlier work, and nowhere is it given a significant role in Heidegger's own thinking. See, for example, Heidegger, 'Über das Zeitverständnis in der Phänomenologie und im Denken des Seinsfrage (1929)', in *Gesamtausgabe*, Vol. 14, *Zur Sache des Denkens*, ed. Friedrich-Wilhelm von Herrmann (Frankfurt: Klostermann, 2007), 148.

56 Martin Heidegger, 'Seminar in Le Thor 1969', in *Four Seminars*, 47.

57 See, for example, Heidegger's comments in *Contributions to Philosophy (of the Event)*, 233; and the comments in Heidegger, 'European Nihilism', in *Nietzsche*, trans. David Farrell Krell, Vol. 4, *Nihilism* (San Francisco: Harper & Row, 1979–87), 141.

58 See Heidegger's reference to the 'distressing difficulty' concerning '*the relation of Being and human being*' that appears in the addendum to 'The Origin of the Work of Art', in *Poetry, Language, Thought*, 87.

59 See Malpas, *Heidegger's Topology*, 155–75.

60 Among other works, see Alfred Schutz, *The Phenomenology of the Social World*, trans. G. Walsh and F. Lehnert (Evanston, IL: Northwestern University Press, 1967). See also, Maurice Natanson, 'Alfred Schutz on Social Reality and Social Science', *Social Research* 35 (1968): 217–44.

61 Peter Berger and Thomas Luckmann, *The Social Construction of Reality: A Treatise in the Sociology of Knowledge* (Garden City, NY: Anchor, 1966).

62 Pau Obrador-Pons, 'Dwelling', in *Companion Encyclopaedia of Geography: From Local to Global*, ed. I. Douglas, R. Huggett and C. Perkins (London: Routledge, 2006), 954.

63 See, for example, Philip Tonner, *Dwelling: Heidegger, Archaeology, Mortality* (London: Routledge, 2017).

64 Tim Ingold, 'Building, Dwelling, Living: How Animals and People Make Themselves at Home in the World', in *The Perception of the Environment Essays on Livelihood, Dwelling and Skill* (London: Routledge, 2000), 172–88.

65 Ingold, 'Building, Dwelling, Living', 153.

66 There is a larger story about the relation between Heidegger and von Uexküll – see Malpas, 'Geography, Biology, and Politics', in *Heidegger and the Thinking of Place*

(Cambridge, MA: MIT Press, 2012), 137–58. See also Anne Harrington, *Reenchanted Science: Holism in German Culture from Wilhelm II to Hitler* (Princeton: Princeton University Press, 1996), esp. 44–7 and Florian Mildenberger, *Umwelt als Vision: Leben und Werk Jakob von Uexkülls (1864–1944)* (Stuttgart: Franz Steiner, 2007).

67 Perhaps ironically, however, although Ingold's turn to von Uexküll arises out of a dissatisfaction with constructionist accounts, the neo-Kantianism of von Uexküll's work can itself tend towards a form of constructionism.

68 'Psychologism' takes psychological structures as the most basic, and 'anthropologism' makes the same move but giving priority to anthropological structures (in both cases, the structures at issue are empirically given). Ironically, even though phenomenology has itself tended to give rise to psychologistic interpretation, what set Husserl on the path towards the development of phenomenology was his abandonment of psychologism (largely as a result of the criticisms advanced by Gottlob Frege in relation to Husserl's first book, *The Philosophy of Arithmetic*, 1891).

69 Martin Heidegger, *Introduction to Metaphysics*, trans. Gregory Fried and Richard Polt (New Haven: Yale University Press, 2000), 159–62.

70 Tim Ingold, 'Epilogue: Towards a Politics of Dwelling', *Conservation and Society* 3 (2005): 503.

71 See Anatoly Liberman, 'Our Habitat: Dwelling', *OUPblog, Oxford University Press's Academic Insights for the Thinking World*, 14 January 2015, accessed, May 2020, https://blog.oup.com/2015/01/dwelling-word-origin-etymology/. This is the most detailed (and convincing) account of the likely origins of 'dwell' that is readily available in the existing research literature.

72 *Oxford English Dictionary*, 3rd ed. (2004), s.v. 'dwell'. The entry is largely unchanged from the first edition of the OED in 1933 to the current edition. See also the entry in Robert K. Barnhart, ed., *Chambers Dictionary of Etymology* (London: Chambers, 2000).

73 Pavlos Lefas, *Dwelling and Architecture: From Heidegger to Koolhaas* (Berlin: Jovis Verlag, 2009).

74 Heidegger, 'Building Dwelling Thinking', 143–4. Interestingly, Heidegger immediately goes on: 'These buildings house man' and the reference to 'these buildings' includes the power station, the spinning mill *and the highway*.

75 Andrew Benjamin seems to suggest just such a translation (despite his title) in 'Who Dwells? Heidegger and the Place of Mortal Subjects', *PIi* 10 (2000): 217–43. He begins his discussion with the questions: 'What is it to inhabit? What is it to inhabit the architectural?'

Chapter 2

1 That the divide between country and city is not a simple nor a new one is a key element of the argument in Raymond Williams, *The Country and the City* (London: Chatto and Windus, 1973).

2 Pau Obrador-Pons, 'Dwelling', 967. Obrador-Pons goes on to list a series of other issues to which the concept supposedly gives rise: 'the "partial eschewing of the visual", the ignorance of bodily movement and the framing of the landscape. While bridging the Cartesian division between the material and the ideal, the dwelling

perspective risks erecting new binarisms between vision and embodied practice, fleeting and enduring life'.
3   Heynen, *Architecture and Modernity*, 222.
4   Adorno, *Minima Moralia*, 38.
5   Heidegger, 'Building Dwelling Thinking', 161.
6   Heidegger, 'Building Dwelling Thinking', 161; Walter Benjamin, *The Arcades Project*, 220, 865. There is also a sense in which Benjamin, too, agrees that 'dwelling' today is impossible – at least if understood in the 'extreme' sense that Benjamin associates with the nineteenth century.
7   Heidegger, 'Memorial Address', 49.
8   Massimo Cacciari, 'Eupalinos or Architecture', *Oppositions* 21 (1980): 106–16; and see Heynen, *Architecture and Modernity*, 19–20.
9   Cacciari, 'Eupalinos or Architecture', 107.
10 There is mention of 'dwelling' in *Being and Time* (see §12 – the passage is quoted in Chapter 10), but it is quite brief, and the same is true of all of the references to the notion prior to 'Building Dwelling Thinking' – including in 'The Thing?', in which the fourfold is discussed, but not in a way that connects it to any detailed analysis of 'dwelling'. There is a further discussion of 'dwelling' in '" … Poetically Man Dwells … "' (first given as a lecture two months after 'Building Dwelling Thinking'), but again there is nothing in that essay that restricts 'dwelling' to the rural or to the past, and the same is true of the other references to 'dwelling' elsewhere. Occasionally, Heidegger does talk about homelesssness as more specifically an affliction of modernity – most directly, as noted above, in the 'Memorial Address'. But the focus of Heidegger's discussion there is specifically on his own relation to his hometown of Messkirch and on the experience of home and homelessness as it seems to be a part of the present. In fact, it is almost certainly the case that homelessness and dwelling, or the lack of it, can refer both to the character of human being irrespective of its historical situation and to a feature of specific situations (including that of modernity). In 'Building Dwelling Thinking', it seems primarily to refer to the former.
11 Heidegger, 'Building Dwelling Thinking', 143 (emphasis added).
12 The bridge goes from one of the old town gates to the road along the river that passes below the Heilegenberg – the wooded hill that stands opposite the town.
13 Heidegger, 'Building Dwelling Thinking', 152.
14 It is important to recognize that, for Heidegger, modern technology is continuous with previous forms of technology, even as it is also a break with it – the break coming about as a result of the radicalization of tendencies present within the technological as such.
15 Something noted in Adam Sharr, *Heidegger's Hut* (Cambridge, MA: MIT Press, 2006), 66.
16 See Martin Heidegger, 'Why Do I Stay in the Provinces', in *Heidegger: The Man and The Thinker*, ed. Thomas Sheehan (Chicago: Precedent, 1981), 27–30 – an essay originally given as a radio talk in Autumn, 1933. Although presented as an almost 'folksy' reflection on the groundedness of his thinking in the landscape of Todtnauberg, the essay is more complicated than it may at first appear, partly because of its public character, and partly because it is also framed by the increasing difficulties surrounding Heidegger's involvement as Rector in Freiburg and his relationship with the National Socialists. See also the discussion in Chapter 10, in which the role of landscape in Heidegger's thinking – and for topology – is further discussed.

17 In 2019, the two huts, Heidegger's and Wittgenstein's, were the focus for an exhibition at the Neubauer Collegium for Culture and Society at the University of Chicago. See the following websites, accessed May 2020, https://news.uchicago.edu/story/big-ideas-tiny-houses and also https://www.anothermag.com/art-photography/10944/an-exhibition-recreating-the-isolated-huts-that-philosophers-worked-in. The exhibition also included a third and 'absent' hut – Adorno's – a hut that Adorno never possessed; the idea being a curatorial conceit.
18 'Our reference to the Black Forest farm in no way means that we should or could go back to building such houses'. See Heidegger, 'Building Dwelling Thinking', 160.
19 See Karsten Harries, 'In Search of Home', *Wolkenkuckucksheim – Cloud-Cuckoo-Land* 2 (1998), accessed May 2020, https://www.cloud-cuckoo.net/openarchive/wolke/eng/Subjects/982/Harries/harries_t.html. See also Brendan O'Donoghue, *A Poetics of Homecoming: Heidegger, Homelessness and the Homecoming Venture* (Newcastle-Upon-Tyne: Cambridge Scholars Publishing, 2011), 28–9. Harries's 'In Search of Home' is one of the very few discussions that address, in any detailed way, the circumstances of Heidegger's original 1951 presentation of 'Building Dwelling Thinking'.
20 See especially Theodor W. Adorno, *The Jargon of Authenticity*, trans. Knut Tarnowski and Frederic Will (Evanston, IL: Northwestern University Press, 1964), esp. 49–59. On the complex relation between Heidegger and Adorno, see Fred Dallmayr, *Between Freiburg and Frankfurt: Toward a Critical Ontology* (Amherst: University of Massachusetts, 1991), 42–71. As Dallmayr points out, for all the polemic on Adorno's part, there are also significant points of affinity between the two thinkers. It is remarkable how much of the recent and contemporary critique of Heidegger, especially in disciplines like architecture, consists in the repetition of criticisms from Adorno, despite the extent to which those criticisms often depend on obvious misreading of the Heidegger's texts. This is made very clear in Hermann Mörchen, *Adorno und Heidegger: Untersuchung einer philosophischen Kommunikationsverweigerung* (Stuttgart: Klett-Cotta, 1981), which is the focus for much of Dallmayr's discussion.
21 Harries, 'In Search of Home'.
22 See Immanuel Kant, *Critique of Pure Reason*, ed. Paul Guyer and Allen W. Wood (1781; Cambridge: Cambridge University Press, 1998).
23 See Dallmayr, *Between Freiburg and Frankfurt*, 47–8.
24 Martin Heidegger, '" … Poetically Man Dwells … "', in *Poetry, Language, Thought*, 228.
25 Heidegger, 'Memorial Address', 45.
26 Heidegger, 'Building Dwelling Thinking', 161.
27 Although, see the comments relating to the 'Memorial Address' in the notes above. Heidegger's critical attitude towards modern technology long predates his discussion in 'Building Dwelling Thinking'. The form in which it appears in his later thinking, however, is more developed and more sophisticated than in the earlier. See Heidegger, 'The Question Concerning Technology', in *The Question Concerning Technology and Other Essays*, trans. William Lovitt (New York: Harper and Row, 1977), 3–35 and 'The Thing', in *Poetry, Language, Thought*, 163–86. It is made very clear in 'The Thing' the extent to which Heidegger's critique of modern technology is bound up with the analysis of its spatial and topological character.
28 Heidegger, 'Building Dwelling Thinking', 157.
29 See Heynen, *Architecture and Modernity*, 23–4.

30 This is an issue that will arise again, in Chapter 3, with respect to the interplay between sameness and difference in Heidegger's thinking – an interplay that he takes to be integral to those very ideas so that there is no sameness without difference nor difference without sameness. And it arises also with respect to the Heidegger's thinking of unity and multiplicity. In a way that draws directly on Aristotle, Heidegger takes unity always to involve multiplicity and complexity, so that the 'pure' unity of that which contains no multiplicity within it – the paradigm being simple numerical unity, the number 'one' – is no genuine unity at all.
31 Heidegger, Heidegger, *Basic Concepts*, trans. Gary E. Aylesworth (Bloomington: Indian University Press, 1993), 75.
32 Heidegger, 'Building Dwelling Thinking', 161.
33 Martin Heidegger, *What Is Called Thinking?*, trans. J. Glenn Gray (New York: Harper and Row, 1968) – the language of 'what is called' comes directly from the German *was heisst* in the original title.
34 Heidegger, 'Building Dwelling Thinking', 161.
35 What marks it out, however, is its refusal to offer any set of ethical principles or precepts, and additionally, its eschewal of the language of 'values' – largely as a result of Heidegger's own critique of the 'value theory' that was so prevalent in German though in the early part of the twentieth century and which he regarded as leading to, and an expression of, a fundamental nihilism.
36 Heidegger, 'Building Dwelling Thinking', 160.
37 Heidegger, " … Poetically Man Dwells … ", 214.
38 Heidegger, " … Poetically Man Dwells … ", 219–20.
39 Heidegger, " … Poetically Man Dwells … ", 227. Hofstadter's translation has 'authentic building' rather than 'genuine building', for *eigentliche Bauen,* as it is in Heidegger's German – the same practice Hofstadter employs in translating *eigentliche Dichten* ('genuine poetry'). Ordinarily, using 'authentic' for *eigentlich* is not unreasonable, but in a Heideggerian context it can be misleading – a point discussed further in Chapter 3.
40 Once again, the English translation uses 'authentic' for *eigentlich* so that *eigentliche Dichten* becomes 'authentic poetry', with the same potential for misreading as noted immediately above.
41 Heidegger, " … Poetically Man Dwells … ", 228–9.
42 Heidegger, 'Building Dwelling Thinking', 149.
43 Heidegger, " … Poetically Man Dwells … ", 229.
44 See Heidegger, *What Is Called Thinking?,* 192ff.

Chapter 3

1 One might also talk of a form of 'emptying' here – or *kenosis* – see Randall Lindstrom, *Kenosis Creativity Architecture: Appearance through Emptying* (London: Routledge, 2021).
2 Sharr, *Heidegger for Architects*, 112. Sharr's comment as to the ease with which Heidegger's thinking can be challenged from 'the perspectives of critical theory' (and despite Sharr's own very broad characterization of what 'critical theory' encompasses) can be seen to highlight a point noted elsewhere; namely, the extent to which the

critique of Heidegger, in architecture especially, is largely a repetition of criticisms enunciated by Theodor Adorno (perhaps the key figure within 'critical theory' as more narrowly understood). Of course, it is easy to repeat such criticisms, but whether they constitute a real challenge, and the exact nature of that challenge, is quite a different matter.

3   See Martin Heidegger, *Nature, History, State: 1933–1934*, trans. and ed. Gregory Fried and Richard Polt (London: Bloomsbury, 2013). As Charles Bambach notes, this material does present some significant interpretive issues (not least because the lectures as they currently exist are derived solely from student notes), and it is not at all clear what significance should be attached to these lectures in relation to Heidegger's work as a whole. See Charles Bambach, review of *Nature, History, State: 1933–1934*, by Martin Heidegger, trans. and ed. Gregory Fried and Richard Polt, *Notre Dame Philosophical Reviews* 9 (June 2014), accessed June 2020, https://ndpr.nd.edu/news/nature-history-state-1933-1934/. Some of what appears in the 1933–4 lectures goes against key notions Heidegger develops even in his early work (including *Being and Time*), but it goes very much against what is developed in the writings after 1947.

4   This has been the focus for the critical reading of Heidegger by commentators such as Peter Trawny and Donatella di Cesare – see Trawny, 'Heidegger and the Shoa', and di Cesare, 'Heidegger's Metaphysical Anti-Semitism', in Farin and Malpas, *Reading Heidegger's Black Notebooks*, 169–94. There are even more extreme readings that treat Heidegger's thinking as irredeemably tied to Nazi ideology, but such extreme readings are hard to sustain (especially in relation to the later thinking), often resting on problematic methods of interpretation and argumentation, and sometimes questionable evidence.

5   There is, however, an indirect connection back to 'Building Dwelling Thinking'. Blundell Jones had a close association with Hans Scharoun, who was present at the Darmstadt meeting, and with whom Heidegger himself engaged directly. See Peter Blundell Jones, 'A Forty Year Encounter with Hans Scharoun' (commentary on PhD diss. by publication, School of Architecture, University of Sheffield, 2013), accessed June 2020, https://core.ac.uk/download/pdf/20344024.pdf; and Peter Blundell Jones, *Hans Scharoun* (London: Phaidon, 1995).

6   Peter Blundell Jones, 'In Search of Authenticity Part One', *Architect's Journal* 194 (30 October 1991): 26. The remaining three parts of the lecture series were published as: 'In Search of Authenticity Part Two', *Architect's Journal* 194 (6 November 1991): 32–6; 'In Search of Authenticity Part Three', *Architect's Journal* 194 (4 December 1991): 22–5; 'In Search of Authenticity Part Four', *Architect's Journal* 195 (8 and 15 January 1992): 29–32. All are available online at https://www.architectsjournal.co.uk/.

7   Blundell Jones, 'In Search of Authenticity Part Four', 32.

8   Blundell Jones, 'In Search of Authenticity Part One', 30.

9   Although the term 'authenticity' is seldom explicitly employed, such conceptions are embedded in heritage documents such as: Australia ICOMOS Incorporated, *The Australia ICOMOS Charter for Places of Cultural Significance, The Burra Charter, 2013* (Burwood, VIC: Australia ICOMOS Incorporated, 2013), originally adopted in 1979. Here, too, the notion of place is directly and explicitly invoked. Thus, *The Burra Charter* declares that 'Cultural significance is embodied in the place itself, its fabric, setting, use, associations, meanings, records, related places and related objects' (p. 1).

10 Tom Spector begins his discussion of authenticity in architecture with just such an idea. See Spector, 'Architecture and the Ethics of Authenticity', *Journal of Aesthetic Education* 45 (2011): 23–33, esp. 23.
11 See, for example, A. M. S. Ouf, 'Authenticity and the Sense of Place in Urban Design', *Journal of Urban Design* 6 (2001): 73–86 and Gunila Jive´n and Peter J. Larkham, 'Sense of Place, Authenticity and Character: A Commentary', *Journal of Urban Design* 8 (2003): 67–81.
12 See, for example, the discussion in M. F. Piazzoni, 'Authenticity Makes the City. How "the Authentic" Affects the Production of Space', in *Planning for Authenticities*, ed. L. Tate and B. Shannon (New York: Routledge, 2018), 154–69, esp. 154–64.
13 Relph argues that the sense of place is tied to a notion of authenticity that he characterizes in terms close to the 'weak' sense distinguished here (Relph refers to Trilling, but does not engage with Trilling's critique of 'strong' authenticity). See Relph, *Place and Placelessness*, 62–78.
14 See Lionel Trilling, *Sincerity and Authenticity* (Cambridge, MA: Harvard University Press, 1971), 131.
15 On the relation between Rand and Wright, see Peter Reidy, 'Frank Lloyd Wright and Ayn Rand', *The Atlas Society* (website), 7 July 2010, accessed June 2020, https://www.atlassociety.org/post/frank-lloyd-wright-and-ayn-rand.
16 Ayn Rand, *The Fountainhead* (1943; New York: Penguin, 1994), 713–14. Joel Sanders takes Roark as the epitome of a certain masculine conception of the architect that also fits with the strong sense of authenticity. See Joel Sanders, Introduction to *Stud: Architectures of Masculinity*, ed Joel Sanders (New York: Princeton Architectural Press, 1996), 11-12.
17 There are readings that do look to find something like this strong notion of authenticity in Heidegger's *Being and Time*, most obviously in connection with the notion of *Entschlossenheit* (often translated as 'anticipatory resoluteness'), and especially as it figures in the discussion of historicity in *Being and Time* §74. Such readings are, however, largely specific to *Being and Time*, and cannot easily be carried over to the later work that is the main focus here, and even within the frame of *Being and Time*, this way of reading *Entschlossenheit* tends to leave out other important elements of the position that Heidegger develops that are inconsistent with that reading.
18 See Randall Lindstrom and Jeff Malpas, 'The Modesty of Architecture', *Political Theory and Architecture*, ed. D. Bell and B. Zacka (London: Bloomsbury, 2020), 225–76.
19 Hans Ulrich Gumbrecht provides an excellent illustration of this in his 'Being Authentic: The Ambition to Recycle', in *Waste-Site Stories: The Recycling of Memory*, ed. Brian Neville and Johanne Villeneuve (Albany, NY: SUNY Press, 2002), 121–30.
20 In defence of Adorno, one might say that the critique that he advances against Heidegger – which focuses primarily on *Being and Time* – is, properly understood, not as a critique of *authenticity*, despite the way that term figures in the English translation of Adorno's title, nor of *eigentlich* in its usual adjectival form. Instead, it is more narrowly directed at the notion that Adorno takes to be embodied in the notion of the *eigentlich*, the proper, as it is 'reified' into *Eigentlichkeit*; namely, a certain sort of state or mode of the proper or the 'own', and so also, a certain mode of subjectivity (which Adorno sees as a continuation of the idea of subjectivity in Husserl), as well as the language ('jargon') associated with it. It is this language of subjectivity that Adorno sees as part of German 'existentialist' thought, as exemplified in Heidegger as well as Karl Jaspers, and as prefigured in Kierkegaard.

21 Heidegger avoids talk of 'reality' and 'the real' partly because of the Latin derivation of these terms (he treats the shift from Greek to Latin in philosophical discourse as associated with philosophical decline), and because he takes the terms to carry a metaphysical sense he eschews.
22 See, for example, Joan Stambaugh, 'Introduction', in Heidegger, *Identity and Difference*, trans. Joan Stambaugh, first published 1969 (Chicago: University of Chicago Press, 2002), 14.
23 Such an idea is consistent with those many accounts of human engagement and activity in which the emphasis is more on a form of 'letting go', or releasement, rather than a 'holding onto' – accounts of religious and spiritual practices (from the liturgical to the meditative), of creative and artistic production, of almost all forms of genuinely skilful making and performance, of genuinely engaged conversation and communal involvement, and even of many accounts of the character of thinking itself.
24 Trilling, in his classic study of sincerity and authenticity, acknowledges that the way authenticity develops as a distinctive notion is through its separation from sincerity, and so also, one might say, from other related notions, but it is in becoming distinctive in this way that authenticity takes on its strong form.
25 See Charles Guignon, *On Being Authentic* (London: Routledge, 2004).
26 An idea suggested by the very title of Natalie M. Fletcher, 'The Challenges of Achieving Authenticity: A Commentary on Gardner and Anderson', *Mind, Culture, and Activity* 22 (2015): 402–7.
27 See, once again, Fred Dallmayr's discussion of this issue in *Between Freiburg and Frankfurt: Toward a Critical Ontology*, 44–71.
28 Sharr, *Heidegger for Architects*, 111.
29 Heynen, *Architecture and Modernity*, 222.
30 See, for example, Heidegger's discussion in 'Nietzsche's Word: "God Is Dead"', in *Off the Beaten Track*, a translation of *Holzwege* by Julian Young and Kenneth Haynes (Cambridge: Cambridge University Press, 2002), 195.
31 See *Being and Time*, H42.
32 'We can only say "the same" if we think difference'. See Heidegger, "' … Poetically Man Dwells … '", 218.
33 See Heidegger, *Identity and Difference*.
34 Ian Hacking, *The Social Construction of What?* (Cambridge, MA: Harvard University Press, 1999), 17.
35 See Dolf Sternberger, response to presentation by José Ortega y Gasset, *Mensch und Raum: Darmstädter Gespräch 1951*, ed. Otto Bartning (Darmstadt: Neue Darmstädter Verlagsanstalt, 1952), 124–9.
36 Sternberger, *Mensch und Raum*, 127.
37 Underlying Sternberger's comments is also a criticism to the effect that Heidegger (and thinkers like him) are neglectful of the concrete realities of human life, ignoring the actual social conditions under which people live. The criticism is a common one – essentially the repetition of one made by Adorno. However, not only does it operate at a very general level, but it is not clear to what extent it really differentiates Heidegger's position from that of someone like Sternberger (or Adorno). The criticism seems actually to amount to the claim simply that Heidegger does not engage in the same kind of social- or political-theoretic enterprise as Sternberger, and, more pointedly, that he adopts a different ideological orientation (one that is not primarily indebted to Marx).
38 Sternberger, *Mensch und Raum*, 127.

39 Interestingly, *Heimat* does not appear in Dolf Sternberger, Gerhard Storz and Wilhelm Emanuel Süskind, *Aus dem Wörterbuch des Unmenschen* [From the Dictionary of the Inhuman] (Hamburg: Claassen, 1945), which lists a set of key terms in the vocabulary of Nazi Germany. Whilst *Heimat* is not listed, *Raum* (Space) is.
40 See Ernst Bloch, *The Principle of Hope*, trans. N. Plaice, S. Plaice and P. Knight, 3 vols. (Cambridge, MA: MIT Press, 1986). Bloch's work is also discussed in Heynen, *Architecture and Modernity*, 118–27.
41 See Wigley, 'Heidegger's House: The Violence of the Domestic', 91–121.
42 Robert Mugerauer provides perhaps the most detailed and careful study of the ideas of home and homecoming in Heidegger's later thinking in his *Heidegger and Homecoming: The Leitmotif in the Later Writings* (Toronto: University of Toronto Press, 2008).
43 First proposed as such by Andy Clark and David J. Chalmers, 'The Extended Mind', *Analysis*. 58 (1998): 7–19.
44 Heidegger, *Being and Time* (Macquarie and Robinson), H109.
45 See Heidegger, 'Seminar in Le Thor 1969', in *Four Seminars*, trans. Andrew Mitchell and François Raffoul (Bloomington: Indiana University Press, 2004), 32; also Heidegger, *Zollikon Seminars*, trans. Franz Mayr and Richard Askay (Evanston, IL: Northwestern University Press, 2001), 86–97.
46 The room is usually taken as the setting for the famous *Meditations* of 1641 – see René Descartes, *Meditations on First Philosophy*, in *The Philosophical Writings of Descartes*, trans. John Cottingham, Robert Stoothoff and Dugald Murdoch (Cambridge: Cambridge University Press, 1984), 2:1–62 – but it is specifically referred to in Descartes, *Discourse on the Method* (1637), in *The Philosophical Writings of Descartes*, 1:116.
47 Indeed, in an essay from 1957, Heidegger is critical of the way the contemporary house has become 'almost a mere container for dwelling'. See 'Hebel – Friend of the House', in *Contemporary German Philosophy*, ed. D. E. Christensen, trans. Bruce Foltz and Michael Heim (University Park: Pennsylvania State University Press, 1983), 3:93.
48 Emmanuel Levinas, 'Heidegger, Gagarin, and Us', in *Difficult Freedom: Essays on Judaism*, trans. Sean Hand (Baltimore: The Johns Hopkins University Press, 1990), 232. Published in 1961, ten years after the Darmstadt meeting, Levinas's essay is clearly directed at exactly the topological thinking that is so prominent in Heidegger's later essays – especially those from the early 1950s, like 'Building Dwelling Thinking'. For a discussion of Heidegger and Levinas on many of the issues at stake here, see David J. Gauthier, *Martin Heidegger, Emmanuel Levinas, and the Politics of Dwelling* (Lanham, MD: Lexington Books, 2011). Gauthier's approach is strongly oriented towards the Levinasian position, reiterating many of the standard criticisms of Heidegger, but although it is a partial account (and gives no real recognition to the questions of the spatial and the topological raised here), it is a useful point of entry into the debate.
49 On 12 April 1961, Gagarin completed a single orbit around the earth aboard the Russian spacecraft Vostok 1.
50 Levinas, 'Heidegger, Gagarin, and Us', 233. There is something peculiar about Levinas's argument here – Heidegger's claim is clearly not such that it involves some human tie to the surface of some particular planetary body, and so the example of Gagarin seems simply irrelevant to the issues at stake. Gagarin is not removed from place, neither in any ordinary sense nor in any sense intended by Heidegger, merely through being lodged within a capsule and shot 300 kilometres into the ionosphere.

However, the reference to Gagarin is indicative both of Levinas's prioritization of spatial extensionality in which there are indeed no places but only locations – often taken to be exemplified in interplanetary space – and of his rejection of Heidegger's critical attitude towards contemporary technology, of which space flight is an especially symbolic.

51 Emmanuel Levinas, *Totality and Infinity: An Essay on Exteriority*, trans. Alphonso Lingis (Pittsburgh: Duquesne University Press, 1969). Levinas devotes an entire chapter of the book to the topic of 'the dwelling' (*la demeure,* in the original French) and, so, to issues of 'home' and 'habitation' (*l'habitation*); see *Totality and Infinity*, 152–74. *Totality and Infinity* is important, as its subtitle suggests, for its analysis of the role of space and exteriority in the constitution of human being and especially of human being in its ethical relation. The problem is thus not that Levinas is blind to the importance of issues of space and place, but that he lacks any real attentiveness to the complexities of the spatial and the topological issues at stake here, insisting on the primacy of displacement and of the unbounded, on a certain autonomous mode of subjectivity and so of the purely spatial. In this, however, his approach is very much in keeping with a certain tendency at the heart of much modern thinking. Modernity, one might say, is defined by the refusal of bounds, even its own.

52 Levinas, *Totality and Infinity*, 172. In this, of course, Levinas is also repudiating Simone Weil and her position as set out in *The Need for Roots: Prelude to a Declaration of Duties toward Mankind,* trans. Arthur Wills (New York: Routledge, 2002).

53 Sternberger, *Mensch und Raum,* 124.

54 See Aristotle, *Physics,* trans. R. P. Hardie and R. K. Gaye, in *The Complete Works of Aristotle: The Revised Oxford Translation*, ed. Jonathan Barnes, Vol. 1, Bollingen Series 71: 2 (Princeton, NJ: Princeton University Press, 1984), bk 4, 212a5 and also 212a20.

55 As indicated above, there is no sense in which Gagarin's flight genuinely involves any 'escape' from place, and neither does it involve any escape from horizonality. The idea of the horizon is often illustrated by reference to the visual horizon – the far distant line that seems to represent the edge of vision for one who is located on a terrestrial surface. But horizonality is not a structure restricted to the visual. The horizon, at its most general, is simply that bound which makes for the possibility of appearance. Horizonality thus operates in space no less than on the earth, and in respect of sound and touch, for example, no less than sight. It is perhaps surprising that Levinas, trained in phenomenology, should treat the idea of the horizon as if it were indeed a phenomenon of vision alone. The phenomenological concept of horizon, largely developed by Husserl (though adumbrated in William James), is part of the structure of meaning presentation – it is exemplified in visual perception but not restricted to it. In a topological context, horizon can be seen as a problematic notion because it is easily assimilable either to a subjective structure or else to part of a transcendental frame of the sort associated with the constitution of 'objects – as noted in Chapter 10, Heidegger is critical of the notion on these grounds in his Country Path 'Conversation' – see Heidegger, 'Αγχιβασιν: A Triadic Conversation on a Country Path between a Scientist, a Scholar, and a Guide', in *Country Path Conversations,* in *Country Path Conversations*, trans. Bret W. Davis (Bloomington: Indiana University Press, 2010), 55–72, esp. 72. For the most part, as it is used here however, 'horizon' is taken to refer simply to the bound that belongs to place – a sense that Heidegger also employs in 'Building Dwelling Thinking'.

56 It is essentially the rejection of ontological horizonality (a rejection that has very different grounds from Heidegger's own critique of horizonality in 'A Triadic

Conversation') that is at the heart of the argument in Emmanuel Levinas, 'Is Ontology Fundamental?', in *Entre Nous: Thinking-of-the-other*, trans. Michael Smith and Barbara Harshav (London: Continuum, 2002), 1–10.
57 Levinas, 'Heidegger, Gagarin, and Us', 233. Although she makes no reference to the issue of spatialization and is more focused on the critique of Heidegger, Chantal Bax also notes the potentially problematic character of Levinas's displaced and unsituated account of the ethical encounter. See Bax, 'Otherwise than Being-with: Levinas on Heidegger and Community, *Human Studies* 40 (2017): 381–400.
58 Although oriented to a rather different end and from within a different frame, Leora Batnitzky provides an intriguing discussion of Levinas's reliance on a Cartesian notion of subjectivity in Batnitzky, 'Encountering the Modern Subject in Levinas', *Yale French Studies* 104 (2004): 6–21.

Chapter 4

1 Petzet, *Encounters and Dialogues with Martin Heidegger, 1929–1976*, 188. It seems most likely that the volume referred to is the 1951 publication of the Darmstadt proceedings – Otto Bartning, ed., *Mensch und Raum*.
2 There was certainly no direct connection between the two men, and the Aalto Archives, at least as they were accessible in 2015, contain no record of any correspondence between them.
3 As in, for example, Colin St John Wilson, *The Other Tradition of Modern Architecture: The Uncompleted Project* (London: Academy Editions, 1995).
4 Heidegger, 'Building Dwelling Thinking', 159.
5 Heidegger sometimes hyphenates *Entwurf* – as *Ent-wurf* or 'pro-jection' – in order to emphasize the idea of the 'forward throw' (*wurfen* being what one does when, e.g., one throws dice) that is at issue here. Often *Entwurf* means something like a 'sketch' or 'preliminary draft', and sometimes, therefore, 'design', and it appears in what is self-evidently this sense in other contributions included in *Mensch und Raum*. What Heidegger does in *Being and Time*, however, is pick up on the idea of *Entwurf* as a throwing forward – something closely captured in the English 'project' and 'projection'. Given that prior usage, it would be a little odd for Heidegger to use *Entwürfen* here to mean *just* 'plan' or 'design' – if anything, it seems more likely that he is interpreting the plan or design as a mode of projection or as related to a mode of projection– and it is thus that the passage resists translation in any straightforward fashion.
6 Residential design was an important part of Aalto's architectural practice. As Markku Lahti notes, Aalto designed around one hundred single family houses during his career, including houses for family and friends, houses that formed part of larger institutional or corporate complexes, and more standardized homes that were wholly or partly mass-produced (of which around one thousand were built). See Markku Lahti, 'Alvar Aalto and the Beauty of the House', in *Alvar Aalto: Towards a Human Modernism*, ed. Winfried Nerdinger (Munich: Prestel, 1999), 49.
7 Le Corbusier, *Towards a New Architecture*, 95. For Heidegger, and perhaps for Aalto, the language of the 'machine' is, however, especially problematic. For a comparative study of Aalto and Le Corbusier, see Sarah Menin and Flora Samuel, *Nature and Space: Aalto and Le Corbusier* (London: Routledge, 2003).

8   Alvar Aalto, 'Instead of an Article', in *Sketches*, ed. Göran Schildt, trans. Stuart Wrede (Cambridge, MA: MIT Press, 1979), 161.
9   Aalto, 'The Architect's Conception of Paradise', in *Sketches*, 158.
10 See Martin Heidegger, 'Letter on "Humanism"', in *Pathmarks*, ed. William McNeill (Cambridge: Cambridge University Press, 1998), 244–6.
11 Aalto was younger than all three, born in 1898 – Le Corbusier in 1887, van der Rohe in 1886 and Gropius in 1883.
12 Aalto, 'The Humanizing of Architecture', in *Sketches,* 76. Here Aalto broadens the concept of functionalism, just as he also broadens (or 'deepens') the concept of rationalism.
13 Aalto, 'Rationalism and Man', in *Sketches*, 51.
14 It is important to stress that the emphasis on the spatial here should not be assumed to exclude the temporal either – there is no space that is not dynamic, while the functional conception is also one that is inherently temporalized.
15 Aalto, 'Art and Technology', in *Sketches*, 127.
16 Heidegger, 'Building Dwelling Thinking', 160.
17 See Aalto, 'The Dwelling as a Problem', in *Sketches*, 33. In Heidegger's case, the fact that he did not address such issues does not, of course, demonstrate that he lacked awareness of them – and in this regard it is worth recalling that his wife, Elfride, was herself an independent and strong-minded woman: she was one of the first women to study economics at a German university, and also one of the first women to gain a driver's license in Freiburg (something her husband never did); it was also Elfride who organized the building of the hut at Todtnauberg. Heidegger was not a feminist, but that he lacked awareness of any feminist issues in the context of his time seems highly improbable.
18 Heidegger, 'Building Dwelling Thinking', 160.
19 Aalto, 'The Humanizing of Architecture', in *Sketches*, 77.
20 Aalto, 'Experimental House, Muuratsalo', in *Sketches*, 115.
21 Aalto, 'Experimental House, Muuratsalo', in *Sketches*, 115.
22 See, for example, Göran Schildt, *Alavar Aalto: The Early Years* (New York: Rizzoli, 1984), 242–59. This is as evident in Aalto's approach to urban planning as in the design of single buildings. See, for example, Aalto, 'National Planning and Cultural Goals', in *Sketches*, 99–110 and Aalto, 'Town Planning and Public Buildings', in *Sketches*, 165–7.
23 Schildt draws attention to the connection to Kropotkin, but argues that it was based only in an interest and acquaintance with Kropotkin's autobiographical *Memoirs of a Revolutionary* (New York: Houghton Mifflin Company, 1899), and so related to Kropotkin's 'personality, philosophy of life and attitudes to certain basic moral values, not his intellectual theories'. See Schildt, *Alvar Aalto: The Early Years*, 242. Clearly, however, Kropotkin's own organicist and mutualist commitments, which are foundational to his thinking, have strong resonances with important aspects of Aalto's thought and practice.
24 See especially Schildt, *Alvar Aalto: The Early Years*, 149–59.
25 See Juahni Pallasmaa's discussion in 'From Tectonics to Painterly Architecture', in *Encounters 1: Architectural Essays* (Helsinki: Rakenustieto Oy, 2013), 212–21.
26 Hartmut Buchner, 'Fragmetarisches', in *Errinerung an Martin Heidegger*, 47; see also Julian Young, *Heidegger's Philosophy of Art*, 151; and Christoph Jamme, 'The Loss of Things: Cézanne – Rilke – Heidegger', *Kunst & Museumjournaal* 2 (1990): 39–40.
27 Schildt, *Alvar Aalto: The Early Years*, 220.

28 See Schildt, *Alvar Aalto: The Early Years*, 223.
29 'Building Dwelling Thinking', 152 (Hofstadter has 'locations' instead of 'places').
30 Here, it is important to give added emphasis to the point, also noted in the text above, that the artistic image does not function here merely as a visual 'representation', offering just a 'view' of the thing or scene. Instead, and in keeping with the broader focus on the engagement with the thing in its concrete situatedness, the image works so as to allow things to come forth in a manner revelatory of the place and space to which the thing belongs as well as of the working of the thing in that place – thereby revealing more than is given in any mere 'view'.
31 Schildt, *Alvar Aalto: The Early Years*, 221.
32 It is this that can be seen partly to underlie Heidegger's account of the nature of Cézanne's achievement in terms of its realization of the twofold unity of 'what is present' (*Anwesendem*) and 'presence' (*Anwesenheit*). See Martin Heidegger, 'Cézanne', in *Aus der Erfahrung des Denkens, 1910–1976, Gesamtausgabe*, Vol. 13, ed. Hermann Heidegger (Frankfurt am Main: Klostermann, 1983), 223; see also Julian Young's discussion of this in *Heidegger's Philosophy of Art* (Cambridge: Cambridge University Press, 2001), 152–3.
33 Heidegger, 'The Thing', in *Poetry Language Thought*, 163–86.
34 See Aalto's own account of the Villa Mairea, as set out in his plan description for the building: 'The Villa Mairea', in *Alvar Aalto in His Own Words*, ed. Göran Schildt, trans. Timothy Binham (New York: Rizzoli, 1998), 225–30. Aalto emphasizes that, although built as a unique dwelling for a wealthy client, the building is nevertheless an opportunity 'to tackle some of the central problems in architecture today'. See Aalto, 'The Villa Mairea', 226.
35 See Schildt, *Alvar Aalto: The Early Years*, 155.
36 See, for example, Aalto, 'Art and Technology', in *Sketches*, 128. Here, Aalto argues that technology itself, 'even the more vulgar, … must in each detail practice the same synthesis: think of man above all'. His comments on planning, in note 41 below, are also of relevance here.
37 Alvar Aalto, 'From Doorstep to Living Room', in *Alvar Aalto in His Own Words*, 55. Thanks to Esa Laaksonen for drawing attention to this passage.
38 The quotation comes from Aalto, 'Culture and Technology', in *Sketches*, 95. Measure is also, of course, an important focus of attention in Heidegger's "' … Poetically Man Dwells … "'.
39 See Karsten Harries, *The Ethical Function of Architecture* (Cambridge, MA: MIT Press, 1998).
40 See Heidegger, 'Letter on "Humanism"', in *Pathmarks*, 269–71.
41 Aalto, 'Between Humanism and Materialism', in *Sketches*, 131. Elsewhere he talks of planning being 'regarded as an ethical means of development that puts a stop to centralization, leading where blind development cannot, and functioning as a guardian of ethics and human freedom'. See Aalto, 'National Planning and Cultural Goals', in *Sketches*, p.101.
42 See, for example, Aalto, 'Art and Technology', in *Sketches*, esp. 127–8.
43 In Heidegger's case, it is crucial to realize (although, again, this is all too often overlooked) that his own critique of technology is not a critique of technology as usually understood, but is indeed directed at a particular mode of ordering of the world (see Malpas, *Heidegger's Topology*, 278–303)– one as much evident in contemporary economic and organizational systems as in particular instances of contemporary technology – and, perhaps, Aalto should be read in similar fashion.

Certainly, one finds an equally trenchant critique of technology, developed over several decades, in the work of Aalto's close friend, the philosopher G. H. von Wright. Von Wright attacks what he refers to as 'the managerial type of rationality of which modern natural science is in origin the outflow', as well as the refusal of limit that appears as a characteristic element in modern technology. See von Wright, 'Dante between Ulysses and Faust', in *Knowledge and the Sciences in Medieval Philosophy*, Vol. 48, *Acta Philosophica Fennica*, ed. Monika Asztalos, John E. Murdoch and Ilkka Niiniluoto (Helsinki: Philosophical Society of Finland, 1990), 1–9.
44   A 'wicked' problem is one that resists solution because of an intrinsic incompleteness or indeterminacy in relation to its characterization.

Chapter 5

1   The question arises explicitly, although (as it often does) in terms of the very possibility of such truth, in the exchange between Jean Baudrillard and Jean Nouvel. Baudrillard comments: 'Can we speak of truth in architecture? No, at least not in the sense that architecture would have truth as its goal or culmination'. See Baudrillard and Nouvel, *The Singular Objects of Architecture*, 37. In addition, see, for example, Karsten Harries, 'On Truth and Lie in Architecture', *Via* 7 (1984): 47–57; Adam Sharr, 'Can Architecture Lie? On Truth, Knowledge and Contemporary Architectural Theory', *Architectural Theory Review* 8 (2003): 164–72; and in the series of discussions by Blundell Jones, 'In Search of Authenticity' Parts One-Four.
2   Pragmatic approaches take truth to be a matter of what 'works' or is useful (whether in the promotion of successful action or in the facilitation of discourse) and 'disquotational' (sometimes also 'deflationary' or 'redundancy') approaches point to the fact that to say that a sentence is true is the same as asserting the sentence ('S is true' is the same as 'S'). Beyond the approaches just listed, there are also, of course, questions as to how truth relates to other notions, and whether truth should be understood to be absolute or relative. None of these questions are directly relevant, however, to what is at issue here.
3   Aristotle, *Metaphysics*, bk. 4, 1011b25-26.
4   Some of these question are famously taken up in Robert Venturi, Denise Scott Brown, and Steven Izenour, *Learning from Las Vegas* (Cambridge MA: MIT Press, 1972).
5   Although there are ways of thinking – especially in pre-modern contexts – that would insist on discourse as infusing the entire world, so that nothing stands apart from discourse (*everything* 'speaks'), such ways of thinking shift the terms of the discussion so much that the question of truth in architecture becomes very different from the sort of discussion pursued here, or that is at issue in most contemporary architectural contexts.
6   It might be objected that the discussion here does not give enough account to the idea of the semiotic as an alternative way of theorizing meaning or content. In fact, attending more closely to the semiotic, although it would complicate the analysis, would not make a great deal of difference to the argument. The primary issue is the way buildings or designs can function in relation to assertoric or declarative content, rather than merely as generating 'meanings'. However, it should also be noted that the broad notion of 'meaning' that often operates in semiotics is so broad as to give rise to problems in itself – it becomes a primitive and ubiquitous notion that, as such, resists any genuine elucidation.

7   On the holistic understanding of meaning at issue here, see Malpas, 'The Weave of Meaning: Holism and Contextuality', *Language and Communication* 22 (2002): 403–19.
8   See Peta Carlin, *On Surface and Place: Between Architecture, Textiles and Photography* (London: Routledge, 2016). The way textile and fabric are related to surface makes for an intriguing relation to place, given that surface is itself connected to place, especially via the Greek *topos*. But there is also a further connection back to meaning, through the connection between text, context and textile. See Malpas, 'The Weave of Meaning: Holism and Contextuality'.
9   Often taken to be expressed in Jacques Derrida's claim that 'there is nothing outside the text' in Derrida, *Of grammatology*, trans. G. C. Spivak (Baltimore: Johns Hopkins University Press, 1976), 158. In fact, rather than implying any form of textual idealism, the claim relates to what can be understood as the autonomy of textuality (thus there is no 'outside' to the text).
10 For more on this notion of 'transparency', see Deborah Ascher Barnstone, *The Transparent State: Architecture and Politics in Postwar Germany* (London: Routledge, 2005).
11 Walter Benjamin, *One-way Street, and Other Writings*, trans. Edmund Jephcott and Kingsley Shorter (London: New Left Books, 1979), 45–103. Other narratives refer to the Star of David, Shönberg's unfinished opera, *Moses und Aaron*, and the *Gedenkbuch* (the Memorial Book for the German Victims of the Holocaust).
12 Although this also leads on, especially given the supposedly *Australian* focus, to the question as to exactly how the references to Libeskind's Jewish Museum in Berlin – or to Le Corbusier's Villa Savoye, which is also there along with still others – function as part of the system of 'ropes' supposedly at work here.
13 See Rob Foot, 'Rehabilitating Australia's National Museum', *Quadrant Online*, 7 October 2008, https://quadrant.org.au/magazine/2008/10/rehabilitating-australia-s-national-museum/.
14 In Miles Glendinning, *Architecture's Evil Empire? The Triumph and Tragedy of Global Modernism* (London: Reaktion, 2010), esp. chap. 5, 'Metaphor versus Meaning in Contemporary Architecture', 98–113. Here, Glendinning explores some of these issues as part of a broader critique of contemporary globalized architecture (Libeskind and Eisenman, as well as Hadid, being particular targets).
15 An underlying problem, however, is that it is impossible to tie a built form to a specific conceptual – or assertoric – content. An idea may give rise to a building, but the building will always be amenable to multiple readings of the idea or ideas (the conceptual or assertoric content) that it supposedly carries. In some circumstances, there may be a widespread tendency to assume certain reading more than others, but the possibility of other readings can never be ruled out.
16 See also Eisenman's account in 'Interview: Peter Eisenman', interview by Iman Ansari, *Architectural Review* 26 (April 2013), accessed January 2020, https://www.architectural-review.com/view/interviews/interview-peter-eisenman/8646893.article?utm_medium=website&utm_source=archdaily.com. Much of this idea, if more developed, also appears (it is suggested in the very title) in Eisenman's *Diagram Diaries* (London: Thames and Hudson, 1999).
17 This is not an arbitrary assumption, since there is good reason to think, as Martin Jay notes – in *Downcast Eyes: The Denigration of Vision in Twentieth-Century French Thought* (Berkeley: University of California Press, 1993), 8–9 – that visuality and linguistically (and hence conceptuality also) are connected, as are visuality and

spatiality. On the latter see, for example, Achille Pasqualotto and Michael J Proulx, 'The Role of Visual Experience for the Neural Basis of Spatial Cognition', *Neuroscience & Biobehavioral Reviews* 36 (2012): 1179–87. There is also an important connection between spatiality and number – see Stanislas Dehaene and Elizabeth M. Brannon, eds., *Space, Time, and Number in the Brain. Searching for the Foundations of Mathematical Thought* (Amsterdam: Elsevier, 2011).

18 See, for example, Claire Zimmerman, *Photographic Architecture in the Twentieth Century* (Minneapolis: University of Minnesota Press, 2014). Zimmerman writes: 'Evidence, visible appearance, and truth constructions in photography and architecture became more causal and direct as the twentieth century advanced, shaping both media as mass publics formed around them' (p. 6). See also David Campany, 'Architecture as Photography: Document, Publicity, Commentary, Art', in *Constructing Worlds: Photography and Architecture in the Modern Age*, ed. Alona Pardo and Elias Redstone (Munich: Prestel, 2014), 27–39. In 'The Aesthetics of Space: Modern Architecture and Photography', *The Journal of Aesthetics and Art Criticism* 69 (2011): 105–14, Filip Mattens argues for photography (and so also a certain abstracted mode of visuality) as playing an important role in allowing the architectural engagement with space.

19 Most notably, perhaps, Juhani Pallasmaa has drawn attention to the issue in his *The Eyes of the Skin*, a book that focuses on the sensory aspects of architecture, giving particular attention to touch and hapticity. Pallasmaa describes the book as having arisen as a result of his becoming 'increasingly concerned about the bias towards vision, and the suppression of other senses, in the way architecture was conceived, taught, and critiqued, and about the consequent disappearance of sensory and sensual qualities from the arts and architecture'. See Pallasmaa, *The Eyes of the Skin: Architecture and the Senses* (Chichester, UK: Wiley, 1996), 10. There is a much larger set of issues here concerning the supposed 'ocularcentrism', not only of architecture, but of European thought and culture more generally. Those issues cannot adequately be addressed in this discussion, but in *Downcast Eyes*, Martin Jay provides both a useful survey of the critique of vision in contemporary theory and a corrective to that critique.

20 Pérez-Gómez notes how the 'sprit of place' that is so central in Norberg-Schulz's work is nevertheless 'transmitted to the reader through black and white (and only later colour) photography, carefully framed and edited'. Alberto Pérez-Gómez, 'The Place Is Not a Postcard: The Problem with *Genius Loci*', in *An Eye for Place: Christian Norberg-Schulz: Architect, Historian and Editor*, ed. Gro Lauvlandet, Karl Otto Ellefsen and Mari Hvattum (Oslo: Akademisk Publisering, 2009), 27. See also Wilken, 'The Critical Reception of Christian Norberg-Schulz's Writings on Heidegger and Place', 340–55.

21 Can it therefore be said that what Eisenman assumes is the primacy of truth as correctness of representation? Eisenman may not have a considered view on this matter, although his Derridean affinities suggest that he would refuse to affirm any substantive theory of truth and may even deny that truth is a significant concept. But that certainly does not mean that there is no notion of truth implied by Eisenman's approach, and his emphasis on conceptuality seems to entail that, inasmuch as there is a concept of truth at work, it must be such as to allow discrimination between modes of conceptual or discursive *adequacy* (where 'adequacy' may be seen as essentially a surrogate for 'correctness').

22 Blundell Jones, 'In Search for Authenticity Part One' and 'In Search for Authenticity Part Four'.

23 See Adrian Forty, *Words and Buildings: A Vocabulary of Modern Architecture* (London: Thames and Hudson, 2000), 289. Forty's three senses may be compared with Blundell Jones's four senses of authenticity as 'truth to the material object … truth to form or arrangement … truth to place or context … truth to use and the meaning of use'. See 'In Search of Authenticity Part One', 30.
24 See John Ruskin, 'The Lamp of Truth', in *The Seven Lamps of Architecture* (London: Smith, Elder & Co., 1849).
25 Louis H. Sullivan, 'The Tall Office Building Artistically Considered', *Lippincott's Magazine* (March 1896): 408. Sullivan's statement of the principle is grounded in the observation of nature, and this is also true of Greenough's formulation of the idea: 'If there be any principle of structure more plainly inculcated in the works of the Creator than all others, it is the principle of unflinching adaptation of forms to functions.' See Horatio Greenough, *Form and Function: Remarks on Art, Design, and Architecture* (Berkeley: University of California Press, 1947), 118. The latter volume is essentially an edited reprinting of Henry T. Tuckerman, ed., *The Memorial of Horatio Greenough* (New York: G. P. Putnam, 1853). For more on Greenough, see Edward Robert DeZurko, 'Greenough's Theory of Beauty in Architecture', in *The Rice Institute Pamphlet: Vol. XXXIX, No. 3, Public Addresses* (Houston: Rice Institute, 1952), 96–121. Neither Greenough nor Sullivan took the emphasis on functionality to mean the complete eschewal of ornamentation.
26 Sullivan's critique of ornamentation was directed at *applied* ornamentation or decoration – ornamentation that was essentially extraneous to the structure – and so was not at all averse to ornamentation that was integral to parts of the design nor to the idea of the ornamental or decorative as such. In contrast, Loos, and many of those who followed him, advocated the abandonment of any and all forms of ornamentation, even of the idea that the unadorned building, in its form and overall configuration, might itself have a certain decorative character (something that was certainly not seen as problematic by modernism more generally – as Aalto, for one, demonstrates).
27 Loos may well have been influenced by American ideas, although Christopher Long suggests that Loos was already working on the ideas expressed in his 1910 lecture, 'Ornament and Crime', for a decade prior to his return from the United States in 1896, and the lecture itself made little or no reference to architecture, but instead responds to an already existing discussion, in German intellectual circles, regarding the role of ornament in art and culture. See Long, 'The Origins and Context of Adolf Loos's "Ornament and Crime"', *Journal of the Society of Architectural Historians* 68 (2009): 200–23 and Long, 'Ornament, Crime, Myth, and Meaning', in *Architecture: Material and Imagined, Proceedings of the 85th ACSA Annual Meeting and Technology Conference* (Washington, DC: Association of Collegiate Schools of Architecture, 1997), 440–5. Not appearing in print until 1929, an English translation of 'Ornament and Crime' is included in Adolf Loos, *Ornament and Crime: Thoughts on Design and Materials*, trans. Shaun Whiteside (Harmondsworth: Penguin, 2019), 187–202.
28 In the first of his *Meditations*, Descartes famously proposes the hypothesis that the world as he knows it is entirely an illusion created by a demon whose aim is solely to deceive – see René Descartes, *Meditations on First Philosophy*, in *The Philosophical Writings of Descartes*, trans. John Cottingham, Robert Stoothoff and Dugald Murdoch (Cambridge: Cambridge University Press, 1984), 2:15. The idea is reworked by the Wachowskis (Lana Wachowski and Lilly Wachowski, then known as the Wachowski Brothers) in the hugely successful 1999 film, *The Matrix*, distributed by Warner Bros.

29 The term used in *Being and Time* is *Unverborgenheit* – see Heidegger, *Being and Time*, H33. Heidegger also talks of disclosedness, *Erschlossenheit* – see *Being and Time*, §44, H212–H230.
30 Unconcealment is a modification of concealment, the point being captured by what Heidegger takes to be the privative character of *aletheia* (the 'a' in *a-letheia* indicating an *un-*concealing). This means that truth is not a matter of simple transparency or complete illumination but is always a *localized* revealing (which means that it occurs against a background of concealment).
31 See Heidegger, *Being and Time*, H133.
32 As it is used to refer to an open bounded space within a town or village, 'place' is common across many European languages. But English, as noted previously, is unusual in also combining many different topological and spatial senses into 'place'. By contrast, Italian has *piazza*, as well as several different terms that capture various senses of 'place' as site, location, position and so forth – primarily, *posto, luogo, posizione* – whilst 'space' is *spazio*.
33 Heidegger, 'The Origin of the Work of Art', 40–2.
34 Vincent Scully, *The Earth, the Temple, and the Gods* (New Haven: Yale University Press, 1962), 2–3.
35 See also Heidegger's analysis in 'The Thing', *Poetry, Language, Thought*, 167–86.
36 On the relation between this twofold and the later fourfold, see Malpas, *Heidegger's Topology*, 225–30.
37 Walter Benjamin, 'The Work of Art in the Age of Mechanical Reproduction', in *Illuminations: Essays and Reflections*, ed. Hannah Arendt, trans. Harry Zohn (New York: Schocken Books, 1986), 240.
38 Mark Meagher and Peter Blundell Jones claim that 'the experience of movement through space … has been neglected or sidelined in much architecture and planning over the past century'. See Meagher and Blundell Jones, *Architecture and Movement: The Dynamic Experience of Buildings and Landscapes* (London: Routledge, 2014), 36. In this volume, they offer an exploration of various aspects of movement as they relate to architecture.
39 The ritual character of the cathedral is not peculiar to it alone. See Peter Blundell Jones's investigation of the many ways in which buildings relate to the activities of human life in *Architecture and Ritual: How Buildings Shape Society* (London: Bloomsbury, 2016).
40 Such 'humanism' is present even in Le Corbusier through his own concern, as noted in Chapter 4, with the way architecture relates to human life. On this, see also Le Corbusier's comments on the possibility that one can 'create drama out of inert stone', in *Programs and Manifestoes on 20th-Century Architecture*, ed. Ulrich Conrads (Cambridge, MA: MIT Press, 1970), 61.
41 In one of his very late essays, and in response to criticism of his treatment of unconcealment as a mode of truth, Heidegger retreats from that claim, but without abandoning the insistence on the primacy of unconcealment. See Heidegger, 'The End of Philosophy and the Task of Thinking', first published in 1964 (in a French translation), in *On Time and Being*, trans. Joan Stambaugh (New York: Harper & Row, 1971), 69–70.

Chapter 6

1 Although, see Véronique M. Fóti, 'Heidegger: Remembrance and Metaphysics', *Journal of the British Society for Phenomenology* 15 (1984): 243–8.

2   Heidegger, *Basic Concepts*, 78.
3   The Apache elder, Dudley, tells Basso: 'Wisdom sits in places. It's like water that never dries up. You need to drink water to stay alive, don't you? Well, you also need to drink from places. You must remember everything about them. You must learn their names. You must remember what happened at them long ago. You must think about it and keep on thinking about it. Then your mind will become smoother and smoother. Then you will see danger before it happens. You will walk a long way and live a long time. You will be wise. People will respect you.' See Keith H. Basso, *Wisdom Sits in Places: Landscape and Language among the Western Apache* (Albuquerque: University of New Mexico Press, 1996), 127.
4   See Frances A. Yates, *The Art of Memory* (Chicago: University of Chicago Press, 1966). The earliest known reference to the 'method of places' is in the *Rhetorica ad Herennium* (once incorrectly attributed to Cicero). See *Rhetorica ad Herennium*, trans. Harry Caplan, Loeb Classical Library (Cambridge, MA: Harvard University Press, 1954).
5   Gaston Bachelard, *The Poetics of Space*, trans. Maria Jolas (Boston: Beacon Press, 1969).
6   Marcel Proust, *In Search of Lost Time*, trans. C. K. Scott Moncrieff and Terence Kilmartin, rev. D. J. Enright (London: Chatto and Windus, 1992).
7   See W. G. Sebald, *Austerlitz*, trans. Anthea Bell (London: Hamish Hamilton, 2001); and also Sebald, *The Rings of Saturn*, trans. Michael Hulse (London: New Directions Books, 1998).
8   See, for example, Dan Hicks and Mary C. Beaudry, eds., *The Oxford Handbook of Material Culture Studies* (New York: Oxford University Press, 2010).
9   Edward S. Casey, *Remembering: A Phenomenological Study*, 2nd ed. (Bloomington: Indiana University Press, 2000), 182.
10 See Malpas, *Place and Experience*, esp. chap. 7, 161–78.
11 Casey, *Remembering: A Phenomenological Study*, 214–15.
12 Casey, *Remembering: A Phenomenological Study*, 215.
13 See Jean Améry, 'How Much Home Does a Person Need?', in *At the Mind's Limits: Contemplations by a Survivor on Auschwitz and Its Realities*, trans. Sidney Rosenfeld and Stella P. Rosenfeld (Bloomington: Indiana University Press, 1998), 41–61. See also Martin Schuster, 'A Phenomenology of Home: Jean Améry on Homesickness', *Journal of French and Francophone Philosophy – Revue de la philosophie française et de langue française* 24 (2016): 117–27.
14 Vidler, *The Architectural Uncanny*, esp. 'Unhomely Houses', 16–44. Vidler bases his analysis (as do so many commentators) on Freud's 1919 discussion in 'The Uncanny', in *The Standard Edition of the Complete Psychological Works of Sigmund Freud*, 17:217–56. However, the uncanny has a deeper connection, largely ignored by Freud (and arguably not restricted to modernity), with the spatial and topological – something evident in the original paper to which Freud's discussion was a response; namely, Ernst Jentsch, 'On the Psychology of the Uncanny (1906)', trans. Roy Sellars, *Angelaki* 2, no.1 (1997): 7–16.
15 Jorge Luis Borges, 'Funes, His Memory', in *Collected Fictions*, trans. Andrew Hurley (Harmonsworth: Penguin, 1996), 131–7.
16 A. R. Luria, *The Mind of a Mnemonist*, trans. L. Solotaroff (Cambridge, MA: Harvard University Press, 1987).
17 See Peter Zumthor, *Thinking Architecture* (Basel: Birkhäuser, 1999).
18 Quoted in Kristiina Lehtimaki and Petri Neuvonen, eds., *Richard Leplastrier: Spirit of Nature Wood Architecture Award 2004* (Helsinki: Rakennustieto Publishing, 2004), 18.

19 Of course, nowadays one tends to think of the surface on the model of the outer 'skin' of the thing whose surface it is, whereas the Aristotelian notion of *topos* is more like the inner 'skin' of the surrounding body. So, in this latter sense, the *topos* of an underwater swimmer is given by the interior surrounding surface of the water as it touches the swimmer's skin rather than by the exterior surface of the swimmer's skin as it touches the surrounding water.
20 See David Leatherbarrow and Mohsen Mostafavi, *On Weathering: The Life of Buildings in Time* (Cambridge, MA: MIT Press, 1993), esp. 118–19.
21 Beatriz Colomina, *Privacy and Publicity: Modern Architecture as Mass Media* (Cambridge, MA: MIT Press, 1994), 14.
22 Especially, of course (but not only), the photographic image – thus David Campany suggests that the experience of architecture 'may now be inseparable from the experience of its imagery, and … photography may now belong to the very same networks of spectacle'. See Campany, 'Architecture as Photography', 38.
23 Colomina, *Privacy and Publicity*, 13–14.
24 Benjamin, 'The Work of Art in the Age of Mechanical Reproduction', 220.
25 Notice that here 'authenticity' is used here to translate a different term, *Echtheit* (which itself has connotations of 'real' and 'true'), from either *Authentizität* or *Eigentlichkeit*.
26 The work's 'unique existence at the place where it happens to be' can be understood in terms of its 'singularity'. Such singularity belongs both to the thing and to place. See Malpas, 'Place and Singularity', in *The Intelligence of Place: Topographies and Poetics*, ed. Jeff Malpas (London: Bloomsbury, 2015), 65–92.
27 See, for example, Jean Baudrillard, *Simulacra and Simulations*, trans. Paul Foss, Paul Patton and Philip Beitchman (New York: Semiotext(e), 1981).

Chapter 7

1 See Malpas, *Place and Experience*, 49–80.
2 See *Being and Time*, H69–H72.
3 Heidegger's emphasis on the primacy of the hand is, as always, ontological in character. That means that it is operative even in the absence of that specific part of human anatomy that the term 'hand' usually designates. So human handedness is not a matter of satisfying a specific anatomical model, even if most humans do satisfy it, but of having a certain way of engaging with the world. Human handedness can thus be realized through the use of the foot or the mouth, as well as prosthetically.
4 Martin Heidegger, *Parmenides*, trans. André Schuwer and Richard Rojcewicz (Bloomington: Indiana University Press, 1992), 80, 81.
5 Heidegger, *What Is Called Thinking?*, 16.
6 See Friedrich A. Kittler, *Gramophone, Film, Typewriter*, trans. Geoffrey Winthrop-Young and Michael Wutz (Stanford: Stanford University Press, 1999). See also, Jacques Derrida, 'Geschlecht II: Heidegger's Hand', in *Deconstruction and Philosophy: The Texts of Jacques Derrida*, trans. John P. Leavey (Chicago: University of Chicago Press, 1987), 161–96.
7 Heidegger, *Parmenides*, 85.
8 The point, more generally, is that pictures are not restricted to the modality of vision (and vision should not itself be construed as 'picture-like'). On this, see the discussion

in Dominic M. M. Lopes, 'Art Media and the Sense Modalities: Tactile Pictures', *Philosophical Quarterly* 47 (1997): 425–40.
9. One may be tempted to say that, strictly, the line does not itself move, but this is arguable depending on exactly how movement and the line are understood. If the line is taken always to involve a movement between two points, then the line moves, but if the line is taken to be an already completed movement, grasped as such in its entirety, then it will be viewed as unmoving.
10. Sixtus's replanning of Rome is discussed by Edmund Bacon, in his classic *Design of Cities* (London: Thames and Hudson, 1967), 131–61. Bacon's larger discussion provides an excellent exploration of many of the issues of orientation and situation in the context of urban design.
11. Le Corbusier, *Towards a New Architecture*, 187.
12. As Flora Samuel and Peter Blundell Jones describe it: 'The whole promenade, which follows the topos of Jacob's ladder so prevalent in the work of Le Corbusier, is a switchback journey from darkness to light in order to "find the sun", augmented by the manipulation of colour, rhythm and proportion.' See Flora Samuel and Peter Blundell Jones, 'The Making of Architectural Promenade: Villa Savoye and Schminke House', *Architectural Research Quarterly* 16 (June 2012): 114. See also Flora Samuel, *Le Corbusier and the Architectural Promenade* (Basel: Birkhäuser, 2011).
13. Le Corbusier, *Towards a New Architecture*, 187. Le Corbusier visited the Acropolis, for the first time, in 1911 – eighteen years before *Towards a New Architecture* appeared – and the visit had an enormous influence upon him. See Sebastian Harris, 'Le Corbusier between Sketches: A Graphic Analysis of the Acropolis Sketches', LC2015: Le Corbusier, 50 Years Later International Congress at Valencia, 18–20 November 2015, sponsored by Universitat Politècnica de València, accessed September 2020, http://dx.doi.org/10.4995/LC2015.2015.911.
14. See Hélène Bauchet-Cauquil, Françoise-Claire Prodhon, Patrick Seguin, Michael Roy, Le Corbusier and Pierre Jeanneret, *Le Corbusier, Pierre Jeanneret: Chandigarh, India, 1951–66*, ed. Laurence Seguin and Patrick Seguin, trans. John Tittensor and Jeremy Harrison (Paris: Galerie Patrick Seguin, 2014).
15. See David K. Connolly, 'At the Center of the World: The Labyrinth Pavement of Chartres Cathedral', in *Art and Architecture of Late Medieval Pilgrimage in Northern Europe and the British Isles*, ed. Sarah Blick and Rita Tekippe (Boston: Brill, 2005), 285–326.
16. See Aristotle, *Physics*, 212a20.
17. Erwin Strauss, *The Primary World of the Senses*, trans. Jacob Needleman (New York: Macmillan, 1963), 244. See the discussion of Strauss in Malpas, *Place and Experience*, 171–2.
18. Strauss, *The Primary World of the Senses*, 243.
19. Strauss, *The Primary World of the Senses*, 244.
20. David Leatherbarrow uses the notion of the 'horizon' to elaborate aspects of the topographical embeddedness of buildings – see Leatherbarrow, 'In and Outside of Architecture', chap. 5 in *Uncommon Ground*, 170–214.
21. 'Movement' here encompasses many different kinds of moving – and again, part of what is issue is how 'movement' should be understood, and whether there is only one unique and exclusive way of characterizing it.
22. Heidegger, 'Building Dwelling Thinking', in *Poetry, Language, Thought*, trans. Albert Hofstadter, 1st Harper Colophon ed. (New York: Harper and Row, 1971; New York: Harper Colophon, 1975), 151.

Chapter 8

1. Government Architect New South Wales, *Better Placed: An Integrated Design Policy for the Built Environment of New South Wales* (Sydney: NSW Government, 2017).
2. Patrik Schumacher, 'Parametricism – The Parametric Paradigm and the Formation of a New Style', chap. 11 in *The Autopoiesis of Architecture: A New Agenda for Architecture*, Vol. 2 (London: John Wiley & Sons Ltd, 2012).
3. 'Parametricism' sits alongside other overlapping terms such as 'parametrics' and 'parametric design', and these terms are also used here, although not in a way that strongly differentiates between them. Nevertheless, these terms are sometimes distinguished – see, for example, Matthew Poole and Manuel Shvartzberg, eds., *The Politics of Parametricism: Digital Technologies in Architecture* (London: Bloomsbury, 2015), 5.
4. So, for example, the first definition listed in the Burra Charter (The Australia ICOMOS Charter for Places of Cultural Significance) is for the term 'place', yet it remains primarily seen as a 'location', rather than as a more encompassing or fundamental notion. See Australia ICOMOS Incorporated, *The Australia ICOMOS Charter for Places of Cultural Significance, The Burra Charter, 2013* (Burwood, VIC: Australia ICOMOS Incorporated, 2013), article 1.1, p. 2, accessed September 2020, http://australia.icomos.org/wp-content/uploads/The-Burra-Charter-2013-Adopted-31.10.2013.pdf. The Burra Charter was originally adopted in 1979.
5. Sometimes these terms are distinguished – 'bound' being taken to imply something *that bounds* and is distinct from what is so bounded, whereas there being no such implication in the case of limit. The Aristotelian sense of *topos* implies a notion of bound in just this sense. Limit can be viewed as the broader term, encompassing instances of bound, but not restricted to such instances. The distinction can be viewed as important in certain contexts, but it does not play a significant role in the discussion here.
6. See Lucretius, *Lucretius on the Nature of Things*, a translation of *De Rerum Naturae* by Cyril Bailey (Oxford: Clarendon Press, 1910), 58–9.
7. For a more detailed discussion of the meaning and etymology of 'space' and 'place', see Malpas, *Place and Experience*, 24–7. See also the entries for 'place' and 'space' in the *Oxford English Dictionary* and the *Chambers Dictionary of Etymology*.
8. See Malpas, *Place and Experience*, 12, 34–5.
9. See Humberto Maturana and Fransisco Varela, *Autopoiesis and Cognition: The Realization of the Living* (1972; repr., Dordrecht: Reidel, 1980).
10. Alberto Pérez-Gómez, *Attunement: Architectural Meaning after the Crisis of Modern Science* (Cambridge, MA: MIT Press, 2017), 130–1.
11. Richard Coyne, 'What's Wrong with Parametricism', *Reflections on Technology, Media & Culture* (blog), 18 January 2014, accessed September 2020, https://richardcoyne.com/2014/01/18/whats-wrong-with-parametricism/.
12. See, for example, Achim Menges, 'Computational Material Culture', in *Parametricism 2.0: Rethinking Architecture's Agenda for the 21st Century*, special issue, *Architectural Design* 86 (2016): 76–83, in which computational robotic design (including certain associated parametric techniques) is seen as part of a purely computation and material design culture.
13. Martin Heidegger, *The Principle of Reason*, trans. Reginald Lilly (Bloomington: Indiana University Press, 1991), 129.

Chapter 9

1. Stuart Elden, *Mapping the Present: Heidegger, Foucault and the Project of a Spatial History* (London: Continuum, 2001), 4.
2. Elden, *Mapping the Present*, 151.
3. In fact, for Elden, it would be a 'platial' history' – 'platial' being the neologism he introduces (see, for example, *Mapping the Present*, 36) to parallel 'spatial'.
4. A topic explored in volumes such as Lawrence J. Vales, *Architecture, Power, and National Identity* (New York: Routledge, 2008) and Michael Minkenberg, ed., *Power and Architecture: The Construction of Capitals and the Politics of Space* (New York: Berghahn, 2014).
5. See Robert R. Taylor, *The Word in Stone: The Role of Architecture in the National Socialist Ideology* (Berkeley: University of California Press, 1974).
6. There have, however, been few studies that try, in any direct fashion, directly to interrogate the relation between power and architecture in this latter sense, and even fewer, if any, that approach the matter from within architectural theory. Notable exceptions include, Thomas A. Markus, *Buildings & Power: Freedom and Control in the Origin of Modern Building Types* (London: Routledge, 1993); Paul Hirst, *Space and Power: Politics, War and Architecture* (Oxford: Polity, 2005); and Kim Dovey, *Framing Places. Mediating Power in Built Form* (London: Routledge, 1999). There is also a considerable literature that addresses specific forms of power as these are worked out spatially and sometimes architecturally. This is especially true in relation to questions of gender. See, for example, Dörte Kuhlmann, *Gender Studies in Architecture: Space, Power and Difference* (London: Routledge, 2013).
7. This is true, to a large extent (and notwithstanding their significance in other respects) of both Markus, *Buildings & Power* and Dovey, *Framing Places*.
8. Elden captures something of the contrast at issue here when he writes: 'Lefebvre suggests "there is a politics of space because space is political". Following Heidegger, we might suggest that "there is a politics of space *because politics is spatial*". See Elden, *Mapping the Present*, 151.
9. Henri Lefebvre, *The Production of Space*, trans. Donald Nicolson-Smith (1974; repr., Oxford: Blackwell, 1991).
10. Louis Kahn, 'The Room, the Street, and Human Agreement', *AIA Journal* 56 (September 1971): 33. See also the discussion in Chapter 10.
11. See Giovanni Batista Piranes, *The Prisons (Le Carceri), The Complete First and Second States* (New York: Dover, 1973). Originally published in 1750.
12. A collaborative project between the University of Melbourne and design and fabrication company United Make has visualized Piranesi's Carceri using contemporary Virtual Reality software. The project, titled 'Re-Imagining Imaginary Prisons', describes itself as having brought to life 'in 3D the 2D spaces of Piranesi's Imaginary Prison, which scholars had previously thought could not feasibly exist as real, constructible spaces'. See http://www.unitedmake.com.au/portfolio/re-imagining-imaginary-prisons/, accessed August 2020. In fact, the shift from a 2-D to a 3-D environment no more establishes that the Carceri could exist as 'as real … spaces' than do Piranesi's original drawings.
13. Jane Jacobs, *The Death and Life of Great American Cities* (New York: Random House, 1961).
14. Kahn, 'The Room, the Street, and Human Agreement', 33.

15 For a discussion of the complex of economic factors, including land values, that bear on high-rise development in one example (though an important one), see Jason Barr, 'The Economics of Skyscraper Construction in Manhattan: Past, Present, and Future', in *Global Interchanges: Resurgence of the Skyscraper City*, proceedings of the CTBUH 2015 International Conference, New York, ed. Antony Wood and David Malott (Chicago: Council on Tall Buildings and Urban Habitat, 2015), 33–9, accessed August 2020, https://global.ctbuh.org/resources/papers/download/2435-the-economics-of-skyscraper-construction-in-manhattan-past-present-and-future.pdf.
16 The role of visual spectacle is an important part of the analysis in Stephen Graham, *Vertical: The City from Satellites to Bunkers* (London: Verso, 2016); and more sympathetically explored, in the case of Pudong, in Anna Greenspan, 'The Power of Spectacle', *Culture Unbound* 4 (2012): 81–95, accessed June 2020, http://www.cultureunbound.ep.liu.se.
17 See Greenspan, 'The Power of Spectacle'.
18 Quoted in Amy Frearson, 'Renzo Piano Draws Up Designs for His Next London Skyscraper', *Dezeen*, 21 October 2015, accessed June 2020, https://www.dezeen.com/2015/10/21/renzo-piano-designs-skyscraper-paddington-station-31-london-street/.
19 See Frearson, 'Renzo Piano Draws Up Designs for His Next London Skyscraper'; see also Cahal Milmo, 'London's New Skyscrapers "Inflict Serious Harm" on Capital's Historic Landscape, Heritage Watchdog Warns', *The Independent*, 10 December 2015, accessed June 2020, https://www.independent.co.uk/arts-entertainment/architecture/londons-new-skyscrapers-inflict-serious-harm-on-capitals-historic-landscape-warns-heritage-watchdog-a6767296.html.
20 Fred A. Bernstein, 'Supersizing Manhattan: New Yorkers Rage against the Dying of the Light', The *Guardian*, 16 January 2015, accessed June 2020, https://www.theguardian.com/cities/2015/jan/16/supersizing-manhattan-new-yorkers-rage-against-the-dying-of-the-light.
21 Bernstein, 'Supersizing Manhattan: New Yorkers Rage against the Dying of the Light'.
22 Broadway Malyan's website (as at August 2020) declares that, 'We design cities, buildings, and places with a strong sense of purpose and identity', at https://www.broadwaymalyan.com/. Such declarations seem to be a standard part of the self-promotion of most contemporary global design firms, and are especially ironic given the almost generic character of the designs that such firms tend to produce – forms geared more to a globalized capitalist aesthetic than to any genuine engagement with place.
23 Rowan Moore, 'How a High-rise Craze Is Ruining London's Skyline', *The Guardian*, 2 December 2012, accessed June 2020, https://www.theguardian.com/artanddesign/2012/dec/02/london-high-rise-craze-ruins-skyline.
24 See Bachelard, *The Poetics of Space*.
25 See Lindstrom and Malpas, 'The Modesty of Architecture'.

Chapter 10

1 Kahn, 'The Room, the Street, and Human Agreement', 33.
2 See Robert McCarter, *The Space Within: Interior Experience as the Origin of Architecture* (London: Reaktion, 2016), esp. chap. 1, 'The Space Within as the Origin of Architecture', 13–24.

3   Frequently through the focus on interior design and ideas of domesticity – a topic explored in Charles Rice, *The Emergence of the Interior: Architecture, Modernity, Domesticity* (London: Routledge, 2006).
4   Eisenman, *Diagram Diaries*, 87.
5   See Heidegger, 'Building Dwelling Thinking', in *Poetry, Language, Thought*, 152. This passage immediately precedes Heidegger's discussion of the productive character of the boundary.
6   Einstein suggests a similar way of arriving at the concept of space by a process of abstraction that depends on identifying the space within a containing object as comparable to the spaces within other containing objects, and as the space is thereby taken to be something common to all those objects, so it allows of being understood as independent of any of the containing objects – see Albert Einstein, foreword to *Concepts of Space: The History of Theories of Space in Physics*, by Max Jammer, 2nd ed. (Cambridge, MA: Harvard University Press, 1969), xv.
7   Although he interprets the implications somewhat differently, Fillip Mattens describes more or less the same process – see Mattens, 'The Aesthetics of Space: Modern Architecture and Photography', 114.
8   McCarter, *The Space Within. Interior Experience as the Origin of Architecture*, 8.
9   Le Corbusier, *Towards a New Architecture*, 187.
10 It is this sort of view, and the spatiality associated with it, that can be said to be implicated in the mode of engagement that is also at work in much digital and parametric design.
11 One might be tempted to treat the first sense as 'objective' and the second 'subjective', except that it is the relation to place that is primarily at issue rather than the relation to a subject. Moreover, the idea of a 'topological space' that is at issue here is not a space that is completely apart from any objective sense of space but, properly understood, involves a complex spatial structure that encompasses both subjective and objective elements. See Malpas, *Place and Experience*, 48–80, especially 67–72.
12 See Malpas, *Place and Experience*, esp. 71–2. To the extent that the space associated with the bird's-eye view is an abstract space, it is so through being abstracted from out of the more encompassing topological structure in which it is already given.
13 Exteriority, as noted above, is itself part of the same structure as interiority – space as extension allowing neither an interior nor an exterior other than as conventionally determined designations of spaces that are essentially no different. It is thus that the bird's-eye view seems less a view that is 'exterior to', as it is a view that is simply 'apart from'.
14 'In-ness' is used here as another way of capturing what is at issue in interiority in a way that echoes Heidegger's focus on 'being-in'. One might also talk of 'insideness', except that this is used in both the Macquarie/Robinson and Stambaugh/Schmidt translations of *Being and Time* to translate *Inwendigkeit*, which Heidegger uses (notably in *Being and Time*, H101) to refer to that mode of spatial containment from which the being-in that is tied to dwelling is so clearly set apart. In fact, he probably ought to be seen as committed to the view that there is no genuine sense of interiority, whether of in-ness, or insideness, in the case of spatial containment at all.
15 See Heidegger, *Being and Time*, H54. It is the 'insideness' associated with this sense of containment that Heidegger refers to as *Inwendigkeit* – see *Being and Time*, H56, H101.
16 Heidegger, *Being and Time*, H54, Stambaugh/Schmidt translation. The Macquarie and Robinson translation differs significantly from the Stambaugh/Schmidt, and effectively de-emphasize the focus on dwelling.

17 See Heidegger, *Being and Time*, H54.
18 See e.g. *Being and Time*, H71–72. 'Ready-to-hand' is from Macquarie/Robinson, Stambaugh/Schmidt have 'handy'.
19 See Heidegger, *Being and Time*, §§22–24, H101–H113.
20 Simmel speaks of the 'merciless separation of space', writing that 'no particle of matter can share its space with another, a real unity of the diverse does not exist in spatial terms'. See Simmel, 'Bridge and Door', 170–1.
21 Heidegger, *Being and Time*, H55. On this basis, and keeping in mind the comments made at the end of Chapter 3, Heidegger's claim sets up a significant issue for that Levinasian mode of thinking that is indebted to and grounded in Cartesian spatiality, as against the mode of topological spatiality that is central in Heidegger. The Levinasian account is, on the one hand, predicated on a fundamental relationality, and yet, on the other hand, its implicit espousal of an essentially Cartesian spatiality makes such relationality problematic.
22 Martin Heidegger, *The Fundamental Concepts of Metaphysics*, trans. William McNeill and Nicholas Walker (Bloomington: Indiana University Press, 1995), 177.
23 See Heidegger, *Being and Time*, §15, H70.
24 See, for example, Hans-Georg Moeller and Andrew K. Whitehead, eds., *About Landscape and Travelling East and West: A Philosophical Journey* (London: Bloomsbury, 2014).
25 Heidegger, 'Why Do I Stay in the Provinces', 27.
26 Landscape is often assumed to be entirely artefactual – always constituted in terms of a 'view' – but, as used here, it refers neither to such a *cultural* construct nor to something that is entirely and unequivocally *natural* (as if that contrast could ever be used in an unqualified sense).
27 Although the recent rise of interest in the idea of 'atmosphere' (especially among phenomenologically inclined designers) ought to bring with it an increased sense of the potential interiority of landscape. Atmosphere brings a sense of interiority with it (partly through the connection between atmosphere and *environment* – the latter being that which *environs* one and, so, holds one *within*), and atmosphere is also an idea as applicable to the conventionally understood 'exterior' spaces of landscapes as to conventionally understood interior spaces. See Tonino Griffero, *Atmospheres: Aesthetics of Emotional Spaces*, trans. Sarah de Sanctis (Farnham, Surrey: Ashgate, 2014), esp. 60–2 (on 'atmosphere and landscape'). See also Peter Zumthor, *Atmospheres: Architectural Environments, Surrounding Objects* (Basel: Birkhäuser, 2006); and Juhani Pallasmaa, 'Place and Atmosphere', in *The Intelligence of Place: Topographies and Poetics*, ed. Jeff Malpas (London: Bloomsbury, 2015), 129–56. From a different direction, Simon Schama's, *Landscape and Memory* (London: HarperCollins, 1998), provides another pathway into the connection between interiority and landscape through its focus on what Schama describes, using a line from Thoreau, as 'the bog in our brain and bowels' (Schama, *Landscape and Memory*, 578).
28 Here, the expansive and seemingly empty character of the landscape draws attention to the boundedness of the landscape – its horizontality – as beckoning towards what lies beyond it. Thus, the horizon can be associated with a sense of spatial immensity or even infinity. But this occurs only when the horizon is understood as it is understood independently of the field that it also makes possible – as attention is turned to the horizon apart from that which it allows to appear within it (i.e. as apart from its own interiority). Of course, the horizon (so long as it is not restricted just to

the horizon of a specific *representation*), and place with it, does have an immensity and even an infinity of its own, but it lies within the opening that occurs within it – its interiority, one might say, is where its genuine infinity is to be found – and this is a key point of the discussion in this chapter.

29 Appearing in several English translations, including 'The Pathway', trans. Thomas F. O'Meara, rev. Thomas Sheehan, in *Heidegger: The Man and the Thinker*, ed. Thomas Sheehan (Chicago: Precedent Publishing, 1981), 69–72, but first published in German in 1949 (after several earlier private editions).

30 Appearing in English, in 1966, as 'Conversation on a Country Path about Thinking', *Discourse on Thinking*, 58–90. The complete version appears as 'Αγχιβασιν [*Anchibasie*]: A Triadic Conversation on a Country Path between a Scientist, a Scholar, and a Guide', in *Country Path Conversations*, 1–104. The shortened version corresponds to 'A Triadic Conversation', 68–103.

31 See Heidegger, 'A Triadic Conversation', 19.

32 This is partly because of its association with a Kantian transcendental framework focused on the structure of objectivity – see Heidegger, 'A Triadic Conversation', 55–72, esp. 72 – but also because of the way it might be taken to suggest a surrounding field with the human being at the centre. Elsewhere, however, Heidegger is less concerned about the use of the term 'horizon', employing it, as noted below, in the discussion of boundary in 'Building Dwelling Thinking', 152.

33 See the note in 'A Triadic Conversation', 73–74n.44.

34 Heidegger, 'A Triadic Conversation', 75.

35 Heidegger, 'A Triadic Conversation', 102.

36 'The door handle is the handshake of the building', writes Juhani Pallasmaa, in *The Eyes of the Skin* (1996, repr., Chichester: Wiley, 2012), 62, echoing an idea that appears at various places in architectural discussion – e.g. Edward A. Sovik talks of 'the door handles … where people shake hands with a building', in 'Five Easy Pieces', *Journal of Architectural Education* 42 (1989): 59. Of course, the idea of entry and of liminality that is at issue here involves more than just a handshake, but it may be taken to include this.

37 See Jean-Pierre Vernant, 'Hestia – Hermes: The Religious Expression of Space and Movement among the Greeks', *Social Science Information* 8 (1969): 131–68.

38 Massimo Cacciari, 'Place and Limit', in *The Intelligence of Place*, ed. Jeff Malpas (London: Bloomsbury, 2015), 15.

39 Heidegger, 'Building Dwelling Thinking', 152.

40 Simmel, 'Bridge and Door', 170–4. The boundary is a focus for Simmel's attention, though in a different way, in 'The Sociology of Space', in *Simmel on Culture*, 137–69, esp. 141–6.

41 Heidegger, 'Building Dwelling Thinking', 150.

42 Simmel, 'Bridge and Door', 170.

43 Heidegger, 'A Dialogue on Language', in *On the Way to Language*, trans. Peter D. Hertz (New York: Harper and Row, 1971), 41.

44 McCahon, quoted in R. N. O'Reilly, Introduction to *Colin McCahon: A Survey Exhibition* (Auckland: Auckland Art Gallery, 1972), 8.

45 McCahon, in O'Reilly, Introduction to *Colin McCahon: A Survey Exhibition*, 19.

46 'I'm finished with frames and all that they imply', says McCahon in 1971. See 'Ideas and Reflections – A McCahon Miscellany', in *Colin McCahon: Gates and Journeys*, ed. Michael Gifkins (Auckland: Auckland City Art Gallery, 1988), 78.

47 *Colin McCahon: Gates and Journeys*, Auckland City Art Gallery, 11 November 1988 to 26 February 1989, and at galleries in Wellington, Christchurch and Sydney. See Michael Gifkins, ed., *Colin McCahon: Gates and Journeys* (Auckland: Auckland City Art Gallery, 1988).
48 In McCahon, 'Ideas and Reflections – A McCahon Miscellany', 78.
49 McCahon (from 1979), quoted in Gordon H. Brown, *Colin McCahon: Artist* (Wellington: A. H. and A. W. Reed, 1984), 54.
50 Taken from the anonymously presented invitation cards for McCahon's first exhibition of his *Gates* paintings, quoted in Tony Green, 'McCahon and the Modern', in *Colin McCahon: Gates and Journeys*, 34. Green himself contests the claim that the *Gates* paintings can be read as landscapes, arguing that they transform landscape into symbol (Green, 'McCahon and the Modern', 34–5). But this is to overlook the way McCahon's own use of words and symbols is transformative of them also. Rather than landscapes becoming symbolic, it is perhaps better to say that, in McCahon's work, landscape is transmuted into its primordial elements.
51 Geoffrey Hill, 'The Mystery of the Charity of Charles Péguy', in *Collected Poems* (Harmondsworth, Penguin, 1985), 188.

Epilogue

1 Although it is probably better to say that, for Heidegger, the ethical is always already encompassed by the ontological, as *ethos* is indeed always already encompassed by *topos*, or, perhaps, is another name for *topos*.
2 Heidegger, 'Letter on "Humanism"', 269, 271.
3 See Harries, *The Ethical Function of Architecture*, chap. 11.
4 Harries, *The Ethical Function of Architecture*, 175.
5 On the relation between Heidegger and Eckhart, see, especially, Reiner Schürmann, *Heidegger on Being and Acting: From Principles to Anarchy*, trans. Christine-Marie Gros (Bloomington: Indiana University Press, 1987); and also Schürmann, *Meister Eckhart, Mystic and Philosopher: Translations With Commentary* (Bloomington: Indiana University Press, 1978).
6 Although one also taken up in Randall Lindstrom, *Kenosis Creativity Architecture: Appearance through Emptying*, esp. chap. 2.
7 *Discourse on Thinking: A Translation of* Gelassenheit, trans. John M. Anderson and E. Hans Freund (New York: Harper & Row, 1966).
8 Corresponding to 'A Triadic Conversation', 68–103.
9 Heidegger, 'Memorial Address', 47.
10 Heidegger, 'Memorial Address', 47.
11 On this notion of groundedness – *Bodenständigkeit* – which is so often misunderstood, see Robert Metcalf, 'Rethinking "Bodenständigkeit" in the Technological Age', *Research in Phenomenology* 42 (2012): 49–66.
12 Heidegger, 'Memorial Address', 49.
13 Heidegger, 'Memorial Address', 54–5.
14 Heidegger, 'Memorial Address', 47.
15 'Conversation on a Country Path about Thinking', 61–2; 'A Triadic Conversation', 70. In its original form, the 'Conversation' has appended as 'supplements' several quotations from Eckhart under the headings 'On Letting Go of Things' and 'Being

of Great Essence', of which the first reads: 'Where I will nothing for myself, there wills instead my God [*Wo ich für mich nichts will, da will statt meiner Gott*]' ('A Triadic Conversation', 103) – perhaps, in the light of the topological character of the 'Conversation' that precedes this line, special attention should be given to the *wo* ('where') and the *da* ('here/there') that appear in it.
16 Heidegger, 'Conversation on a Country Path', 65; 'A Triadic Conversation', 73.
17 Heidegger, 'Conversation on a Country Path', 73 and 82–3; 'A Triadic Conversation', 79 and 95.
18 See Malpas, 'Placing Understanding/Understanding Place', *Sophia: International Journal of Philosophy and Traditions* 56, no. 3 (2017): 379–91.
19 See Heidegger, 'Building Dwelling Thinking', 145–61.
20 See 'Conversation on a Country Path', 89, and 'A Triadic Conversation', 102.

BIBLIOGRAPHY

Aalto, Alvar. *Alvar Aalto in His Own Words*. Edited by Göran Schildt. Translated by Timothy Binham. New York: Rizzoli, 1998.

Aalto, Alvar. *Sketches*. Edited by Göran Schildt. Translated by Stuart Wrede. Cambridge, MA: MIT Press, 1979.

Adorno, Theodor W. *The Jargon of Authenticity*. Translated by Knut Tarnowski and Frederic Will. Evanston, IL: Northwestern University Press, 1964.

Adorno, Theodor W. *Minima Moralia: Reflections from Damaged Life*. London: Verso, 2005.

Alexander, Christopher, and Peter Eisenman. 'Contrasting Concepts of Harmony in Architecture: The 1982 Debate between Christopher Alexander and Peter Eisenman'. Edited by Lucien Steil, Brian Hanson, Michael Mehaffy and Nikos Salingaros. *Katarxis*, no. 3 (2004). Accessed May 2020, http://www.katarxis3.com/Alexander_Eisenman_Debate.htm.

Améry, Jean. 'How Much Home Does a Person Need?' In *At the Mind's Limits: Contemplations by a Survivor on Auschwitz and Its Realities*, translated by Sidney Rosenfeld and Stella P. Rosenfeld, 41–61. Bloomington: Indiana University Press, 1998.

Aristotle. *The Complete Works of Aristotle: The Revised Oxford Translation*, 2 vols. Edited by Jonathan Barnes. Bollingen Series 71: 2. Princeton, NJ: Princeton University Press, 1984.

Australia ICOMOS Incorporated. *The Australia ICOMOS Charter for Places of Cultural Significance, the Burra Charter, 2013*. Burwood, VIC: Australia ICOMOS Incorporated, 2013. http://australia.icomos.org/wp-content/uploads/The-Burra-Charter-2013-Adopted-31.10.2013.pdf. Originally adopted in 1979.

Bachelard, Gaston. *The Poetics of Space*. Translated by Maria Jolas. Boston: Beacon Press, 1969.

Bacon, Edmund. *Design of Cities*. London: Thames and Hudson, 1967.

Bambach, Charles. Review of *Nature, History, State: 1933–1934*, by Martin Heidegger, translated and edited by Gregory Fried and Richard Polt. *Notre Dame Philosophical Reviews* 9 (June 2014). Accessed June 2020, https://ndpr.nd.edu/news/nature-history-state-1933-1934/.

Barnhart, Robert K., ed. *Chambers Dictionary of Etymology*. London: Chambers, 2000.

Barnstone, Deborah Ascher. *The Transparent State: Architecture and Politics in Postwar Germany*. London: Routledge, 2005.

Barr, Jason. 'The Economics of Skyscraper Construction in Manhattan: Past, Present, and Future'. In *Global Interchanges: Resurgence of the Skyscraper City*, proceedings of the CTBUH 2015 International Conference, New York, edited by Antony Wood and David Malott, 33–9. Chicago: Council on Tall Buildings and Urban Habitat, 2015. Accessed August 2020, https://global.ctbuh.org/resources/papers/download/2435-the-economics-of-skyscraper-construction-in-manhattan-past-present-and-future.pdf.

Bartning, Otto, ed. *Mensch und Raum: Darmstädter Gespräch 1951*. Darmstadt: Neue Darmstädter Verlagsanstalt, 1952.

Basso, Keith H. *Wisdom Sits in Places: Landscape and Language among the Western Apache*. Albuquerque: University of New Mexico Press, 1996.

Batnitzky, Leora. 'Encountering the Modern Subject in Levinas'. *Yale French Studies* 104 (2004): 6–21.

Bauchet-Cauquil, Hélène, Françoise-Claire Prodhon, Patrick Seguin, Michael Roy, Le Corbusier and Pierre Jeanneret. *Le Corbusier, Pierre Jeanneret: Chandigarh, India, 1951–66*. Edited by Laurence Seguin and Patrick Seguin. Translated by John Tittensor and Jeremy Harrison. Paris: Galerie Patrick Seguin, 2014.

Baudrillard, Jean. *Simulacra and Simulations*. Translated by Paul Foss, Paul Patton and Philip Beitchman. New York: Semiotext(e), 1981.

Baudrillard, Jean, and Jean Nouvel. *The Singular Objects of Architecture*. Translated by Robert Bononno. Minneapolis: University of Minnesota Press, 2002.

Bax, Chantal. 'Otherwise than Being-with: Levinas on Heidegger and Community'. *Human Studies* 40 (2017): 381–400.

Benjamin, Andrew. 'Who Dwells? Heidegger and the Place of Mortal Subjects'. *PIi* 10 (2000): 217–43.

Benjamin, Walter. *One-way Street and Other Writings*. Translated by Edmund Jephcott and Kingsley Shorter. London: New Left Books, 1979.

Benjamin, Walter. 'The Work of Art in the Age of Mechanical Reproduction'. In *Illuminations: Essays and Reflections*, edited by Hannah Arendt, translated by Harry Zohn, 217–51. New York: Schocken Books, 1986.

Benjamin, Walter. *The Arcades Project*. Translated by Howard Eiland and Kevin McLaughlin. Cambridge, MA: Harvard University Press, 2002.

Berger, Peter, and Thomas Luckmann. *The Social Construction of Reality: A Treatise in the Sociology of Knowledge*. Garden City, NY: Anchor, 1966.

Bernstein, Fred A. 'Supersizing Manhattan: New Yorkers Rage against the Dying of the Light'. The *Guardian*, 16 January 2015. Accessed June 2020, https://www.theguardian.com/cities/2015/jan/16/supersizing-manhattan-new-yorkers-rage-against-the-dying-of-the-light.

Bloch, Ernst. *The Principle of Hope*. Translated by N. Plaice, S. Plaice and P. Knight. 3 vols. Cambridge, MA: MIT Press, 1986.

Blundell Jones, Peter. *Architecture and Ritual: How Buildings Shape Society*. London: Bloomsbury, 2016.

Blundell Jones, Peter. 'A Forty Year Encounter with Hans Scharoun'. Commentary on PhD diss. by publication, School of Architecture, University of Sheffield, 2013. Accessed June 2020, https://core.ac.uk/download/pdf/20344024.pdf.

Blundell Jones, Peter. *Hans Scharoun*. London: Phaidon, 1995.

Blundell Jones, Peter. 'In Search of Authenticity', 'Parts One-Four'. *Architect's Journal* 194 (30 October, 1991): 26–30; 194 (6 November 1991): 32–6; 194 (4 December 1991): 22–5; 195 (8 and 15 January 1992): 29–32.

Borges, Jorge Luis. 'Funes, His Memory'. In *Collected Fictions*, translated by Andrew Hurley, 131–7. Harmondsworth: Penguin, 1996.

Borgmann, Albert. 'Cosmopolitanism and Provincialism: On Heidegger's Errors and Insights'. *Philosophy Today* 36 (1992): 131–45.

Brown, Gordon H. *Colin McCahon: Artist*. Wellington, NZ: A. H. and A. W. Reed, 1984.

Buchner, Hartmut. 'Fragmetarisches'. In *Errinerung an Martin Heidegger*, edited by Günther Neske. Pfullingen: Verlag Günther Neske, 1977.

Buttimer, Anne. 'Grasping the Dynamism of Lifeworld'. *Annals of the Association of American Geographers* 66 (1976): 277–92.

Buttimer, Anne. *Geography and the Human Spirit*. Baltimore: Johns Hopkins University Press, 1994.
Cacciari, Massimo. 'Eupalinos or Architecture'. *Oppositions* 21 (1980): 106–16.
Cacciari, Massimo. 'Place and Limit'. In *The Intelligence of Place*, edited by Jeff Malpas, 12–22. London: Bloomsbury, 2015.
Campany, David. 'Architecture as Photography: Document, Publicity, Commentary, Art'. In *Constructing Worlds: Photography and Architecture in the Modern Age*, edited by Alona Pardo and Elias Redstone, 27–39. Munich: Prestel, 2014.
Carlin, Peta. *On Surface and Place: Between Architecture, Textiles and Photography*. London: Routledge, 2016.
Carr, David. 'Husserl's Problematic Concept of the Life-World'. *American Philosophical Quarterly* 7 (1970): 331–9.
Casey, Edward S. *Remembering: A Phenomenological Study*. 2nd ed. Bloomington: Indiana University Press, 2000.
Casey, Edward S. *Representing Place: Landscape Painting and Maps*. Minneapolis: University of Minnesota Press, 2002.
di Cesare, Donatella. 'Heidegger's Metaphysical Anti-Semitism'. In *Reading Heidegger's Black Notebooks, 1931–1941*, edited by Ingo Farin and Jeff Malpas, 181–94. Cambridge, MA: MIT Press, 2015.
Clark, Andy, and David J. Chalmers. 'The Extended Mind'. *Analysis*. 58 (1998): 7–19.
Colomina, Beatriz. *Privacy and Publicity: Modern Architecture as Mass Media*. Cambridge, MA: MIT Press, 1994.
Connolly, David K. 'At the Center of the World: The Labyrinth Pavement of Chartres Cathedral'. In *Art and Architecture of Late Medieval Pilgrimage in Northern Europe and the British Isles*, edited by Sarah Blick and Rita Tekippe, 285–326. Boston: Brill, 2005.
Conrads, Ulrich, ed. *Programs and Manifestoes on 20th-Century Architecture*. Cambridge, MA: MIT Press, 1970.
Coyne, Richard. 'What's Wrong with Parametricism'. *Reflections on Technology, Media & Culture* (blog), 18 January 2014. Accessed September 2020, https://richardcoyne.com/2014/01/18/whats-wrong-with-parametricism/.
Dallmayr, Fred. *Between Freiburg and Frankfurt: Toward a Critical Ontology*. Amherst: University of Massachusetts Press, 1991.
Dehaene, Stanislas, and Elizabeth M. Brannon, eds. *Space, Time, and Number in the Brain: Searching for the Foundations of Mathematical Thought*. Amsterdam: Elsevier, 2011.
Derrida, Jacques. 'Khôra'. In *On the Name*, edited by Thomas Dutoit, 89–130. Stanford: Stanford University Press, 1993.
Derrida, Jacques. 'Geschlecht II: Heidegger's Hand'. In *Deconstruction and Philosophy: The Texts of Jacques Derrida*, translated by John P. Leavey, 161–96. Chicago: University of Chicago Press, 1987.
Derrida, Jacques. *Of Grammatology*. Translated by G. C. Spivak. Baltimore: Johns Hopkins University Press, 1976.
Descartes, René. *The Philosophical Writings of Descartes*. Translated by John Cottingham, Robert Stoothoff and Dugald Murdoch, 3 vols. Cambridge: Cambridge University Press, 1984.
DeZurko, Edward Robert. 'Greenough's Theory of Beauty in Architecture'. In *The Rice Institute Pamphlet: Vol. XXXIX, No. 3, Public Addresses*, 96–121. Houston: Rice Institute, 1952.
Dovey, Kim. *Framing Places: Mediating Power in Built Form*. London: Routledge, 1999.

Dreyfus, Hubert. *Being-in-the-World: A Commentary on Heidegger's Being in Time, Division I*. Cambridge, MA: MIT Press, 1990.
Einstein, Albert. Foreword to *Concepts of Space: The History of Theories of Space in Physics*, by Max Jammer. 2nd ed. Cambridge, MA: Harvard University Press, 1969.
Eisenman, Peter. *Diagram Diaries*. London: Thames & Hudson, 1999.
Eisenman, Peter. 'Interview: Peter Eisenman'. By Iman Ansari. *Architectural Review* 26 (April 2013). Accessed January 2020, https://www.architectural-review.com/view/interviews/interview-peter-eisenman/8646893.article?utm_medium=website&utm_source=archdaily.com.
El-Bizri, Nader. 'Ὀν καὶ χώρα: Situating Heidegger between the *Sophist* and the *Timaeus*'. *Studia Phaenomenologica* 4 (2002): 73–98.
Elden, Stuart. *Mapping the Present: Heidegger, Foucault and the Project of a Spatial History*. London: Continuum, 2001.
Evers, Hans Gerhard, ed. *Neue Darmstädter Sezession: Das Menschenbild in unserer Zeit*. Darmstadt: Neue Darmstädter Verlagsanstalt, 1951.
Fell, Joseph P. 'The Familiar and the Strange: On the Limits of Praxis in the Early Heidegger'. In *Heidegger: A Critical Reader*, edited by Hubert L. Dreyfus and Harrison Hall. Oxford: Blackwell, 1992.
Fletcher, Natalie M. 'The Challenges of Achieving Authenticity: A Commentary on Gardner and Anderson'. *Mind, Culture, and Activity* 22 (2015): 402–7.
Foot, Rob. 'Rehabilitating Australia's National Museum'. *Quadrant Online*, 7 October 2008. https://quadrant.org.au/magazine/2008/10/rehabilitating-australia-s-national-museum/.
Forty, Adrian. *Words and Buildings: A Vocabulary of Modern Architecture*. London: Thames and Hudson, 2000.
Fóti, Véronique M. 'Heidegger: Remembrance and Metaphysics'. *Journal of the British Society for Phenomenology* 15 (1984): 243–8.
Frampton, Kenneth. 'On Reading Heidegger'. *Oppositions* 4 (1974): n.p.
Frearson, Amy. 'Renzo Piano Draws Up Designs for His Next London Skyscraper'. *Dezeen*, 21 October 2015. Accessed June 2020, https://www.dezeen.com/2015/10/21/renzo-piano-designs-skyscraper-paddington-station-31-london-street/.
Freud, Sigmund. '*The Standard Edition of the Complete Psychological Works of Sigmund Freud*. Edited by James Strachey in collaboration with Anna Freud, 24 vols. London: Hogarth Press, 1955–74.
Gauthier, David J. *Martin Heidegger, Emmanuel Levinas, and the Politics of Dwelling*. Lanham, MD: Lexington Books, 2011.
Gumbrecht, Hans Ulrich. 'Being Authentic: The Ambition to Recycle'. In *Waste-Site Stories: The Recycling of Memory*, edited by Brian Neville and Johanne Villeneuve, 121–30. Albany, NY: SUNY Press, 2002.
Gifkins, Michael, ed. *Colin McCahon: Gates and Journeys*. Auckland: Auckland City Art Gallery, 1988.
Glendinning, Miles. *Architecture's Evil Empire? The Triumph and Tragedy of Global Modernism*. London: Reaktion, 2010.
Government Architect New South Wales. *Better Placed: An Integrated Design Policy for the Built Environment of New South Wales*. Sydney: NSW Government, 2017.
Graham, Stephen. *Vertical: The City from Satellites to Bunkers*. London: Verso, 2016.
Green, Tony. 'McCahon and the Modern'. In *Colin McCahon: Gates and Journeys*, edited by Michael Gifkins. Auckland, NZ: Auckland City Art Gallery, 1988.

Greenough, Horatio. *Form and Function: Remarks on Art, Design, and Architecture*. Edited by Harold A. Small. Berkeley: University of California Press, 1947. Edited reprint of the 1853 publication of *The Memorial of Horatio Greenough*, edited by Henry T. Tuckerman, published by G. P. Putnam (New York).
Greenspan, Anna. 'The Power of Spectacle'. *Culture Unbound* 4 (2012): 81–95. Accessed June 2020, http://www.cultureunbound.ep.liu.se.
Griffero, Tonino. *Atmospheres: Aesthetics of Emotional Spaces*. Translated by Sarah de Sanctis. Farnham, Surrey: Ashgate, 2014.
Grosz, Elizabeth. *Architecture from the Outside: Essays on Virtual and Real Space*. Cambridge, MA: MIT Press, 2001.
Guignon, Charles. *On Being Authentic*. London: Routledge, 2004.
Hacking, Ian. *The Social Construction of What?* Cambridge, MA: Harvard University Press, 1999.
Harries, Karsten. *The Ethical Function of Architecture*. Cambridge, MA: MIT Press, 1997.
Harries, Karsten. 'In Search of Home'. *Wolkenkuckucksheim – Cloud-Cuckoo-Land* 2 (1998). Accessed May 2020, https://www.cloud-cuckoo.net/openarchive/wolke/eng/Subjects/982/Harries/harries_t.html.
Harries, Karsten. 'On Truth and Lie in Architecture'. *Via* 7 (1984): 47–57.
Harrington, Anne. *Reenchanted Science: Holism in German Culture from Wilhelm II to Hitler*. Princeton: Princeton University Press, 1996.
Harris, Sebastian. 'Le Corbusier between Sketches: A Graphic Analysis of the Acropolis Sketches'. Presented at LC2015: Le Corbusier, 50 Years Later International Congress at Valencia, 18–20 November 2015, sponsored by Universitat Politècnica de València. Accessed September 2020, http://dx.doi.org/10.4995/LC2015.2015.911.
Heidegger, Martin. *Aus der Erfahrung des Denkens, 1910–1976*. Vol 13 of *Gesamtausgabe*. Edited by Hermann Heidegger. Frankfurt: Klostermann, 1983.
Heidegger, Martin. 'Bauen Wohnen Denken'. In *Mensch und Raum: Darmstädter Gespräch 1951*, edited by Otto Bartning, 72–84, Darmstadt: Neue Darmstädter Verlagsanstalt, 1952.
Heidegger, Martin. *Being and Time*. Translated by Joan Stambaugh. Revised by Dennis Schmidt. Albany, NY: SUNY Press, 2010.
Heidegger, Martin. *Being and Time*. Translated by John Macquarie and Edward Robinson. New York: Harper & Row, 1962.
Heidegger, Martin. *Basic Concepts*. Translated by Gary E. Aylesworth. Bloomington: Indiana University Press, 1993.
Heidegger, Martin. *Contributions to Philosophy – From Enowning*. Translated by Kenneth Maly and Parvis Emad. Bloomington: Indiana University Press, 1999.
Heidegger, Martin. *Contributions to Philosophy (of the Event)*. Translated by Richard Rojcewicz and Daniela Vallega-Neu. Bloomington: Indiana University Press, 2012.
Heidegger, Martin. *Country Path Conversations*. Translated by Bret W. Davis. Bloomington: Indiana University Press, 2010.
Heidegger, Martin. *Discourse on Thinking: A Translation of* Gelassenheit. Translated by John M. Anderson and E. Hans Freund, 43–57. New York: Harper & Row, 1966.
Heidegger, Martin. *The End of Philosophy*. Translated by Joan Stambaugh. New York: Harper and Row, 1973.
Heidegger, Martin. *Four Seminars*. Translated by Andrew Mitchell and François Raffoul. Bloomington: Indiana University Press, 2004.
Heidegger, Martin. *The Fundamental Concepts of Metaphysics*. Translated by William McNeill and Nicholas Walker. Bloomington: Indiana University Press, 1995.

Heidegger, Martin. 'Hebel – Friend of the House'. In Vol. 3 of *Contemporary German Philosophy*, edited by D. E. Christensen, translated by Bruce Foltz and Michael Heim, 89–101. University Park: Pennsylvania State University Press, 1983.
Heidegger, Martin. *The Heidegger Reader*. Edited by Günter Figal, translated by Jerome Veith, 305–9. Bloomington, IN: Indiana University Press, 2009.
Heidegger, Martin. *Identity and Difference*. Translated by Joan Stambaugh. Chicago: University of Chicago Press, 2002.
Heidegger, Martin. *Introduction to Metaphysics*. Translated by Gregory Fried and Richard Polt. New Haven: Yale University Press, 2000.
Heidegger, Martin. *Nature, History, State: 1933–1934*. Translated and edited by Gregory Fried and Richard Polt. London: Bloomsbury, 2013.
Heidegger, Martin. *Nietzsche*. Edited by David Farrell Krell. 2 vols. San Francisco: Harper & Row, 1979–87.
Heidegger, Martin. *Off the Beaten Track*. Translated by Julian Young and Kenneth Haynes, 157–99. Cambridge: Cambridge University Press, 2002.
Heidegger, Martin. *On the Way to Language*. Translated by Peter D. Hertz. New York: Harper and Row, 1971.
Heidegger, Martin. *Parmenides*. Translated by André Schuwer and Richard Rojcewicz. Bloomington: Indiana University Press, 1992.
Heidegger, Martin. *Pathmarks*. Edited by William McNeill, 239–76. Cambridge: Cambridge University Press, 1998.
Heidegger, Martin. 'The Pathway'. Translated by Thomas F. O'Meara. Revised by Thomas Sheehan. In *Heidegger: The Man and the Thinker*, edited by Thomas Sheehan, 69–72. Chicago: Precedent Publishing, 1981.
Heidegger, Martin. *The Principle of Reason*. Translated by Reginald Lilly. Bloomington: Indiana University Press, 1991.
Heidegger, Martin. *The Question Concerning Technology and Other Essays*. Translated by William Lovitt. New York: Harper and Row, 1977.
Heidegger, Martin. *What Is Called Thinking?* Translated by J. Glenn Gray. New York: Harper and Row, 1968.
Heidegger, Martin. 'Why Do I Stay in the Provinces?' In *Heidegger: The Man and the Thinker*, edited by Thomas Sheehan, 27–30. Chicago: Precedent, 1981.
Heidegger, Martin. *Zollikon Seminars*. Translated by Franz Mayr and Richard Askay. Evanston, IL: Northwestern University Press, 2001.
Heidegger, Martin. *Zur Sache des Denkens*. Vol. 14 of *Gesamtausgabe*. Edited by Friedrich-Wilhelm von Herrmann. Frankfurt: Klostermann, 2007.
Heynen, Hilde. *Architecture and Modernity*. Cambridge, MA: MIT Press, 1998.
Heynen, Hilde. 'Worthy of Question: Heidegger's Role in Architectural Theory'. *Archis* 12 (1993): 42–9.
Hicks, Dan, and Mary C. Beaudry, eds. *The Oxford Handbook of Material Culture Studies*. New York: Oxford University Press, 2010.
Hill, Geoffrey. *Collected Poems*. Harmondsworth: Penguin, 1985.
Hirst, Paul. *Space and Power: Politics, War and Architecture*. Oxford: Polity, 2005.
Husserl, Edmund. *The Crisis of European Sciences and Transcendental Phenomenology*. Translated by David Carr. Evanston, IL: Northwestern University Press, 1954.
Illies, Christian, and Nicholas Ray. *Philosophy of Architecture*. Cambridge: Cambridge Architectural Press, 2014.
Ingold, Tim. 'Building, Dwelling, Living: How Animals and People Make Themselves at Home in the World'. In *The Perception of the Environment: Essays on Livelihood, Dwelling and Skill*, 172–88. London: Routledge, 2000.

Ingold, Tim. 'Epilogue: Towards a Politics of Dwelling'. *Conservation and Society* 3 (2005): 501–8.
Jacobs, Jane. *The Death and Life of Great American Cities*. New York: Random House, 1961.
Jamme, Christoph. 'The Loss of Things: Cézanne – Rilke – Heidegger'. *Kunst & Museumjournaal* 2 (1990): 33–44.
Janicaud, Dominique. *Heidegger in France*. Translated by François Raffoul and David Pettigrew. Bloomington: Indiana University Press, 2015.
Jay, Martin. *Downcast Eyes: The Denigration of Vision in Twentieth-Century French Thought*. Berkeley: University of California Press, 1993.
Jentsch, Ernst. 'On the Psychology of the Uncanny (1906)'. Translated by Roy Sellars. *Angelaki* 2, no. 1 (1997): 7–16.
Jive'n, Gunila, and Peter J. Larkham. 'Sense of Place, Authenticity and Character: A Commentary'. *Journal of Urban Design* 8 (2003): 67–81.
Kahn, Louis. 'The Room, the Street, and Human Agreement'. *AIA Journal* 56 (September 1971): 33–4.
Kant, Immanuel. *Critique of Pure Reason*. Edited by Paul Guyer and Allen W. Wood. Cambridge: Cambridge University Press, 1998.
Kant, Immanuel. *Theoretical Philosophy, 1755–1770*. Translated and edited by David Walford in collaboration with Ralf Meerbote. Cambridge: Cambridge University Press, 1992.
Keiller, Patrick. *London*. Written, photographed, and edited by Patrick Keiller. Narrated by Paul Scofield. London: BFI and Koninck Studios, 1994. Released on video, London: BFI Video, 2012. DVD, 85 min.
Keiller, Patrick. *Robinson in Ruins*. Written, photographed, and edited by Patrick Keiller. Narrated by Vanessa Redgrave. London: Royal College of Art/Illuminations Films, 2010. Released on video, London: BFI Video, 2011. DVD, 101 min.
Keiller, Patrick. *Robinson in Space*. Written, photographed, and edited by Patrick Keiller. Narrated by Paul Scofield. London: BBC and Koninck Studios, 1997. Released on video, London: BFI Video, 2012. DVD, 82 min.
Kipnis, Jeffrey, and Thomas Leeser. *Chora L Works: Jacques Derrida and Peter Eisenman*. New York: Monacelli Press, 1997.
Kittler, Friedrich A. *Gramophone, Film, Typewriter*. Translated by Geoffrey Winthrop-Young and Michael Wutz. Stanford: Stanford University Press, 1999.
Korab-Karpowicz, W. Julian. 'Schopenhauer's Theory of Architecture'. In *A Companion to Schopenhauer*, edited by Bart Vandenabeele, 178–92. Malden, MA: Wiley-Blackwell, 2012.
Kropotkin, Pyotr. *Memoirs of a Revolutionary*. New York: Houghton Mifflin Company, 1899.
Kuhlmann, Dörte. *Gender Studies in Architecture: Space, Power and Difference*. London: Routledge, 2013.
Lahti, Markku, 'Alvar Aalto and the Beauty of the House'. In *Alvar Aalto: Towards a Human Modernism*, edited by Winfried Nerdinger. Munich: Prestel, 1999.
Le Corbusier (Charles Edouard Jeanneret). *Towards a New Architecture*. Translated by Frederick Etchells. New York: Dover Publications, 1986.
Leach, Neil. 'The Dark Side of the *Domus*'. *The Journal of Architecture* 3 (1998): 31–42.
Leach, Neil, ed. *Rethinking Architecture: A Reader in Cultural Theory*. New York: Routledge, 1977.
Leatherbarrow, David. 'In and Outside of Architecture'. In *Uncommon Ground: Architecture, Technology, and Topography*, 179–214. Cambridge, MA: MIT Press, 2000.

Leatherbarrow, David, and Mohsen Mostafavi. *On Weathering: The Life of Buildings in Time*. Cambridge, MA: MIT Press, 1993.
Lefas, Pavlos. *Dwelling and Architecture: From Heidegger to Koolhaas*. Berlin: Jovis Verlag, 2009.
Lefebvre, Henri. *The Production of Space*. Translated by Donald Nicolson-Smith. Oxford: Blackwell, 1991.
Lehtimaki, Kristiina, and Petri Neuvonen, eds. *Richard Leplastrier: Spirit of Nature Wood Architecture Award 2004*. Helsinki: Rakennustieto Publishing, 2004.
Levinas, Emmanuel. *Difficult Freedom: Essays on Judaism*. Translated by Sean Hand. Baltimore: The Johns Hopkins University Press, 1990.
Levinas, Emmanuel. *Entre Nous: Thinking-of-the-Other*. Translated by Michael Smith and Barbara Harshav. London: Continuum, 2002.
Levinas, Emmanuel. *Totality and Infinity: An Essay on Exteriority*. Translated by Alphonso Lingis. Pittsburgh: Duquesne University Press, 1969.
Liberman, Anatoly. 'Our Habitat: Dwelling'. *OUPblog, Oxford University Press's Academic Insights for the Thinking World*, 14 January 2015. Accessed May 2020, https://blog.oup.com/2015/01/dwelling-word-origin-etymology/.
Lindstrom, Randall. *Kenosis Creativity Architecture: Appearance through Emptying*. London: Routledge, 2021.
Lindstrom, Randall, and Jeff Malpas. 'The Modesty of Architecture'. In *Political Theory and Architecture*, edited by D. Bell and B. Zacka. London: Bloomsbury, 2020.
Long, Christopher. 'The Origins and Context of Adolf Loos's "Ornament and Crime"'. *Journal of the Society of Architectural Historians* 68 (2009): 200–23.
Long, Christopher. 'Ornament, Crime, Myth, and Meaning'. In *Architecture: Material and Imagined, Proceedings of the 85th ACSA Annual Meeting and Technology Conference*, 440–5. Washington, DC: Association of Collegiate Schools of Architecture, 1997.
Loos, Adolf. *Ornament and Crime: Thoughts on Design and Materials*. Translated by Shaun Whiteside. Harmondsworth: Penguin, 2019.
Lopes, Dominic M. M. 'Art Media and the Sense Modalities: Tactile Pictures'. *Philosophical Quarterly* 47 (1997): 425–40.
Lucretius. *Lucretius on the Nature of Things*. A translation of *De Rerum Naturae* by Cyril Bailey. Oxford: Clarendon Press, 1910.
Luria, A. R. *The Mind of a Mnemonist*. Translated by L. Solotaroff. Cambridge, MA: Harvard University Press, 1987.
Lyotard, Jean-François. 'Domus and the Megalopolis'. In *The Inhuman: Reflections on Time*, 191–204. Cambridge: Polity Press, 1991.
Malpas, Jeff. 'The Beginning of Understanding: Event, Place, Truth'. In *Consequences of Hermeneutics*, edited by Jeff Malpas and Santiago Zabala, 261–80. Chicago: Northwestern University Press, 2010.
Malpas, Jeff. *Heidegger and the Thinking of Place: Explorations in the Topology of Being*. Cambridge, MA: MIT Press, 2012.
Malpas, Jeff. *Heidegger's Topology: Being, Place, World*. Cambridge, MA: MIT Press, 2006.
Malpas, Jeff. 'On the Reading of Heidegger: Situating the Black Notebooks'. In *Reading Heidegger's Black Notebooks, 1931–1941*, edited by Ingo Farin and Jeff Malpas, 3–22. Cambridge, MA: MIT Press, 2015.
Malpas, Jeff. *Place and Experience: A Philosophical Topography*. 2nd ed. London: Routledge, 2018.
Malpas, Jeff. 'Place and the Problem of Landscape'. In *The Place of Landscape: Concepts, Contexts, Studies*, edited by Jeff Malpas, 3–26. Cambridge, MA: MIT Press, 2011.

Malpas, Jeff. 'Place and Singularity'. In *The Intelligence of Place: Topographies and Poetics*, edited by Jeff Malpas, 65–92. London: Bloomsbury, 2015.
Malpas, Jeff. 'Place and Situation'. In *The Routledge Companion to Hermeneutics*, edited by Jeff Malpas and Hans-Helmuth Gander, 354–66. London: Routledge, 2017.
Malpas, Jeff. 'Placing Understanding/Understanding Place'. *Sophia: International Journal of Philosophy and Traditions* 56, no. 3 (2017): 379–91.
Malpas, Jeff. 'The Weave of Meaning: Holism and Contextuality'. *Language and Communication* 22 (2002): 403–19.
Mattens, Filip. 'The Aesthetics of Space: Modern Architecture and Photography'. *The Journal of Aesthetics and Art Criticism* 69 (2011): 105–14.
Maturana, Humberto, and Fransisco Varela. *Autopoiesis and Cognition: The Realization of the Living*. Dordrecht: Reidel, 1980.
McCahon, Colin. 'Ideas and Reflections – A McCahon Miscellany'. In *Colin McCahon: Gates and Journeys*, edited by Michael Gifkins. Auckland, NZ: Auckland City Art Gallery, 1988.
McCarter, Robert. *The Space Within: Interior Experience as the Origin of Architecture*. London: Reaktion, 2016.
McCarthy, Christine. 'Toward a Definition of Interiority'. *Space and Culture* 8 (2005): 112–25.
Meagher, Mark, and Peter Blundell Jones. *Architecture and Movement: The Dynamic Experience of Buildings and Landscapes*. London: Routledge, 2014.
Menges, Achim. 'Computational Material Culture'. In *Parametricism 2.0: Rethinking Architecture's Agenda for the 21st Century*. Special issue, *Architectural Design* 86 (2016): 76–83.
Menin, Sarah, and Flora Samuel. *Nature and Space: Aalto and Le Corbusier*. London: Routledge, 2003.
Metcalf, Robert. 'Rethinking "Bodenständigkeit" in the Technological Age'. *Research in Phenomenology* 42 (2012): 49–66.
Mildenberger, Florian. *Umwelt als Vision: Leben und Werk Jakob von Uexkülls (1864–1944)*. Stuttgart: Franz Steiner, 2007.
Milmo, Cahal. 'London's New Skyscrapers "Inflict Serious Harm" on Capital's Historic Landscape, Heritage Watchdog Warns'. *The Independent*, 10 December 2015. Accessed June 2020, https://www.independent.co.uk/arts-entertainment/architecture/londons-new-skyscrapers-inflict-serious-harm-on-capitals-historic-landscape-warns-heritage-watchdog-a6767296.html.
Minkenberg, Michael, ed. *Power and Architecture: The Construction of Capitals and the Politics of Space*. New York: Berghahn, 2014.
Mitias, Michael, ed. *Philosophy and Architecture*. Amsterdam: Rodopi, 1994.
Moeller, Hans-Georg, and Andrew K. Whitehead, eds. *About Landscape and Travelling East and West: A Philosophical Journey*. London: Bloomsbury, 2014.
Moore, Rowan. 'How a High-Rise Craze Is Ruining London's Skyline'. *The Guardian*, 2 December 2012. Accessed June 2020, https://www.theguardian.com/artanddesign/2012/dec/02/london-high-rise-craze-ruins-skyline.
Mörchen, Hermann. *Adorno und Heidegger: Untersuchung einer philosophischen Kommunikationsverweigerung*. Stuttgart: Klett-Cotta, 1981.
Mugerauer, Robert. *Heidegger and Homecoming: The Leitmotif in the Later Writings*. Toronto: University of Toronto Press, 2008.
Mugerauer, Robert. *Interpreting Environments: Tradition, Deconstruction, Hermeneutics*. Austin: University of Texas Press, 2014.

Mugerauer, Robert. *Responding to Loss: Heideggerian Readings of Literature, Architecture, and Film*. New York: Fordham, 2015.
Natanson, Maurice. 'Alfred Schutz on Social Reality and Social Science'. *Social Research* 35 (1968): 217–44.
Neske, G. *Errinerung an Martin Heidegger*. Pfullingen: Neske, 1977.
Nietzsche, Friedrich. *The Genealogy of Morals/Ecce Homo*. Translated by Walter Kaufmann. New York: Vintage, 1989.
Norberg-Schulz, Christian. *The Concept of Dwelling: On the Way to Figurative Architecture*. New York: Rizzoli, 1985.
Norberg-Schulz, Christian. *Existence, Space and Architecture*. London: Vista, 1971.
Norberg-Schulz, Christian. *Genius Loci: Towards a Phenomenology of Architecture*. New York: Rizzoli, 1980.
Norberg-Schulz, Christian. 'Heidegger's Thinking on Architecture'. *Perspecta* 20 (1983): 61–8.
Norberg-Schulz, Christian. *Intentions in Architecture*. Cambridge, MA: MIT Press, 1962.
Obrador-Pons, Pau. 'Dwelling'. In *Companion Encyclopaedia of Geography: From Local to Global*, edited by I. Douglas, R. Huggett and C. Perkins. London: Routledge, 2006.
O'Donoghue, Brendan. *A Poetics of Homecoming: Heidegger, Homelessness and the Homecoming Venture*. Newcastle-Upon-Tyne: Cambridge Scholars Publishing, 2011.
O'Reilly, R. N. Introduction to *Colin McCahon: A Survey Exhibition*. Auckland, NZ: Auckland Art Gallery, 1972.
Ouf, A. M. S. 'Authenticity and the Sense of Place in Urban Design'. *Journal of Urban Design* 6 (2001): 73–86.
Pallasmaa, Juhani. *The Eyes of the Skin: Architecture and the Senses*. Chichester, UK: Wiley, 2012. First published 1996.
Pallasmaa, Juhani. 'From Tectonics to Painterly Architecture'. In *Encounters 1: Architectural Essays*, 212–21. Helsinki: Rakenustieto Oy, 2013.
Pallasmaa, Juhani. 'Place and Atmosphere'. In *The Intelligence of Place: Topographies and Poetics*, edited by Jeff Malpas, 129–56. London: Bloomsbury, 2015.
Pérez-Gómez, Alberto. *Attunement: Architectural Meaning after the Crisis of Modern Science*. Cambridge, MA: MIT Press, 2017.
Pérez-Gómez, Alberto. 'The Place Is Not a Postcard: The Problem with *Genius Loci*'. In *An Eye for Place: Christian Norberg-Schulz; Architect, Historian and Editor*, edited by Gro Lauvlandet, Karl Otto Ellefsen, Mari Hvattum. Oslo: Akademisk Publisering, 2009.
Petzet, Heinrich. *Encounters and Dialogues with Martin Heidegger, 1929–1976*. Translated by Parvis Emad and Kenneth Maly. Chicago: University of Chicago Press, 1993.
Piazzoni, M. F. 'Authenticity Makes the City. How "the Authentic" Affects the Production of Space'. In *Planning for Authenticities*, edited by L. Tate and B. Shannon, 154–69. New York: Routledge, 2018.
Piranesi, Giovanni Battista. *The Prisons (Le Carceri): The Complete First and Second States*. New York: Dover, 1973.
Poole, Matthew, and Manuel Shvartzberg, eds. *The Politics of Parametricism: Digital Technologies in Architecture*. London: Bloomsbury, 2015.
'Power and Architecture: Public Space and the Post-Soviet City'. Report on events presented at Calvert 22, 10 June to 9 October 2016. *The Calvert Journal*. http://www.calvertjournal.com/features/show/6155/special-report-power-and-architecture.
Proust, Marcel. *In Search of Lost Time*. Translated by C. K. Scott Moncrieff and Terence Kilmartin. Revised by D. J. Enright. London: Chatto and Windus, 1992.
Rand, Ayn. *The Fountainhead*. New York: Penguin, 1994.
Rapaport, Amos. *House Form and Culture*. Englewood Cliffs, NJ: Prentice-Hall, 1969.

Rasmussen, Steen Eilar. *Experiencing Architecture*. Cambridge, MA: MIT Press, 1962.
Reidy, Peter. 'Frank Lloyd Wright and Ayn Rand'. *The Atlas Society* (website), 7 July 2010. Accessed June 2020, https://www.atlassociety.org/post/frank-lloyd-wright-and-ayn-rand.
Relph, Edward. *Modern Urban Landscapes*. Baltimore: Johns Hopkins University Press, 1987.
Relph, Edward. *Place and Placelessness*. London: Pion, 1976.
Relph, Edward. *Rational Landscapes and Humanistic Geography*. New York: Barnes and Noble, 1981.
Rhetorica ad Herennium. Translated by Harry Caplan. Loeb Classical Library. Cambridge, MA: Harvard University Press, 1954.
Rice, Charles. *The Emergence of the Interior: Architecture, Modernity, Domesticity*. London: Routledge, 2006.
Richardson, William. *Heidegger: Through Phenomenology to Thought*. The Hague: Martinus Nijhoff, 1963.
Ruskin, John. *The Seven Lamps of Architecture*. London: Smith, Elder & Co., 1849.
Samuel, Flora. *Le Corbusier and the Architectural Promenade*. Basel: Birkhäuser, 2011.
Samuel, Flora, and Peter Blundell Jones. 'The Making of Architectural Promenade: Villa Savoye and Schminke House'. *Architectural Research Quarterly* 16 (June 2012): 108–24.
Samuels, Marwyn S. 'Existentialism and Human Geography'. In *Human Geography: Problems and Prospects*, edited by David Ley and Marwyn S. Samuels, 23–40. London: Croom Helm, 1978.
Sanders, Joel. Introduction to *Stud: Architectures of Masculinity*. Edited by Joel Sanders, 11–12. New York: Princeton Architectural Press, 1996.
Schama, Simon. *Landscape and Memory*. London: HarperCollins, 1998.
Sharr, Adam. *Heidegger for Architects*. London: Routledge, 2007.
Sharr, Adam. *Heidegger's Hut*. Cambridge, MA: MIT Press, 2006.
Schildt, Göran. *Alavar Aalto: The Early Years*. New York: Rizzoli, 1984.
Schilli, Hermann. *Das Schwarzwaldhaus*. Stuttgart: W. Kohlhammer, 1953.
Schopenhauer, Arthur. *The World as Will and Representation*. Translated by E. F. J. Payne. New York: Dover, 1969.
Schumacher, Patrik. *The Autopoiesis of Architecture: A New Agenda for Architecture*. 2 vols. London: John Wiley & Sons Ltd, 2012.
Schürmann, Reiner. *Heidegger on Being and Acting: From Principles to Anarchy*. Translated by Christine-Marie Gros. Bloomington: Indiana University Press, 1987.
Schürmann, Reiner. *Meister Eckhart, Mystic and Philosopher: Translations with Commentary*. Bloomington: Indiana University Press, 1978.
Schuster, Martin. 'A Phenomenology of Home: Jean Améry on Homesickness'. *Journal of French and Francophone Philosophy – Revue de la philosophie française et de langue française* 24 (2016): 117–27.
Schutz, Alfred. *The Phenomenology of the Social World*. Translated by G. Walsh and F. Lehnert. Evanston, IL: Northwestern University Press, 1967.
Scruton, Roger. *The Aesthetics of Architecture*. Princeton, NJ: Princeton University Press, 1979.
Scully, Vincent. *The Earth, the Temple, and the Gods*. New Haven: Yale University Press, 1962.
Seamon, David. *A Geography of the Lifeworld: Movement, Rest and Encounter*. London: Croom Helm, 1979.

Seamon, David. *Place: Phenomenology, Lifeworlds and Place Making.* London: Routledge, 2018.
Seamon, David, and Robert Mugerauer. *Dwelling, Place and Environment: An Introduction.* Dordrecht: Martinus Nijhof, 1985.
Sebald, W. G. *Austerlitz.* Translated by Anthea Bell. London: Hamish Hamilton, 2001.
Sebald, W. G. *The Rings of Saturn.* Translated by Michael Hulse. London: New Directions Books, 1998.
Seyfarth, Robert M., and Dorothy L. Cheney. *The Social Origins of Language.* Edited by Michael L. Platt. Princeton, NJ: Princeton University Press, 2017.
Sharr, Adam. 'Can Architecture Lie? On Truth, Knowledge and Contemporary Architectural Theory'. *Architectural Theory Review* 8 (2003): 164–72.
Simmel, Georg. *Simmel on Culture.* Edited by David Frisby and Mike Featherstone. London: Sage, 1997.
Snodgrass, Adrian, and Richard Coyne. *Interpretation in Architecture: Design as a Way of Thinking.* London: Routledge, 2006.
Sovik, Edward A. 'Five Easy Pieces'. *Journal of Architectural Education* 42 (1989): 58–60.
Spector, Tom. 'Architecture and the Ethics of Authenticity'. *Journal of Aesthetic Education* 45 (2011): 23–33.
Spector, Tom. *The Ethical Architect: The Dilemma of Contemporary Practice.* New York: Princeton Architectural Press, 2001.
Sternberger, Dolf. 'Response to presentation by José Ortega y Gasset'. In *Mensch und Raum: Darmstädter Gespräch 1951*, edited by Otto Bartning, 124–9. Darmstadt: Neue Darmstädter Verlagsanstalt, 1952.
Sternberger, Dolf, Gerhard Storz and Wilhelm Emanuel Süskind. *Aus dem Wörterbuch des Unmenschen* [From the Dictionary of the Inhuman]. Hamburg: Claassen, 1945.
Strauss, Erwin. *The Primary World of the Senses.* Translated by Jacob Needleman. New York: Macmillan, 1963.
Sullivan, Louis H. 'The Tall Office Building Artistically Considered'. *Lippincott's Magazine,* March 1896, 408.
Taylor, Robert R. *The Word in Stone: The Role of Architecture in the National Socialist Ideology.* Berkeley: University of California Press, 1974.
Tonner, Philip. *Dwelling: Heidegger, Archaeology, Mortality.* London: Routledge, 2017.
Trawny, Peter. 'Heidegger and the Shoa'. In *Reading Heidegger's Black Notebooks, 1931–1941,* edited by Ingo Farin and Jeff Malpas, 169–94. Cambridge, MA: MIT Press, 2015.
Trilling, Lionel. *Sincerity and Authenticity.* Cambridge, MA: Harvard University Press, 1971.
Vales, Lawrence J. *Architecture, Power, and National Identity.* New York: Routledge, 2008.
Venturi, Robert, Denise Scott Brown, and Steven Izenour. *Learning from Las Vegas.* (Cambridge MA: MIT Press, 1972).
Vernant, Jean-Pierre. 'Hestia – Hermes: The Religious Expression of Space and Movement among the Greeks'. *Social Science Information* 8 (1969):131–68.
Vidler, Anthony. *The Architectural Uncanny: Essays in the Modern Unhomely.* Cambridge, MA: MIT Press, 1992.
Vidler, Anthony. 'Nothing to Do with Architecture'. *Grey Room* 21 (2005): 112–27.
Virilio, Paul. *Speed and Politics: An Essay on Dromology.* Translated by Marc Polizzotti. New York: Semiotext(e), 1986.
Vycinas, Vincent. *Earth and Gods.* The Hague: Martinus Nijhof, 1961.
Weil, Simone. *The Need for Roots: Prelude to a Declaration of Duties toward Mankind.* Translated by Arthur Wills. New York: Routledge, 2002.

Wigley, Mark. *The Architecture of Deconstruction: Derrida's Haunt*. Cambridge, MA: MIT Press, 1993.
Wigley, Mark. 'Heidegger's House: The Violence of the Domestic'. *Columbia Documents of Architecture and Theory* 1 (1992): 91–121.
Wijdeveld, Paul. *Ludwig Wittgenstein, Architect*. London: Thames & Hudson, 1994.
Wilken, Rowan. 'The Critical Reception of Christian Norberg-Schulz's Writings on Heidegger and Place'. *Architectural Theory Review* 18 (2015): 340–55.
Williams, Raymond. *The Country and the City*. London: Chatto and Windus, 1973.
Wilson, Colin St John. *The Other Tradition of Modern Architecture: The Uncompleted Project*. London: Academy Editions, 1995.
Wirth, Arthur G., and Carl Bewig. 'John Dewey on School Architecture'. *The Journal of Aesthetic Education* 2 (1968): 79–86.
Wittgenstein, Ludwig. *Philosophical Investigations*. Translated by G. E. M. Anscombe. Oxford: Blackwell, 1953.
Wocke, Brendon. 'Derrida at Villette: (An)aesthetic of Space'. *University of Toronto Quarterly* 83 (2014): 739–55.
Woessner, Martin V. *Heidegger in America*. Cambridge: Cambridge University Press, 2011.
Wrathall, Mark A. *Heidegger and Unconcealment: Truth, Language, and History*. Cambridge: Cambridge University Press, 2011.
Von Wright, G. H. 'Dante between Ulysses and Faust'. In *Knowledge and the Sciences in Medieval Philosophy*. Vol. 48, *Acta Philosophica Fennica*, edited by Monika Asztalos, John E. Murdoch and Ilkka Niiniluoto, 1–9. Helsinki: Philosophical Society of Finland, 1990.
Yates, Frances A. *The Art of Memory*. Chicago: University of Chicago Press, 1966.
Young, Julian. *Heidegger's Philosophy of Art*. Cambridge: Cambridge University Press, 2001.
Zimmerman, Claire. *Photographic Architecture in the Twentieth Century*. Minneapolis: University of Minnesota Press, 2014.
Zumthor, Peter. *Atmospheres: Architectural Environments, Surrounding Objects*. Basel: Birkhäuser, 2006.
Zumthor, Peter. *Thinking Architecture*. Basel: Birkhäuser, 1999.

INDEX

Aalto, Alvar 2, 40, 75, 102, 167, 206n6, 207n23, 208n34
   and art 82–4, 86
   and function/functionalism 78–9, 82 (*see also* functionalism)
   and Martin Heidegger 75–88, 102–3
   and materiality 84–5
   and nature 77–9, 82, 83, 86
   and the sketch/the act of sketching 84
   and spatialized thinking 84–5
   and technology/rationalization 86, 87, 208n43
Aboriginal culture, Australia 107
Acropolis 126, 216n13
Adorno, Theodor 24, 37, 38, 41, 57–62, 70, 199n20, 200n2, 202n20
aesthetic theory 94
Alexander, Christopher 18
Améry, Jean 111
anarchism 82
Anchibasie or Αγχιβασιν 176
Apache, the (Native American peoples) 107
appearance/coming to presence 69, 83
architecture (also design, and architectural design):
   as active engagement in the world 86, 146, 185
   and authenticity 53–60, 89
   boundedness of 142, 148, 154–7, 165, 167, 187–8
   and 'Building Dwelling Thinking' 45, 51–2, 71–2, 75–6, 135
   building(s) in the domain of dwelling 39, 51, 77–8, 122–3, 135, 165, 187
   and built form 10, 25, 39–40, 62, 80–2, 97, 113, 123
   and its constituting surfaces (walls, floors, ceilings, etc.) 155
   and the contemporary situation 16–17, 18, 111, 116–17, 169
   in contemporary urban settings 155, 157–65
   and drawing 123–4, 139 (*see also* line, surface)
   as *Ereignis* (event of appropriation) 58–9
   its ethical function 87, 97, 181–2 (*see also* ethics/ethical)
   and function (*see* functionalism, functionality/utility)
   its groundedness in thinking 87–8
   heritage or historical 54
   high-rise (verticality) (*see* architecture in contemporary urban settings)
   and the human 80, 85–6, 123 (*see also* human, humanism)
   and 'iconic' buildings 56
   interiority of 168–9, 175
   line and surface in (*see* line, surface)
   and materiality 84–5, 96–7, 112–14, 114–16
   and memory (via place) 106–7, 112, 119–20, 121 (*see also* memory, place)
   and Modernism 77, 78, 102, 157–65, 167
   narrative/storytelling in 118–19, 144–6
   ontology (fundamental nature) of 10, 89, 95, 120
   and ornamentation 96, 133, 212n26
   and philosophy in practice 76
   and place, situatedness 10, 35–6, 45, 51, 71–2, 75, 85–6, 103, 120, 135, 140, 148, 165, 182–5, 188 (*see also* place)
   and 'play' or artistic playfulness 81–2
   as poetic measure-taking 49–50
   and prioritization of the representational, conceptual, visual 93–5, 97, 116, 145, 170
   and releasement 187–8 (*see also* releasement/releasing, Heidegger and *Gelassenheit*)

and representational/reproduced
modes (i.e., photography) (*see*
representation/reproduction)
as response to the question of human
dwelling, human living 46, 75,
76–7, 80, 85–6, 86–7, 103, 120, 185,
187–8
and romantic materialism 112–14
as sensory experience 84, 211n19,
222n36
and 'simple oneness' 15–16
and 'starchitects' 56
and the street (withdrawal from)
156–7, 160–5
and 'strong' authenticity 55–6, 58–9
as structures of power (*see* power)
and technological interconnection
164–5
as textual or discursive practice 84,
118–19, 210n8
topology of 50, 102–3
and transparency 92
truth in 89–103, 209n5 (*see also*
truth (and assertion, appearance,
opening))
and the uncanny 17, 31, 111
and the vernacular, indigenous or
traditional 40, 54, 80
viewpoints *of* and *in* ('bird's-eye', or
apart, and 'located', or within)
169–70, 172, 179, 220n12
as visualizing and imagining 84
Aristotle 69, 90, 115, 131, 143, 176
ars memorativa 107
Augé, Marc 152
authenticity 52–3, 53–60, 64
Authentizität vs. *Eigentlichkeit* (also
eigentlich) 57–9, 200n39
and *Echtheit* 215n25
and *Ereignis* 58–9
and the Greek *authentes* 55
and sincerity 203n24
its 'strong' sense 55–7, 58–9, 95,
202n16
and truth 89, 95, 117 (*see also* truth
(and assertion, appearance,
opening))
in urban planning and design 54–6
its 'weak' sense 53–4, 58–60, 95

Bachelard, Gaston 26, 107, 110, 152, 163
Baroque planning and design 124
Bartning, Otto 19–20, 24, 65, 71
Basso, Keith 107
Baudrillard, Jean 1, 118
Bauhaus movement 96
being, being-in-the-world 9–10, 20–3, 45, 66,
77, 105, 121, 149, 170–2, 175–6, 183
Benjamin, Walter 24, 38, 67, 101, 107, 117,
157, 193n29, 193n30, 198n6
'One-Way Street' 92
Berger, Peter 29
Bergson, Henri 82
Bernstein, Fred A. 162
Bloch, Ernst 65
Blundell Jones, Peter 53–5, 201n5
Borges, Jorge Luis 112
Borgmann, Albert 193n15
bound(s), boundedness (and limits) 67,
69–72, 142–4, 184–5, 187–8, 217n5
in creating inner and outer 154–7,
164–5, 167–8 (*see also* interiority)
and entry, threshold, liminality 167,
176–7 (*see also* liminality)
modernity's antagonism towards 69
restrictive vs. productive 69, 154, 177
of truth 103
Bourdieu, Pierre 152
Braque, George 179
Broadway Malyan, architects 162–3, 219n22
Bruno, Giordano 124
building (*Bauen*), to build:
as active engagement in the world
85–6, 122, 146, 185
as attentiveness to place 102–3, 188
and design or project/projection
(*Entwurf*) 76, 206n5
as embodied action/activity 66, 121–3
ethics of 181–2
as grounded in dwelling, to 'let dwell'
(*Wohnenlassen*) 20, 22, 76–7, 80, 86,
105, 187
and language 122
and memory 105–20
as memory-forming 113–14
as opening up of place 113, 132
and thinking and dwelling 48–50, 66,
105, 122, 134, 182–3, 188
(*see also* dwelling, thinking)

'Building Dwelling Thinking' ('Bauen
  Wohnen Denken', 1951) 1–5, 8–11,
  16–36, 38–9, 51–2, 57, 64, 66–7, 69,
  71–2, 75–6, 98, 101–2, 105–6, 120,
  121, 133–4, 135, 151, 170–1, 181–3
Burra Charter (Australia ICOMOS
  Charter) 201n9, 217n4
Buttimer, Anne 25–7, 35, 41, 52, 195n44,
  195n51

Cacciari, Massimo 38, 41–3, 49, 52, 110
Canary Wharf (London) 158, 162
capitalism (contemporary, technologized,
  globalized) 118, 155, 163, 164–5
Cartesian thought *See* Descartes, René,
  and Cartesian thought
Casey, Edward 108, 110
Cézanne, Paul 82–4, 208n32
Char, René 174
Chartres Cathedral (labyrinth) 128–9
chora 2
Citicorp Building (now 601 Lexington,
  NYC) 163–4
cognitive science/philosophy of mind (and
  Extended Mind Thesis) 66, 71, 151
Colomina, Beatriz 116
constructionism (and essentialism) 61–2
correlationism 8
Coyne, Richard 145–6
critical engagement, critique 43, 53, 62
Critical Regionalism 135, 195n37
critical theory 200n2

Dasein (being here/there) 21, 28–9, 31, 46,
  56–8, 66, 76, 121, 170–2 *See also*
  interiority
de Certeau, Michel 152
Debord, Guy 152
democracy 92
Derrida, Jacques 1, 2
Descartes, René, and Cartesian thought
  20–1, 31, 66–7, 70–1, 97, 124, 151,
  171–2, 212n28
design thinking 87–8
Dewey, John 1
Docklands (Melbourne) 158, 160–3
Doha 163
Dreyfus, Hubert 39
Dubai 162–3

dwelling *(Wohnen)*, to dwell 3–5, 198n10
  articulation in built form 39–41, 77–8,
    80, 187–8
  as being in place, at home, in the
    world 17, 45, 51, 68–9, 77, 106, 122,
    170–2, 187
  definitions 32–3, 194n34
  and embedded contrasts 17–18, 37
  as embodied action/activity 122–3, 133–4
  failure of 38, 42
  in geography 25–26, 30, 41
  and home or *domus* 34, 65
  vs. at home *(zu Hause)* 33–4, 39, 45, 77
  in Levinas 205n51
  and modernity 15–18, 24, 26, 36, 37,
    38–41
  as necessarily constitutive of human
    being 42, 47
  and notions of homeland *(Heimat)*,
    nationalism, and the static 17 (*see
    also* home, homeland)
  and notions of past, romantic,
    nostalgic, provincial and the like
    15–19, 39–41, 52
  and place 5–6, 16–36, 17–19, 45, 72,
    77, 135, 188
  and the poetic 48–9
  and possibility 46, 133
  and proper measure 149
  quantitative vs. qualitative definition 25
  as relating human being and place,
    space, world 25, 51, 68, 78–82, 85–6
  stereotypical view of 41
  and thinking and building 45–50, 105,
    134, 182–3, 188
  as translation of *Wohnen* 18, 24, 31–5,
    41, 170, 183, 188, 193n30
  and truth 102
  (*see also* building, thinking)

Eckhart, Meister 185–7, 223n15
Eisenman, Peter 1, 18, 93, 97, 101, 168,
  211n21
Elden, Stuart 151
environmental thought 173
Ereignis (event of appropriation) 58–9, 175
essence, essential, essentialism (also
  foundationalism 19, 43, 52–3,
  60–3, 64

ethics/ethical/ethos 10–11, 47, 110, 181–3, 223n1
  as the function of architecture/building 87, 97, 181–4, 188
  Levinasian ethics of hospitality 67
exclusion 52, 60, 62–3, 64–9
  in architecture 155, 158
exile/displacement 15–16, 18, 68
existential (vs. ontological) 27
extension 20, 83

Foster, Norman 92
Foucault, Michel 151, 154
The Fountainhead 55–7
fourfold, the 21–3, 39, 49, 58, 63, 69, 78, 83, 84, 101, 134
Frampton, Kenneth 24–5, 135, 195n37
Frankfurt School 41
functionalism, functionality/utility 54, 78–82, 93, 181, 188
  and form 95

Gagarin, Yuri 68, 70, 121, 204n50, 205n55
Gehry, Frank 135
Gelassenheit See releasement/releasing, Heidegger and *Gelassenheit*
God 187
Greenough, Horatio 95
Gropius, Walter 79
groundedness or rootedness (*Bodenständigkeit*) 38, 111
grounds, beginnings, origins, (first) principles 9–10, 105, 186, 188
Guignon, Charles 59

Hacking, Ian 64
Hadid, Zaha 135–6
Harries, Karsten 11, 41, 87, 182–5
Heidegger, Martin 1
  and Alvar Aalto 75–88
  and architecture 1–2, 71–2, 76, 86, 181
  and art/artists 82–3, 190n12, 208n32
  and authenticity *see* authenticity
  Being and Time (1927) 20–1, 28, 31, 46, 56–8, 66, 76, 121, 151, 170–2, 175, 185, 191n23
  birthplace *see* Messkirch, Germany
  and the Black Forest farmhouse 15–16, 22–3, 39–41, 43, 80
  and the bridge, the *Alte Brücke* (Old Bridge) 22–3, 39, 177
  and building (*see* building, to build)
  and 'Building Dwelling Thinking' (1951) (*see* 'Building Dwelling Thinking')
  and the country path conversation 173–6, 185–7
  and *Dasein* (*see Dasein*)
  and dwelling (*see* dwelling)
  and English language, engagement with 194n35
  and *Ereignis* (event) 58–9, 175
  and essentialism (*see* essence)
  and exclusionary thinking (*see* exclusion)
  and the fourfold (*see* fourfold)
  and *Gelassenheit* (releasement) 185–8
  and gender 207n17
  and the Greek temple 99–100
  and the hand, handiness, ready-to-hand, present-at-hand 121–3, 171–2, 215n3
  and his hut at Todtnauberg 40
  and home, homeland (*see* home, homeland *(Heimat)*)
  and homelessness (*see* homelessness)
  and human freedom 7, 110, 186
  and humanism/the human (*see* human (human being), 'Letter on "Humanism"')
  and identity and belonging (*see* identity and belonging)
  and language (incl. word) 8–9, 122–3, 191n26 (*see also* language)
  and Le Corbusier 190n13
  and Meister Eckhart (*see* Heidegger and *Gelassenheit*, Eckhart)
  and Nazism, anti-Semitism 3, 52, 65, 201n4
  and nostalgic, provincial, mystical or poetic thinking 23, 33, 38, 39–40, 43, 110, 173
  and ontological inquiry 62, 105, 191n29
  and philosophical anthropology 7
  and place (*see* place, topology)
  and reality/the real 203n37, 230n21
  and 'simple oneness' 15–16

and spatialized thinking 84–5
and technology, critique of 138, 198n14, 199n27, 208n43
and thinking (also poetizing) 4–5, 8–9, 48–50, 105–6, 149, 151 (*see also* thinking/rethinking)
and truth 90, 98–103 (*see also* truth (and assertion, appearance, opening))
and wartime destruction 193n19
and 'Why Do I Stay in the Provinces?' (radio talk) 198n16
Heidelberg 22
Heraclitus 176
hermeneutics 28, 66, 191n26
Hermes 176
Hestia 176
Heydar Aliyev Center, Baku (Hadid) 135–6
Heynen, Hilde 16–19, 37, 38, 41, 45, 49, 60–62
Hill, Geoffrey 179
Hirst, Paul 158
Hitler, Adolf 152
Hölderlin, Friedrich 48
home, homeland (*Heimat*) 17, 51, 68, 80, 110–11, 185–6, 188
and place 64–9, 77, 111
and self 65
as something chosen 68
homelessness: as ancient, inevitable and surmountable 43–4, 46
as both 'physical' and 'intellectual/spiritual' 19–20, 37
and the contemporary condition 37–50, 51–2, 68, 198n10
giving thought to 46–7, 52
and home 44–5, 68–9
(*see also* uncanny/unhomely (*unheimlich*), *or* homeless)
horizon/horizontality 68–9, 70, 83, 86, 106, 175–6, 177–9, 205n55, 205n56, 221n28, 222n32
human (human being):
biological 6–7, 31
and the body, embodiment 27, 66, 106, 121–3, 133–4
and bounds or limits ('between') 7, 177–9, 186
and *Dasein* 21, 46, 66

and freedom/questionability 7, 46, 68–9, 110, 177, 188
and its grounding in and through dwelling 51, 186
and its placed/topological character 45, 65–6, 85–6, 119–20, 121, 146, 151, 184–5
and the world (externalized or extended into, internalized or separated from) 20–3, 35, 66–7, 75, 78, 108, 146
humanism 3, 7, 26–7, 78–82, 102
Husserl, Edmund 28

identity and belonging/sameness and difference 53, 60, 62–3, 69, 188, 200n30
Ingold, Tim 30, 35, 46, 197n67
interiority (and exteriority) 2, 106, 108–9, 130, 131, 155, 220n13, 220n15
and boundedness 167
as 'in-ness' (and 'there-ness' or 'here-ness') 170–2, 193n22, 220n14
and landscape 172–6, 221n27
and the 'room' 155, 167, 168

Jacob, Jane 157
Jaspers, Karl 64
Jewish Museum Berlin 92
Johnson, Philip 164

Kahn, Louis 155, 157, 167, 168, 176
Kantian thought 176, 222n32
Keiller, Patrick 15–16, 26, 37, 38, 39, 49, 65
kindness (*Freundlichkeit*) 49
Kittler, Friedrich 122
Koolhaas, Rem 93
Kropotkin, Pyotr 82, 207n23

La Défense (Paris) 158, 160–61, 163
landscape and nature 172–6, 221n26, 221n28 (*see also* Aalto and nature)
language 8–9, 42, 97, 109, 122
of/in architecture 89–95, 144–6
Le Corbusier (Charles-Édouard Jeanneret) 53, 77, 79, 124–6, 129, 167, 169, 216n13
Leach, Neil 17–18, 34, 37, 38, 49, 58
Leatherbarrow, David 116, 190n15

Lefas, Pavlos 33
Lefebvre, Henri 152, 154
Léger, Fernand 82
LeMessurier, William 163
Leplastrier, Richard 113–14
'Letter on "Humanism"' 3, 78, 183
letting be (in place) 49, 52, 69–70, 142
Levinas, Emmanuel 67–9, 121, 205n56
    spatial vs. topological perspective 70–2, 94, 205n51, 221n21
Libeskind, Daniel 92–3
lifeworld 25–8, 196n55
liminality 176–9
    as door, threshold, entry into 176
    and horizon *(horismos)* 177–9 (*see also* horizon/horizonality)
    as opening, freeing 177
    as separating and connecting 177
        (*see also* Heidegger and the bridge)
    (*see also* bound(s), boundedness (and limits))
line 123–30; in architecture 124–6, 129–30
    as connecting/delimiting 124–6
    in maritime charting 126–7
    as moving (or representing movement), journeying, and orienting 124, 128, 155, 216n21, 216n9
    its shape and direction 128
    and surface 129–31, 155
    in topographic mapping 127–8
Loos, Adolf 96, 97, 212n26
Lovett Bay House (Leplastrier) 113–14
Luckman, Thomas 29
Lucretius 140
Luria, Alexander 112

'Man and Space' (Darmstadt conference, 1951) 19–20, 24, 35, 37, 40, 64–5, 71, 181–2
Mannheim, Karl 29
Massey, Doreen 15–16
material culture studies 107
materiality *See* Aalto and materiality, architecture and materiality, memory and materiality, power and materiality, romantic materialism, surface materiality, truth and appearance of built form and materiality

McCahon, Colin 177–9, 223n50
McCarter, Robert 169
meaning *(Bedeuting* or *Sinn)* and content 28–30, 153
    in things vs. *of* things 25, 29–30
    (*see also* truth and assertion, meaning and content)
measuring, taking measure (of life, the human) 48–9, 57, 142, 148–9
memory:
    and building 105–20, 121, 182
    dynamic and performative 112
    and fixity 110–12
    and forgetting 105–6, 112, 120
    and materiality (of things) 107–8, 117
    and place 107–12, 121
    refusal of (and presentism) 114–19
    and self 108
    subjective vs. constructed 109
    and time/temporality 107
Merleau-Ponty, Maurice 151, 152
Messkirch, Germany 38, 41, 173–4, 185
method of places (method of *loci*) 107, 214n4
Moore, Rowan 162
Mostafavi, Mohsen 116
Mugerauer, Robert 26, 41, 52, 135, 195n51
Muuratsalo Experimental House (Aalto) 81–2

National Museum of Australia 92
nature *See* landscape and nature
Nazism 3, 52, 65
New York City (and Manhattan) 162–3
Newton, Isaac 124
Nietzsche, Friedrich 173
non-human 22, 41, 78
Norberg-Schulz, Christian 5, 29–30, 35, 38, 41, 49, 52, 54, 135, 211n20
nostalgia/nostalgic (also melancholic) 38, 40, 43, 68, 110
Nouvel, Jean 1

objectification 9
Obrador-Pons, Pau 30, 37, 41
ontology 9–11, 61, 191n28, 191n29, 196n53
    and the ethical 10–11, 97, 119–20, 181, 223n1

and the existential 27
and memory 112
relational structure of 21–3
and topology 8–11
(*see also* grounds, beginnings, (first) principles)
openness, bounded openness of place and world 5, 46, 69, 83, 87, 99, 101, 111, 141–2, 168-9, 178, 184–6
Ortega y Gasset, Jose 64

Paddington Cube (Piano) 162
Paimo Tuberculosis Sanatorium (Aalto) 80–1
Pallasmaa, Juhani 135, 211n19
parametricism (the parametric):
    and *autopoiesis* 143
    and bounds or limits 142
    and computational technologies 138–9, 142, 147–9
    definitions, views and uses of (ontology of) 136–9, 217n3, 220n10
    and globalism 147
    and language, narrative 144–6
    and place 135–49
    and proper measure 142, 148–9
Parc de la Villette 1
Petzet, Heinrich 75, 82, 88
phenomenology/phenomenological 25–31, 66, 75, 93, 101–2, 112, 197n68, 205n55
Piano, Renzo 162
Picasso, Pablo 179
Piranesi, Giovanni Battista 155, 168, 218n12
place *(Ort)*, in philosophical topology 2, 5, 16–36, 54, 60, 64, 139–42, 217n4
    and agency 131–2
    and its boundedness 67, 69–72, 83, 85–6, 106, 140–3, 167, 184, 186 (*see also* openness, bounded openness of place and world)
    distorted 'sense of' 162
    and dwelling 5–6, 35, 77, 170, 188
    as dynamic and indeterminate 111–12, 131, 132–4
    and exclusion 64–9
    and the human 6–7, 106, 119–20, 146

and interiority 170–1
and liminality 176–9
and memory 105–6, 107–12, 119–20
as opening up 98–102, 108, 110
and orientation/orientating 25, 30, 51, 86, 102, 110, 133
and parametricism 135–49
and *piazza,* opening, clearing 99, 141, 213n32
and placelessness 45, 54
and power (*see* power)
as qualitative 142
and region 175–6, 183–4, 186–7
and releasement 187
responsiveness to 49, 51, 75, 105, 187–8
and self, others, other things (incl. the social) 65–7, 108, 110
vs. space 5, 69, 70–2, 80, 83, 94, 102, 140, 169, 184
and subjectivity 141
and time 83, 179
(*see also* space, topology)
platial 218n3
poetry, the poetic (also *poiesis*) 48–9
Pope Sixtus IV 124
post-structuralism 92
power:
    expression of (direct and indirect) 152
    and materiality, materialized 153, 155, 157
    and space and place 152–4, 218n6
    spatialized 155
    understood topologically 154–7
    (*see also* bound(s), boundedness (and limits))
pragmatism 209n2
presentism 114–19
Proust, Marcel 107
psychologism 197n68
Pudong New District (Shanghai) 158, 160–63

question/questionability 7, 35, 46, 69, 86, 98, 110

Rand, Ayn 55–7, 59, 67, 202n16
region *See* place and region

Reichstag (Berlin) 92
relationality/relatedness 21–3, 31, 45,
    48–9, 51, 65–6, 69–72, 78–82, 84,
    112, 167, 171–2, 178–9, 221n21
releasement/releasing (also freeing) 99,
    185–8, 203n23
Relph, Edward 26–7, 35, 41, 52, 54, 135,
    195n47, 195n51, 202n13
representation/reproduction 116–19, 168,
    208n30, 211n20, 215n8
resoluteness *(Entscholssenheit)* 202n17
Rockefeller Center (NYC) 163
romantic materialism 112–14
Ronchamp, Chapelle Notre-Dame du
    Haut (Le Corbusier) 53
Rousseau, Jean-Jacques 173
ruins/ruination 113
Ruskin, John 95–6, 97

sameness and difference See identity and
    belonging
Samuels, Marwyn 196n52
Sartre, Jean-Paul 3
Schama, Simon 221n27
Scharoun, Hans 2, 24, 201n5
Scheler, Max 29
Schildt, Göran 83, 84
Schilli, Hermann 192n4
Schopenhauer, Arthur 1
Schumacher, Patrik 135, 136, 143, 147
Schutz, Alfred 29, 109
Scully, Vincent 99–100
Seagram Building (NYC) 164
Seamon, David 26, 41, 52, 135, 195n51
Sebald, W. G. 107
self/individual: expressivist view of 55–6
    and place 65–7, 120
The Shard (London) 162
Sharr, Adam 17–18, 40, 52, 56, 58, 60, 62,
    72
Simmel, Georg 171–2, 177, 184
sincerity See authenticity and sincerity
singularity 215n26
social constructionism 29–31, 109
space 5
    abstracted view of 94–5, 101, 220n12,
        220n6
    as extension 20, 140, 168

grounded in place 20, 70–2, 83, 107,
    184–5
and interiority 167–79
and movement/activity 131, 132–4
and objective exteriority 108
and power see power
as quantitative 141–2
and room *(Raum)* 83, 168, 171, 177
and time 69, 83, 207n14
topological (and non-topological) 5,
    167–70, 175, 176, 220n11
and visuality 210n17
(*see also* place, topology, openness)
St George Wharf Tower or Vauxhall Tower
    (London) 162–3
Sternberger, Dolf 64–5, 66–7, 68, 86
Strauss, Erwin 131–2
street, the See architecture and the street
    (withdrawal from)
Stubbins, Hugh 163
subjectivism/subjectivity 28–9, 35, 108–9,
    132, 141, 167, 220n11
Sullivan, Louis 95, 97, 212n26
surface 129–32
    creating within and without 131
    and the line 129–31
    and space, place 130–2, 215n19
surface materiality (and depth of surface)
    114–16

Taylor, Charles 59
telos 182, 188
Therme Vals spa (Zumthor) 136–7
thing/things 8, 23, 27, 44–5, 49, 82–6, 101,
    117
thinking/rethinking 4–5, 8–9, 23, 35, 175
    of architecture 50
    as attending and responding
        to place, dwelling and their
        bounds 52, 57, 72, 87, 149, 175, 182,
        187–8
    and building and dwelling 182–3, 188
    as grounding design 87–8, 175
    and homelessness 46–7, 52
    in the poetic 48
    as relatedness in and to the world
        48–50, 106, 175
    and releasement 186

as remembering or overcoming forgetting 105–6
(*see also* building, dwelling)
Thoreau, Henry David 173
time/temporality: in relation to space and place 83, 107–8
and subjective interiority 108–9; and surface(s) 115
topology *(Topologie)* or topological thinking 19, 23, 45, 105, 151, 154, 173, 183–5, 190n15, 191n26
as mnemonical/recollective 106
and ontology 8–11
and power (*see* power understood topologically)
vs. spatialized thinking 70–2
and truth 102–3
topos 2, 115, 131, 182–3, 188, 215n19, 217n5, 223n1
Trilling, Lionel 55, 59
truth *(Wahrheit)* 28
truth and appearance 95–8
of built (vs. represented) form and materiality 96–7, 117, 211n21
as honesty or integrity (vs. the lie) 95–6
truth and assertion 89–95
Aristotelian view 90
correctness, correspondence, coherence 89–90
Heideggerian view 90
meaning and content (symbolic, semiotic) 91–4, 153, 209n6, 210n15
textuality and conceptuality (esp. in architecture) 91–5
truth and opening 98–102
as 'at work' (in a Greek temple) 99–101
of relations and possibilities 101
as topological 99, 101–3

as unconcealment, *aletheia, Lichtung* 98–9, 213n30
Tschumi, Bernard 1

uncanny/unhomely *(unheimlich),* or homeless 4, 17, 19–20, 31, 46, 111, 214n14
(*see also* homelessness)
unitary complexity 79, 84, 200n30

values 200n35
van der Rohe, Mies 79, 164
Vesely, Dalibor 25
Vidler, Anthony 17, 31, 111
Villa Mairea (Aalto) 84–5, 208n34
Villa Savoye (Le Corbusier) 125, 129
vitalism 82
von Uexküll, Jakob 31, 197n67
von Wright, G. H. 208n43

Wachowski, Lana and Lilly 97, 212n28
Weil, Simone 111
Whitman, Walt 95
Wigley, Mark 17, 40
Wittgenstein, Ludwig 1, 40
world 20–3, 35, 209n5
being at home in the 34, 51
and human activity 28–31, 35–6, 121, 146
and the human body 27, 121–3
and human relatedness to 21, 31, 65–6, 85–6, 121, 175
as near and far 174
opening of the 23, 31, 49, 69–70, 98–101
understood topologically 21–3, 175, 193n22
Wright, Frank Lloyd 55–6, 167
writing, mechanization of 122–3

Zumthor, Peter 113, 135–7

www.ingramcontent.com/pod-product-compliance
Lightning Source LLC
Chambersburg PA
CBHW062135300426
44115CB00012BA/1937